AF478149

RESOLVING THE CYPRUS CONFLICT

Resolving the Cyprus Conflict

Negotiating History

Michális Stavrou Michael

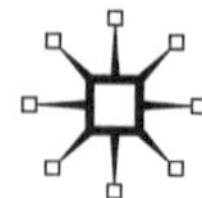

RESOLVING THE CYPRUS CONFLICT
Copyright © Michális Stavrou Michael, 2009.

First published in 2009 by
PALGRAVE MACMILLAN®
in the United States—a division of St. Martin's Press LLC,
175 Fifth Avenue, New York, NY 10010.

Where this book is distributed in the UK, Europe and the rest of the world,
this is by Palgrave Macmillan, a division of Macmillan Publishers Limited,
registered in England, company number 785998, of Houndmills,
Basingstoke, Hampshire RG21 6XS.

Palgrave Macmillan is the global academic imprint of the above companies
and has companies and representatives throughout the world.

Palgrave® and Macmillan® are registered trademarks in the United States,
the United Kingdom, Europe and other countries.

ISBN: 978–0–230–62002–5

Library of Congress Cataloging-in-Publication Data

Michael, Michális S.
    Resolving the Cyprus conflict : negotiating history / Michalis Stavrou
  Michael.
        p. cm.
    Includes bibliographical references and index.
    ISBN 978–0–230–62002–5 (alk. paper)
    1. Cyprus—History—Cyprus Crisis, 1974– 2. Cyprus—Politics and
  government—1960– 3. Cyprus—International status. I. Title.
DS54.9.M535 2009
956.9304—dc22   2009011017

A catalogue record of the book is available from the British Library.

Design by Newgen Imaging Systems (P) Ltd., Chennai, India.

First edition: November 2009

10 9 8 7 6 5 4 3 2 1

Printed in the United States of America.

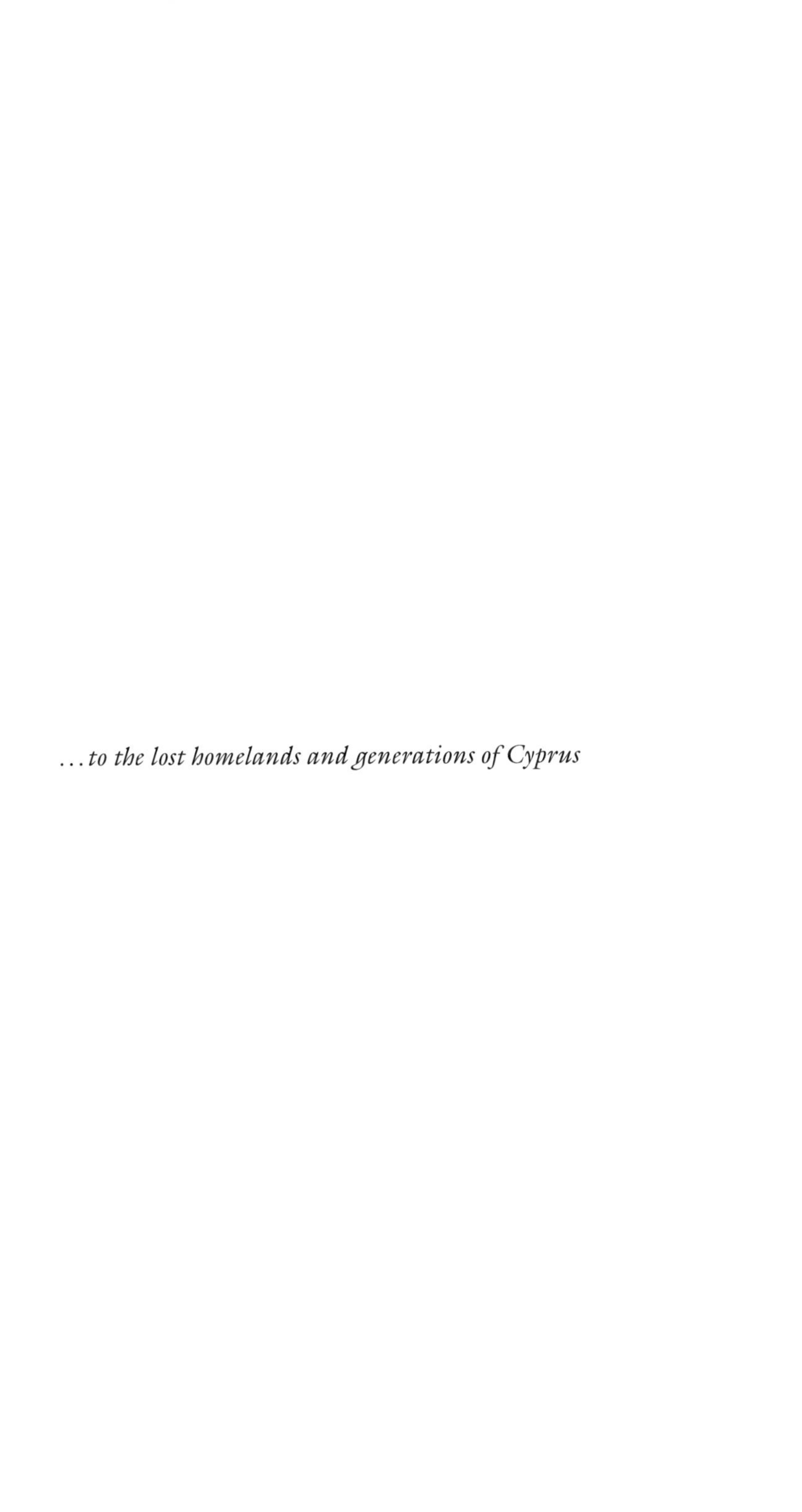

...to the lost homelands and generations of Cyprus

Contents

List of Maps

Acknowledgments

This book has been a part of my life for many years. Its completion brings to an end what has been a long but rewarding path of research, discovery, memory, narrative, and finally conclusion. It was not often easy to maintain the momentum, and certainly there were times when I felt it would never come to fruition. In this respect the project threatened to emulate its subject matter.

There are many people who, in various ways and at different junctures, contributed to this project. Foremost I wish to thank my colleague, friend, and teacher Joseph Camilleri, who guided me through this scholastic journey and constantly challenged my thinking and presumptions. The support of my family was crucial at all times, in particular during the final stages. I want to especially thank my wife Maria Vamvakinou for her support, tolerance, and encouragement throughout this endeavor.

I also want to acknowledge the assistance of Alexander Kouttab, Larry Marshall, and Alex Keeble for their invaluable assistance and excellent work as they proofread their way through hundreds of pages. I am indebted to Anastasia Andreou for her thorough resolve and audacious persistence to trace several minute details for me, including the number of the elusive Nicosia-Rome Alitalia flight scheduled for July 20, 1974.

The author and publishers wish to thank Cartographer Vladimir Bessarabov and the Cartography Section, Department of Peacekeeping Operations, at the United Nations, for permission to reproduce copyright material: "Cyprus post-1974," "1977 Greek Cypriot Map," "1978 Turkish Cypriot Map," "Boutros-Ghali's Map of 1992," and the "Annan Map 2004"; thanks also to Map Librarian Brenda Brookes, at the Dag Hammarskjöld Library, and Alex Skevofylakas for their assistance in providing access to, converting, and supplying the aforementioned maps.

Every effort has been made to trace the rights holders of copyright material, but if any have been inadvertently overlooked, the publishers would be pleased to make the necessary arrangements to obtain permissions at the first opportunity.

This book would not have been possible without the foresight and commitment of my publishers, Palgrave Macmillan. In particular I wish to thank Farideh Koohi-Kamali, her capable assistants Asa Johnson and later Robyn Curtis, as well as Samantha Hasey for all their assistance, professional dedication, and guidance. I am also indebted to the reviewers for their commentary, which has helped improve the original manuscript. The views conveyed in this book are exclusively those of the author.

Finally, I wish to dedicate this work to my late father, Stavros, and to my mother Xenia, who, having endured dislocation from their beloved Ayios Epiktitos,[1] Kyrenia, never lost hope that one day the partition of Cyprus would cease. As each generation invests its hopes and aspirations in the hands of their children, I also dedicate this book to my children Stavros and Stella, in the hope that their generation will learn to live in peace and harmony in a world without borders.

Introduction: The Cyprus Conflict

With mischievous wit, humorist George Mikes, commenting on the Cyprus conflict, remarked that "Cypriots know that they cannot become a World Power; but they have succeeded in becoming a World Nuisance, which is almost as good."[1] Undertones of comic relief aside, Mikes's quip encapsulates both the entrenched nature and the longevity of the Cyprus conflict. When Cypriots are frustrated by a difficult situation, they often exclaim "it has become like the Cyprus problem!" Such a comment is indicative of the way the conflict has embedded itself in the everyday cultural milieu of its constituents.

With this idea as our starting point, we begin an explorative journey into the puzzle that is the Cyprus conflict. Renowned as the birthplace of Aphrodite, a heaven of archaeological debris, and a tourist resort for affluent northern holidaymakers, Cyprus is in many respects the quintessential Mediterranean paradox. Locked in a historical impasse, its geographical predicament exposes centuries-old footprints of commerce, discourse, and conquest. Cyprus's strategic position has throughout history rendered it a conduit for civilizations. At the crossroads of three continents, Cyprus's European demeanor does not overshadow Alasiya's[2] oriental heritage and many links to the Balkans, the Aegean, and Asia Minor. Cyprus has become a metaphor for the encounter, over time and space, between civilizations; a repository of cultural remnants where East meets West. In many respects, Cyprus's tumultuous political history reflects its geocultural ambiguity. Measuring 9,251 square kilometers, with an estimated population of 784,301, this island-state has frustrated the United Nations (UN) for over half a century, accruing in excess of 120 UN Security Council resolutions between 1960 and 2008.

Cyprus occupies a prominent position among a group of seemingly intractable international conflicts, including Palestine, Northern Ireland, Sri Lanka, Eritrea, Lebanon, and Bosnia, all of which transcend their national borders and whose sustainable resolution has eluded third-party mediation.[3] The Cyprus dispute has preoccupied theorists and practitioners of conflict resolution ever since the United Nations stationed its peacekeeping force on the island in 1964. In its wake, the Cyprus problem has challenged conventional international analysis and defied traditional approaches to negotiation and peacemaking.

Despite the fact that the Cyprus question has engaged international diplomacy for over half a century, it is the events of 1974 that have dramatically changed the nature of the problem and propelled it in an entirely new direction. Since 1974, negotiations over the Cyprus problem have proceeded through UN-sponsored intercommunal talks between the Greek and Turkish Cypriot communities. This book examines the various proposals that have unfolded in the ensuing thirty years, concentrating on the post-1974 period because this constitutes the latest manifestation of the Cyprus problem and is the focal point for peace negotiations.

The Structural Logic of the Book

Although this book professes to be an investigative account of the Cyprus peace talks, it cannot disguise its underlying motive—as the title alludes—of serving a pedagogical function for policy makers and practitioners of conflict resolution. This book revolves around a central question: Why, despite endless negotiations and numerous proposals, has resolution of the Cyprus problem eluded the various parties and mediators involved since 1974? Put another way: Why is this small island-state still physically divided, despite decades of persistent UN efforts to bring about a negotiated settlement? Is there anything new in this conflict that explains why Cyprus is hitting the headlines? Why is there a renewed bout of optimism during each initiative, followed by the sense of failure and anxiety that a solution will never be achieved? Is the systemic impasse at the intercommunal talks best explained in terms of the shortcomings of the mediating strategy or more fundamentally because the negotiating process itself is inadequate/insufficient in effectively addressing the deeper causes of the conflict? What can Cyprus teach us about the nature of protracted conflicts and ways of resolving them?

In answering these questions, this book comes at a critical time for the partitioned island-state and for those parties associated with the conflict. By analyzing current developments, this book has both a practical and theoretical relevance. Placing the Cyprus conflict in its historical, ideological, ethno-political, and geostrategic context, this book explains why the Annan initiative failed, and examines the resultant implications for Cyprus, Greece, and Turkey, as well as for the UN and the European Union (EU).

From an intergovernmental perspective, the Cyprus dispute presents itself as a test case for the role of regional organizations in conflict resolution. Whether deliberate or not, the inclusion of Cyprus in its latest round of enlargement has saddled the European Union with a divided state, part of whose territory is occupied by a potential member (Turkey), while two of its member-states (Greece and the United Kingdom) remain guarantor powers. The book explores the external and internal dimensions of this dilemma and, in particular, considers the implications for Turkish Cypriots in the north who, for 30–40 years (depending on one's historical vantage point) lived in protective isolation and international illegality.

To make sense of recent developments and imagine future prospects, we need to establish the nature, sources, and dynamics of the conflict, and ground our analysis in an examination of the negotiating process's various phases. To understand the trends as they have emerged over the past three decades, this study reveals both the impeding and facilitating factors that have framed the intercommunal negotiating process, and explains why impediments to resolution have thus far proved decisive. It asks whether recent developments point toward a new and substantive breakthrough in the conflict or toward a quagmire for the EU—as the conflict has been for the UN.

Addressing these core questions, this book explores three closely interrelated themes: the role of key protagonists and third parties; the dialectic of continuity and change; and the nexus/tension between the domestic and external environments. By weaving these themes into the narrative of intercommunal talks and by exposing those hidden dimensions that are often ignored by analysts and policy makers alike, the analysis extends beyond conventional realist approaches.

The first of the above-mentioned themes analyzes the motivations and expectations of the various parties involved in the Cyprus conflict, the roles they have played, and limitations on their freedom of action. These actors are classified in four categories: the primary internal parties, that is, the Greek and Turkish Cypriot communities; the principal external powers, namely, Greece and Turkey; the secondary external powers (the United States, Britain, and the Soviet Union/Russia); and the multilateral institutions (primarily the UN, NATO, and the European Union). The delineation between the principal and secondary external powers does not necessarily reflect the order of their importance to the conflict. Rather, principal powers are those parties that have played a more central role in the conflict and its origins. All players who do not satisfy the above definition—although very important—are classified as secondary powers. The various parties are examined in terms of their interactions at different levels, stages, and junctures. The aim here is to determine how their convergence or divergence has impacted on the intercommunal negotiations.

The second theme examines the elements of continuity and change that have marked these negotiations to ascertain the extent and manner in which the expectations, perceptions, and strategies of the various actors have changed over time and as the Cyprus problem evolved. The aim of this examination is to identify those instances where most progress has been made, and why.

Closely connected with the question of change and continuity is a third theme concerning the interaction between internal and external factors. Defining Cyprus's internal and external realm as all interactions, developments, and events that occur within and beyond the physical and legal boundaries of Cyprus, we soon discover the limitations of such an approach. The contradictions between the conflict's internal and external dimensions form the very basis of the conflict's irresolution. By engaging, however, in Cyprus's internal-external debate, we are able to comprehend the power structures that underpin the conflict. Two questions assist us in this line of thought: To what extent has the internal/external environment impeded and/or facilitated the resolution of the conflict? How have particular internal and external influences impacted on the negotiating process across its various phases?

The methodological approach here is to apply these three themes, and the core question from which they derived, to the entire post-1974 period, which, for purposes of analytical convenience, has been subdivided into four distinct phases: 1974–1981, 1982–1989, 1989–1994, and 1995–2008. These four periods have been delineated by employing two sets of criteria: the first pertains to the endogenous factors associated with the actual cycle of negotiations; and the second refers to those exogenous factors that arose from the domestic or external environment and impacted on the negotiating process.

By addressing the three themes, this book intends to trace, in chronological sequence, the course of the intercommunal talks, through its four phases, as the epicenter of its inquiry, and then to incorporate other events and developments that have impacted on the negotiations. The analysis will extend beyond the conventional approach to the study of negotiations by exposing those hidden components that are often ignored by analysts and policy makers.[4] Starting from the premise that these political units cannot be treated as monolithic entities, the study will probe the internal political dynamics of the two main parties (i.e., the Greek and Turkish Cypriot communities). The internal tensions and contradictions, which have characterized the two communities, hold an important key to any explanation of the Cyprus problem and the obstacles to conflict resolution.[5]

This book is therefore structured around a two-pronged approach. The first consists of a chronological account outlining the historical background of the conflict and assigning a chapter to each of the major phases. We may label this the vertical axis of the study. Complementing and illuminating this inquiry is a horizontal strand dealing with the three themes mentioned above.

As noted above, the primary focus of this book is the dialectical relationship between the two parties that has developed throughout the intercommunal negotiations. All other actors, primary and secondary, are viewed from a similarly concentric perspective. The best way to understand the structural model adopted here is to conceptualize the history of the intercommunal talks as an ever-expanding circle. Each phase constitutes a different layer in the circle, and each layer is examined in terms of the three themes (parties involved, continuity/change, and internal/external factors) that shape and give content to the negotiations at any given time. With this dual approach, we seek to uncover those influences, factors, and events that, though at first sight may appear to fall outside the parameters of this book, are nevertheless integral to the story. Delving into the internal dynamic of the principal parties' decision-making processes allows us to better understand alterations in their political behavior and subsequent transformations in their relationship. This vertical/horizontal approach—a three-dimensional perspective—paves the way for a more complex but also more illuminating analysis, hopefully shedding new light on what remains one of the world's most intractable conflicts.

Chapter 1

Identifying the Sources of the Conflict

"The English want Cyprus, and they will take it as compensation"
—Disraeli, *Tancred,* Book IV (1847)[1]

When Sir Garnet Wolseley arrived in Cyprus on July 22, 1878, as the first British High Commissioner, he did not realize he would assist in bringing modernity to this languishing Ottoman province. On that crisp summer morning, as the *Himalaya* sailed into the derelict Larnaca harbor, winds of change signaled things to come. Waiting by the pier, in full regalia, the Bishop of Kitium displayed his Byzantium heritage, cherishing the suppressed aspirations of Cypriot Hellenism. Despite the widespread reservations of Latin Christians, Bishop Kyprianos viewed these latter-day crusaders as European saviors from Ottoman despotism.

After more than three centuries of medieval Ottoman rule, Cyprus had returned to Europe.[2] By laying claim to this provincial backwater, British imperial design found in Cyprus an offshore *place d'armes* to one of the most turbulent regions of the twentieth century. Yet Cyprus's annexation, steeped in geopolitical expediencies, diplomatic intrigue, and adversarial politics, unwittingly served as a signpost for British imperial fate. Once again, history conspired with geography to garner the three forces that have determined the fate of the island and its people, often transforming the serene isle into a quagmire of violence, suffering, and injustice.

Colonialism, Modernity, and Nationalism

Any serious examination of the Cyprus conflict cannot take place without first considering its historical origins. If the history of the Cyprus conflict was reduced to a single diagram, it would be a triangular trajectory of colonialism, nationalism, and modernity. Nowhere is the clash between colonialism and nationalism more eloquently displayed than in the literary interplay between Lawrence Durrell's *Bitter Lemons* (1957) and Rodis Roufos's *The Age of Bronze* (1960). Written in an orientalist vernacular, Durrell's narrative of a benevolent colonial ruler provides insight into the benign British liberalism that shifted from nostalgic fatalism to a third-party adjudication between two squabbling ethnonationalisms. Roufos's *The Age of Bronze*, written in a postwar liberal idiom, attempts to rebuff *Bitter Lemons*, providing us with an intuitive—almost spiritual—rendition of Greek Cypriot nationalism, encapsulated by its campaign for union with Greece—*enosis*.

The clash between *enosis* and British strategic interests in Cyprus reflected the much broader historical confrontation between third-world nationalism and waning colonialism (the collapse of empire) within the dialectical compulsions of modernity. Unlike other twentieth-century national liberation movements, *enosis* was fundamentally an extension of nineteenth-century Greek irredentist nationalism and subsequent struggles to incorporate Greek-speaking regions of the old Ottoman Empire into the modern Greek state. Although Greek nationalism first appeared in Cyprus as a consequence of the 1821 Greek revolution, it was swiftly suppressed and did not manage to establish itself until the arrival of the British. By contrast, Turkish Cypriot nationalism, imbued by Kemalism, did not fully emerge until the 1940s.[3] This delay was due to the late development of Turkish nationalism itself, and to the fact that the Islamic Turkish-speaking minority in Cyprus did not immediately endear itself to secular Kemalism.[4]

Nonetheless, locating Turkish nationalism in Cyprus's contested history has proven to be an elusive expedition. Unnoticed by Greek Cypriot historiography, Turkish Cypriot nationalism cannot be merely explained as a "top-down" manifestation of Turkey's geopolitical interests. Its steady politicization eventually rendered it, in addition to the British, the *enosists*, and the communists, a fourth force to be reckoned with. Using *enosis* as a benchmark, we are able to gauge Turkish Cypriot nationalism's limitations and exhortations. As a susceptible minority in the triangular—or quadrangular—power struggle, Turkish Cypriots allied themselves with the most powerful and least threatening force—the British colonial rulers.[5]

One cannot appreciate Greek Cypriot nationalism—or Cypriot history for that matter—without grasping the effect of *enosis*. Attempting to explain *enosis*, Peter Loizos aptly noted that it meant "different things, at different times, to different...people."[6]

Moreover, one cannot understand the contradictions of modern Cyprus without first delving into the ideological underpinnings of British colonialism. While a mischievous Durrell quipped that "there is nothing anti-English in Enosis,"[7] British attitudes toward Greek Cypriot nationalism rested on an ideological perspective, as rendered in English literature and imagery through the centuries. Although, over time, various arguments were mounted by Whitehall rejecting *enosis* on security, strategic, political, and economic grounds, underpinning British refusal was an unrelenting cultural ambivalence about whether Cyprus was a Greek island.

Such ambivalence rested largely on what Robert Holland and Dianna Markides identified as Cyprus's "peculiarity" amongst other British possessions in the Hellenic world. In contrast to the Ionian (1864) and Cretan (1913) *enosis* movements, Greek Cypriot nationalism was distinctive for its fatalistic marginalization from mainstream political discourse. Cyprus's exceptionalism was compounded by the Church's leading role and the fact that primarily the Greek Cypriots determined the initiative, instead, and often in defiance, of the metropolitan national centre of Athens.[8]

Relevant to our discussion, British oriental perception and depiction of Cyprus, as framed originally around its acquisition, conceived the island as a semimythical geographic and communal construct. Nowhere is this more telling than in the images of the John Thomson photo-collection *Through Cyprus with the Camera in the Autumn of 1878*. As the first visual "outsider" interpretation of Cyprus and Cypriots, Thomson's work was paramount in shaping domestic public and elite opinion on the eve of British possession of the island.[9] Such images attached particular characteristics, which were typically negative, setting "those" Orientals in contrast to Westerners (those of the Occident). At their worst incarnation, such "demeaning generalizations," as Edward Said calls them, attributed exoticism, threat, violence, backwardness, and deviousness to the people of the Orient.[10] Over time, this conception became the lens through which all Cypriots were perceived.

It is worth stressing, though, that orientalist representations are seldom motivated by a calculated intent to denigrate, rather the distortions are structurally imbedded, a product of cultural assumptions, ideas, and representations. This orientalist template serves to frame the Cyprus conflict in inherently violent, chaotic, and problematic terms. In its British manifestation, the orientalist template helps to frame the "history wars" in a manner that projects an adversarial "pick a side." Attached to this orientalist frame is a confused and misplaced philhellenism—whereupon British intellectual tradition is seen as reclaiming and reasserting ancient Greek norms upon the Greek Cypriots' culture and society "contaminated" by eastern malaise.[11]

Clearly, orientalist narrative on Cyprus predates its modern rendition. References to Cyprus appeared in English texts only after the first crusades. Travelers, pilgrims, merchants, surveyors, and adventurers such as John Mandeville (1322–1356), William Wey (1458), M. John Locke (1553), Thomas Dallam (1596), George Sandys (1610), and Benjamin Disraeli (1830) cited Cyprus in their diaries, as it lay *en route* to Jerusalem. But books on Cyprus only emerged after its annexation, resulting from the British public's fascination with this exotic acquisition.

The most representative text of this genre is English explorer Samuel White Baker's account of his ten-month pilgrimage, *Cyprus, As I Saw It in 1879*. Baker's book was significant for its vast influence among British opinion and policy makers; it was heralded as the most thoughtful book on Cyprus.[12] Yet Baker's text was condescending, depicting Cypriots as ugly and dirty, even if they were good-natured and hospitable. The notion that local inhabitants needed both Westernizing and civilizing was a familiar cultural presumption, judging from W. Hepworth Dixon's remark that Wolseley had the arduous task of "quickening a torpid Oriental body like these Cypriotes into an active and progressive state of life."[13] Baker considered the "Greek element" of Cyprus vulnerable to nationalist exploitation by Athens-inspired agitators. During the first year of British occupation, taking advantage of the regime's liberal nature, various discontents awakened "philhellenic" aspirations in certain urban circles. This campaign was led by the Cypriote Fraternity Society, which established clubs in various districts to inspire Greek Cypriots to take up the "noble" cause of union with the Greek kingdom. This political agitation found support among the Greek clergy and some British parliamentarians who maintained a romantic *Byronesque* philhellenism. Baker did not attach much importance to the movement, considering Greek Cypriots too "shrewd" to sacrifice the benefits they enjoyed under the British for the shadowy prospects of attaching their fate to Greece.[14]

Complementing Baker's early account of *enosist* agitation is Esmé Scott-Stevenson's book, *Our Home in Cyprus*, which was also published in 1880. The wife of a Black Watch captain stationed in Kyrenia, Scott-Stevenson remarked that *enosis* was propagated by certain members of the urban-educated well-to-do classes—Christians spurred-on by Greek intellectuals who considered the "Cypriote Christians" as

Hellenes. Claiming that the English favored the "Osmani" more than the Christians, nationalist agitation accentuated ethno-religious differences in order to entice—without success—support from the peasant population. This campaign was organized by the Cypriote Brotherhood Society, whose headquarter was in Alexandria, with branches in Larnaca, Limassol, and Nicosia. Collecting money to outbid the British government when time came for the final acquisition of the island from the Sultan, the Brotherhood gained limited support among the population.[15]

British Changes to the Cypriot Landscape

The British administration introduced changes that led to structural transformations in Cyprus's social, political, and economic spheres, paradoxically fostering the growth of *enosis*. New laws, institutions, and processes challenged the traditional authority of the autocephalous Church of Cyprus, which under the Ottoman millet system was not only the spiritual head of the Greek Cypriots as Orthodox Christians but also the civil head of the Greek *ethnos* (nation). This duality conferred on the Archbishop the Byzantium title of *ethnarhis* (ethnarch, or head of the nation), which the British—with their secularist separation of state and church—did not grasp. British reforms challenged the Church in three main ways. Politically, the establishment of a Legislative and Executive Council, and a new Constitution (1882), reflected and encouraged the emergence of the urban elite as a political entity. Economically, the Church was no longer in charge of collecting taxes, as it had been during Ottoman rule. Lastly, the British attempted, unsuccessfully, to detach education from the influence of the Church. These structural changes alienated the Church from the governing process, leading it to resume its traditional role as an advocate of Greek nationalism and the main exponent of *enosis*. As a social movement, *enosis* became essentially an effort by the traditional elite, especially the Church of Cyprus, to retain/regain their legitimacy and authority.[16]

In a broader context, British reforms improved living standards on the island. According to the 1946 census, Cyprus experienced a dramatic population increase, from 185,630 in 1881 to 274,108 in 1911, and to 450,114 in 1946. Education received a major impetus. In 1881, for example, there were only ninety-four Greek schools in Cyprus, which under the Ottoman system were maintained by the Church. Twenty years later, there were 238 schools, and by 1951, there was a primary school in every village, with 1,584 elementary teachers—1,218 of whom were Greek. The British also established transportation and telecommunication on the island. Under the Ottomans, Cyprus had only one asphalt road, twenty-six miles in length, connecting Larnaca with Nicosia, and no motor vehicles or telephones. By 1951 there were 741 asphalted highways, with over 1,800 miles of subsidiary roads linking every village to its main town. There was also a comprehensive telephone network, connecting all the main towns and 123 villages.[17]

Modern infrastructure was instrumental in creating the social and ideological processes for spreading *enosis*, especially among the rural population. The great majority of Cypriots lived in rural areas (in 1953 it was 78 percent)[18] and the village was the major community unit of Cypriot society. The importance of the village as a social-communal construct cannot be underrated; its centrality in Cypriot social discourse is evident. Its influence was felt well beyond its physical confines, extending into urban and migrant settings. The British were fully aware of the importance of rural Cyprus, both as a bulwark against urban-centered discontent and as a potential hub for nationalist discord. With its agrarian loans, expansion of educational and health infrastructure, and agricultural and farming improvements, British colonial policy assumed that rural Cyprus was more preoccupied with material issues and less susceptive to nationalist—and communist—propaganda. As communication and transportation improved between the rural periphery and the urban centers, however, so did the transmission of political ideas.[19] This analysis is supported by Kyriacos C. Markides' profiling of EOKA (*Ethniki Organosi Kiprion Agoniston* [National Organization of Cypriot Fighters]) recruits. Scanning the *Cyprus Police Gazette* of 1955–1959, Markides found that the average EOKA member was a young, working-class male technician who had migrated from the village to the city.[20]

The existing network of churches and schools in rural Cyprus formed a complementary process by which the *enosis* message was transmitted to a younger generation of Greek Cypriots. Within the village-community, the priest and the teacher were the most important and respected bearers of norms and beliefs. Although the government-appointed *muktar* (a local agent for the central authority) had considerable administrative authority, this was founded on fear rather than respect. The priest and the teacher—as nationalist agents in the village-community—must be viewed as conduits of Greek consciousness.[21] For the villagers, language, faith, and (ethno) nationalism were so interconnected that a Greek Cypriot found them impossible to differentiate. As John G. Peristiany observed, the priest was "always a firm believer" of *enosis* and was also a "propagandist for the conservative movement," which had always been zealously pro-*enosis*.[22]

In addition to the clergy, two other groups were strong advocates of *enosis*. The educated elite and urban intelligentsia, exasperated by the fact that the British occupied all senior administrative posts, saw *enosis* as a way of demonstrating their "glorious and civilized connection" to their Greek heritage. As already mentioned, teachers—most of whom were educated at Greek tertiary institutions—also saw *enosis* as the realization of their historical destiny.

Another consequence of British rule that unwittingly aided the proliferation of *enosis* was the introduction of printing presses and newspapers. The first printing press and newspaper appeared in Larnaca a few months after the British arrived. Apart from the English Cypriot newspapers, there was a flurry of Greek newspapers. By 1911, there were fifteen Greek newspapers and magazines, and only one in Turkish. Notwithstanding their fluctuating circulation, they were the only non-state communications media available to Cypriots and, as such, wielded enormous power. Over time, newspapers offered alternative, even dissident, points of view to the official British position. Given to polemical editorials and embellished news coverage, they became beacons of nationalist, and later communist, ferment.

British economic policy also had an unintended impact on the growth of *enosis* and the sharpening of class conflict. For the first fifty years of British rule, the imposition of the tribute, or the Turkish Debt Charge, dominated domestic politics. Eventually, this led to the 1931 riots, which fused anti-British slogans against colonial oppression with the demands of *enosis*, lending it a militancy and popular appeal that would funnel future armed insurrections.[23]

British rule fostered the emergence of a capitalist class and the formation of a secular elite that intended to challenge the Church's political and economic monopoly. The conservatives' inability, however, to confront the emergence of an effective labor movement, led them to seek the patronage of the Church. In doing so, they willingly surrendered leadership to the Church, giving rise to the formation of the *Ethnarhiko Simvoulio* (ethnarchy council). When Archbishop Makarios II, together with the young Bishop of Kitium, Makarios III, established the Ethnarchy Council, its anticommunist position became clear: its membership comprised of clergy, conservative politicians, and candidates who had lost to the communist mayors at the 1946 municipal elections. With the organization of the Ethnarchy, the scene was set for a power struggle between the left and the right over leadership of the *enosis* movement, and subsequently over Greek Cypriot society.

Clash of Enosis and British Strategic Interests

In his first proclamation, Wolseley promised Cypriots that "attention will be paid to their wishes" and that their "ancient customs" would be respected—provided these were "consistent with civilization and liberty."[24] This type of oratory would have been fashionable in Victorian times: imperial paternalism with liberal overtones.

After 300 years of Ottoman rule, the arrival of the British was welcomed by the Greek and the Turkish Cypriot populace. Greek Cypriot leaders wasted no time in declaring their aspiration for *enosis*, which was synonymous with national liberation for the Greek Orthodox Christian millet. But no sooner had Wolseley disembarked at Larnaca than two differing views of *enosis* emerged. Whereas Bishop Kyprianos welcomed the British with a succinct *enosist* message, Archbishop Sofronios, although hinting at *enosis*, stressed the people's attachment to the new administration and their expectation for a libertarian and equitable government.[25] For the next 100 years, sharpened by external events and local conditions, these two tendencies would merge and divide—at various historical junctures, and over strategy and tactics—in their understanding and pursuit of *enosis*. Until the mid-1970s, *enosis* was the hallmark of Greek Cypriot political and cultural discourse.

Initially, *enosis* was contested by the British on legal grounds, who argued that under the 1878 Cyprus Convention, they did not have the jurisdiction to cede Cyprus to another state, since it was still a territory of the Ottoman Empire. Yet beneath such legalistic edicts, the real motives for holding on to the island were purely strategic and geopolitical.[26] Captain J. M. Kinneir, an officer of the East India Company, visiting Cyprus sixty-four years before British acquisition, extolled the island's strategic virtues:

> The possession of Cyprus would give England a preponderating influence in the Mediterranean, and place at her disposal the future destinies of the Levant. Egypt and Syria would soon become her tributaries, and she would acquire an overawing position in respect to Asia Minor, by which the Porte might at all times be kept in check, and the encroachments of Russia, in this quarter, retarded if not prevented.[27]

This view was shared by Disraeli, who secured the island as part of a defensive alliance with Turkey against Russian encroachment.

There has been much speculation over Disraeli's motives for acquiring Cyprus—searching for hints in his romantic novel *Tancred*. Although Disraeli was in search of a *place d'armes* to defend Asia Minor and the Persian Gulf, Cyprus competed with Batoum, Mohammerah, Limnos, and Alexandretta as possible options. Harold Temperley argues that the final selection of Cyprus was the result of a last-minute coup—by the Foreign Secretary Robert A. T. Gascoyne-Cecil and the Ambassador to Constantinople, Austen Henry Layard—rather than any preplanned policy.[28] But Lord Derby's resignation as Secretary of State reveals a more fixed determination to acquire Cyprus. He cited the cabinet's decision to seize and occupy Cyprus (and Alexandretta) to use as a base in the eastern Mediterranean for its secret naval expedition from India. Disraeli himself, writing to the Queen, considered the acquisition of Cyprus as the "key of Western Asia," which would "weld together" the Indian Empire and Great Britain, while enormously increasing England's power in the Mediterranean.[29]

Cyprus's strategic importance to British regional and imperial geopolitics has been the subject of much historical conjecture. In many respects, the debate surrounding the acquisition of Cyprus came to epitomize two opposing views of empire exemplified by the Gladstone-Disraeli enmity: "Little Englandism" and "New Imperialism." Cyprus features prominently in both the empire's expansion and retraction, and its acquisition has to be placed in the context of Britain's imperial expansion. Cyprus's annexation came at a time of popular domestic support for New Imperialism, between 1852 and the outbreak of the First World War.

Without doubt, the acquisition of Cyprus was linked to the opening of the Suez Canal (1869) and the occupation of Egypt (1882). The acquisition of Cyprus, as well as of Palestine (1917–1918), was designed to protect the vital Mediterranean-Suez route. Cyprus became the third of Britain's island-bases in the Mediterranean, which included Gibraltar (from 1704) and Malta (from 1800)—an assessment validated by Britain's Consul to Cyprus, R. Hamilton Lang, who in praising the benefits of Cyprus said that:

It forms an invaluable outpost for the defence of the Suez Canal; it will protect the Asiatic terminus of a possibly future Euphrates Valley Railway; it will prove a convenient starting-point as well as a depot for whatever operations may become necessary in the future in Asiatic Turkey. All the great aggressive dynasties of the world—Assyrian, Babylonian, Persian, and Macedonian—have found the capture or subjection of Cyprus a first necessary step in the approach upon Egypt.[30]

Nevertheless, from the outset, many questioned Cyprus's strategic value for British imperial designs. Cyprus's critics argued that the island lacked adequate fortification, or a deepwater harbor in which British naval vessels could dock. In addition, the occupation of Egypt three years later offered Alexandria as a better-positioned and better-equipped proposition for Britain's Middle East interests. After the acquisition of Egypt, British thinking about Cyprus's strategic function became vague—which accounts for it abandoning the clearing of the Famagusta harbor. Such policy inertia relegated Cyprus to a second-string support base—at least until the fall of the Suez in 1956. The answer to why the British were reluctant to relinquish Cyprus is located in the imperial mindset of retaining territorial possessions. There was also the desire to deprive other powers from possessing Cyprus. Maintaining Cyprus was a kind of insurance policy for British interests in the Middle East.

Early accounts epitomized British imperial thinking toward the island, which subsequently dictated colonial policy on the *enosis* issue. The idea that *enosis* could be utilized first appeared in British policy when foreign secretary Edward Grey offered Cyprus to Greece in order that Greece enters the First World War on the allied side.[31] Britain's 1915 offer is a landmark in Greek Cypriot nationalist discourse. Its dual recognition as both precedent and "lost opportunity" lends support to the view that Greek Cypriot nationalists were the driving force behind *enosis*, rather than the reluctant Greek state. Yet Grey's offer was symbolic rather than substantial. Closer scrutiny of the events reveals that it was one of many overtures made to entice Greece into the war throughout the 1914–1915 period. Grey's offer was tangled up with the Entente's diplomatic machinations to balance the conflicting and overlapping interests, insecurities, and territorial aspirations of Russia, Romania, Serbia, and Greece, while simultaneously trying to induce Ottoman Turkey and Bulgaria to remain neutral. Turkey's eventual entry into the war provided British policy makers with the opportunity to barter the future division of Ottoman territory in a manner that would aid them in the war.

The next turning point to have a profound impact on Greek Cypriots was the riots of 1931. The 1931 crisis was significant for the fact that it saw the first riots against British authority. The crisis began when a tax bill, already defeated by the Cyprus Council, was nevertheless imposed by the British-appointed governor as an Order of the Council, overruling the only representative legislative institution on the island. The intervention, aggravated by a world economic crisis, sparked an island-wide uprising and brought the demand for *enosis* back to the forefront of the political agenda. The Greek Cypriot members of the Council withdrew. Riots broke out in Nicosia and the Governor's House was burned to the ground. The riots, however, were soon suppressed and emergency regulations enforced. The governor abolished the Council, censored the press, and deported many leading Greek Cypriot instigators. Furthermore, Governor Herbert Richmond Palmer enacted sixteen draconian laws, four of which were aimed at curbing the authority of the Church by requiring that the governor approve the election of the new archbishop. The Church responded by not electing a new archbishop for eleven years—until the edicts were eventually modified.[32] The regulations also targeted the newly formed communist movement. As with 1915, the 1931 *Oktovriana* (October) riots entered the *enosis* lexicon, forming a reference point, sharpening the conflict, and setting a precedent for the ensuing 1950s Greek Cypriot armed struggle.

The Second World War saw an end to the draconian "Palmerian Era." During this period, the island's domestic political environment was largely shaped by external forces. The war persuaded all the political players in Cyprus (British, nationalists, and communists) into cooperation, since their patrons (a neutralist Turkey, Britain, Greece, and the Soviet Union) had become allies. In the case of the *enosists*, the war determined the extent of pressure to be exerted against British rule, moderated by the belief that, as allies, the British would "reward" Greece by granting it Cyprus. The British capitalized on this sentiment by recruiting Cypriots with the slogan, "Fight for Freedom and Greece." Many Cypriots joined the specially formed Cyprus Regiment in the hope that the Greek-British partnership would aid the realization of *enosis*.

At the end of the war, the Greek government prepared its territorial claims—the acquisition of Cyprus was second on their list after the Dodecanese. Greece evidently had "no desire" to embarrass Britain and believed an arrangement could be found by which "certain strategic rights and bases could be leased (back) to Britain."[33] U.S. policy at the time favored the island's cession to Greece, provided this was satisfactory to Britain, and that it "protected the security of non-Greek inhabitants and...the lines of communication in the eastern Mediterranean."[34]

The Cold War further catapulted Cyprus's strategic significance beyond the British realm into the Western Alliance's frontline. In a major policy revision, the new Labour Cabinet was adamant that the Middle East would remain under Britain's sphere of influence, and that it would resist U.S. infiltration. The Middle East was vital to British imperial interests: it formed a central junction of land, air, and sea communication, linking Britain with India, the Far East, and Australasia; and it constituted the empire's main oil reserve. In this highly sensitive region, Cyprus was the only territory under full British sovereignty. In 1946, the Attlee Government considered Cyprus to be one of the six vital points in its global empire strategy. Planning against a possible clash with the Soviet Union in the oil-rich Middle East, Cyprus was considered even "more important than Haifa."[35]

Probing British decision-making at the time, we can ascertain that Britain's refusal to cede Cyprus to Greece stemmed from its desire to remain a power in the Eastern Mediterranean and the Middle East, particularly in the face of a Soviet threat to that predominance. A third geopolitical factor accompanied these two considerations: the fear that Greece might succumb to communist control.[36] This view was shared by the United States, which by September 1947 was making contingency plans in the event that Greece fell to communism.[37] By 1948, the State Department and the British Foreign Office jointly assessed that the "security of the whole Eastern Mediterranean and Middle East would be jeopardized if the Soviet Union should succeed in its efforts to obtain control" of either Italy, Greece, Turkey, or Iran. As a result, the State Department recommended that the United States should "support the security of the Eastern Mediterranean and the Middle East" and that such a policy was impractical unless Britain retained its "strong strategic, political and economic position" in the region.[38]

On reflection, C. M. Woodhouse believes that "in 1945 the cession could have been carried out painlessly, and even with public approval."[39] And although interdepartmental rivalry between the Colonial and Foreign offices is revealing, in the end it was Cabinet that determined governmental policy, adopting the military's position, which was consistently anti-*enosis*. Official British views on *enosis* still resembled those of Lord Reginald Fletcher Winster: that it "was a completely rhetorical and emotional cry on the part of a few people, which had no real reflection in the minds of the great majority" and that *enosis* was supported only by the middle class. British officials considered that the "agricultural population" was not interested in politics, and that the business community "would leave Cyprus if ENOSIS came about."[40] The search for the "eternal Cypriot"—pro-British, anti-*enosis*, and anticommunist—became a salient feature in most British deliberations on the Cyprus question.[41] This "silent majority" was situated amongst the ex-soldiers, rural population, the petty bourgeoisie, trade and small business community, the urban-educated elite, those who had relatives in the United Kingdom (UK), and those employed in the colonial administration. For John Reddaway, postwar British reforms' failure to "mobilize" this constituency was paramount for the ascendancy of "frenzied" nationalism in Cyprus.[42]

Despite Greek Cypriot expectations that Attlee's Labour government would implement its commitment to self-determination in the colonies, ultimately the British government was unwilling to relinquish Cyprus. The absence of any serious outbreak of violence in Cyprus in the preceding years had spared the British Labour Party the need to choose between "pragmatic" strategic considerations and the party's commitment to the principle of liberating the colonies.

In Search of a Cyprus Policy

Domestically, the end of the Second World War found Cyprus in a precarious juxtaposition. External developments in Greece and Britain, as well as in the Middle East, were linked to an internal political rivalry between the Left and the Church. Against this backdrop, the 1947 Winster proposals for limited self-government represented the first British attempt to resolve the Cyprus problem. While the Church and the right boycotted the process, the Left, led by AKEL (*Anorthotiko Komma Ergazomenou Laou* [Progressive Party of the Working People]), initially agreed to discuss the proposals, assuming a more moderate approach to *enosis*. Rebuked by their brethren communists in Greece, and suffering from their 1949 municipal electoral setback, AKEL's acrimonious change of leadership resulted in an ambiguous and often uncomfortable policy on *enosis*. The militant slogan of "*enosis* and only *enosis*," declared by newly elected Archbishop Leontios, had entered into the nationalist lexicon.[43] By the late 1940s, the Church had assumed leadership of the *enosis* movement and regained the political initiative within the Greek Cypriot community.

British attempts to settle the Cyprus problem during the postwar period were clearly a response to *enosis*. For, as Thomas Ehrlich pointed out, until 1958 *enosis* was the only noteworthy alternative to British sovereignty.[44] But the British "began by badly underestimating the strength of Enosist feeling"[45] and treated it "as if it were a kind of hobby of Greek-Cypriots and far too insignificant to affect the majesty of worldwide British rule."[46] Initially, the British misjudged the allure of *enosis* among the masses and hastily dismissed its capacity to mobilize Greek Cypriots and seriously challenge British hegemony.[47] The British proposals and the emergence of communism on the island contributed to the Church's militancy. In retrospect, the British would have been better able to deal with the pragmatic autonomist communists than with the "absolute" nationalistic Right. Failure of Britain's reform radicalized and consolidated the nationalist *enosists*, sharpening the schism with the autonomists who were largely dominated by the Left.

The Suez crisis once again determined Britain's policy toward Cyprus. British withdrawal from the Suez Canal and Egypt, in conjunction with political uncertainty over its other bases, provoked the first public debate over the whole question of its overseas bases. The Foreign Office argued for the continued stationing of British troops in Cyprus, as the only non-Arab territory that exercised real influence on the surrounding region.[48] The British Government was adamant that its overseas bases must be retained, even against their inhabitants' wishes. Military advice to Prime Minister Anthony Eden was that Cyprus was "an essential point for the maintenance of [the British] position in the Middle East, including the Persian Gulf."[49] Given Britain's and the North Atlantic Treaty Organization's (NATO) dependence on Middle East oil, Britain had to retain its "influence and prestige in the region," and Cyprus had to be maintained as "the only possible base for operations in that part of the world."[50] Between 1954 and 1956 Britain evacuated its Suez Canal Base and transformed Cyprus into its Middle East Army and Air Force Command Headquarters. After the Suez debacle, Harold Macmillan concluded that the United States was more important than Europe for Britain's Middle East military policy. As an air base, Cyprus would support the southern flank of NATO and the Baghdad Pact, with the clear understanding that Cyprus's future in any Middle East defense plan would remain a British prerogative.[51] Furthermore, the military's assessment was that after the losses of the Suez Canal and the Indian subcontinent, Britain's strategic position was at a "bare minimum." The loss of any of their bases in Gibraltar, Malta, Cyprus, Aden, or the Maldive Islands would have created "an irreparable gap" in Britain's global defense capability.[52]

After 1951, the United States urged Britain to improve its "Air Force facilities in Cyprus"[53] in order to link the island into a comprehensive Allied Mediterranean command, in which the role of Greece and Turkey would be crucial. For President Dwight Eisenhower, the Cyprus question was important only with respect to its potential impact on the British-Greek-Turkish NATO relationship. The United States was unwilling to allow the Cyprus dispute to disrupt its relations with Britain, which was seen as the main protector of the West's interests in the Middle East.[54]

By the mid-1950s, recognition of Cyprus's strategic importance to the Western Alliance in the Middle East was firmly entrenched in British-American military policy assessment. This assessment clearly impacted any political consideration of the future status of the island. Britain's rule over Cyprus was always dictated by its strategic interests in the region, which required "no change" to the island's sovereignty, thereby putting it on a collision course with the *enosists*.

The Lion and the Scorpion

On the dawn of April 1, 1955 a series of explosions across the island by militant *enosists* disrupted the tranquility of Cyprus once and for all. Initially dismissed by the British authorities as an April-Fools' Day hoax, for the next four years EOKA's guerrilla warfare focused international attention on British rule in Cyprus. Five years earlier, the Ethnarchy had held a plebiscite in which 95 percent of all Greek Cypriots voted for *enosis*. This was the brainchild of a dynamic new presence in the *enosist* camp—the Bishop of Kitium, and later Archbishop Makarios—who transformed the *enosis* campaign, beginning with persuading the Greek government to pursue Cyprus's case for self-determination at the UN General Assembly.

Confronted with these difficulties, the British government began to seek a political solution to the Cyprus crisis. To defuse the looming interalliance crisis, Britain invited Greece and Turkey to a tripartite conference, where Macmillan tabled his proposals. The Macmillan plan introduced a new constitution for internal self-government. More importantly, Macmillan proposed that a special tripartite committee be established, comprised of Britain, Greece, and Turkey, to oversee the constitutional proposals, consider the system of guarantees, and supervise "self-government in Cyprus."[55] Despite the collapse of the tripartite conference, its residual significance lies in the way it officially brought Turkey into the Cyprus equation and introduced the concept of tri-condominium over sovereignty of the island.

Failure to settle the dispute amongst the motherlands saw an internalization of the negotiating process to Cyprus as the British realized Makarios's influence with Greece. The new governor of Cyprus, John Harding, was instructed by London to engage in direct discussions with Makarios, while pursuing a tough law-and-order policy against the insurgents. London, nevertheless, viewed the Makarios-Harding talks with cynicism, and Eden was convinced that the Cyprus problem would only be resolved by agreement between the British, Greek, and Turkish governments. Eden also believed that Makarios "would not budge" on the question of self-determination and that he wanted to exclude the Turkish and even the Greek governments from the negotiations.[56]

Limited by their colonial outlook, Britain throughout these talks failed to grasp the shift in Makarios's position. For the first time, he abandoned the demand for immediate *enosis* and accepted a transitional constitution for self-government.[57] Neither did the British appreciate the intergroup dynamics at play, which required Makarios to win over his hard-line *enosists*, beginning with EOKA's military leader, Colonel George Grivas, "Dighenis."[58] Rather, as the talks reached a stalemate over the question of self-determination, Makarios's brinkmanship was misconstrued as obstinacy.[59] British frustration resulted in their halting negotiations and exiling Makarios, and with Harding declaring a state of emergency and banning AKEL as an "unlawful association."[60]

Eden's decision to exile Makarios came under severe criticism both internationally and from the Labour opposition. Attempts by the British to find "moderate" Greek Cypriots with whom they could deal over the Radcliffe proposals proved elusive, and it became abundantly clear that no one but Makarios had the authority to negotiate on behalf of the Greek Cypriot community. Makarios's absence from Cyprus had another profound effect: it provided Grivas with greater latitude for military action and consolidated his political authority over EOKA. In course of time, solidifying his political position, Grivas was elevated to coleader status of the entire *enosist* movement, and he became the principle agent and symbol of militant *enosis*.

During this political hiatus, the ill-fated Radcliffe proposals for internal self-government were introduced. As with the Macmillan plan, the Radcliffe plan was significant for serving as a constitutional blueprint for self-government, elements of which can be found in the final settlement of 1959. In line with previous British proposals on self-government, Radcliffe introduced a constitution that regulated "the exercise of political power" in Cyprus.[61] The central tenet of his power-sharing model rested on diarchy between the British governor and a Cypriot parliament. The plan, however, was tainted by the British government's redefinition of its self-determination policy: that power should be exercised equally by both the Greek and Turkish communities and that, for the first time, the policy should include partition as an option.[62]

Partition had in fact been an option for the British government as early as 1956, when Macmillan mused that it "might prove the only solution."[63] In more blunt terms, Eden's ultimate view was that "Greeks and Turks could be associated with the British in control of the island, or the island could be partitioned."[64] The seriousness of the "partition option" was such that Macmillan, a few days after becoming prime minister, "sent a minute to the Foreign Secretary, reverting to the possibility of a settlement on the lines of partition." Furthermore, he "asked that the Minister of Defence…set up an urgent inquiry into [British] military needs, and whether the base could be carved out of the territory without too much difficulty and effectively defended."[65]

Whether a sign of policy fatigue or a tactical "divide-and-rule" ploy to blackmail the Greeks into compromise, partition emerged as Turkey's predominant Cyprus policy (*taksim*) to negate *enosis*. British engagement with Turkey and Turkish Cypriots in negotiations, on their own counterclaim of partition, created a triangular relationship that enabled Britain to redefine its role as a mediator with muscle. The British concept of the tripartite prevailed, becoming the dominant process by which a Cyprus settlement was negotiated. By abandoning its policy of retaining exclusive sovereignty over Cyprus, Britain could then, as Harding argued, "dovetail" its military requirements into any agreement.[66]

In Search of an Exit Strategy

While on the island, EOKA and the Turkish Cypriot nationalist underground group TMT (*Türk Mukavemet Tehşkilati* [Turkish Resistance Organization]) intensified their armed conflict, resulting in the island's first intercommunal violence, British policy had shifted: they were satisfied with having only a base in Cyprus, and were prepared to relinquish sovereignty over the whole island. Specifically, British objectives were to protect the island from communist infiltration; retain "minimum essential military facilities" under its sovereignty; "achieve a permanent settlement" acceptable to both communities, Greece and Turkey; and strengthen security and cooperation between Britain and its allies in a vital area.[67]

As with his first proposal, Macmillan's "partnership plan" proposed that a Greece-Turkey-Britain troika rule Cyprus, while internally a dual governmental system would allow each community to exercise autonomy over its own affairs. Britain was prepared, subject to retaining "such bases and facilities" that it deemed necessary, to share sovereignty of the island with Greece and Turkey.

By 1958, it became apparent that Macmillan intended to push forward with his plan.[68] NATO's subsequent failure to intervene compounded Greek fears of a British unilateral implementation. When Makarios—who was released from exile but was not allowed to return to Cyprus—decided to switch to a call for independence, it caught both the Konstantinos Karamanlis government and Grivas by surprise. Meanwhile, international pubic opinion, the United States, and the British Labour Party had grown weary of the Cyprus conundrum, which was generally seen to be separate from other national liberation movements. As Makarios frantically tried to convince Grivas of the independence option as the only way to avert the British plan, Greek Cypriot discord had embarked on a collision path with history.

Transformation of the Conflict: Phases and Thresholds

One of Cypriologists' favorite past-times is to quarrel over when the Cyprus problem started. Various historical thresholds are asserted: 1571, 1821, 1878, 1915, 1931, 1945, 1955, 1960, 1964, and 1974. As with any other protracted conflict, the Cyprus dispute comprises of a series of turning points—mostly violent events—that catapulted the conflict in new directions. In addition to 1878, three other major turning points have clearly and radically transformed Cyprus: independence in 1960, the collapse of first Republic in 1963–1964, and partition in 1974 (the latter two, despite contestations between Greek and Turkish Cypriot historiography)—subsequently, as we will see further down, the events of 2003–2004 may also prove to be a significant reference point in the post-Cold War incarnation of the Cyprus conflict.

The Dawn of Independence

The idea of independence, albeit as a second-best solution, had been strongly advocated by India and gained traction among various third parties, including the British Labour opposition and the United States. By the time the London Conference (February 19, 1959) took place to formally sign the Cyprus Agreement, the three governments had reached agreement on the main terms of a settlement. Britain had secured its strategic needs, with the retention of ninety-nine square miles for two sovereign bases of Akrotiri and Dhekelia. Makarios's last-minute objections to certain aspects of the Zurich Agreement—drafted eight days before the London Conference by the prime ministers of Greece and Turkey—were thwarted by Karamanlis, who warned that if Makarios did not sign, Greece would not be responsible for the conference's failure, or for the consequences (meaning partition).[69] Renditions of Makarios agonizing between pragmatic compromise and obstinate resistance have entered the annals of Greek Cypriot nationalist folklore; and his historical dilemma has recast itself at every momentous juncture when major decisions are called for by the Greek Cypriot leadership.

The 1959 Cyprus settlement ushered in a new state of affairs. Cyprus became a presidential republic, the president being a Greek Cypriot and the vice-president a Turkish Cypriot with veto rights. The Council of Ministers comprised seven Greek Cypriot and three Turkish Cypriot ministers; legislative power would be vested in a House of Representatives comprising 70 percent Greek Cypriots and 30 percent Turkish Cypriots; all laws would be adopted by "a simple majority," except for the basic articles, electoral law, municipalities, duties, and taxes, which would require separate majorities; there would be two Communal Chambers with the right to impose taxes and levies on its community; the public service would be 70 percent Greek Cypriot and 30 percent Turkish Cypriot; the Cyprus Army would be 60 percent Greek Cypriot and 40 percent Turkish Cypriot; the security forces would be 70 percent Greek Cypriot and 30 percent Turkish Cypriot; the High Court of Justice would have two Greek Cypriots, one Turkish Cypriot, and a neutral judge as president, with two votes; separate municipalities, created in the five largest towns with Turkish Cypriot inhabitants, were to be reviewed in four years; the "total or partial union of Cyprus with any other State, or a separatist independence (i.e., the partition of Cyprus into two independent States) [was to] be excluded."[70]

Finally, the republic's constitutional arrangement incorporated the Guarantee and Alliance treaties. The most significant and controversial of the two, the Treaty of Guarantee, between Cyprus, Britain, Greece, and Turkey, undertook to ensure the republic's "independence, territorial integrity, security and respect for its Constitution," and prohibited "all activity to promote directly or indirectly either union or partition of the Island." In case of a breach, Britain, Greece, and Turkey undertook to consult each other and take the "necessary steps" needed to rectify the situation. If "common or concerted action [was to] prove impossible, each of the three" reserved the "right to take action with the sole aim of re-establishing the state of affairs established by the present Treaty."[71]

In its attempt to reconcile inherently paradoxical principles, Cypriot independence still remains a by-product of its postcolonial constellation. Post-colonialism saw the emergence of a contradictory order, in which the Republic of Cyprus typified the irresolvable tension between the compulsion toward sovereignty and the benefits of limited self-determination under hegemonic oversight. As it rendered *enosis* illegal, few Greek Cypriot nationalists embraced the Republic of Cyprus as a final solution. Rather, independence was viewed as an intermediate step toward self-determination and *enosis*. On the other hand, despite its clumsiness, the Republic of Cyprus was an attempt at power-sharing among Greek and Turkish Cypriots. The 1960 model promised to usher in a new era of cooperation, collaboration, peaceful coexistence, and prosperity among Cypriots. And although a second-best solution, the Republic of Cyprus served as both a source of dispute and a reference model into the future.[72]

Nominally, 1960 heralded the end of British colonial rule, the relinquishing of its hegemonic role and setting the scene for a triangular showdown between *enosist*, republicans, and *taksimists*. Reviewing the British colonial period, there is no doubt that along with transforming the Cyprus problem from a colonial to a regional dispute, British policy also converted it into an interethnic conflict. The process of ethnic division and segregation began with British colonial policies and practices that shaped the social system in such a way that the evolution of distinct Greek and Turkish nationalisms in Cyprus was inevitable.[73] In many respects, the Cyprus conflict is anchored in the legacy of British colonialism. That legacy included an unworkable constitution that institutionalized ethno-communalism, because it failed to take into account "the psychological and sociological fact that the power-protection system" increased "suspicions, antagonism and conflict between the communities because of the discriminations and uncertainties involved."[74] The sectarian and divisive provisions of the 1960 arrangement constituted the seeds that led to its collapse three years later.

Collapse of the First Republic

Three years after independence, the crisis of 1963–1964 and the collapse of the first republic saw another transformation of the conflict. From the beginning of the young republic, contentious issues (such as the integrated Cypriot Army, quotas for the public service, tax legislation, separate municipalities and communal chambers) emerged between the two communities. Each tested the effective functioning of the constitution. Against a background of constitutional gridlock, Makarios's attempts to amend the constitution, and their subsequent rejection by Turkish Cypriots, exposed the frailty of the Zurich regime. The political crisis flared to violent conflict when fighting broke out between armed irregulars, while Turkish jet fighters flew threateningly low over Nicosia. As fighting on the island threatened to escalate and embroil mainland Greek and Turkish troops stationed there, a UN cease-fire paved the way for failed negotiations between the guarantor powers.

It is difficult to overestimate the magnitude of the 1964 crisis for the Turkish Cypriot community. This was a seminal event for them. The Greek Cypriots failed to comprehend the significance of 1964 crisis in the Turkish Cypriot national narrative. Their inability to grasp the centrality of this "chosen trauma" only compounded the "mistrust factor" in any prospective endeavor toward coexistence and reunification.[75] Cast in bereaved language, the 1964–1974 trial would underline all future negotiating predispositions for the Turkish Cypriots.

Turkish Cypriot withdrawal from the state apparatus and retraction into concentrated enclaves brought about a political, social, and demographic separation. Makarios's overtures to the Soviets prompted the British to seek a U.S.-NATO intervention. The NATO plan, which entailed a peacekeeping force and a mediator, was intended to diffuse the Cyprus crisis before it reached the United Nations. The internationalization of the Cyprus problem would have unleashed a Pandora's Box of Soviet and Nonaligned meddling in what was considered a Western prerogative. The plan's rejection by Makarios, alongside Soviet warnings, however, saw the Cyprus problem being referred to the United Nations, resulting in the establishment of a United Nations Peacekeeping Force in Cyprus (UNFICYP) and the appointment of a mediator. Essentially, UNFICYP originated from Britain's assessment that the ad hoc peacekeeping set up by the three guarantor powers was unsustainable, given the failure by NATO countries to supplement it. As the situation in Cyprus deteriorated, Britain feared unilateral action by Turkey if a solution on the ground was not found quickly.[76]

Another significant feature of the 1964 crisis was that it ushered in the direct involvement of the United States in the Cyprus conflict. An extension of the Truman doctrine to include Cyprus within its ambit saw the British relinquishing primacy to the Americans. In their account of U.S. foreign policy during the 1960s, award-winning journalists Edward Weintal and Charles Bartlett judged America's first foray into the Cyprus conflict as an unmitigated success. Basking in a Kennedy-like, Peace Corps naiveté, Weintal and Bartlett echoed prevailing U.S. liberalism at the time, which measured diplomatic success in terms of military and expenditure commitment.[77] In the short term, this assessment was not totally unfounded: U.S. policy did manage to keep the Soviets from gaining a foothold in a strategically placed East Mediterranean/Middle Eastern outpost; it deterred Turkey from invading the island;[78] and it also averted intercommunal hostilities from spilling over into a broader Greco-Turkish war.

The 1964 crisis is renowned for prompting U.S. intervention in the Cyprus problem. The United States was determined to remove Cyprus as an unremitting source of tension between Greece and Turkey. To achieve their overarching objective of eliminating the Republic of Cyprus, U.S. Undersecretary of State George Ball and former Secretary of State Dean Acheson advanced various alternatives of "double enosis" to solve the Greek-Turkish quagmire.[79] The main tenets of the Acheson plan were the union of Cyprus with Greece, in exchange for the Greek island of Kastellorizo and a military base on the island for Turkey. In addition, there would be two Turkish Cypriot enclaves and resettlement provisions for those wishing to emigrate. In pursuit of the Acheson plan, Ball engaged in clandestine dealings with Makarios's nemesis Grivas, who adopted it as his own plan, with the amendment that the Turks take over one of Britain's bases and the supplementary ousting of Makarios, an attractive proposal for the United States.[80] For various reasons, the scheme was unacceptable to both Greece and Turkey, and was eventually superseded by situational events.

The year 1964 cemented U.S. policy on Cyprus. Makarios was castigated as a "spoiler" whom Acheson blamed for throwing "monkey wrenches" into his plan.[81] Until the mid-1970s, 1964 was the benchmark by which all future U.S. intervention would be judged. It also set the model for the U.S.-UN relationship over the Cyprus problem—epitomized by the setting-up of Acheson's consultancy office adjacent to the main UN-negotiations office in Geneva.

A less notorious intervention, but one that left an indelible imprint on the peace process, was that of the UN mediator on Cyprus, Galo Plaza. An antidote to the Acheson model, the Plaza plan favored "an independent Cyprus with adequate safeguards for the safety and the rights of all its people," and the exclusion of *enosis*, which he considered as "the most divisive and...explosive aspect" of the conflict. He dismissed federation and the "geographical separation of the two communities," which would "inevitably lead to partition," and supported the protection of Turkish Cypriot minority rights, designating the United Nations as a guarantor of the settlement.

More significantly, Plaza outlined the process that all future UN mediations would follow. Plaza thought mediation should be conducted in two stages: first, between the two main Cypriot communities, followed by the other parties agreeing to any settlement. Within such a framework, he recommended that a series of meetings between the Greek and Turkish Cypriot representatives would be most productive.[82] Despite its rejection, the value of the Plaza plan rests with its residual impact on future UN-led negotiations.

Inward and Outward

The crisis of 1967 saw another transformation of the conflict. The withdrawal of the Greek secret army and the removal of Grivas from Cyprus as head of the Greek Cypriot National Guard changed the balance of power on the island. It also led Makarios to adopt a new policy, defined by his "feasible" doctrine, which further sharpened opposition from the hard-line *enosists*.

Encouraged by Galo Plaza's recommendations, Security Council Resolution 244 (1967) called on the conflicting parties to enter into intercommunal talks by availing "themselves of the good offices proffered by the Secretary-General."[83] Although the intercommunal talks were conducted on the basis of competing interests, as we saw in the introduction, theoretically at least they contained the potential for what Fred Charles Iklé termed "identical common interests," provided the environment was politically conducive.[84]

Supported by Greece and Turkey, the intercommunal talks took place between 1968 and 1974. Initially the Greek Cypriots were steadfast that the 1960 Constitution needed amendment based on Makarios's thirteen points. The Turkish Cypriot side, on the other hand, pressed for an early agreement, and was prepared to concede on most points in exchange for local government entailing the communal grouping of villages.

In what was to become a familiar pattern, the second and third phases saw an exchange of proposals on the executive government, police, legislature, justice, and local government. The Turkish position hardened demanding that local government be included in the constitution, and a Turkish map regrouping Turkish Cypriot villages into specifically defined local government areas was discovered.[85]

During the fourth phase, the Greek Cypriot negotiator Glafkos Clerides offered his Turkish Cypriot counterpart Rauf Denktash a package deal in which the Greek Cypriots accepted, in principle, the "communal groupings" of Turkish Cypriot villages in exchange for a 60:15 composition of the legislature.[86] Denktash indicated that he was prepared to accept the abolition of the vice-president's veto; proposed the reestablishment of the two communal chambers as separate legislative assemblies in charge of communal matters; and most importantly, proposed that local government's powers, duties, and jurisdiction be embodied in the constitution, coordinated by central authorities rather than district instrumentalities.[87]

By the time the talks had broken down in 1971 it became apparent that the stumbling block to any agreement was over the question of local government. Denktash narrowed the point of disputation even further, for although there was "a fair degree of agreement on what the functions appertaining to local autonomy" should be, there was also a "sharp disagreement on the nature of the organs which [were] to manage such affairs."[88] Polyvios G. Polyviou concurred with Denktash that disagreement was specifically over the "type of power" to be exercised by the local organs and the government's central controls upon it.[89] Following the intervention of UN Secretary-General, U Thant, the talks were reactivated on June 8, 1972 and broadened to include the Secretary-General's Special Representative in Cyprus, B. F. Osorio Tafall, and the Greek and Turkish constitutional experts Michael Dekleris and Orhan Aldiçasti.[90]

The tense political climate of the early-1970s, however, undermined the intercommunal talks. Especially for Greek Cypriots, it was a time of violent tension, as the hard-line *enosists* resorted to open terrorism against the Republic of Cyprus and the Zurich regime— referred to as *tafopetra tis* (tombstone of) *enosis*. Grivas had arrived secretly in Cyprus on August 31, 1971 and formed the pro-*enosis* terrorist group EOKA-B, which was determined to fight for "*enosis* and only *enosis*," and which opposed the intercommunal talks as well as Makarios's "feasible" doctrine.[91] As Dekleris noted, the situation directly impacted the intercommunal talks, in that it undermined Greece's credibility, made Makarios more reluctant to renounce *enosis* and pursue a settlement, and stirred Turkish suspicion regarding Greek duplicity.[92]

Despite political instability, the 1974 model brought the talks very close to a settlement, with agreement on local government remaining the only obstacle. Indicative of the progress achieved was sufficient for the new UN Secretary-General, Kurt Waldheim, to confidently report to the Security Council that:

> agreement was being reached on a "package deal" concerning the structure of the State, the division of powers and the degree of local

authority to be granted to the Turkish Cypriot community in exchange of their renunciation of a number of rights embodied in the 1960 Constitution.[93]

As local government constituted a new layer of government, there were differences over its supposed function. The Greek Cypriots viewed it as a way of decentralization, by delegating power to local units for the discharge of local functions, while the Turkish Cypriots saw it as an alternative power structure organized on communal lines and free of state control.[94]

The last meeting of the intercommunal talks (June 11, 1974) was dominated by the Bülent Ecevit-Turan Günes statements that the best solution for Cyprus was federation.[95] In April, Denktash repeated this view that since there was no "unitary Cypriot people" a "unitary State as envisaged by the Greek-Cypriots cannot be created."[96] The view of a federal solution "based on a cantonal system" was a prevalent view at the time amongst Turkish decision and opinion makers. Reflecting the post-1964 manifestation of the conflict, federation was considered by the Turks as a realistic compromise that would "reconcile cultural, ethnic and geographical differences [reference to Turkish Cypriot enclaves]" whilst retaining the political unity of the state.[97]

In retrospect, the first intercommunal talks clearly presented a unique opportunity for resolving the internal aspect of the Cyprus problem. This assessment is supported by the fact that, except for the issue of local government, a settlement was almost reached in 1974. Whether such a settlement would have circumvented the Greek junta's *coup d'etat*, and subsequently the Turkish invasion, is subject to conjecture. Given Ioannides's ideological (and pathological) nationalism with respect to Cyprus, a settlement during his reign would have been unlikely to deter his plans and would have probably expedited his decision to move against Makarios. The same cannot be said for the circumstances prevailing in Greece prior to November 1973, when his predecessor George Papadopoulos, who supported the intercommunal talks, would have welcomed a settlement.

The Road to Partition

When the Cyprus crisis exploded in the summer of 1974, unevenly matched and differently motivated forces came together to divide the island. As Christopher Hitchens' "collusion theory" suggests, these forces had one thing in common: their fear or dislike of an independent Cyprus.[98] There is no doubt that the most important turning point in the modern incarnation of the Cyprus conflict are the events of 1974 and their dual significance: the socio-demographic impact of partitioning the island's ethnic populations, and the fact that all subsequent peace negotiations attempted to address the consequences flowing from these events.

To appreciate 1974's impact on the Greek Cypriot psyche, we need only to glance ahead thirty years to those emotionally charged weeks before the April 2004 referendum on the Annan plan. Soliciting support for the "Yes" cause, U.S. Secretary of State Colin Powell remarked during a television interview that "2004 (is) not 1974."[99] Echoing Monty Python's "don't mention the war," Powell's uttering unleashed fears and insecurities harbored by Greek Cypriots for three decades. The psychological effect of 1974 was exacerbated by parallels drawn with the fall of Constantinople in 1453 and the Asia Minor Catastrophe of 1922. The year 1974 perpetuated the image of the "unspeakable" Turk as Orthodox Hellenism's eternal enemy, out to expel them from their ancestral homeland, in a melancholic fatalism colored by betrayal, defeat, and loss. Within this context, 1974 represents the apex of national treachery for Greek determinism, which reverberates through Greek Cypriot political culture and haunts their decision-making throughout the peace process.

Conversely, 1974 is heralded as a "peace operation" and celebrated by Turkish Cypriots as an antidote to Greek Cypriot oppression. In Vamık D. Volkan's diagnosis, 1974 served a therapeutic—almost cathartic—function for the Turkish Cypriot community. Its ego-syntonic resonance and its aggressive quality provided a liberating, cleansing sensation for a minority suffering from low esteem and a victim mentality.[100]

The events of the summer of 1974 were set in motion eight months earlier, with a change of guard in the Greek junta. The new regime was led behind the scenes by the mysterious and ruthless chief of military police, Brigadier-General Dimitrios Ioannides, who considered Makarios a "crypto-communist" and was credited with masterminding the 1970 assassination attempt on him. Ioannides's ascension to power aggravated the already strained relationship between Athens and Nicosia, and the rift culminated in a head-on collision on July 15, 1974, when Greek officers of the National Guard mounted a *coup d'etat* ousting President Makarios, who fled to Britain. Citing its right to intervene under the Treaty of Guarantee, Turkey invaded the north of Cyprus five days later.[101]

While armed hostilities transformed Aphrodite's tourist-favored island into an anarchic war zone, the international community scrambled for an expedient cease-fire. Security Council Resolution 353 provided the legal basis for a two-tiered UN-Anglo/American diplomatic initiative, which secured a cease-fire—but not before the Turkish forces established a bridgehead at Kyrenia-Nicosia. Confronted with the possibility of going to war with Turkey unprepared and risking national humiliation, the military junta surrendered political power back to civilian rule in both Greece and Cyprus.

As had often happened before, and after, Switzerland offered itself as a venue for Cyprus peace talks. The first Geneva conference, attended by the guarantors' three foreign ministers—Britain's James Callaghan, Greece's Giorgos Mavros, and Turkey's Günes— endorsed the UN cease-fire and called for the immediate commencement of negotiations. These talks also included Greek and Turkish Cypriot representatives and addressed the "immediate return to constitutional legitimacy," the role of the vice-president, and "the existence in practice in the republic of Cyprus of two autonomous administrations."[102]

The Geneva conference was viewed as a modest success for Anglo-American diplomacy: according to Callaghan's graphic depiction, "America...provided the muscle while Britain...provided the brains."[103] As Callaghan revealed, the agreement created a climate of stabilization "under which Greece and Turkey [could] draw back honourably from making war with each other."[104] A more jubilant Ecevit declared with nationalistic pride that "Turkey did not lose at the conference table what it had gained on the field."[105] In the meantime, Turkish forces began to expand eastward and westward from their Kyrenia-Nicosia bridgehead, doubling the area under their control and unleashing the first wave of refugees.[106] Ecevit justified Turkey's refusal to withdraw, or to stop reinforcing its troops, citing his country's need for a military presence if it was "to contribute to establishing constitutional order in Cyprus." Specifically, Ecevit envisaged a "new constitutional solution for Cyprus" with "separate government for Greeks and Turks on the island," which he saw as "essential after all that has happened."[107] The Greeks, on the other hand, were relieved that war with Turkey had been averted, but they were in no way elated by the costs incurred. Premier Karamanlis—who was brought out of exile—expressed satisfaction with the agreement, as it "[put] an end to the hostilities" and acted as a "starting point for a fair settlement of the Cyprus question."[108] Privately, though, he conceded stoically, "all mistakes must be paid for."[109]

When the Geneva conference reconvened, it became apparent that Günes's intention was to impose Turkey's preferred plan. Essentially,

Günes's plan called for a bicommunal independent state comprised of two autonomous zones, in which the Turkish Cypriot sector, of six districts, amounted to 34 percent of the island. Each administration would control "its own area within its geographical boundaries," with movement between the districts of the same zone secured by a central government.[110]

Having tabled his cantonment plan, Günes gave twenty-four hours notice for acceptance. Despite attempts by both Callaghan and Clerides to propose alternative constitutional and territorial arrangements, the Turks were steadfast on their demands.[111]

An epigraph to the failed peace talks in Geneva was the impudent role played by the superpowers. In a last ditch effort, 'Clerides' sought Soviet military intervention, only to be asked by their representative, Victor Menin, "whether (the) request had been cleared with the Americans." Menin's question indicated that there was an "understanding" between the two superpowers over Cyprus, which effectively barred unilateral Soviet intervention.[112]

In terms of U.S. concerns, Henry Kissinger's message at the last session of the conference recognized that the "position of the Turkish community in Cyprus require[d] considerable improvement and protection" and supported "a greater degree of autonomy for them." The U.S. position was that the parties "negotiat[e] on one or more Turkish autonomous areas." Finally, the United States believed that diplomatic avenues had not been exhausted and considered "a resort to military action unjustified."[113] Günes, who read Kissinger's message, mistook this to be a confirmation of his plan.

It became apparent that Kissinger had counseled President Gerald Ford to "tilt toward Turkey as the lesser political evil" in what constituted Ford's first international crisis.[114] Ecevit later claimed that Kissinger was in favor of "separate, geographically autonomous administrations" to be obtained by "negotiations instead of militarily."[115] Günes insisted that Turkey "would not be satisfied with ending the conference with a bland declaration of good will." Turkey already considered its plan a "big concession" and insisted on Greek agreement.[116]

At 01.20 GMT on Wednesday, August 14, 1974, the talks collapsed after Günes refused British and Greek requests for an adjournment. Immediately, Ecevit ordered Turkish troops in Cyprus to gain control of a "fair share" of territory.[117] Although Callaghan ruled out unilateral British involvement in the fighting, he angrily blamed Turkey for the collapse. Three hours after the breakdown of the Geneva Conference, Turkish military forces—in an operation codenamed

ZAFER—with heavy air and artillery cover, broke through the cease-fire line and opened up two fronts: toward Famagusta in the east and Morphou/Lefka in the west. Having gained control of nearly 37 percent of Cyprus, Ecevit declared a cease-fire on August 16, stating that the "foundations have been laid for the new federal state of Cyprus."[118]

Chapter 2

A Prisoner's Dilemma

On the eve of Leonard W. Doob's foray into the Cyprus conflict, piercing Starfighters of the Turkish Air Force ensured his Track Two negotiations would be aborted. With Alitalia Flight 709 posed to take two dozen Greek and Turkish Cypriots to northern Italy for Doob's workshop, Turkey invaded Cyprus.[1] Malvern Lumsden's premonition of three years earlier had come true: war was not the worst possible outcome.[2] Though the Cyprus conflict had engaged international diplomacy since the 1950s, the events of 1974 dramatically changed the nature of the problem, compounding the difficulties facing all subsequent attempts at mediation. Partition, dislocation, and militarization imposed a new set of variants and metamorphosed the conflict from any previous incarnation. Well-versed in these "new realities," the UN-mediated intercommunal talks emerged as the common denominator for all future negotiations. In light of these "new realities," a survey of the parties' predicaments offers insight into their attitudes toward each other and the negotiating process.

Enunciation of Positions:
Greek and Turkish Cypriot Perspectives

The occupation of 37 percent of the island's territory by Turkish troops, and the exodus of approximately 200,000 Greek Cypriot refugees, divided the island along demographic lines into two homogeneous parts (see Map 2.1). The Greek Cypriot community found itself in a more precarious position than prior to 1974, and in contrast to past seminal events the social consequences of 1974 were felt beyond the traditional elite, shadowing an entire generation of Cypriots.

The Greek Cypriot leadership quickly realized that these "new realities" required a new policy and a new strategy. They became

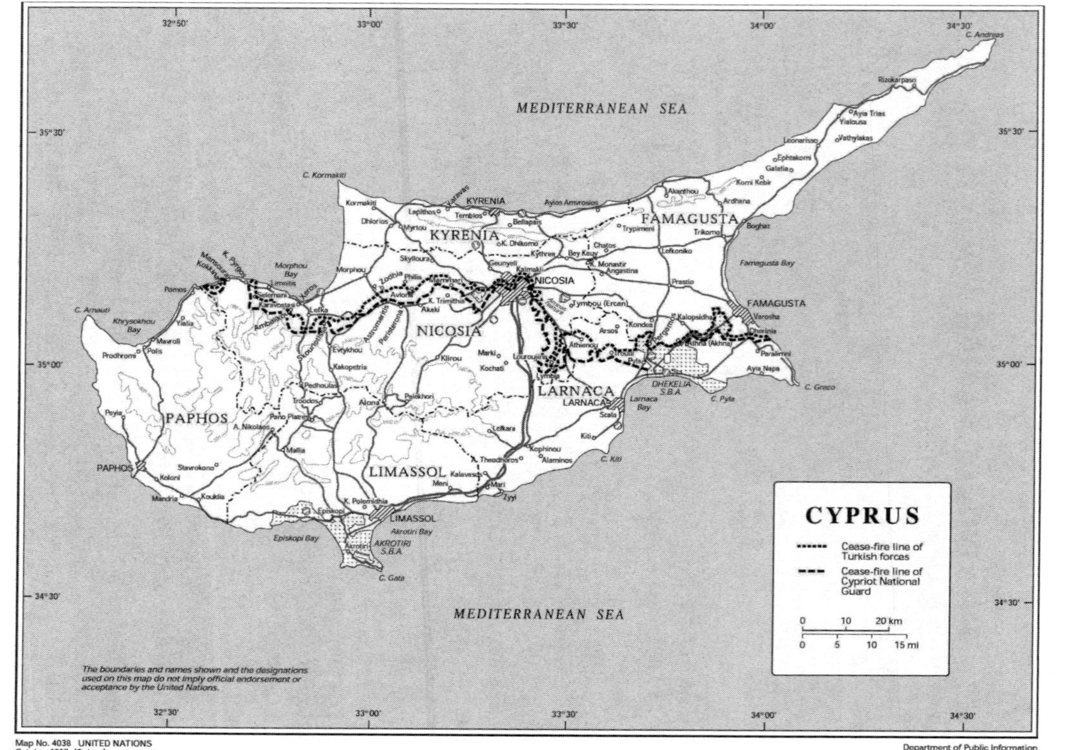

Map 2.1   Cyprus Post-1974

Source: UN Map Cyprus, no. 4038, October 1997.

aware of their limited capacity to bring about a settlement, which was ultimately dependent on external forces. They also realized that any attempt to continue the 1968 intercommunal talks was futile. UN resolutions, however, meant they could not reject the call for intercommunal talks, for fear of alienating the international community in general and the influential Western powers in particular. The intercommunal talks also operated within an environment where their negotiating counterpart was dependent politically, militarily, economically, and psychologically on Turkey. For the Greek Cypriots, Turkey would need to be pressured to instruct the Turkish Cypriots to make concessions at the negotiations. The main agents capable of applying such pressure were the United States, a core of Western European powers, and the international community, in that order.

The call to recommence intercommunal negotiations required an urgent reassessment of the Greek position. But a dilemma confronted both the Greek and Greek Cypriot leaderships: should they hold to the original objectives, or should they develop a new set of objectives? In the latter case, what kinds of objectives should, and could, be sought? At any rate, it quickly became evident that their pre-1974 position was no longer feasible, especially given the threat that the existing *de facto* situation could become, in time, permanent.

At an Athens summit in November–December 1974, this dilemma confronted the Greek and Greek Cypriot leaderships. The Greek premier, Karamanlis, set the tone for national unity. Clerides, who had stewardship of the negotiations and Karamanlis's backing, had made his position clear prior to the summit. He believed that the Greek side should strive for a mutually acceptable settlement, recognizing that Turkish Cypriots would accept federation only if it was established on some sort of geographical division. This position was fiercely opposed by the small but influential socialist party EDEK (*Eniea Dimokratiki Enosis Kentrou* [Unified Democratic Centre Union]), one of Makarios's strongest supporters. Makarios had in fact previously indicated his willingness to discuss federation, provided it entailed a strong central government.[3] In any event, Makarios's precondition that any settlement should include the return of all Greek Cypriot refugees to their homelands—therefore ruling out geographical division on bizonal lines—was incorporated in the new policy.

The policy framework that emerged from the Athens summit became the bedrock of the Greek national position on Cyprus. Heavily influenced by a need for redemption—encapsulated in the slogan "Cyprus decides and Greece follows"—the Athens doctrine advocated a multiregional bicommunal federation, with essential powers vested in the central government; the premise that the total area under Turkish Cypriot administration should be equal to their proportion of the population, or at least not exceed 25 percent of the island; the repatriation of the Greek Cypriot population; the right of property and freedom of movement; and the withdrawal of all foreign troops from Cyprus.[4]

The negotiating framework established by the Athens summit—this early in the process—cannot be underestimated. The prevailing assessment was that comprehensive concessions were necessary if negotiations with the Turkish side were to have any chance of success. The meeting was central for its grounding in the Makarios-Karamanlis policy of realism: accepting federalism as the basis for a negotiated settlement. Ambiguity, however, over the nature of Cypriot federalism and its implementation became the hallmark of the Cyprus dilemma for decades.

Functional federation, embodied territorially as multiregionalism, became the Greek Cypriots' earliest position. The argument for a multiregional federation, and a critique of "classical" federation, was best articulated by the geographer George Karouzis, who proposed a functional federation for the administrative and constitutional aspects of the state, and a multiregional federation for the territorial component. Multiregional federalism, however, would only be feasible if all refugees were allowed to return to their homelands.[5]

The federalist position merged with another social consequence of 1974: the ideological reconfiguration of Cypriot consciousnesses. The events of 1974 accelerated the growth of Cypriotism as a sociopolitical movement at the expense of Greek ethno-nationalism. Cypriotism was not a new phenomenon, and in the historical context of Cyprus's "culture wars" held modest appeal as an antidote to both Greek and Turkish ethno-nationalism. Traditionally the domain of Cypriot communists, Cypriotism had resonated with the KKK (*Kommounistiko Komma Kiprou* [Communist Party of Cyprus])-AKEL, who, as Marxist-Leninists, viewed nationalism as a wedge that divided the working class. Adopted by certain liberal circles, Cypriotism coexisted uncomfortably with ethno-nationalism after independence. Nevertheless, Cypriotism was effectively promoted after 1974, especially by the New Cyprus Association, with the distinct purpose of safeguarding Cyprus's independence. Despite its small size, throughout the 1970s the association had an immense impact on the public policy of denationalizing the Cyprus problem.[6]

The Athens summit and Makarios's return to Cyprus gave rise to two opposing political positions in the Greek Cypriot community, which clashed over the general question of strategy. Known as the *pragmatistes* (pragmatists) and the *mahitikoi* (militants), they were also referred to by detractors as the *endotikoi* (submissive) and the *aporiptikoi* (rejectionists). Neither faction ever had total influence over government policy; their impact depended on domestic and external circumstances as well as the status of the intercommunal talks. Nevertheless, the political and ideological dynamics of these two tendencies shed important light on both the Greek Cypriot and Greek positions; they were capable of influencing the decision-making process and public opinion, at the centre of which was Makarios.

Renowned as a Western-style moderate, Clerides was the leading advocate of the pragmatist position that—until his fallout with Makarios in 1976—was the dominant influence on the official Greek Cypriot position. Essentially, Clerides's view was "that every proposal was worse than the previous," and that in the past, Greek Cypriots had lost opportunities to resolve the Cyprus problem. Convinced that time was against them, he favored a "quick solution," and "the only viable solution [was] a federation on a geographical basis."[7]

Before Makarios's return, this perspective was not hampered by ideological restraints, as Clerides—the ex-officio leader of the conservative right—enjoyed support from AKEL. Despite its political alliances, AKEL remained a fundamental pillar of Cypriot pragmatism. AKEL strongly supported the intercommunal talks as the only feasible and tested procedure, believing that a multiregional federation was the best model that would guarantee the return of all refugees, offer a strong central government, and create the conditions for a harmonic coexistence between Greek and Turkish Cypriots. AKEL also endorsed the Soviet proposal for a UN-sponsored international conference as an alternative procedure if the intercommunal talks failed.[8]

EDEK and its leaders Vassos Lyssarides and Takis Hadjidemetriou spearheaded opposition to the pragmatists. They were later joined by several centralists, including Spyros Kyprianou and Tassos Papadopoulos, as well as the leadership of the Church of Cyprus. Nevertheless, the pragmatists' strongest supporter was Andreas Papandreou and his socialist party PASOK (*Panellinio Socialistiko Kinima* [Panhellenic Socialist Movement]). EDEK was highly critical of Clerides during his tenure as acting president, holding him responsible for the subsequent population transfers, whilst castigating his pragmatism as "subservient realism" and his moderation as "defeatism." Attacking Clerides and the pragmatists, Lyssarides declared that "geographical federation" was "the pseudonym for the total Turkish occupation [of Cyprus] or of partition."[9] As one of the main leaders of the militant faction, Lyssarides considered the intercommunal talks a failure and advocated a policy of a "fighting realism" based on the triptych of internationalization, utilization of all external assistance, and the struggle of the people.[10] Lyssarides favored internationalizing the Cyprus problem by way of an international conference that would implement the UN resolutions; and he opposed further calls for compromise. The militants were even prepared to question Makarios. Hadjidemetriou, for example, criticized the archbishop over his tacit acceptance of the Kissinger initiative, as well as the general policy of moderation adopted after the Athens summit. Hadjidemetriou argued that such a policy placed the Cyprus problem outside the United Nations and allowed NATO to subsume it by treating Cyprus as a problem between Greece and Turkey.[11]

The militants managed to gain more influence following the Clerides-Makarios fallout. After Makarios's death, notwithstanding AKEL's influence, Kyprianou and his centre-Right DIKO (*Dimokratiko Komma* [Democratic Party]) gravitated toward the school's central tenet. After 1981, Papandreou's government significantly boosted the militants. Even Clerides's conservative Right party DISY (*Dimokratikos Sinagermos* [Democratic Rally]) adopted the militants' defiant rhetoric during the resurgence of Greek Cypriot nationalism in the 1990s.

The events of 1974 also had a tremendous impact on the Turkish Cypriot community and were a catalyst for the community's political transformation. The new security afforded to the Turkish Cypriot community by the presence of Turkish troops, and their concentration in one geographical area, meant that internal differences soon emerged. The relocation of Turkish Cypriots into enclaves during 1964–1974 had brought about a certain political homogeneity and united Turkish Cypriots as an isolated minority.[12] The effects of 1964–1974 on the political elite sharpened and solidified the partition ideology as advocated in the 1950s, which had become the vehicle for separating the Greek and Turkish Cypriot communities. The Greek Cypriot economic and political embargo, aimed at preventing recognition of the Turkish Cypriot "state," only compounded the ideology of separateness.

In 1975, Turkish Cypriots proclaimed the Turkish Federal State of Cyprus (TFSC)—a precursor to their Unilateral Declaration of Independence (UDI) eight years later. In the counter vernacular that characterizes the political discourse between the two communities, Denktash blamed Makarios for "making provocative statements about the futility of the [intercommunal] talks" and specified the Greek Cypriots' adoption of the "long struggle" doctrine as Turkish Cypriots' impetus for desiring an autonomous administration.[13]

The Turkish Cypriot leadership's consolidation of its political power was aided by the emergence of a new commercial bourgeoisie imbued with nationalism. Denktash emerged as the founding figure of the new Turkish Cypriot "state" and its official policy was that pursued by himself and Osman Orëk, who advocated non-coexistence. Eventually, such rigidity encouraged the emergence of a political opposition, which originated from the 1973 Turkish Cypriot vice-presidential elections, although it was marginalized by the state apparatus and severely restricted by the influence of mainland Turkey.

Besides their military relationship, the Turkish Cypriot community was also heavily dependent on Turkish aid, which accounted for 80 percent of the community's budget. This economic association was first institutionalized in the 1960s through the formation of the *Koordinasyon Komitesi* (Coordinating Committee), consisting of officials from the prime minister's office and Turkish Cypriot members of the executive branch of the administration. Economic dependency expanded into the political and administrative realms, and from 1974 until 1983 Turkish officials directly participated in the Turkish Cypriot cabinet. This political dependency was exemplified by the fact that announcements pertaining to Turkish Cypriot negotiations were first broadcasted by Ankara—lending weight to Greek Cypriot contention that there was no autonomous Turkish Cypriot policy.

Despite challenges from the Left, there was a commonly held perception of the Turkish Cypriot national question. There was agreement on maintaining the ethnic homogeneity of northern Cyprus and on the need for a Turkish military guarantee. This view maintained that since the 1964 crisis Turkish Cypriots had disputed the legality and legitimacy of the Republic of Cyprus. Turkish Cypriots had been forced to form their own administration, and the 1968–1974 intercommunal talks were conducted on the basis of resolving the 1964 constitutional crisis. For Turkish Cypriots, Turkey's intervention in 1974—referred to as a "Peace Operation"—was legal under the Treaty of Guarantee, and morally justified as it protected them from the Greek *enosists*. Turkish Cypriots argued that since 1964 there had been two administrations on the island, and that the internationally recognized Republic of Cyprus had in essence been the Greek Cypriot state. Turkish Cypriots claim their state was created within the context of both sides endeavoring to establish a federation in partnership. In relation to Greek Cypriot refugee and territorial claims, these matters were supposedly settled on August 2, 1975 with an exchange of population agreement.[14] Given the above situation, Turkish Cypriots argued that only a bicommunal and biregional federation was feasible—not a unified state or a multiregional federation, as advocated by the Greek Cypriots.[15]

In an interview, even the opposition leader Özker Özgür confirmed his adherence to this perspective. Outlining the opposition's policy in 1976, Özgür declared that while Greek Cypriots did not accept the new realities to emerge from 1974, coexistence between the two communities could never be successfully implemented. He believed that withdrawing Turkish troops before a solution would be dangerous, even though it worried him that some people in the Turkish government embraced Pan-Turkism. Özgür did not support the Soviet proposal for a multiparty international conference and accepted the presence of the British bases.[16] Justifying the Turkish Cypriot Left's position at the time, Özgür explained thirteen years later that although the long-term aim was toward the unification and demilitarization of the island, suspicion between the two communities made a bizonal federation solution necessary, so that each community could live in its own area with a sense of security. Simultaneously, though, conditions for cooperation between the two communities needed to be created.[17]

Turkish Cypriot opposition emerged around the economy and corruption; dependency on Turkey; coexistence with the Greek Cypriots within a bizonal federal system; and the fact that Denktash was propped up by the settlers and the Turkish armed forces.[18] By 1978, even the former vice-president, Fazıl Kütchük, broke his silence and spoke against importing settlers from Turkey, stating that "these newcomers will be a nuisance to our decent citizens...stop before it becomes too late."[19] Nevertheless, it was Ahmet Mithat Berberoglu's party CTP (*Comhuriyetçhi Türk Partisi* [Republican Turkish Party]),[20] which continued to be the most outspoken critic of Denktash's policy. In 1979, during an opening of a TMT center in Famagusta, Denktash attacked the opposition's views as nothing short of treason, declaring that such a policy "would surrender the Turkish Cypriots to the Greek Cypriots by deceiving the former with talk appealing to their stomachs."[21]

The two communities' initial proposals to the United Nations reflected these early attitudes. Clerides submitted the Greek Cypriot proposals, amounting to general principles, on February 10, 1975.[22] These proposals clearly defined Greek Cypriot priorities from the outset: the territorial percentage allocated to the Turkish Cypriot areas;

the powers of the central government; the three freedoms of movement, settlement, and property; the model for a bicommunal multiregional federal republic; the withdrawal of Turkish troops; and the return of all refugees to their homelands. These proposals reflected both the Athens summit national policy and what amounted to a consensus between the pragmatists and Makarios. This initial exchange of proposals made it evident that for the first time Greek Cypriots accepted a geographical federation and the bicommunal nature of the proposed state.

Similarly, the Turkish Cypriot proposals reflected their newfound status, their penchant for separation, and their preference for a minimalist federal arrangement.[23] This first attempt at negotiations came to an abrupt end when the Turkish Cypriots proclaimed the Turkish Federal State of Cyprus as an autonomous Turkish Cypriot administration. Justifying this maneuver, Denktash argued that since "the principle of a federal solution had been accepted," their action "was merely to establish the Turkish wing of the envisaged Federal Republic of Cyprus."[24]

Comparing both sets of documents, the gulf between the two communities is immediately apparent. In this first exchange, there was a clear division between the Greek Cypriot's multiregional and the Turkish Cypriots' bizonal federal model. In contrast to the Greek Cypriot side, Denktash made no proposal on the territorial question. While Clerides advocated a strong central government, Denktash pushed for a "loose" federation in which state rights superseded those of the federal government, based on a firm belief that the central government derived its power from the two communal administrations, and not the reverse, as attested by Clerides. Furthermore, Denktash perceived the federation as a partnership of two equals, with adequate constitutional provisions to prevent domination of one community over the other. Clerides supported the implementation of the three freedoms, while Denktash only accepted freedom of movement, making no mention of settlement and property. The Turkish Cypriots introduced the concept of a transitional government until a final agreement was reached. Finally, Denktash wanted the 1960 international regime retained, while Clerides considered that the issue of guarantees rested outside the jurisdiction of the intercommunal talks.

Defining the UN's Role: Mediation in Progress

To understand the evolution of the intercommunal talks, we need to trace their conception in UN resolutions made immediately after the

Turkish invasion. These resolutions dealt with three essential components of the dispute: they provided guidelines upon which a solution should be based, regarding both its long-term settlement and specific crises as they emerged; they recommended the negotiating procedure; and they defined and endorsed the role of the UN Secretary-General.

When hostilities erupted on July 20, 1974, the UN Security Council maintained its encouraging, if passive, position, urging the three guarantor powers to enter into negotiations. Resolution 353 assigned the Secretary-General to monitor the tripartite talks and report back with a view to adopting further measures/resolutions to restore peaceful conditions as soon as possible. The Secretary-General's role was further expanded in Resolution 359, requesting that he "take appropriate action" in respect of political developments in Cyprus.[25]

In accordance with resolutions 359 and 360, Secretary-General Waldheim visited the region to arrange a meeting between the leaders of the two communities, Clerides and Denktash, to address the serious humanitarian problems resulting from the July-August hostilities. Waldheim hoped that the talks would present an opportunity to discuss broader issues, paving the way toward negotiations for a political settlement.[26] Welcoming these meetings, the Security Council incrementally enhanced both Waldheim's role and the status of the talks. From September 6 until the end of 1974, "pre-intercommunal talks" were conducted between Clerides and Denktash at the arrangement of the Secretary-General's Special Representative to Cyprus, Luis Weckmann-Muñoz.

General Assembly Resolution 3212 (XXIX) of November 1974 officially endorsed these preliminary intercommunal talks as the main negotiating model for resolving the Cyprus problem. Specifically, the General Assembly considered "that the constitutional system of the Republic of Cyprus" concerned both the Greek and the Turkish Cypriot communities. Having commended these preliminary meetings, Resolution 3212 called "for their continuation with a view to reaching freely a mutually acceptable political settlement." The resolution also legitimated the Secretary-General's role, requesting that he continue "to lend his good offices to the parties concerned." The resolution called for the respect of Cyprus's sovereignty, independence, and territorial integrity; it urged the withdrawal of all foreign troops; and considered "that all refugees should return to their homes in safety." In conclusion, it encouraged further UN mediation, expressing the "hope that, if necessary, further efforts including negotiations can take place, within the framework of the United Nations, for the purpose of implementing the provisions of the present resolution."[27]

On December 13, 1974 the Security Council adopted two resolutions pertaining to the General Assembly's November proposals. The first, Resolution 364, cautiously agreed that the principles put forward by the General Assembly "intended to facilitate a solution." Satisfied that the General Assembly's model had been "adopted unanimously," in Resolution 365 the Security Council finally endorsed it and urged all "the parties concerned to implement it as soon as possible." The resolution also requested that the Secretary-General report on its implementation.

Finally, after the first round of intercommunal talks, Resolution 367 requested that the Secretary-General undertake a new mission and convene the "parties under new agreed procedures," placing himself personally at their disposal "so that the resumption, the intensification and the progress of comprehensive negotiations…under his auspices and with his direction as appropriate, might thereby be facilitated." It also called on the two communities to accord these negotiations a high priority.[28] Significantly, Resolution 367 established the intercommunal talks as the sole legitimate negotiating process and confirmed the Secretary-General as convener and facilitator of this process.

The Vienna Talks: Facilitative Approach

In pursuit of Resolution 367, Waldheim reconvened the intercommunal talks—known as the Vienna Talks. According to the communiqué issued at the end of the first round of these talks, there was "an exchange of views on the powers and functions of the central government." It was agreed that a combined expert committee would be set up to "examine detailed proposals, and report back to the negotiators at their next meeting." An in-principle agreement was reached to reopen the Nicosia International Airport under a joint committee. The two negotiators also undertook to examine suggestions, exchanged during the meetings, on the territorial and refugee issues and return with specific proposals at the next session. Finally, the issue of missing persons was also discussed and an undertaking made to investigate whatever information was provided, including any request from the International Committee of the Red Cross.[29]

Despite several meetings, the views of the expert committee remained highly divergent; it became clear that no progress could be achieved without firm instructions regarding the kind of federation they should be discussing. These directions could only be supplied by higher political processes, and since such a framework could not be agreed upon, the expert committee soon ground to a halt.

The second round of Vienna Talks was dominated by reports regarding Turkish settlement of the Greek sector of Famagusta. The Turkish Cypriots presented their views on the composition and the powers of the federal government, which essentially restated their position for political equality. Negotiations reached an impasse when Denktash refused to reveal his territorial proposals before Clerides accepted bizonality.

Eleven days after the breakdown of the discussions, the Turkish Cypriots proposed the establishment of a Transitional Joint Federal Government, arguing it would create "an atmosphere of confidence and mutual trust" by bringing the two communities together.[30] The Greek Cypriots rejected the proposal, since acceptance would have meant dismantling the Republic of Cyprus and thus relinquishing their only negotiating advantage—the legitimacy they derived from being internationally recognized as the sole legal state of Cyprus.

During the third round of the Vienna talks, however, Clerides and Denktash reached their first "Agreement on Voluntary Regrouping of Populations."[31] Conflicting interpretations meant the agreement became highly controversial. As far as the Turkish Cypriots were concerned, this was an "Exchange of Populations Agreement"— supervised by UNFICYP—which sealed the demographic question by resolving the "problem of displaced persons."[32] Denktash himself considered that the agreement "tackled and settled" the refugee problem—thus removing it as an issue for negotiation.[33]

Clerides firmly disputed this interpretation and characterized the agreement as simply a humanitarian arrangement.[34] Although Clerides was supported by Makarios and most of the *Ethniko Simvoulio* (National Council), he was fiercely criticized by the militants. Spearheading the attack, Lyssarides' believed that the transfer of Turkish Cypriots residing in the south to the north was in essence implementing the demographic partition of Cyprus. With hindsight, there is no doubt that the agreement was a dramatic development that, in conjunction with the transfer of Turkish Cypriots into self-contained enclaves during the 1960s, completed the division of Cyprus.

Evidently, the prevailing military situation on the island meant both communities entered into the agreement with different intentions. In particular, as Robert McDonald noted, the "Turkish-Cypriots were intent on segregating the communities while the Greek Cypriots sought to restore the heterogeneous distribution of populations by preventing the movement of settled communities and pressing for the safe return of refugees to their homes."[35] In any event, Waldheim observed that Turkish Cyprus did not adhere to the agreement and that the Greek Cypriots residing in the north did not receive any of the requisite assistance. As a result, many Greek Cypriots "gave up their homes…to migrate, often under destitute conditions, to the south."[36]

The fourth round of Vienna Talks produced no progress, as Denktash refused to present any territorial proposals. It became obvious that the midterm Turkish senate elections had hardened the Turkish position at the talks, as Süleyman Demirel's government wanted to avoid any electoral exploitation of the issue by his opponents. The Turkish Cypriot side led the discussions toward generalities and proposed that the various issues be undertaken by subcommittees, which would present submissions in the future.

Four weeks after the General Assembly resolution, the Greek and Turkish governments signed an accord on Cyprus during the NATO summit in Brussels. The accord endorsed a package deal approach at the intercommunal talks to resolve territorial and federal issues. Greece and Turkey would review the progress and attend to any arising difficulties.[37]

Clerides believed that Greece and Turkey had come under considerable pressure from NATO, and especially the United States, to resolve the procedural breakdown of the intercommunal talks.[38] The militants viewed the Brussels accord as undermining the thrust of General Assembly Resolution 3395, which could have been utilized as a negotiating weapon to redefine the terms and conditions for the recommencement of the intercommunal talks.

After the Brussels accord, both sides agreed to simultaneously submit proposals to the new Special Representative of the Secretary-General, Javier Pérez de Cuéllar. Clerides resigned as chief negotiator during this period, after having committed the Greek Cypriot side to be the first to submit territorial proposals. Clerides's political opponents attacked him for entering into a "secret pact" with Denktash. Clerides later said he was under enormous pressure from the Greek government and Waldheim not to allow the negotiations to collapse, as the Greek Cypriots would be held responsible at the Security Council.[39] Clerides's resignation was a clear political victory for the militants who, in alliance with AKEL, had managed to remove the key advocate of the pragmatists from Makarios's inner circle.

Elaborating on their previous positions, the Greek Cypriot proposals dealt with the constitutional and territorial issues, including the powers of the federal and regional administrations. From the outset, the proposals made it clear that all elements were interrelated and put forward on a "package deal" basis. They also stipulated that the federal republic of Cyprus should be the sole subject of international law, preserving the economic unity of the Republic of Cyprus, with human and political rights safeguarded for all citizens irrespective of where they lived. Participation of the "two communities in federal organs should be proportionate according to their ratio of population"; however, constitutional arrangements would provide for "equitable safeguards on certain matters." The Greek Cypriots proposed that the territory of the Turkish Cypriot administration be extended to 20 percent of the island, comprising three areas, as suggested by the Secretary-General at the fifth Vienna round. Finally, on the question of federalism, the proposals made it clear that the federal government should "exercise power on all matters other than those specifically and expressly assigned to its constituent members (regions)."[40]

Subsequently, the Turkish Cypriot proposals reiterated their earlier call for a transitional government and for the retention of the 1960 guarantees. The Turkish Cypriots proposed that Cyprus should be a federal republic composed of two states: one in the north for their community and one in the south for the Greek Cypriots. They reiterated their earlier position that there should be equality between the two states and that sovereignty be shared by the two communities as cofounders. Regarding property rights, these should be "settled by mutual agreement between the parties concerned," including compensation. The proposed powers and function of the federal government recalled their previous proposals. On the territorial issue, the Turkish Cypriots agreed to a "package deal" approach that would "adjust" the border between the two federated states according to a set of criteria.[41]

Comparing the two communities' proposals with their initial positions indicates a slight shift in the Greek Cypriots' original territorial requirements from a multiregional federation to a three-area Turkish Cypriot state. The Turkish Cypriots also seemed to have accepted the Greek Cypriot proposal that a resettlement fund be established to compensate those refugees who did not wish to return to their homes. There had been no change, however, on the substantial territorial and constitutional issues.

The Quest for Federalism

Kurt Waldheim's foray into the Cyprus conflict is now part of UN folklore. His association with the intercommunal talks since their inception saw him visit the island five times, four in an official capacity. Exasperation at the repeatedly failed peace efforts had him anoint Cyprus the "orphan child" of the United Nations.[42] Waldheim's fourth visit to the island in 1977, to chair a meeting between Makarios and Denktash, illustrates his point. Initially, the Secretary-General was to land at the defunct Nicosia International Airport, the expectation being that this symbolic gesture would somehow generate optimism throughout the island. Yet just before Waldheim was scheduled to depart for Cyprus, a fracas over where his plane would land jeopardized his whole mission. Daunted by the prospect of circling forever over the eastern Mediterranean or discarding the concluding leg of his Middle East trip, Waldheim opted for a convoluted compromise that saw him greeted at Larnaca airport by the Greek Cypriots, and then flown by helicopter to Nicosia airport to be received by Turkish Cypriot officials.[43] After this display of diplomatic aerobatics, Waldheim chaired the first meeting between Makarios and Denktash since 1974, which resulted in a landmark four-guideline agreement.[44]

Despite this breakthrough, the agreement's ambiguity rendered it open to conflicting interpretations, and it soon fell into controversy. Fierce debate occurred over the second guideline, and whether it introduced the concept of "bizonality," thus relinquishing the Greek Cypriot claim for multiregional or cantonal federation. Although the term "bizonal" was not in the wording of the agreement, much argument took place over whether the use of "bicommunal" in this context could also be taken to mean "bizonal." Even the Secretary-General bought into the argument. Asked during a press conference whether the use of the term "bicommunal" signified a major shift from "cantonal" towards "bizonal," Waldheim recalled that Makarios used the term "bicommunal," though the Secretary-General thought that what was meant was a bizonal federal constitution.[45]

Waldheim's statement did little to clarify the situation. If "bizonal" was the intended effect, why was the term not used in the actual text of the agreement? Subsequent events demonstrated that the Greek Cypriot side did in fact accept the concept of bizonality, even though it was not directly mentioned in the 1977 agreement.

The Turkish Cypriots, on the other hand, did not doubt that the agreement provided for a bizonal solution with its reference to "territory under the administration of each community" in guideline two.[46] This position was officially communicated by Denktash to Waldheim in a memorandum on the questions of "bizonality" and "security" of June 28, 1979. Denktash argued that the guidelines should be read "in the context of the factual position, i.e. that two Autonomous Administrations are administering two zones of the Republic"; "the word "territory," which appears in Guideline 2,…is in the singular and not in the plural"; and at the summit the agreement intended the establishment of a federation that was not only bicommunal but "also…bi-zonal," but that Makarios had requested the actual word not be used in the text for domestic political reasons.[47]

From the Greek Cypriot side, Criton Tornaritis countered that "the question of territory to be administered by the constituent members of the proposed Federal Republic is not settled by the guidelines but under guideline 2…was left for discussion between the two Communities."[48]

Irrespective, the agreement did represent a major concession by Makarios, which perplexed many Greek Cypriots. Some considered the agreement "a serious error" by Makarios and yet another concession by the Greek Cypriots, without an equivalent one from the Turkish Cypriots.[49] Subsequently, Makarios was strongly criticized by the Turkish Cypriots for backtracking on the agreement, after he stated in an interview with a Greek Cypriot daily that he would not sign any agreement giving even a piece of stone to the Turks.[50]

The political climate of the time, especially externally, sheds crucial light on Makarios's concessions. The new U.S. president, Jimmy Carter, who had been very critical of Kissinger's policy, demanded that Turkey agree to a settlement if its relations with the United States were to improve. It appears that three factors contributed to Makarios's assessment that conditions were ripe for a dramatic gesture in the Cyprus negotiations: pressure by the Greek American lobby on the new U.S. administration; indications by Turkey that progress was in motion regarding Cyprus (no doubt in order to reverse the arms embargo imposed by the United States); and U.S. pressure on Greece and Turkey to solve their differences. Makarios later admitted that his concessions were a dramatic gesture of conciliation to "win over" the new U.S. President and to persuade him to intensify pressure on Turkey to reach a settlement.[51]

As envisaged by the agreement, when the intercommunal talks resumed in Vienna both sides presented proposals on various aspects of the Cyprus problem. The Greek Cypriot side submitted its territorial offer, including a map (see Map 2.2), proposing that, as in 1975, the Turkish Cypriot administrated area be 20 percent, but that, in contrast to its previous position, this would constitute a single territorial entity rather than a composition of regions.

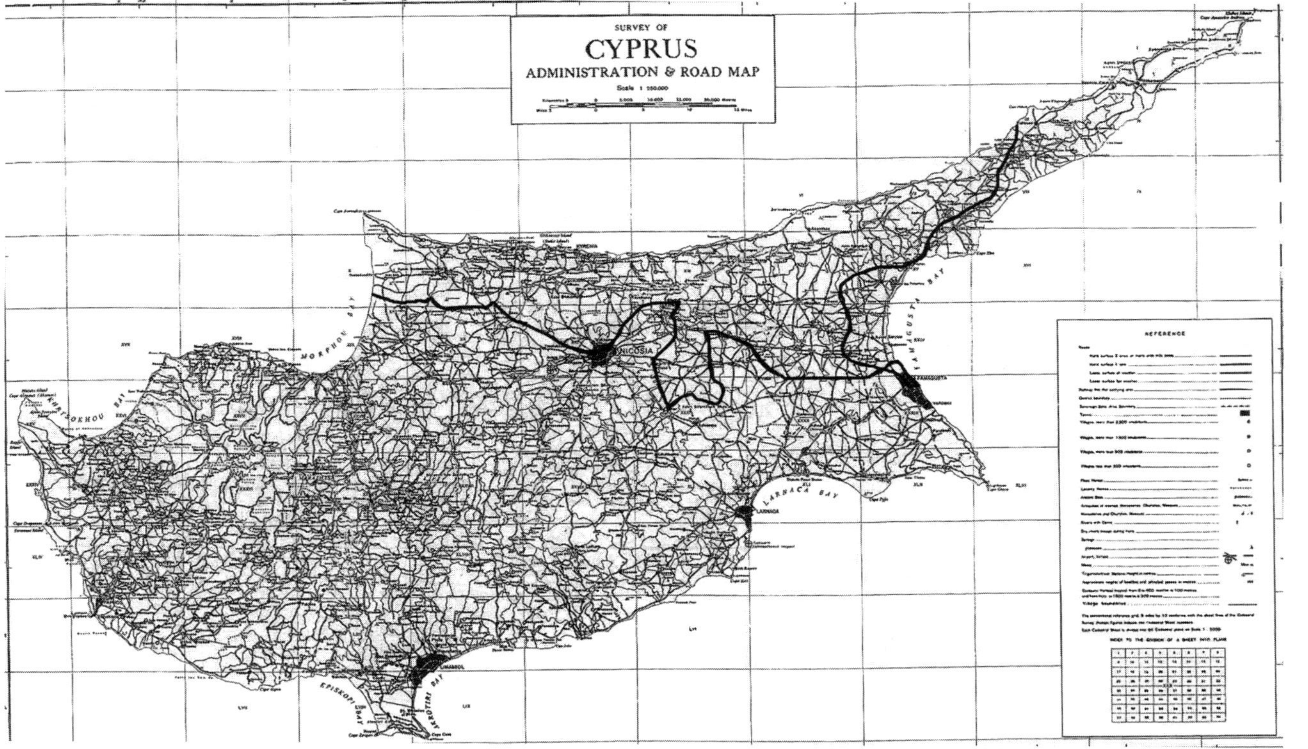

Map 2.2   1977 Greek Cypriot Map

Source: UN S/12323/Annex II, 1977.

Under this proposal, an estimated 120,000 Greek Cypriots would return to their homes under a Greek Cypriot administration, with 50,000 having the option to return to their homes under a Turkish Cypriot administration. In order to allay Turkish Cypriot fears that they would become a minority in such a settlement, Tassos Papadopoulos, who had replaced Clerides as the Greek Cypriot chief negotiator, assured them that "even if they [Greek Cypriot]s all decided to return, the effective majority of the Turkish Cypriots in the Region under their administration would still be maintained."[52]

On the constitutional issue, the Greek Cypriots elaborated their previous principles, arguing that the federal government be headed by a president and vice-president from each of the communities, irrespective of their order of appointment. Despite the fact that Papadopoulos knew the president would be a Greek Cypriot—given their majority—he did not rule out the possibility that a popular Turkish Cypriot could one day be elected president. The legislature would have two chambers: a federal council representing the regions and a house of representatives elected by all Cypriots.[53]

The following day, the Turkish Cypriots submitted their own constitutional proposals, reiterating their previous position that the two states would confer powers and functions to the federal apparatus.[54] Although there were provisions ensuring respect for human rights, these were subservient to the overriding principle of bizonalism and the "territorial integrity and population homogeneity of the Turkish Federated State of Cyprus." On the question of property rights and claims, the Turkish Cypriots proposed they be "settled by mutual agreement," including compensation.[55]

Regarding the federal structure, the Turkish Cypriots proposed a rotating federal presidency that would have "solely representati[ve] powers." The federal legislature would "consist of members elected separately by the two communities" and be restricted to legislating on matters relating to the specifically defined federal areas. Matters pertaining to foreign affairs, the ratification of international agreements, and defense would require separate communal majorities.

The Turkish Cypriots were critical of the Greek Cypriot territorial proposals, arguing that the proposed 20 percent was contrary to the economic viability or productivity and land ownership stipulated in the Makarios-Denktash agreement. Countering this argument, Papadopoulos maintained that in an "island as small as Cyprus," its overall economic viability and productivity took precedence over any specific sector.[56] Furthermore, Papadopoulos maintained that the economic viability of the Turkish Cypriot region could not depend exclusively on agriculture, and that within a politically and economically integrated federation they would be largely funded by federal revenue.

In return, the Greek Cypriots chastised the Turkish Cypriots for coming to the negotiations without any territorial position, arguing it meant that no "meaningful and substantive negotiation" was possible. In relation to federalism, Papadopoulos attacked the Turkish Cypriots for not complying with the guidelines, as their proposals were not compatible with the concept of a federal state but were rather aimed at a confederation; and that they made no mention of a federal Cyprus "except only in name."[57] Justifying the Turkish Cypriot position, Zaim Necatigil explained that a "federation by evolution" was envisaged, in which the role of the federal government would initially be "purely advisory," but that it might evolve as confidence and cooperation between the two communities developed.[58] The Turkish Cypriot approach to federation obviously derived from the point that two existing administrations would come together to form a loose federation.

Comparing the proposals, the two communities were evidently unable to synchronize their negotiations and focus on the same subject. When the Greek Cypriots submitted a map outlining territorial proposals, the Turkish Cypriots concentrated on the constitutional and structural framework of the federation. And although the proposals were extensively discussed and clarifications made, the considerable gap between the two sides was not possible to bridge. Although the Greek Cypriots insisted on their previous constitutional principles of 1976, they did supplement them with specific proposals. The major breakthrough was that for the first time the Greek Cypriots accepted the establishment of two federal regions—a departure from their original multiregional or cantonal position. In general, Turkish Cypriot failure to produce counterproposals was considered as blocking progress during the talks at the very moment when the Greek Cypriots had made significant advances "in the direction of reality and compromise."[59]

Although three more meetings followed, no progress was made in narrowing the gap. Once again, the impasse led the parties to pursue external courses of action. The collapse of the Vienna talks was heavily overshadowed by Makarios's death on August 3, 1977—marking the end of an era. The Greek Cypriots again returned to the United Nations and secured General Assembly Resolution 32/15, which called on both parties to submit "comprehensive and concrete proposals."[60]

In a familiar pattern, Waldheim visited the Cyprus-Greece-Turkey triangle in early 1978 to reactivate the intercommunal talks. While in Ankara, the recently elected Ecevit reassured Waldheim that the Turkish side would submit fresh proposals, including on the territorial issue. The fact that Ecevit announced the Turkish intention gave credence to the Greek Cypriot claim that Ankara, and not the Turkish Cypriots, determined policy on Cyprus. Once Waldheim obtained Ecevit's commitment, and Karamanlis pledged that he would support the resumption of the talks, he then secured agreement over the procedure to be followed: the Turkish Cypriots would first submit their proposals to the Secretary-General. Having studied them, Waldheim would consult both sides on the best way to prepare for recommencing the talks.[61]

On April 13, 1978, the Turkish Cypriot proposals were submitted to Waldheim. Although there was little change from previous positions, the Soysal proposals—named after the Turkish constitutional expert, Mümtaz Soysal—did present a comprehensive account of Turkish Cypriot views on the structural arrangements of the federation, including specific territorial proposals.[62]

Turkish Cypriot constitutional proposals were premised on the "powers and functions" of the "already existing…administrations" being transferred to the central government.[63] Soysal proposed that Cyprus be governed by a federal executive "under the joint direction of the two Presidents of the Federated States," whose role would be ceremonial.[64]

The Turkish Cypriots also proposed a legislative structure comprising three assemblies: two state and one federal. State parliamentarians would be elected by their respective constituents and the federal assembly would be composed of twenty parliamentarians—ten from each state, with five proxies. Federal parliamentarians would be elected by their state colleagues, while the state presidents would not be from the same community as the president of the federal republic. Legislation of federal bills could be initiated by either state assemblies or jointly by the two state presidents. After a proposed bill had been agreed by both the state assemblies and presidents, the bill would be tabled at the federal assembly for a second reading. Approval of the bill would require a simple majority in the federal assembly, but if the bill was passed by the casting vote of the president, then either state president would have the right to put the matter to a referendum in both states.[65]

For the first time, the Turkish Cypriots submitted a map (see Map 2.3) illustrating their proposed territorial adjustments in overall

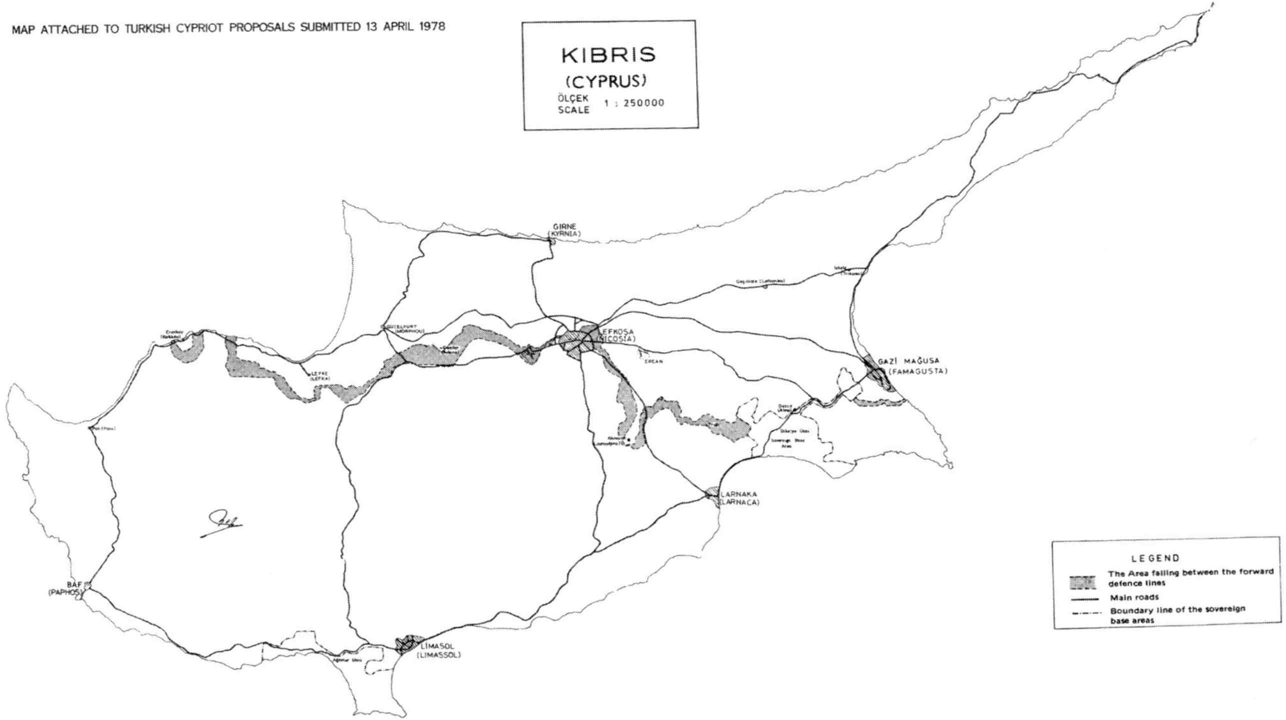

Map 2.3   1978 Turkish Cypriot Map

Source: UN S/12723, 1978.

Cyprus, as well as a detailed town plan of Varosha. The proposals provided for minor border readjustments. The areas of Kokkina, Avlona, Louroujina, Trulli, Ahna and the area south of Varosha and Dherinia, as well as the areas "between the Forward Defence Lines" (meaning the UN-patrolled buffer zone) would be returned to the Greek Cypriots. Once a settlement was reached, Turkish Cypriots who owned property within the British bases would relinquish their proprietary rights. To enhance the productivity of the land available to both communities, a joint project to bring water from Turkey would be discussed.[66] In relation to the resettlement of Varosha, Turkish Cypriots proposed that those Greek Cypriots who returned would "settle to the South of Demokratia and Asteroskopiou Avenues and East of Dherinia Avenue" and "be subject to the laws and regulations of the Turkish Federated State of Cyprus." To assist owners restart their businesses, and to promote the area as a tourist resort, the TFSC would consider providing owners with tax relief and other assistance.[67]

The Greek Cypriots rejected the Soysal proposals on the same day that Spyros Kyprianou—Makarios's replacement—received them. In a press statement, Kyprianou depicted the Turkish proposals as "an attempt to legalize the *fait accompli* and stated that "in no way [could they] form the basis for resumption of the intercommunal talks." Kyprianou described the philosophy of the Soysal proposal's constitutional arrangements as amounting to confederation, and the territorial adjustments as "ridiculous," essentially granting the buffer zone to the Greek Cypriots, thus reducing Turkish territorial concessions to 1 percent of the occupied island. Kyprianou chastised the proposed return of some refugees to Varosha, but under Turkish administration, as an attempt to create "a new enclave . . . to help the Turkish side in the tourist development of the town."[68]

The Soysal proposals lacked any significant shift from previous positions and made no contribution to advancing the negotiations. Nevertheless, it became apparent that the Turkish Cypriots perceived the state parliaments as the principal legislative institutions, with the federal assembly acquiring the character of an upper chamber (senate) in which the two states would be represented on an equal basis. Although the Turkish side was expected to make considerable territorial concessions to offset their constitutional position, these were so small as to be insignificant in the overall package. Despite Turkish claims that their territorial adjustments amounted to 5 percent, this figure was misleading as it included the UN-supervised buffer zone. All this added to the doubt raised in the *Times* as to whether the

Soysal proposals really strove for a "genuinely functioning federation" or were simply a political document to impress the U.S. Congress ahead of its debate to lift the Turkish arms embargo.[69]

Rejection of the Soysal proposals saw Waldheim embark on a fresh initiative to convene a high-level meeting that would set the agenda for negotiations. To this end, the Secretary-General submitted a tentative discussion paper—known as the Waldheim Working Paper—which led to the Denktash-Kyprianou agreement of May 19, 1979.[70]

Despite the resumption of negotiations, as required by the agreement, the talks were postponed without progress. During the four meetings, chaired by UN Under Secretary-General Pérez de Cuéllar, there was disagreement over the agenda's order. Specifically, George Ioannidis, the new Greek Cypriot negotiator, insisted that as per point five of the agreement, the Varosha issue should be discussed first. The new Turkish Cypriot interlocutor Ümit Süleyman Onan argued, however, that point two be agreed on before proceeding to the other items: Onan demanded that Ioannidis acknowledge that "the 1977 agreement comprised also the concepts of 'bi-zonality' and of the 'security of the Turkish Cypriot community.'"[71]

Denktash expressed his disappointment to Waldheim that the talks were being "stalled on account of the Greek Cypriot side's decision to renege on [our] clear understanding" of "bizonality" and "security." The Turkish Cypriot leader reminded the Secretary-General of his assurance that the issues of "bizonality" and "security" had been settled at the 1977 summit. Denktash also reminded the Secretary-General that at the May 1979 press conference he had been prepared to confirm that these two issues were no longer under dispute. Finally, the Turkish Cypriot leader made it abundantly clear that without unequivocal agreement on these fundamental issues "it [would] be very difficult to conduct meaningful" negotiations.[72] On July 30, 1979, Denktash reiterated his demand to Waldheim that the Greek Cypriots publicly confirm their 1977 pledge to a bizonal territorial solution.[73]

Greek Cypriot reluctance to formally endorse "bizonality" did not so much reflect their tendency to revert to their original position—a multiregional federation—as their concern that, once they had conceded, Turkish Cypriots would redefine the term itself. As far as Greek Cypriots were concerned, "bizonal" was synonymous with "biregional," as opposed to "multiregional." Eventually, on August 2, Ioannidis informed Waldheim that in principle the Greek Cypriots accepted the term "bizonal," but clarified that they did not accept Denktash's definition.[74]

There was some basis to Greek Cypriot concern: originally, Turkish Cypriots had used the term "bizonality" to mean the existence of two regions. Soysal, for example, stated that both leaders initially "used the term 'bi regional' but later the Turkish side began to use the word "bizonal." "At first both connoted the same concept but presently they [have] gained different meanings."[75] By 1979, Denktash had clarified the Turkish Cypriot definition of "bizonal" during an interview with the Turkish Cypriot magazine *Olay*:

> The meaning of "bi-zonal" is that I am a state that has territory as one of the two federated states. I am sovereign on many things within this territory. My sovereignty is absolute, no one can take it away from me.[76]

Soysal was blunter than Denktash, suggesting that the concept of "bizonal" implied the existence of a "border."[77]

The failure of Waldheim's Working Paper was attributed mainly to Kyprianou's reluctance to commit himself to substantial negotiations on a "give and take" basis—he was apparently not convinced of the value of abandoning alternative approaches to the Cyprus issue. Even Kyprianou's political backers, AKEL, castigated him for procrastinating over the issue of bizonality.[78] Significantly, AKEL's attack foreshadowed the emergence of a united front by the pragmatists against Kyprianou's handling of the negotiations.

Pérez de Cuéllar then visited the region to reactivate the flagging intercommunal talks. Both sides agreed that negotiations would resume with an opening statement by Waldheim outlining the common ground between the two communities.[79] As a sign of goodwill, the Greek Cypriots agreed that the statement should contain references to "bizonality" and "security." At the first meeting, the Secretary-General's Special Representative to Cyprus, Hugo Juan Gobbi, read Waldheim's statement. In it, Waldheim described the communities' "common ground" as the reaffirmation of the 1977 and 1979 agreements, support for a federal solution to the constitutional aspect and a bizonal solution to the territorial aspect of the Cyprus problem. He also indicated that the issue of security could be discussed, both in relation to certain practical difficulties that might arise for the Turkish Cypriot community as well as the island's security as a whole.

Waldheim's statement outlined the four major areas of concern: (1) the resettlement of Varosha by Greek Cypriots; (2) the identification of practical measures to promote goodwill and build confidence between the two sides; (3) constitutional issues; and (4) territorial issues. Both sides endorsed the Secretary-General's assessment and agreed that these four issues would constitute the agenda whereby each item would be discussed on a rotating basis during weekly meetings, with the submission of various proposals by both sides.[80]

The West, noting developments in both Greece and Turkey, welcomed the new round of intercommunal talks with optimism. In particular, Greece had reentered the military wing of NATO under the Rogers Plan, and there was a new military government in Turkey. Furthermore, for the first time since 1974 the Greek Cypriots did not appeal to the United Nations.

When the Greek Cypriots submitted their constitutional proposals, it became apparent that they had accepted bizonality as referring to two provinces. Regarding individual rights, they stipulated that "every citizen shall enjoy and exercise his (sic) political rights, insofar as the federal government is concerned, irrespective of his (sic) place of residence," but that these might be "regulated by the . . . Provincial Constitution." This was not, however, the concession to Turkish Cypriot desire for regional autonomy that it first appeared to be, as the Greek Cypriots insisted that the three freedoms would apply not only to the federal but also to the provincial tier. Regarding federalism, their only notable addition was the proposal that the president be elected by all Cypriots from a common electoral roll, with the vice-president being elected from the community other than that of the president.[81]

Although there was nothing new in the Turkish Cypriot proposals, they provided further insight into the logic of their position. They pursued their claim for equal representation, aiming to revoke the 1960 constitutional tenet that saw the division of power "not on the basis of the population ratio but on the basis of an agreed fixed ratio."[82] Admitting that a common "identity of views" had not been reached over the question of federation, they offered their own definition of federalism as the:

> establishment of a federal state by the union of two or more federated states. Federated states retain their autonomous status while entering into such union. Each federated state has its own territory, people and government . . . [It] was agreed that the two communities should have territory under their own administration. The word "territory" . . . has a different meaning from the word "land" which is used in private law. The word "territory" here implies land, sea and air space under the administration of the federated state.[83]

The Turkish Cypriots advanced a draft constitution that adamantly safeguarded the communal status quo. For example, in reference to freedom of ownership, Article 22 stipulated that it was "subject to such restrictions" deemed necessary to maintain the "bi-zonality of the Federal Republic."[84] Equally, restrictions applied to the freedoms of movement and settlement, which would be regulated by each federated state. The proposals tended to encroach on other civil liberties such as religion, speech, education, and peaceful assembly—including joining a union—via the caveat that "restrictions may be imposed" for security purposes.[85] Finally, in a departure from their 1978 proposals, the Turkish Cypriots proposed the annual rotation of the federal presidency among the ministers.[86]

Turkish Cypriot territorial proposals represented a modest improvement on their 1978 map. The main map outlined the overall "boundary line between the two federated states" and proposed the return of six regions to the Greek Cypriots. Based on the pre-1974 population figures, an estimated 28,885 Greek Cypriot refugees would return to their homes, and the Turkish Cypriot province would constitute 33 percent of Cypriot territory. However, out of the proposed nineteen villages/towns to be returned to the Greek Cypriots, seven of them (Kokkina, Amadhies, Xerovounos, Limnitis, Louroujina, Pergamos, and Kouklia—with a combined population of 4,656) were, prior to 1974, exclusively inhabited by Turkish Cypriots.

The Mediator Intervenes: Waldheim's Evaluation

With each side rejecting the other's proposals, the intercommunal talks had by October 1981 again reached an impasse. In an effort to retain the momentum, Waldheim put forward some new ideas by way of an evaluation. Waldheim intended "only to establish a method of negotiation," not to "introduce proposals as a basis for the solution of the Cyprus Problem," and his evaluation was by no means exhaustive.[87] His approach was to list all points where the two sides were either in agreement (coincidence) or disagreement (equidistance). In the latter category, he proposed median positions as "working hypotheses" for further deliberation. This matrix was applied to the whole spectrum of the negotiations, which he divided into six sections: general provisions, fundamental rights and liberties, organs of the federal government, provincial government, transitional provisions, and territorial adjustments.[88]

As expected, most points of coincidence were in the general provisions, the main ones stipulating that Cyprus should be an independent, sovereign, bicommunal, and nonaligned federal republic, comprised of a southern and a northern province, with a federal district being the seat of the federal government. The southern province would be divided into four administrative districts and the northern into two. The possible secession, integration, or union of the republic, in whole or in part, with any other state was excluded. The federal republic, comprised of the people of the provinces, with a single citizenship regulated by federal law, would have an "international personality," with the federal government exercising sovereignty over all the territory.

Other points of coincidence detailed Greek and Turkish as the official languages and held that the two provinces would agree on a "neutral flag and national anthem," with each province having its own flag, using "as far as possible elements from the federal flag," with each province observing federal holidays, in addition to those it established for itself. Responding to the main point of equidistance within the general provisions, the deployment of armed forces, Waldheim suggested that except for the police force, Cyprus be demilitarized.

Regarding fundamental rights and liberties, Waldheim listed articles 6 to 35 of the 1960 Constitution as being subject to minor drafting changes or reinforcement. There were two points of equidistance, the first of which debated whether the provinces, in accordance with the federal constitution, should regulate educational and marital matters, and whether higher education should be a federal matter. The second, and more important, related to articles 13(1) and 23 of the 1960 Constitution, which essentially referred to freedom of movement, possession, and settlement. Waldheim proposed that any negotiation on these provisions should take into account Guideline 3 of the 1977 agreement.

The majority of Waldheim's ideas related to the organs of the federal government. He identified only three points of coincidence: (1) the president of the federal council should represent the republic at home and abroad; (2) the federal council should appoint the federal attorney general, federal auditor general, the governor of the reserve bank, and the federal accountant general and their deputies, and that the deputies should not be from the same province as their superiors; and (3) elections should be direct and for all citizens over the age of eighteen.

On the points of equidistance, Waldheim proposed, as median solutions, that federal executive authority be exercised by a federal council (government) comprising six members (two Turkish Cypriot and four Greek Cypriot)—one from each of the administrative districts; that there be six ministerial portfolios (foreign affairs; defense, citizenship, and immigration; justice and higher education; coordination of international trade and tourism, telecommunications and postal services, international navigation; federal finance, central banks, currency, customs, weights, measures, and patents; coordination of environmental matters, natural resources, health, labor, and social services); that ministers be elected for five years; that the federal council's terms of reference should promulgate federal statutes and decisions, appoint ambassadors and perform other diplomatic activities, be in charge of national emergency measures, devise general administrative principles, and formulate federal government policy; that a federal public service commission be established, comprising one member from each administrative district nominated by the federal council; that the federal legislature be composed of two chambers, a chamber of provinces of ten members from each province, and a "popular chamber" acting as a house of representatives, with a ratio of one member per 10,000 electors.

Waldheim proposed that each province draft its own constitution in conformity with the federal constitution. The provinces would elect their own chamber without discrimination and applying the principle of universal suffrage. They would establish their own judicial administration and a provincial police force. The provinces would have no jurisdiction over federal matters but would have jurisdiction over all other matters not listed above. Regarding transitional measures, the Secretary-General suggested the establishment of a joint board to hear compensation claims for those persons adversely affected by the settlement, with the supreme court acting as a court of appeals; a federal agency to provide credit and economic assistance to refugees; and a development fund for the north to "deal with the socio-economic consequences of the territorial adjustment" and as an instrument to achieve economic equilibrium between the two provinces.

On the question of territorial adjustments, Waldheim acknowledged that there was an enormous gap between the two sides, as the Greek Cypriot objective was to resettle the largest possible number of refugees in their province, while the Turkish Cypriots advocated retaining most of northern Cyprus for economic and security reasons. For "illustrative purposes" and as a minimum offer to the Greek Cypriots, Waldheim suggested a territorial breakdown of the two provinces in the ratio of 70 percent to 30 percent.[89] Finally, the questions of international guarantees, taxation, and constitutional amendments were to be discussed at a later stage.

In subsequent informal discussions, both sides sought amendments to several points of coincidence. In general, the Greek Cypriots preferred the term "province" while the Turkish Cypriots favored the term "federated state." The Turkish Cypriots also insisted on the inclusion of the words "territorially bi-zonal" and wished to study further the use of the term "only" in reference to the general provisions. Overall, through these modifications, the Greek Cypriots attempted to strengthen the central federal powers while the Turkish Cypriots sought to increase the regulatory rights of the provinces, especially in relation to the three freedoms. This process, however, was abruptly terminated when major internal and external developments overshadowed the Secretary-General's initiative. With hindsight, it seems clear that Waldheim's evaluation assisted future mediating efforts by structuring the negotiating agenda and setting a precedent for future Secretaries-General to intervene and propose median solutions to intractable issues.

U.S. Intervention

Another process parallel to the intercommunal talks sought to resolve the Cyprus problem, and it involved the two principal external powers, Greece and Turkey, as well as the United States. Although the United States has been classified as an external secondary power in relation to the Cyprus conflict, there is no doubt that it has been the most important non-primary player in the dispute. From its first engagement, the prime objective of U.S. policy was to diffuse the Cyprus issue as a source of tension between its two allies. The United States also desired to keep Cyprus within the Western sphere of influence, preventing Soviet interference and safeguarding British military installations on the island. Its preference was for the Cyprus problem to be settled in a way that was acceptable to both Greece and Turkey. As long as these conditions were met, the United States supported the intercommunal talks as the prime negotiating process and provided, where necessary, political "muscle" to the efforts of the UN Secretaries-General.

After the Cyprus invasion, relations between the two neighboring NATO allies deteriorated even further. Since imposing the U.S. arms embargo on Turkey, Kissinger had been forced into "damage control" mode, trying to establish a dialogue between Greece and Turkey. He realized that a breakthrough on Cyprus was essential if relations between the United States and its two allies were to improve. At Kissinger's instigation, Greece and Turkey entered into a series of meetings that culminated in the Brussels accord. His initiative had two objectives: to appease anti-American feeling in Greece and thereby assist Karamanlis in reviewing his withdrawal from NATO's military command; and to enable Ford to pacify Congress before the presidential suspension of aid to Turkey expired in December. For the initiative to have any prospect of success, Turkey needed to make some concessions on Cyprus in order to make a favorable impression on the Greeks. Essentially, Kissinger's proposals entailed a package arrangement that would have seen the limited resettlement of Greek Cypriot refugees and the establishment of an ethnic federation.[90]

It soon became apparent, however, that both parties had divergent expectations and interpretations of the dialogue. The Greeks interpreted Turkey's support for the talks as an indication of possible concessions, whereas Turkey believed that its willingness to negotiate was sufficient to ensure the lifting of the U.S. embargo.

The Greek-Turkish rapprochement of 1975 was the result of a series of separate but interrelated issues, all of which had Cyprus at their centre. Since Ecevit's resignation in November 1974, Turkey had been in a deep political crisis over its inability to form a stable civilian government. The inability of either Ecevit's CHP (*Cumhuriyet Halk Partisi* [Republican People's Party]), Demirel's National Front coalition, or the smaller DP (*Demokratik Partisi* [Democratic Party]) to form a coalition government compounded the political malaise, while in the background the Turkish army grew restless, increasing the possibility of a military *coup d'état*. When eventually Demirel was able to form a coalition government, his key partners—Necmettin Erbakan's pro-Islamic MSP (*Milli Selâmet Partisi* [National Salvation Party]) and Alparslan Türkes's neo-fascist MHP (*Milliyetçi Hareket Partisi* [National Action Party])—demanded a tougher line on foreign policy and opposed any territorial concessions in Cyprus.

With Turkey in the middle of a political crisis, the U.S. Congress imposed an arms embargo for its illegal use of U.S. arms during the Cyprus invasion. Immediately, Turkey terminated a scheduled meeting between the foreign ministers of Greece and Turkey, arranged by Kissinger.

U.S.-Turkish relations were at their lowest ebb since the 1964 Johnson letter. The relationship soured even further when President Ford's proposal to lift the arms embargo was defeated in the House of Representatives. In retaliation, Demirel abrogated the 1969 Turkish-American Joint Defense Co-Operation Agreement and took over all twenty-five U.S. bases, except for the Izmir and Incirlik NATO installations. Although both Demirel and Turkey's military command had been reluctant to take such extreme action, public opinion—spurred on by a jingoistic media—demanded some sort of governmental reprisal. In the meantime, Ecevit rode the wave of nationalism sweeping Turkey calling for nonalignment. Despite assurances to Kissinger from the Turkish government, the political situation became increasingly unpredictable and, combined with a parallel situation in Greece, seriously threatened the stability of NATO's southeastern flank.

On the other side of the Aegean, anti-American sentiment had been raging since August 1974. The first democratic elections for a decade made this clear, with the issue of Greece's relationships with NATO, the European Community (EC), and the United States dominating. Karamanlis's new party, ND (*Nea Dimokratia* [New Democracy]), declared that Greece's participation in NATO and the future of the U.S. bases were subject to negotiation, and that it supported forging closer relations with Europe. Until then, Greece's EC stratagem had been fundamentally economic, and Karamanlis injected its campaign with a political content that proved crucial to its eventual success. Prominent opposition was driven by PASOK, which, together with the Left parties, advocated an unequivocal withdrawal from NATO. PASOK favored nonalignment and was less enthusiastic about the EC. The election gave the ND a clear majority.

After the collapse of the junta, Greece's European prospects rose dramatically, not least because many European leaders regarded Greece as the birthplace of democratic values and were eager to strengthen the new democracy. Karamanlis took advantage of this climate and within Greece promoted the idea that Europe was a real friend, citing its non-complicity in the Central Intelligence Agency's machinations with the junta, and pointing to its rigorous campaign to restore democracy in Greece. Consequently, at the May 1977 NATO summit, Greece managed to secure British support for its membership to the EC. Karamanlis had already obtained French support and by the end of the year had also secured Germany's vote.

As with 1975, the United States' next venture into the Cyprus conflict was predicated on its broader strategic considerations and its effort to stabilize its alliance with Turkey. Rejection of the Soysal proposals saw the intercommunal talks enter a new impasse, suggesting once again that the gap between both sides was impossible to bridge. Within this void, the U.S. congressional debate to lift the Turkish arms embargo influenced the intercommunal talks. Unlike 1975, when Congress was willing to punish the Ford administration over its special relationship with Turkey, the election of a Democratic president found Congress amenable to White House requests to lift the embargo. It soon became clear that U.S. domestic politics was interfering in the internal dynamic of the Cyprus talks. Clearly referencing the congressional arms embargo debate, the Secretary-General suggested that these external events had "created a situation" in which resumption of the intercommunal talks was impossible.[91]

This was made apparent when, hours before the Congressional House International Relations and the Senate Foreign Affairs committees were scheduled to vote on lifting the arms embargo, the Turkish side requested resumption of the intercommunal talks. Denktash offered to discuss an array of issues such as Varosha, troop withdrawal, freedom of movement, the Nicosia Airport, and to meet Kyprianou "anywhere, any time," with or without an agenda for discussions.[92] Not convinced of Denktash' sincerity, Kyprianou rejected the overture and returned to the UN General Assembly, proposing the demilitarization of Cyprus.[93] Although Resolution 32/15 was ignored by the Security Council, it was, as the *Times* noted, "an impressive reminder of Turkey's virtual isolation" by the international community.[94]

On July 25 and August 1, 1978, the U.S. Senate and House of Representatives acceded to Carter's request and lifted the arms embargo on Turkey, signaling the beginning of the U.S. Cyprus initiative. When the embargo was eventually lifted on August 14, it had two provisos attached: that the president assist in the search for a peaceful resolution to the Cyprus conflict, and that he submit to Congress a progress report on the Cyprus issue every two months.[95]

On November 10, 1978 an American-British-Canadian plan was submitted to the two communities and communicated to Athens, Ankara, and the UN Secretary-General. The aim was to stimulate the resumption of talks by providing a framework for a settlement. Despite enjoying the support of Britain and Canada, the plan was the work of a lawyer in the U.S. State Department, Matthew Nimetz— and it subsequently became known as the Nimetz proposals.

The plan proposed that Cyprus "be a bi-communal federal state with two constituent regions" inhabited predominantly by Greek Cypriots and Turkish Cypriots; and that a new constitutional arrangement, guided by the Makarios-Denktash agreement, the 1960 Constitution, and the relevant UN resolutions, be negotiated. It proposed that a federal constitution would safeguard the three freedoms, subject to modification preserving the "character of each region," with jurisdiction over foreign affairs, defense, communications, civil aviation, immigration, customs, federal finance, currency, foreign commerce, and federal banking. All other powers would be the reserve of the constituent regions and, upon agreement, these could be assumed by the federal government.

As for the federal structure, Nimetz proposed two legislative chambers: an upper house, where the two communities would be represented on an equal footing, and a lower house, whose members would be elected in proportion to the two populations. A bill rejected by the upper house might be passed by a two-thirds majority of the lower house, provided that at least three-eighths of each community's representatives support it. A democratically elected president and vice-president, from each community, would jointly appoint cabinet, which would include a minimum 30 percent representation from each community. Both the president and vice-president would have the joint right of veto over legislation, but this might be overridden by a two-thirds majority in each chamber. The federal supreme court, comprising a Greek Cypriot, a Turkish Cypriot, and a jointly appointed non-Cypriot, would interpret the constitution and act as the highest court of appeal.

The U.S. plan stipulated that the territory of each region would be subject to negotiations "on the basis of criteria such as economic viability and productivity, land ownership, security, population patterns, and historical factors." It was understood that the Turkish Cypriot side would make "significant geographical adjustments" favoring the Greek Cypriot side. Provision would be made "for the return of displaced persons to their properties," which was consistent with the bicommunal constitutional prerequisites of the republic. Those who were unable or did not wish to return would receive some compensation. A jointly administered "Cyprus reconciliation fund" would be established with external contributions to assist with economic and social readjustment, and an "agency for regional cooperation and coordination" would also be set up. Finally, as a goodwill measure, Varosha would be resettled by the Greek Cypriots, under the auspices of the United Nations, at the resumption of the intercommunal talks.[96]

The Greek Cypriots' official response was that Waldheim must undertake a new initiative incorporating the various suggestions in the U.S. plan. But AKEL had condemned the Nimetz proposals as an attempt by the "American imperialist factor" to "derail the Cyprus problem from the United Nations" by diverting it to a Camp David type process.[97] A clearer analysis of the Greek Cypriot position can be found in an internal government paper compiled by the offices of the interlocutor and the attorney general.[98] The paper concluded that the U.S. plan was unbalanced as it heavily detailed the constitutional issues (the Turkish Cypriots' main interest) while paying only light attention to the territorial or refugee issues (the Greek Cypriots' main concerns). The plan only referred to border adjustments, and clearly stated that not all refugees could return to their homes. This disparity would provide Turkish Cypriots with an advantage since they knew from the outset exactly what would be discussed regarding the constitution, while Greek Cypriots would have no idea what would be discussed on the territorial issue.

Other critics suggested that the proposals contained divisive elements that were in conflict with UN resolutions and the Makarios-Denktash agreement. In particular, Yiannos Kranidiotis argued that the requirement for a two-thirds majority and at least three-eighths of each community's parliamentarians to pass a bill would divide the parliament on ethnic rather than political lines.[99] Others were concerned with the ambiguity of concepts such as "substantial powers and responsibilities," "inhabited predominantly" and "nearly exclusively," and wondered who would determine the criteria of "security," "population patterns," and "historical factors" with respect to "geographical adjustments." There was a concern that listing the three freedoms as subject to modification compromised them.[100]

The militants' strongest criticism, however, was for the plan's political motivation. They were convinced that the U.S. purpose for recommencing the intercommunal talks was to undermine UN debate on Cyprus and divert international attention away from Turkey after the lifting of the arms embargo.

The right-wing of the pragmatists advocated an opposite view; Clerides and his party DISY supported the Western plan. In their paper, "Analysis of a Mistake: The Rejection of the Western Plan for Cyprus," they considered it to be consistent with the framework of the UN resolutions and the Makarios-Denktash agreement. They argued that the U.S. proposals formed the basis for negotiations and should not be considered a "take it or leave it" document or draft constitution. Clerides argued that the territory of the federal regions proposed by the plan was consistent with the three criteria agreed to by Makarios and Denktash. The fact that the plan included "security," "population patterns," and "historical factors" as additional criteria did not necessarily disadvantage the Greeks, he argued, and pointed out that if the plan was more specific on the territorial issue there would be less room to maneuver. Regarding the limitation on the three freedoms, the plan had to be examined within the context of the Makarios-Denktash agreement, which would regulate individual rights within a federal system comprising the two communities with respective territorial regions. Clerides argued that those who criticized the U.S. plan were in essence criticizing the Makarios-Denktash agreement. Finally, the pragmatists pointed out that the withdrawal of foreign troops formed an "integral part of a final agreement" under the U.S. plan.[101]

In contrast, the Turkish response to the U.S. framework was initially guarded and low key. They viewed the Nimetz Plan as favoring a strong federal government, reflecting the Greek Cypriot position. Denktash avoided commenting on the plan, for several reasons. First, the Greek Cypriots' quick rejection of the plan preempted any Turkish Cypriot response. The time frame was further restricted by the emergence of Waldheim's "tentative paper," which essentially rendered the U.S. initiative redundant. Second, at the time Denktash was preoccupied with an internal political crisis: growing discontent within his own party, the UBP (*Ulusal Birlik Partisi* [National Unity Party]), erupted and eventually led his entire cabinet to resign. Dissatisfaction among liberal elements of the UBP had been growing for some time over Denktash's authoritarianism and his tendency to be tougher than Turkey regarding the Greek Cypriots. Returning from New York, Denktash threatened to declare his "state" independent in response to Greek Cypriot intransigence, and this further infuriated his party's liberal wing. Some liberal Turkish Cypriots also appeared favorably disposed to the U.S. plan.

Two aspects emerge from any assessment of the plan's impact on the Cyprus negotiations during this time. The first relates to the content of the document and the second to prevailing political circumstances and the purpose of the U.S. initiative. The Nimetz Plan was undoubtedly aimed at producing a package that would satisfy Turkish Cypriot demand for political and territorial autonomy; their concern for security; and their fear of economic domination by the Greek Cypriots. At the same time, it attempted to accommodate Greek Cypriot interests in the three freedoms; territorial adjustments; the return of refugees; and their desire for a strong central government. In essence, the proposals were a trade-off between the territorial and constitutional aspects of the problem, in the hope that this exchange would lead to a settlement. Despite its rejection, the thrust of the Nimetz Plan served as the basis for Pérez de Cuéllar's proposals in the 1980s. Politically, the Americans were undoubtedly concerned that Kyprianou was moving away from the intercommunal talks—and therefore away from acceptance of a bicommunal/bizonal federation—toward an exclusive policy of internationalization. The fact that Kyprianou did not replace Papadopoulos with a new interlocutor, and that he adamantly pursued sanctions against Turkey at the United Nations, confirmed this hypothesis to the Americans. Carter also believed that the repeal of the Turkish arms embargo "created fresh opportunities for progress on the Cyprus issue."[102]

The U.S. proposals have been the subject of much debate and speculation. Timing of the initiative was directly related to developments in U.S.-Turkish relations and the UN debate on Cyprus. The U.S. administration's desire to convince Congress to lift the arms embargo against Turkey was closely linked to its attempt to disengage the Cyprus conflict from the realm of the United Nations. The short-term goals of the Nimetz Plan became obvious in its abrupt abandonment when confronted with its first obstacles. Unlike, for example, its Middle East campaign, the U.S. venture into the Cyprus problem was short-lived, and its stewardship was relegated to middle-ranking State Department officials.

After the failure of the Nimetz Plan, the United States confined its role to quiet diplomacy, working behind the scenes and aiding the UN Secretary-General's efforts. By this stage, their immediate objective of restarting the intercommunal talks, and thus bypassing a fully fledged debate of the Cyprus issue at the United Nations, had been achieved. Furthermore, with the 1979 agreement, Carter could illustrate to Congress that his policy of persuading rather than pressuring Turkey was the best contribution the United States could make toward resolving the Cyprus problem.

Peripheral Issues: Varosha and "Goodwill" Measures

Nowhere is the tragedy of Cyprus more succinctly encapsulated than in the city of Famagusta. Located on the eastern coast of the island, between the Greco and Eloea capes, Varosha—the new city of Famagusta—had been a thriving cosmopolitan town, a tourist and trade hub with a population of over 39,000. Since August 1974, however, Varosha (or Maraş), fenced off by the Turkish military, has remained a derelict ghost town. The image of Varosha as a "hostage city" occupies a special space in the Greek Cypriot psyche. The Famagusta Refugee Movement has argued that there is no logical reason why the Varosha issue should remain unresolved for so long, considering that the city holds no strategic value for the Turks. On the contrary, they have argued, and quite convincingly, that its resettlement offers significant benefits for both communities, such as the immediate reduction of Greek Cypriot refugees by one-third and the revitalization of the city as a tourist centre, boosting intercommunal confidence in the island and acting as a catalyst for an overall settlement.[103]

The idea to resettle Varosha first emerged in 1978 during the Soysal proposals, and it continued to gather momentum throughout the year as a result of Denktash's and Kyprianou's offer and counteroffer.[104] This impetus continued when Nimetz attached the issue of Varosha to his proposals.[105] Despite its failure, one of the unintended consequences of the U.S. plan was to catapult Varosha into the forefront of the Cyprus negotiations. Varosha's acquired negotiating value was also due to Waldheim's strategic change from conducting negotiations over a wide range of complex issues, carefully integrated into an overall agreement, to focusing attention on a single practical matter. Waldheim had decided to switch tack by dealing with one aspect of the stalemate, which if successful would create an "opening for further significant steps."[106] He believed that a breakthrough on an issue such as the resettlement of Varosha would generate sufficient goodwill between the two sides to improve the prospects of a general settlement. The mediators failed to understand, however, that Varosha constituted a bargaining chip for the Turkish side: they required a counteroffer as a sufficient incentive to relinquish the town. There appeared to be signs from Denktash that the lifting of the arms embargo might have constituted such an incentive. Once the arms embargo was lifted, Waldheim attempted to link Varosha with the reopening of the Nicosia airport, considered to be in the economic interest of the Turkish Cypriots. The trade-off, however, progressed no further when Denktash withdrew his Varosha offer.

Throughout 1978 and 1979, Varosha was at the center of all negotiations and proposals, as per the U.S. plan and the 1979 agreement. The last initiative on the Varosha issue during this period took place on August 9, 1980 when Waldheim explored with both sides the prospects for a partial interim agreement (or mini-package). The mini-package involved the resettlement of Varosha in exchange for the reopening of the Nicosia airport, both under an interim UN administration. This cycle of talks produced new Turkish Cypriot proposals in January 1981 when Denktash stipulated quite clearly that Varosha would remain under Turkish Cypriot security control with supervised entry and exit checkpoints and would comply with TFSC taxation laws. Municipal matters would be run by a three-member council (one Greek Cypriot, one Turkish Cypriot, and one from UNFICYP), and if an overall agreement was not achieved, this interim arrangement would be reviewed.[107] The Greek Cypriots rejected these proposals on the grounds that they only offered a small coastal strip for resettlement that was located in Turkish-held territory, accommodating only 10,000 refugees and providing them no access to southern Cyprus. The Varosha approach to the negotiations ended in April-May 1981 when it was decided that the Cyprus discussions should revert to searching for an overall settlement.

Comparing Denktash's 1981 Varosha proposals with his previous 1978 proposals, there can be little doubt that domestic pressure from his nationalist supporters had hardened his position. Indeed, he went to considerable lengths to persuade his constituents that "according to the provisional status agreement, Varosha [would] remain part of the TFSC and Turkish Cypriot laws [would] apply."[108] He reassured his support base that the Greek Cypriot resettlement of Varosha would not constitute territorial concessions, since the town would remain under Turkish Cypriot jurisdiction; the settlers would abide by their laws, security and administration would lie firmly under Turkish Cypriot control, and all visitors to Varosha would enter through their own airport in Tymbou or the Famagusta port.[109] Finally, Denktash attempted to paint his Varosha proposal as a gain, since it would result in revenue through the taxation of Greek Cypriot owned hotels and businesses.

Varosha is significant to the Cyprus negotiations because it is a secondary issue uniquely placed to be resolved. It is of little military worth to the Turkish side, although it has immense political value as a bargaining commodity; the fact that since 1974 Varosha has not been settled by the Turkish Cypriots supports this theory. As the largest town under Turkish Cypriot control, its resettlement would considerably reduce the number of Greek Cypriot refugees, and it would be an ideal area of economic cooperation between the two communities. Waldheim's decision to switch the negotiating emphasis from the broader aspects of the Cyprus problem to more tangible issues such as Varosha was a sensible tactic. Yet the various sides failed to comprehend that Varosha was a bargaining item requiring a corresponding offer to the Turkish side. This could have been achieved by linking it with the reversal of the U.S. arms embargo on Turkey or, since this was complicated, with the reopening of the Nicosia airport.

Negotiation Impact Assessment: Adapting to the "New Realities"

A first glance at the immediate post-1974 period suggests that the overall conditions were conducive to a settlement: the period was characterized by fluidity and the main actors appeared more open to change. There was a high level of external involvement in the search for a solution to the Cyprus conflict, which was made possible by the fact that channels of communication were at their embryonic stage and had not yet entrenched themselves as the sole negotiating process.

As the intercommunal talks got underway it became apparent that, despite minor breakthroughs, such hopes were unfounded. The gap between both sides over key issues remained impossible to bridge. Yet the period was crucial for the Cyprus conflict as it established the intercommunal talks as the sole negotiating process and defined the agenda upon which all future talks would be based. The institutionalization of the intercommunal talks resulted from the convergence of a number of internal and external factors, and it may be characterized as the lowest common denominator upon which all parties could agree.

Changes during this period within the Greek Cypriot community saw its political mood defined by the contest between the pragmatists and the militants. Makarios, however, whose presence prevented either faction from dominating the political agenda, managed to synthesize both parties' basic tenets into a common strategy. The main thrust of this strategy was to internationalize the Cyprus issue by securing a series of favorable UN resolutions. Utilizing the Greek Cypriots' diplomatic leverage, which they enjoyed as the sole legal representative of Cyprus, Makarios pursued a confrontational line against Turkey. His aim was to gather enough diplomatic pressure on Turkey to force it into making concessions on Cyprus. Although he knew that Turkey determined the overall Turkish position on Cyprus, he could not avoid direct negotiations with the Turkish Cypriots through the UN-sponsored intercommunal talks. Makarios feared that accepting the intercommunal talks as the sole negotiating process ran the risk of compromising the Greek Cypriots' international status and therefore reducing the Cyprus problem to a domestic, intercommunal, ethnic conflict.

Makarios death signaled the end of an era, and of the post-1974 patriotic solidarity, with the leadership beginning to erode. The changing political landscape seriously impacted on his successor's behavior during the negotiations. Unlike Makarios, Kyprianou did not enjoy the passionate support of the overwhelming majority of Greek Cypriots, and he therefore had to depend on alliances for his political survival. Although Kyprianou was methodical in his analysis and policy preparation, he lacked the lateral and quick thinking of the more visionary Makarios. Where Makarios was the undisputed

Ethnarch of the Greek Cypriots and commanded the obedience and loyalty of other political leaders, Kyprianou was considered as just one political personality among many others, whose elevation to the office of president was little more than accidental. The post-Makarios era also heralded a maturing of the Greek Cypriot political system, with its electoral contests and acceptance of open challenges to the president. As soon as Kyprianou took over leadership, he had to contend with permanent opposition from Clerides and open criticism from both the militants and the pragmatists if they disagreed with his handling of the Cyprus negotiations.

In contrast, territorial control over some 37 percent of the island and a heavy Turkish military presence provided Turkish Cypriots with a new sense of power. The Turkish Cypriots' prime objective was to solidify their administration and gain recognition as an autonomous political unit. In the absence of international acceptance, the intercommunal talks placed them on an equal footing with the Greek Cypriots. Although they were prepared to negotiate a partnership state with the Greek Cypriots, their insistence on retaining the maximum autonomy rested on their fear that the Greek Cypriots would dominate any unified Cyprus and subsequently reduce the Turkish Cypriot community to minority status.

As occurred for Greek Cypriots, although to a lesser degree, dissatisfaction began to emerge within the Turkish Cypriot community over Denktash's paternalistic rule, which occasionally overflowed to his management of the intercommunal negotiations. Although cautious, the Turkish Cypriot Left echoed wider Turkish Cypriot dissatisfaction over the economic situation.[110] On the other side of the political spectrum, Denktash came under fierce pressure from the nationalists when he proposed the Greek Cypriot resettlement of Varosha. Finally, discontent also emerged among liberal elements of his own party, who were interested in the economic benefits that might derive from the unification of the island.

The change of leadership in the Greek Cypriot community was not particularly conducive to a successful outcome of the intercommunal talks. Yet continuity in the Turkish Cypriot leadership was no more advantageous.

An assessment of both sides indicates little change in their respective positions. The two dominant issues that emerged—territorial and constitutional—were to pervade all future negotiations. Once both sides accepted the principle of federalism, discussions focused on defining the relationship between the states and the central government. On the constitutional issue, the Greek Cypriots still advocated a strong central government based on communal proportional representation, with safeguards for the Turkish Cypriot minority, and the implementation of the three freedoms throughout the island. The Turkish Cypriots, on the other hand, proposed strong federated states within a "loose" federation that entailed equal power sharing. They ruled out the return of all refugees, as unrealistic, given the demographic changes that had taken place and the fact that Turkish Cypriots had settled on Greek Cypriot property. The Turkish Cypriots also considered the refugee matter as having been resolved by the 1975 exchange of population agreement. With regard to the three freedoms, Turkish Cypriots envisaged that these could gradually be restored as the federation evolved.

Linked with the constitutional issue was the territorial composition of the federation. Until the Greek Cypriots accepted the concept of bizonality, there was not enough clarity to proceed to the next stage of the negotiations regarding the establishment of an acceptable federal model. Much of the period was consumed by the Greek Cypriots' gradual shift from a multiregional or cantonal federation to a biregional federation as they eventually agreed to in their 1977 territorial proposals. In contrast, the territorial issue was not a priority for the Turkish Cypriots, as they were aware they had to make serious concessions on this question. For them, the important issues pertained to the structure of the federation and, in particular, to the relationship between the states and the central federal apparatus. Denktash avoided making any concessions because he firmly believed that time was on his side, and because he anticipated further concessions from the Greek Cypriots. The absence of any substantial territorial proposals from the Turkish Cypriots clearly impeded progress in the negotiations, especially after the Greek Cypriots had accepted bizonality as the basis for federation.

On the territorial issue, the submission of the 1978 and 1981 Turkish Cypriot maps illustrated the gap between both sides. There was some movement during this phase on the part of the Greek Cypriots, who finally abandoned their previous position and accepted both the concept and the reality of biregionalism. Regarding the actual size of these provinces, the official Greek Cypriot position was that the Turkish Cypriots should retain 20 percent of the island— privately they were prepared to settle for 25 percent. The Turkish Cypriots proposed retaining 30 to 35 percent, but their two maps included the UN buffer zone within this territory. While their 1981 map was slightly more accommodating, it fell short of meeting the Greek Cypriots' minimum territorial expectations, which envisaged acquiring the Morphou and Famagusta areas to allow for the resettlement of a considerable number of their refugees.

Overall, the negotiations were plagued by uncertainty, interruptions, and a lack of cohesion. By the time the Secretary-General attempted to inject some structural discipline into the talks, the psychology of preserving the status quo was deeply entrenched. There was no progress during this period, and the complacency of all parties reflected the undisciplined mood of the negotiations and ensured a lack of movement on the major issues. As the talks progressed, in fact, previous commitments were revoked. A combination of external and internal factors caused the malaise contaminating the negotiations. Broadly speaking, this period witnessed significant changes in the procedural aspects of the negotiations, but there was little progress on the substantive issues that continued to divide the two sides.

Chapter 3

Faltering UN Involvement

By the end of his tenure as the UN Secretary-General, Waldheim would have taken little solace from Matthew 5:9 ("blessed are the peacemakers") as far as the Cyprus conflict was concerned. Having described the Cyprus problem as one of the most complicated and emotionally loaded problem he came across,[1] Waldheim accredited the prevailing status quo as the main bulwark preventing a solution to this problem. In particular, commenting on the subjective nature of the negotiations, Waldheim stated that "the existing *status quo* [tended] to create a dynamic of its own, which [did] not necessarily facilitate an agreed solution." He identified two sets of difficulties for this predicament. The first concerned the positions of the two communities during the negotiations. The other related to the political problems "they faced in tackling the compromises and accommodations" essential to achieving progress toward a negotiated solution.[2] By the 1980s it became evident that the impasse at the intercommunal talks was primarily because a psychology of complacency had set in on all parties. This was reflected in the undisciplined mood of the negotiations and punctuated by lack of movement on the major issues. With the passage of time, the negotiations became retrospective as they revoked previous commitments and became more susceptible to an ad hoc combination of external and internal factors.

Waldheim's departure also marked the end of the 1968 negotiating model. His evaluation managed to enhance the mediating role of the Secretary-General's "good offices" by becoming the official channel of communication between the two leaders. This structural change completed the transformation of the Secretary-General as a third party to the conflict and kept the negotiations going by instigating their own proposals and ideas. However, by the time the Secretary-General attempted to inject a structural discipline into the talks, the psychology of preserving the status quo was deeply entrenched. As both sides grew disenchanted with the stagnation of the intercommunal talks, they hardened their positions at the negotiating table and began to pursue alternative courses to achieve their separate ambitions.

Hardening of Dispositions: *Allagi* and Unilateralism

The election of PASOK in Greece had an enormous impact on the Cyprus talks as it transformed Athens engagement with the Greek Cypriot community. Within the Cyprus spectre, the significance of PASOK's slogan of *Allagi* (change) could only be appreciated by first understanding its ideological overview of national policy, especially the Greek-American axis that had dominated Greek affairs since 1947. Prime Minister Andreas G. Papandreou viewed Greece's national security woes as stemming from its postwar dependence on the U.S. alliance. On this assessment he questioned the benefit of the relationship by challenging the presence of the U.S. bases, Greece's membership of NATO, and even of the EC. Although U.S. officials publicly played down PASOK's anti-Americanism as nothing more than oppositionist rhetoric, its election clearly signalled a new era in U.S.-Greek relations.

Throughout the first year of the PASOK government, U.S. officials sought to ascertain Papandreou's position on the triangular nexus between Cyprus, Turkey, and the U.S. bases. The change of government had a major effect on the course of the Cyprus peace talks as it firmly repositioned Greece's role. Papandreou immediately discarded the Karamanlis's doctrine as a renunciation of Greece's moral, political, and military obligations to the Greek Cypriots. Immediately the Cyprus problem was reinstated as the principal *ethniko zitima* (national issue) with the PASOK government pursuing the matter vigorously at every opportunity. Papandreou did not have much confidence in the ongoing intercommunal talks, which, in his view, disengaged the Cyprus problem from its essence, namely, as a question of invasion and occupation.[3] He therefore favored its internationalization as a strategy of refocusing attention on Turkey as the aggressor. Both these policies created a new relationship between Athens and Nicosia and were instantly embraced by Kyprianou. PASOK's election also impacted on the domestic Greek Cypriot political scene as it strengthened the militants with Kyprianou's party, DIKO, siding with EDEK and even found adherence amongst nationalist elements of DISY.

By the end of 1982, the lack of progress at the intercommunal talks prompted the new UN Secretary-General Javier Pérez de Cuéllar—who, as Waldheim's special representative, was well versed on the Cyprus problem—to warn that time was eroding the "window of opportunity" to resolve the dispute.[4] Encouraged by the UN Security Council, he launched a major diplomatic offensive aimed at synthesizing the parties' various positions. However, when Pérez de Cuéllar met with Kyprianou and Denktash he discovered that both leaders had hardened their positions. Any attempts to reignite the intercommunal talks came to an abrupt end once the Cyprus issue went before the General Assembly, resulting in Resolution 37/253.[5] In rejecting the resolution, the Turkish Cypriots immediately withdrew from the intercommunal talks, claiming that it undermined their negotiating position.

In an effort to inject new impetus into the flagging intercommunal talks, Pérez de Cuéllar undertook his "indicators" initiative. Essentially this approach involved holding informal soundings with both sides in order to reduce the gap between them. The Secretary-General sought to establish a contextual framework based on three indicators that covered the major issues left unresolved in Waldheim's evaluation. These indicators dealt with three issue areas—the executive government, the legislature, and the question of territory—and were put forward in a two-option format.[6]

With minor altercations, both Kyprianou and Denktash accepted the Secretary-General's new initiative and agreed to the convention of a high-level meeting. However, when the Secretary-General's assistant, Hugo Gobbi, called on Denktash for further consultation, he was informed that the "Turkish Federated State of Cyprus" unanimously declared "before History" and the world the creation of the "Turkish Republic of Cyprus as an Independent State."[7] Based on their firm belief "that the two Peoples of Cyprus each [had] the right to live and govern" their "own territory," the Turkish Cypriots were convinced that their unilateral declaration of independence (UDI) would "not hinder but facilitate" the federal process.[8]

Pérez de Cuéllar considered the decision to be contrary to the UN resolutions, the two high-level agreements, and that it would adversely affect the situation by complicating his efforts. Subsequently the UN Security Council, in resolution 541 (1983), deplored the Turkish Cypriots' decision to formalize the partition of the Republic of Cyprus, which it considered illegal, called for its withdrawal, and stipulated that "all states not to recognise any Cypriot state other than the Republic of Cyprus."[9]

Despite the challenge to the intercommunal talks by Papandreou and the UDI, these same impediments provided the stimulus for an intense effort on the part of both internal and external actors to refocus the negotiations on a more competent basis. In retrospect, the UDI proved to be a turning point in the negotiating process, forcing Pérez de Cuéllar to adapt his mediation to the prevailing circumstances of a breakdown in communication between the two sides. The changing nature of the negotiations effectively meant the end of the 1968 model, conducted primarily by the two interlocutors. The emphasis of the negotiations now shifted through the Secretary-General directly to the two leaders.

In the aftermath of the UDI, the Greek Cypriots submitted a new set of proposals. Kyprianou's framework—as they were known—rendered the demilitarization of Cyprus as a fundamental prerequisite to resolving the problem.[10] To facilitate an agreement, Kyprianou was prepared to increase the Turkish Cypriot federal province to 25 percent provided that highly populated Greek Cypriot areas such as Famagusta and Morphou were returned. The executive would retain the 1960 presidential system. As for the legislature, Kyprianou proposed a unicameral system or alternatively a bicameral system consisting of a lower chamber that represented the two communities on the basis of population ratio, and an upper chamber. On the question of the three freedoms, Kyprianou emphasized that they needed to be safeguarded at both national and provincial level. Arrangements pertaining to their implementation would be made with a view to "overcoming certain practical difficulties." Finally, the federal government would be committed to a social justice platform that entailed providing economic assistance to less developed areas.[11]

Two weeks after the release of Kyprianou's proposals, the oppositionist Clerides plan was leaked to the media. Clerides was confident that the Turkish Cypriots would be receptive to his plan since it did not require them revoking their UDI, and would be enticed by the financial benefits entailed from lifting the economic embargo. Furthermore, all that had been proposed, with the exception of the 70:30 distribution of federal power and the presidency, had been previously accepted by the Turkish Cypriots. It entailed the phased, but eventual, withdrawal of the Turkish troops and allowed for the return of a substantial number of refugees. Clerides believed that under the circumstances his plan was the best settlement that the Greek Cypriots could aim for. He warned that any other proposition by the Greek Cypriots would lead to the gradual recognition of the

Turkish Cypriot UDI and the "total loss of 37 percent of Cypriot territory."[12]

In essence, both of these documents reflected the growing internal rift between Kyprianou and the pragmatists. The militants argued that the timing of Clerides' plan was not coincidental and sought to undermine Kyprianou's efforts. The fact that the Clerides plan was not criticized by AKEL implied that it constituted the position of the pragmatists. Clerides' objective was to convince the Turks and the West that there was an alternative Greek Cypriot position to that advocated by its official leadership.

Sensing that the Turkish side was willing to make some concessions in order to retrieve its lost credibility with the international community, Pérez de Cuéllar took advantage of Denktash's offer for the resettlement of Varosha and reopening the Nicosia airport,[13] and developed it into a "mini package." He knew that the Greek Cypriots would reject Denktash's overture so he adopted it as his own proposal. Essentially it consisted of a five-point confidence-building package suggesting that there be no further internationalizing of the Cyprus problem, a freeze of the Turkish Cypriot declaration, no military increase on the island, transfer of Varosha to the UN, and the recommencement of negotiations.[14]

As with previous initiatives, Pérez de Cuéllar's efforts was complicated when its political setting became adversely imbued by a series of relevant developments. For example, Denktash announced his intention to proceed with a constitutional referendum and elections, whilst Turkey exchanged diplomatic credentials with the Turkish Republic of Northern Cyprus (TRNC). Furthermore, whilst the Secretary-General's "mini package" was under way, congressional developments once again linked the Cyprus issue with U.S. military aid to Turkey, leading to the United States abstaining from voting on Resolution 550.[15]

Like his predecessor, Pérez de Cuéllar experimented with a "mini package" proposal in an attempt to exploit the Turkish side's vulnerability after it had been internationally condemned for the Turkish Cypriot UDI. However, Pérez de Cuéllar's "mini package" suffered the same fate as Waldheim's attempts to settle the Varosha issue. Initially Denktash would offer Varosha, only to effectively withdraw it by attaching conditions that he knew would be unacceptable to the Greek Cypriots.[16] Denktash's behavior led the Secretary-General to state that in pursuing his "mini package" he had been "under the impression...that he could count on the sympathetic consideration of the scenario by the Turkish Cypriot community."[17]

Proximity Talks and the New York High-Level Meeting: Lessons Learned

Failure of the "mini package" saw the Secretary-General revert to a comprehensive approach with his "working points." His strategy was to revitalize the negotiations by conducting proximity talks that would eventually lead to a high-level meeting.

The "working points" began with a recommitment to the 1977 and 1979 agreements and the notion that Cyprus should be a constitutionally bicommunal and territorially bizonal federation. They then proceeded by codifying the five confidence-building measures previously flagged. Further territorial adjustments would include enlargement of the areas already proposed by the Turkish Cypriots on the proviso that the criteria for resettlement would not be based on percentages but rather on the number of refugees. The three freedoms and demilitarization issues would be discussed and integrated into the final timetable of implementation. But the centerpiece of the "working points" was the proposal to set up joint technical working groups to deliberate on those unresolved issues that prevented agreement on a common governmental structure. A transitional federal government would come into being when the government institutions and territorial adjustments were finalized.[18]

From the moment Pérez de Cuéllar submitted his "working points," disagreement intensified amongst the Greek Cypriots. Despite the Secretary-General's repeated appeal for confidentiality, details of the negotiations were leaked to the Greek Cypriot media, with AKEL issuing a press release in support of the Secretary-General's initiative. The political crisis intensified when both AKEL and DISY requested an extraordinary sitting of parliament to discuss the "working points." The situation escalated when EDEK criticized AKEL, and Kyprianou questioned the motive for the parliamentary debate.

To conduct negotiations in the face of the difficulties created by UDI, the Secretary-General adopted a two-way communication system known as proximity talks. This method of negotiation involved the two leaders being assigned to separate rooms while the Secretary-General went from one to the other. The purpose of the proximity talks was to resolve a number of substantial issues by elaborating further on the "working points." It was hoped that this process would result in a preliminary draft that would be submitted to a high-level meeting.

Initially Pérez de Cuéllar sought discussion on the confidence-building measures, but after resistance from both sides he concentrated exclusively on the substantive questions. By the end of the first round of the proximity talks in 1984, the two sides had essentially reiterated their respective positions on the contentious issues. The Turkish Cypriots made it clear that any concessions on the territorial issue depended on progress in the constitutional arrangements. On the other hand, the Greek Cypriots reiterated their latest proposals as found in the Kyprianou framework.

With a disappointing start to the proximity talks, there was an immediate diplomatic intervention by high-ranking U.S. officials in what constituted the third American post-1974 initiative on Cyprus. The Americans urged the parties to take advantage of this opportunity to reach a final settlement, and they constantly put their weight behind Pérez de Cuéllar's efforts.

Despite Pérez de Cuéllar warning that he would cast blame on the intransigent side, by the end of the second round of the proximity talks, differences were still too wide to make the prospect for a summit meeting at all feasible. Disagreement between the two sides still persisted over the powers and functions of the central government, especially over the question of residual power. The Greek Cypriots flatly rejected the concept of a rotating presidency, and on territorial arrangements they insisted that the Turkish Cypriot area should be 25 percent whilst they persisted on 30 percent. The Secretary-General's documents raised several new questions for the Turkish Cypriots. If the head of the executive government belonged to one community, would the deputy be from the other? Would the executive be responsible to the parliament? Would the mode of decision-making process, both at the executive and parliamentary levels, be by consensus or would it encompass separate majorities on certain issues?[19] The Greek Cypriots were also concerned about the sort of mechanism for deadlock resolution that would be instituted to resolve any difference between the two chambers.

In the interim, Kyprianou sought a consensus amongst the Greek Cypriot political parties. At a summit with the political leaders in November 1984, they resolved that there would be no transitional government before a comprehensive solution was reached, and that no settlement would be accepted without the prior withdrawal of all the Turkish troops. As for the timetable, DISY and AKEL accepted their gradual withdrawal after the installation of a transitional government, provided that a comprehensive agreement on all other matters had been reached. EDEK, DIKO, and Kyprianou opposed this view, insisting that the Turkish troops withdraw before the introduction of a transitional government. On all other major issues they agreed that all settlers should be withdrawn from Cyprus; besides the actual figure of the territorial adjustments, what was of equal concern was the number of refugees that were to be resettled and the specific areas that would be returned; there could be no agreement without the total return of the Greek Cypriot sector of Famagusta; "equal political status," as advocated by the Turkish Cypriots to mean equal participation in decision making, with veto rights on all issues, was unacceptable; and there could be no rotation of the presidency. Finally, it was generally held that a high-level meeting should not proceed until a comprehensive preliminary agreement was reached.

In an attempt to expedite the negotiations Pérez de Cuéllar submitted, at the third round of the proximity talks, a preliminary draft agreement aimed at a high-level meeting. Overall he proposed an integrated package with the distinct aim of resolving those points of disagreement by applying direct pressure on both sides to compromise. The draft agreement incorporated all the points that were agreed to during the previous two rounds and identified the unresolved issues.[20]

Denktash accepted the preliminary draft agreement provided that it was ratified at the summit without any further negotiations, whilst Kyprianou submitted revised constitutional proposals. To narrow the gap further, Pérez de Cuéllar sought from the Turkish Cypriots "understandings," which he communicated to Kyprianou, in the form of two "non-papers": the first being Denktash's informal proposals, whilst the second was his assessment. Denktash suggested that the 1960 presidential and cabinet system be retained, with decisions of special concern taken by weighted voting. According to Pérez de Cuéllar, this would be exchanged for the foreign ministry being given to the Turkish Cypriots. With respect to the legislature there would be a conciliation committee of three Greek Cypriots and two Turkish Cypriots with weighted voting, with separate majorities in both houses on major matters. Other matters would require a simple majority with at least 30 percent of each community in the upper chamber. On territorial adjustments Denktash recommended 29 to 71 percent division, and Pérez de Cuéllar believed that the 1981 Turkish Cypriot map was not the "last word." In order to enhance trust between the two sides Denktash also proposed the setting up of "special status areas" adjacent to each other.[21]

Kyprianou's response was more substantial. He was critical that there was no mention of the UN resolutions, that the delineation between federal and provincial jurisdictions, including the vexed question of residual power, was not settled. He insisted that the withdrawal of non-Cypriot troops, including settlers, should be completed prior to the establishment of a transitional government. Kyprianou rejected the proposed legislative voting system, agreeing that a working group should deliberate on it. On the territorial issue, he wanted that the actual areas to be placed under Turkish Cypriot administration should also be discussed taking into consideration the number of Greek Cypriot refugees to be returned as well as the nature of the special status areas. Finally, Kyprianou also responded to the "non-papers," indicating that he was willing to discuss at the high-level meeting matters that were of special concern to the Turkish Cypriots. The Greek Cypriots did not accept the proposition that the foreign minister always be a Turkish Cypriot but were prepared to discuss the issue of the Turkish Cypriot ministries.[22]

By the end of 1984 Pérez de Cuéllar was convinced that the documentation was sufficient to render the submission of a draft agreement to a high-level meeting. Closer examination of the relevant documentation indicates that there were still significant differences that required further negotiations before reaching the final stage of a summit. By agreeing to attend the high-level meeting Kyprianou inevitably encouraged Pérez de Cuéllar's assessment that, confronted by the pressure of international expectations, the Greek Cypriots would overcome their reservations.

The announcement of a high-level meeting was welcomed by the United States, who had applied a lot of pressure on the various parties to reach a negotiated settlement. Indicative of this was U.S. President Ronald Reagan's letter to his counterpart Kenan Evren, urging the Turkish side to adopt a conciliatory attitude toward the Greek Cypriots in order to create a federal state and end the division on the island.[23] The Americans realized that for a breakthrough to occur during these negotiations the Turkish side had to be pressured to abandon its intransigence and be more forthcoming with its concessions. Reagan's letter, together with a $500 million U.S. aid package and the intensity of diplomatic activity, epitomized Reagan's Cyprus initiative. The president's initiative reflected a policy shift on Cyprus by which the Americans realized that it was not merely an ethnic conflict but also an issue that for the past thirty years had been manipulated by outside actors. To achieve a breakthrough the two communities had to be "freed." The American shift was due to three considerations: Reagan's battle with Congress over aid to Turkey, which was traceable to the Cyprus conflict; the increasing turmoil in the Middle East, which demanded that tension within the northeastern flank of NATO be relaxed; and, that settlement of the Cyprus problem would enable the U.S. Rapid Deployment Force to use the huge new air base at Lefkoniko in the Turkish occupied sector, which could only be achieved with the Greek Cypriots' approval.[24] Margaret Thatcher's Government, as a guarantor power, also strongly supported the Secretary-General's initiative based on the assessment that whilst it condemned the Turkish Cypriot UDI it accepted the "effective partition" of Cyprus as a reality.[25]

At the opening of the high-level meeting in New York on January 17, 1985, the Secretary-General tabled an amended draft agreement. Denktash was of the understanding that all that the sides had to do was agree upon three dates, set up the working groups that would elaborate the details, and sign the agreement. According to Denktash, this belief was based on Pérez de Cuéllar's statement that only one hour was needed for the conclusion of the summit. Kyprianou, on the other hand, stated that he did not come to New York to sign a "ghost paper" and insisted on negotiations. Denktash responded by saying that these matters were to be dealt with by the working groups, and in any case if renegotiations were to occur then the Turkish Cypriots would demand the reassessment of all the points agreed to thus far. Confusion and uncertainty prevailed over the summit's precise purpose. Unable to get the two parties to issue a joint communiqué, Pérez de Cuéllar issued his own press release noting that the gap had "never been so narrow" and appealing to the participants that the progress achieved be preserved for another meeting.[26]

Several factors contributed to the failure of the New York summit, the most notable being the Secretary-General's mishandling of the last phase of the proximity talks and the premature scheduling of the meeting. Leading up to the high-level summit, Pérez de Cuéllar knew that the major issues were not addressed and that consigning them to working groups would be unacceptable to the Greek Cypriots. Kyprianou believed that these outstanding issues would be subject to further negotiation during the high-level meeting. Once Denktash had indicated that he was unwilling to discuss them, Pérez de Cuéllar, in order to retain the momentum, tried to secure an in-principle agreement. This tactical manoeuvre nearly succeeded when Kyprianou proposed a constitutional working group and four discussion areas.[27] With Denktash also rebuffing this offer, Pérez de Cuéllar tried to avoid a breakdown of the negotiations by rescheduling another meeting.

Assuming that both Denktash and Kyprianou were sincere about their dealings with the Secretary-General during the proximity talks, a series of questions arise regarding Pérez de Cuéllar's handling of the negotiations. In particular, why did he give two totally different impressions regarding the purpose of the summit meeting? And what led the Secretary-General to the view that an agreement could be achieved at a high-level meeting when the Greek Cypriots were clearly not convinced that all major issues had been satisfactorily resolved? It is likely that Pérez de Cuéllar believed that once he had secured Denktash's acceptance of his draft agreement, then Kyprianou could be persuaded within a summit environment to follow suit. This assessment was based on the belief that Kyprianou would bow to internal and external pressure and for fear of being cast as the intransigent figure at the discussions. However, in his assessment of Kyprianou the Secretary-General failed to allow for two important considerations: Papandreou's attitude to the draft agreement, which strengthened Kyprianou's resilience; and the likelihood that pressuring Kyprianou to make fundamentally unacceptable concessions would only have the opposite effect. Pérez de Cuéllar misjudged Kyprianou's psychological circumstances. As one of Makarios' close advisers during the London agreements, he was deeply affected by the fact that the archbishop, under extreme duress, eventually succumbed to accepting the unacceptable. Amid the tension of the New York summit, Kyprianou may have seen parallels between 1959 and his current predicament, the only difference being that in 1985 the Greek government advised him against conceding. The prevailing view in the West was that Kyprianou "rejected a good deal" because he steered the "cautious middle path" to avoid offending the militants. Opposition by the militants was complicated by Papandreou's strident anti-Turkish rhetoric, criticism of UN proposals, and insistence that all Turkish troops be removed from Cyprus.[28]

Yet, responsibility for the failure of the high-level meeting should also be placed at Kyprianou's door. He agreed, after all, to attend the summit without having sought clearer assurances from Pérez de Cuéllar that the outstanding issues would be effectively dealt with prior to any agreement. Kyprianou's justification for attending the high-level meeting was that he had succumbed to the pressure generated by the general euphoria suggesting that a breakthrough was imminent. He did not therefore wish to appear to the rest of the world as the one who had torpedoed the Secretary-General's initiative. In this regard, at least, Pérez de Cuéllar's assessment was correct. Finally, it is also the case that Denktash could have assisted the process by accepting Kyprianou's last-minute offer of conditional agreement. Instead, sensing that international opinion had focused on the Greek Cypriots' procrastination, he hardened his position in order to win an important political battle.

In addition to the above factors, timing proved to have a major detrimental effect on the mediatory effort. Besides the need for more preparatory work, the fact that the meeting occurred at a time when Greek-Turkish relations were strained reduced considerably the chances of success. On a broader level, the summit's failure proved to be a major setback for the negotiations, for it exhausted the political will of both parties, as well as the energy invested by various external powers. Much of the capital earned during the proximity talks had been depleted, thereby dissipating the psychological as well as political momentum created during that cycle of negotiations.

Overall, compared to previous negotiations the progress achieved during the proximity talks had narrowed the gap between the two sides to such an extent that a settlement seemed feasible. Despite Pérez de Cuéllar's optimistic postmortem suggesting that both sides were interested "in solving the problem,"[29] subsequent events suggested that, as UN sources privately conceded, the draft agreement "was virtually dead."[30]

Challenging the President:
Greek Cypriot Domestic Political Crisis

Exhausted by the peace process, the Greek and Turkish Cypriot communities entered an introverted phase dominated by internal disputes, as opposition forces within both communities began to challenge the prevailing orthodoxy of the governing leadership.

Within the Greek Cypriot community, the collapse of the 1985 high-level meeting unleashed the political forces of the pragmatists and the militants, with AKEL and DISY directly disputing Kyprianou's legitimacy as chief negotiator. Although there was empathy for Kyprianou not succumbing to the immense pressure to sign an agreement, the Greek Cypriots were blamed for the collapse of the summit. Despite Kyprianou's repeated stress on the need for "guarded optimism" in the lead up to the New York summit, the Greek Cypriot community felt terribly let down, precisely because there had been such high expectations for a settlement.

In what emerged as a common front by the pragmatists, AKEL and DISY chastised Kyprianou as a "minority president" since he did not enjoy majority support amongst the Greek Cypriot electorate. The pragmatists intensified their campaign when the two parties combined their majority numbers in parliament to pass a resolution calling on the president to sign the Secretary-General's draft agreement. Kyprianou dismissed the resolution as unconstitutional and declared that he was willing to work with all the political parties to achieve a united position. In late March, AKEL and DISY increased the pressure by adopting another parliamentary resolution that called on Kyprianou to resign and hold presidential elections within forty-five days.

Kyprianou's strongest defender during this crisis was militant EDEK, which urged him not to succumb to pressures to sign an agreement. In a further attempt to diffuse the crisis, Kyprianou proposed to reestablish the national council. To make the offer more appealing to the pragmatists, Kyprianou intended to strengthen the body, allowing for disagreements between the president and the majority to be referred to a reconciliation committee, and if the differences persisted, to be put to a referendum. Both AKEL and DISY rejected Kyprianou's overtures and reiterated their call for Kyprianou to resign.

Although Kyprianou managed to fend off the assault at the time, the incident inflicted considerable political damage on the president's credibility as the expression of the Greek Cypriot collective will. Denktash seized upon this weakness and constantly hammered Kyprianou throughout his presidential term. The political crisis also undermined Kyprianou's efforts to concentrate on Pérez de Cuéllar's new initiative.

If the 1985 parliamentary elections were considered as a quasi-referendum, then Kyprianou would have felt vindicated that he had acted wisely both at the high-level meeting and in taking on the pragmatists. Kyprianou's party had increased its vote by 8 percent and doubled its parliamentary seats. The major development was that, despite their ideological and historical antipathy, the two advocates of the pragmatists formed a political alliance that was not restricted to streamlining their positions on the Cyprus negotiations but also embarked on a joint strategy to force Kyprianou into submission or to oust him from the presidency. Indicative of their intentions was AKEL's and DISY's failed attempt in 1984 to engineer early parliamentary elections in order to gain a two-thirds majority by which they could amend the constitution and thereby impose their will on the president. However, the merits of such a partnership did not resonate well with AKEL's traditionally disciplined constituency. As a result, AKEL suffered its biggest electoral upset as 5 percent of its base vote abandoned the party in protest over its political alliance with the conservative Right. A year after the elections, AKEL admitted that its "co-direction" with DISY led the party "to make wrong decisions" and "its actions were misunderstood."[31]

What also emerged from the Greek Cypriot political crisis of 1985 was that, irrespective of the president's constitutional powers, any major decision pertaining to the Cyprus problem would need the support of the great majority, if not all, of the main political forces. In what constituted the clearest electoral clash between the pragmatists and the militants, the elections of 1985 proved that, despite the strong machinery of the two largest parties of Cyprus, the militants were supported by approximately 40 percent of the Greek Cypriots.

The crisis of 1985 signaled the beginning of Kyprianou's defeat at the next presidential elections. The withdrawal of Kyprianou's main backer, AKEL, meant that for him to advance to the second round of the election process he needed to attract an additional 10 percent to his party's maximum base vote of 25 percent. As a seasoned politician, Kyprianou would have anticipated that this additional support would have derived from EDEK, which polled around that mark. However, in 1988 EDEK contested the presidential elections with its own candidate. Kyprianou fared much better than anticipated by increasing his primary vote considerably, but he fell short of outpolling AKEL's candidate George Vassiliou for the second spot. With EDEK's support and enough leakage from DIKO, Vassiliou defeated Clerides in the second round.

Turkish Cypriot Opposition and the Politics of Population

As with the Greek Cypriots, the Turkish Cypriot community was undergoing a transitional phase characterized by the progressive erosion of political singularity underscored by internal socioeconomic contradictions.

As Denktash prepared for a constitutional referendum and fresh parliamentary elections, he also confronted political opposition of his own with the growing strength of the two main opposition parties: the left-wing CTP and the center-left TKP (*Toplumcu Kurtulus Partisi* [Communal Liberation Party]). As a result of the 1981 parliamentary elections the two opposition parties held nineteen votes out of forty, with a higher percentage of the overall vote than Denktash's UBP.

In examining the parliamentary elections conducted in the northern Cyprus after 1976, Denktash would have been concerned that if the electoral trend continued, the opposition could soon gain control and threaten his handling of the peace talks. The collapse of the New York summit provided Denktash with the opportunity to consolidate his new "state" whilst taking the necessary measures to stem the influence of the opposition in northern Cyprus.

To curtail the prospect of an electoral threat to the doctrine of separateness, Denktash empowered the mainland settlers by granting them citizenship, in the firm belief that they would be strongly pro-Turkey and less receptive to the opposition's call for the reintegration of the island. He also prepared a constitution that provided protection against acts committed by any individual or group against the TRNC.

The internal dynamics of Turkish Cypriot politics, in particular the opposition to Denktash's authority, was significant in that it pointed to policy differences and to the ability of opposition forces to influence the Turkish Cypriot stance in the negotiations. The relevance of this opposition to the future course of the intercommunal negotiations, although operating in different circumstances to those of the Greek Cypriot community and in a context of interdependence with Turkey, cannot be overlooked.

The strongest opponent to *taksim* and Turkish Cypriot nationalism was, in its various manifestations, the Turkish Cypriot left. The campaign to silence the Turkish Cypriot Left reached its peak in 1965 with the murders of two outspoken Turkish Cypriot trade unionists, Fazil Onder and Dervish Kavazoglu. These acts preceded the execution of *Cumhuriyet* editors Ayhan Hikmet and Ahmet Gürkan in 1962. During this period Turkish Cypriot Marxists were politically isolated as they soon disagreed with AKEL's ambiguity on *enosis* whilst at the same time they were persecuted by Turkish Cypriot extremists.

In the aftermath of 1974, the Turkish Cypriot opposition occupied an obscure presence in northern Cyprus. A decade later the political landscape changed dramatically and there emerged a distinct opposition to Denktash's rule comprised of the CTP and the TKP.

Ever since its formation in 1970 the CTP led the Turkish Cypriot opposition. Although it has never described itself as a communist party, it was pro-Soviet and under Özgür's leadership sharpened its left-wing ideology. Given its "one people" viewpoint, the CTP (together with AKEL) was the strongest advocate of communal rapprochement and the forging of a genuine federal state. On the Cyprus conflict the CTP maintained a consistent position that, in many ways, correlated with that of AKEL. It supported a federal, bicommunal, bizonal, nonaligned, independent Cyprus, opposed the British bases, and favored the continuation of the intercommunal talks. On the question of the Turkish occupation troops, the CTP's official policy was that they should remain until a solution was found, and it supported Turkey's rights as a guarantor power. Despite its previous opposition to an independent Turkish Cypriot state, the CTP voted for its establishment under the threat of being outlawed. After 1983, the CTP toned down its criticism on the sensitive issues of statehood and the role of the Turkish troops. Instead, it concentrated its attention on the lack of democracy in northern Cyprus, the importation of settlers, and on the progressive integration of the TRNC with Turkey, leading to the partition of Cyprus.

Formed in 1976, the other opposition party, the TKP, was viewed as a social democratic party influenced by Atatürk's reformism. The UDI caused a split in the TKP over whether or not independence was the best way to proceed toward a federal Cyprus. Prior to 1983, its founder Alpay Durduran was adamantly opposed to the declaration of statehood, stressing that it would "be an adventure with unpredictable consequences."[32] As with the CTP, the TKP also voted in favor of UDI.

Notwithstanding its internal rift over the question of independence, the TKP was against the division of the island and did not consider the post-1974 separation of the two communities as a permanent solution. It supported the gradual integration of the two communities by fostering trust and encouraging contact and interaction between them especially on practical matters. By way of example, its next leader Mustafa Akinci, whilst being mayor of Nicosia, cooperated with his Greek Cypriot counterpart and the UN to establish a joint sewage system and prepared for the urban unification of the capital. Akinci strongly advocated open boundaries between the two sides and did not reject, at least in principle, the freedoms of settlement and ownership, provided they could be applied in a way that safeguarded the bizonal character of the federation. Under Akinci, the TKP also proposed property-swap and compensation for those refugees who would not be able to return to their properties. With respect to security matters, the TKP supported the mutual reduction of forces to nonthreatening levels and the retention of Turkey's guarantee rights so long as these were invoked by the Turkish Cypriots rather than Ankara. While he did not advocate the expulsion of the settlers, as this would create a new refugee problem, Akinci opposed any further immigration. The TKP was opposed to settler parties and challenged the nationalist presumption that the Turkish Cypriots' economic troubles were due solely to the Greek Cypriot embargo.

As with the Greek Cypriots, two political groupings existed within the Turkish Cypriot community regarding the Cyprus problem. The first grouping could be called separatists (*ayrılıkcı*), who essentially encapsulated the official Turkish Cypriot position as pursued by

Denktash and the nationalists. The second grouping, the integrationalist (*birliktelik*), consisted of the main Turkish Cypriot opposition parties CTP and TKP. The relevance of the integrationalist for the peace process was not that they could radically alter Turkish national policy on Cyprus. As in many third world countries, the Turkish military in Cyprus performed a dual role in that they were prepared to intervene in the domestic political process if they perceived a threat to their national interest. In this respect the Turkish army was aided by the military, economic, and political integration of northern Cyprus with Turkey, by its military presence in such a small territory, and by the emotional attachment of the majority of Turkish Cypriots who viewed Turkish officers as their guardians.[33]

The significance of the integrationalist to the Cyprus conflict, then, is to be found outside the formal negotiating process. From the late 1970s, unions and political parties from both sides met several times in an effort to demonstrate the case for reunification and coexistence to their respective communities. Among all the possible configurations between the Greek and Turkish communities, AKEL and the CTP maintained the strongest links. In any federal arrangement they would presumably evolve into a coalition. It was also conceivable that the integrationalist could increase their political influence in the post-Denktash era by aligning themselves with moderate Turkish Cypriot political forces.

Opposition to Denktash stemmed not only from his hard line at the peace talks but also from his manipulation of the power structures within the TRNC to retain electoral power through the naturalization of the settlers. Although the "settlers" issue was considered by many outsiders of secondary importance, it had the potential to emerge as a major stumbling block to any final settlement of the conflict.

On a broader level, the politics of population constitutes an important feature of the Cyprus conflict. It impacts on the question of majority versus minority rights and is reflected throughout the course of negotiations in recurring discussions over percentages and the ratio distribution of power, entitlements, and territory. Any alteration of the demographic composition of the island's population would therefore be expected to have a severe impact on any attempt to resolve the Cyprus problem. At the core of this debate was the arrival, after 1975, of large numbers of Turkish nationals who settled in northern Cyprus and the social and political impact on the Turkish Cypriot community. The "settler question" was of great concern not only to the Greek Cypriots but also to the Turkish Cypriot opposition, which feared that the community was being socially engineered for political and indeed electoral purposes.

Although the U.S. State Department dismissed the settler issue as insignificant to the overall Cyprus dispute,[34] former Vice-President of the Republic of Cyprus Fazıl Kütchük was so concerned about the settlers that in 1978 he wrote several critical articles on the matter.[35] In 1984 a series of mainland Turkish newspapers reported that friction had developed between the Turkish Cypriots and the settlers on the island.[36] By 1986 the settler question had become so divisive within the Turkish Cypriot community that Özgür declared that if the "situation continues, it will before long be impossible to talk about the presence of Turkish Cypriots in Northern Cyprus."[37] These suspicions were compounded by the fact that the Turkish and TRNC authorities had initially attempted to conceal the situation by denying access to, or publication of, comprehensive population statistics.

When the settler issue was first raised, the TFSC's official position was that owing to a labor shortage "skilled technicians and workers" were being imported from Turkey on a "seasonal basis" as "guest workers." Furthermore, it was claimed, those who were migrating back to Cyprus were amongst the 300,000 Turkish Cypriots living in Turkey.[38] In 1975 Denktash himself stated that during 1954–1959 EOKA "caused nearly 30,000 Turks to leave the island," of whom 10,000 subsequently returned.[39]

However, statistical information provided by the British Colonial Office reveals that during 1955–1959 only 4,539 Turkish Cypriots departed from Cyprus.[40] Furthermore, the Department of Statistics and Research of the Republic of Cyprus for the years 1960–1973 indicated that a total of 11,980 Turkish Cypriots emigrated from Cyprus during those thirteen years.[41] Though the accuracy of the 1963–1973 figures may be questioned, since they were controlled by the Greek Cypriots, the figure of 6,086 Turkish Cypriots departing Cyprus for 1960–1963 is less contestable as this was the period of bicommunal participation in the public service, which at that time included the Department of Statistics. In 1989 the Turkish Cypriot newspaper *Yenidüzen*, having investigated police and immigration records, revealed that approximately 6,000 Turkish Cypriots had emigrated from Cyprus during the period of 1963–1974. This confirmed the original findings of the Department of Statistics that 11,980 Turkish Cypriots had emigrated from Cyprus between 1960 and 1973 (by subtracting the

1960–1963 figure of 6,086 from 11,980 we are left with 5,894). *Yenidüzen* also contradicted Denktash's second assertion by disclosing that 24,152 Turkish Cypriots had emigrated from northern Cyprus during 1974 to 1986[42]—a figure that is believed to have risen to 30,000 by 1989.[43]

The settler theory is substantiated by the following statistics. In 1974 both the Republic of Cyprus and the Turkish Cypriot Ministry of Justice estimated the Turkish Cypriot population to be around 116,000. In 1987 the TRNC authorities reported that this figure had increased to 165,000.[44] After subtracting those Turkish Cypriots who emigrated from northern Cyprus during 1974–1987 (24,152) from the 1974 Turkish Cypriot figure of 116,000, then we are left with a figure that places the Turkish Cypriot population in the north closer to 100,000. This leaves us with a discrepancy between the figures for 1974 and 1987 of 65,000, for which no satisfactory explanation was offered by the Turkish and Turkish Cypriot authorities.

Though there may be legitimate disagreement over the actual figure, the above hypothesis is substantiated by a number of credible sources.[45] If one adds the number of Turkish armed personnel—conservatively estimated at around 30,000—to that of the settlers, then we can appreciate that mainland Turks could seriously rival the total number of Turkish Cypriots in northern Cyprus.

Even by conservative estimates the settlers' electoral power may have been as high as one-third of the TRNC electoral constituency.[46] By 1980, over 30,000 Turkish nationals had been granted TRNC citizenship and were entitled to vote.[47] In establishing their voting intention there is no doubt that the great majority would have voted for Denktash, especially in any contest against CTP and TKP candidates. This assertion is based on the fact that they were indebted to, and dependent on, Denktash' administration for providing them with homes, land, and political patronage. Furthermore, the settlers were in accord with Denktash's nationalist conviction and opposed to any of integrationists' rapprochement.

Given their electoral strength, and the intention that any prospective settlement would first have to be approved by a referendum of both communities, the settlers indubitably constitute a third party in the communal conflict. In addition, the manner in which they were settled and naturalized in northern Cyprus by the authorities weakened the integrationists' forces and raised questions, at least in the longer term, regarding the representation of Turkish Cypriot interests in any negotiated settlement.

Pérez de Cuéllar's Draft Agreement

Whilst both communities were preoccupied with their domestic affairs, Pérez de Cuéllar launched a new initiative. In an attempt to salvage the basic tenets of his preliminary agreement, the Secretary-General presented his consolidated draft agreement. As with the draft agreement, Pérez de Cuéllar foresaw the need for four working groups to deal with the unresolved issues as well as elaborate on the details of the agreement. Pérez de Cuéllar attached great significance to these working groups; he wanted to maintain stewardship over them and insisted that a joint high-level meeting ratify their deliberations.

Wheeling from the New York debacle, Kyprianou immediately accepted the draft agreement, whilst Denktash delayed his response. As Necatigil explained, the Turkish Cypriots objected to the changes made by the Secretary-General, about which they were not consulted, especially those concerning the upper chamber voting system, which no longer required separate majorities but only the consent of at least 30 percent of the Turkish Cypriot deputies. More importantly was the departure from the principle that residual powers would remain with the provinces. It soon became apparent that the Turkish Cypriots were not interested in discussing the new document and considered it a political ploy to deter them from consolidating their state.[48]

Encouraged by Security Council Resolution 578, Pérez de Cuéllar continued to lobby both sides to sustain the dialogue through two rounds of "low level" talks. After the rejection of his two previous proposals, Pérez de Cuéllar sought, through a third document—the Draft Framework Agreement on Cyprus—a compromise position. Overall, the draft framework amalgamated his 1985 January and April proposals and included those procedural aspects contained in his 1985 statement.

Pérez de Cuéllar proposed that in accepting the Draft Framework Agreement they also agree to the adoption of a three-stage negotiating process. The first stage required acceptance of those elements on which there was already agreement; the second entailed negotiations through working groups and joint high-level meetings of the unresolved issues; and the final stage involved ratification of the overall agreement, which would only come into effect as an integrated whole.

Denktash replied to Pérez de Cuéllar's proposals by confirming his understanding of the terms of the draft agreement. That the Turkish Cypriot community would enjoy equal political status in terms of its participation in all aspects and structures of the federation, and

Turkey's guarantee rights would be retained. In relation to the withdrawal of the Turkish troops, Denktash reiterated that this could only occur once there was a settlement and a transitional government. He also clarified his position on the question of the three freedoms that they be regulated in a way that will not infringe on the Turkish Cypriot's security nor threaten the bicommunal-bizonal nature of the federation. Denktash added that all elements of the document had to be treated as an integral whole and the summit meeting would deal only with the establishment of the working groups and "filling...the blanks" in the document. He stipulated that removal of the economic embargo and cessation of provocative actions, both domestically and internationally, by the Greek Cypriots was imperative for progressing toward a peaceful solution. He concluded by stating that in case the Greek Cypriots rejected the proposals, then "the Turkish Cypriot side [would] no longer be bound" by any of the concessions it had made. With these understandings, Denktash accepted the Draft Framework Agreement.[49]

Kyprianou insisted that before the Greek Cypriot side expressed its views on the Draft Framework Agreement it was imperative that there first be "agreement on the basic issues of the Cyprus problem." These priority matters constituted the withdrawal of the Turkish troops and settlers, effective international guarantees, and the application of the three freedoms. According to the Draft Framework Agreement, these three priority matters would have been dealt with by working groups and subsequently by the joint high-level meetings. Kyprianou sought to have them resolved in the first stage of Pérez de Cuéllar's proposed negotiating process. To appear accommodative, Kyprianou was willing to have the constitutional and territorial issues discussed at the second stage of the negotiations. Kyprianou then proposed the adoption of "one of two alternative procedures." Either an international conference would be convened or, if this was not possible, a high-level meeting would be called to deal with the above matters.[50]

As both sides disagreed on the procedural provisions, the Secretary-General's initiative, yet again, had reached an impasse.

Alternatives: International Conference and Beyond

At first sight it seems as if the Secretary-General's two draft agreements had narrowed the gap on the territorial and constitutional questions and managed to reduce the outstanding issues. However, this was a misleading impression, as the most contentious issues had not been tested at a negotiating forum and the working groups had not started their deliberations. Despite Pérez de Cuéllar's attempts to revive momentum, the negotiating process exhibited signs of fatigue and eventually grounded to a halt.

The impasse in the intercommunal talks allowed outside initiatives to emerge, with a range of ideas advocating a radical departure from the UN-sponsored intercommunal talks. The most important of these alternatives was the Soviet idea of a UN-sponsored international conference that would deal with the external aspects of the Cypriot dispute. Such a conference could result in the signing of a treaty that would see the demilitarization of the island and the installation of an effective regime of guarantees. The guarantor powers could be the permanent members of the Security Council, Greece, and Turkey, as well as some nonaligned states. However, any decision for intervention required the consent of all guarantor powers and Cyprus was not to be subjected to the threat or use of force. Finally, participants to the international conference could include the Republic of Cyprus (representatives from both communities), Greece, Turkey, all members of the Security Council, and some nonaligned countries.[51]

This was not the first time the Soviet Union had called for an international conference on Cyprus, but this version was far more specific in its structure and substance. The primary Soviet aim was to disengage the Cyprus problem from the political confines of the NATO quadrangle, which had constrained it since the 1950s. This required the dismantling of the 1960 regime of guarantees and the removal of British bases from the island. Essentially, the Soviet Union sought not only to internationalize the process of resolving the Cypriot dispute, but also to approach the problem from a different perspective. Soviet policy was premised on the demarcation between the internal and the international aspects of the Cyprus problem.

The manner in which Pérez de Cuéllar handled the Soviet call for an international conference suggests that he did not view it as a serious proposition. Although he acknowledged the circulation of the Soviet proposal and provided an outline of its content in his report, no indication was given of its fate. As the Soviet proposal coincided with Pérez de Cuéllar's framework, its timing raises certain questions as to Moscow's actual intention. It is reasonable to assume that the Secretary-General kept the Soviets informed of his desire to launch a new initiative and so prevent any unforeseen developments from compromising his efforts. Although we can only speculate about Soviet motives, the initiative was riddled with political paradoxes. Whilst the Soviet Union most likely knew of Pérez de Cuéllar's intended proposals, it nevertheless proceeded with its own submission. It may be that it was trying to ingratiate itself with the Papandreou Government, hence the support given by Soviet proposals to the militant's contention that the intercommunal talks as a negotiating process were deficient in addressing the core of the Cyprus problem, namely, its external dimension. One can also assume that the Soviet Union, under Mikhail Gorbachev's leadership, was trying to convince nonaligned states that it was still a superpower capable of promoting their interests against Western influences. In any case, by April 1987 the Soviet Union had clearly abandoned its historical anti-Western attitude to the Cyprus issue and signaled that it would not necessarily be adverse to a Western-based plan simply because of its origin.

Having rejected Pérez de Cuéllar's latest proposals, Kyprianou embraced the Soviet idea for an international conference with ferment vigor. There is no doubt that in the lead-up to the 1988 presidential elections, Kyprianou's tenacious pursuit of the international conference constituted a deliberate attempt aimed at the pro-Soviet constituency of AKEL. He first raised the issue with Pérez de Cuéllar in April 1986 and sought support for the idea during his address to the General Assembly. Having promised that he would consult the members of the Security Council, the Secretary-General reported that there was "lack of agreement" over Kyprianou's proposal for an international conference. Undeterred by the Secretary-General's soundings, Kyprianou called upon Pérez de Cuéllar to endorse the convening of an international conference and "to convince those members of the Security Council who appear[ed] to be unfavorable."[52] In the meantime, Denktash informed the Secretary-General that the Turkish Cypriot side was against an international conference.

Given the split within the Security Council and Pérez de Cuéllar's unwillingness to pursue the matter, Kyprianou contemplated taking the issue directly to the General Assembly. The aim was to incorporate the convening of an international conference into the operative segment of the General Assembly's resolution on Cyprus.[53] However, Kyprianou did not persevere with his campaign as traditionally friendly governments were not so encouraging and, in any case, by then Moscow itself had moderated its support. Although Vassiliou, who succeeded Kyprianou, supported the convening of an international conference, once in government he abandoned the idea as the Cypriot negotiations entered a new phase.

Another contribution to the discussion of alternatives came from the former Cyprus Coordinator of the State Department, Richard Haass. In rejecting the call for an international conference, Haass agreed that the UN was intellectually exhausted, and that there was a need to search for other options. One such option, he argued, involved a more active role for the United States. He dismissed outright the option of a grand U.S. diplomatic initiative (such as a Camp David on Cyprus), which he considered too risky for American interests as it might negatively impact on bilateral relations with Greece and Turkey. He advocated instead a low-key diplomatic approach designed to create the necessary conditions for a settlement. In this respect the Haass doctrine supported the retention of the UN peacekeeping force in Cyprus, which served as a military buffer zone between the Greeks and Turks, and discouraged the view that another major crisis—similar to 1974—would force an American intervention. Haass believed that the United States should restrain from any new UN initiative until the two communities—especially the Greek Cypriots—demonstrated a greater willingness for a solution. Haass also argued that the United States should prevent the recognition of the TRNC as this would transform a temporary situation into a permanent one, and that the United States should channel the $250 million Cyprus Fund and congressional aid toward encouraging joint projects, enterprises, and other measures that aimed at reunification. Finally, in addition to the official processes, Haass maintained that the United States should exercise secondary diplomacy with the objective of achieving confidence-building measures, such as Turkish troop reductions, relaxation of the Greek Cypriot trade embargo, and the reopening of the Nicosia airport.[54]

The Haass doctrine did not profess to offer a solution to the Cypriot conflict, nor did it seek to place the United States into a predicament—as in the past—by getting it embroiled in a dispute between two of its allies. Its aim was to remove from the Cyprus problem potential sources of friction that could provoke a conflict on the island, which could in turn escalate into a broader Greek-Turkish crisis—in which case the Americans would be forced to intervene. His formula was a combination of preventative measures and the provision of economic and political incentives to construct a climate of confidence between the communities until they were ready for a solution.

Davos and Greek-Turkish Rapprochement

Undoubtedly the most serious conflict in relations between Greece and Turkey during the postwar period has been the Cyprus problem. Many analysts consider the Cyprus dispute as constituting the core of the Greek-Turkish problem, which effectively dismembered the 1930 Greek-Turkish détente of Atatürk and Eleftherios Venizelos. Although the Cyprus question is technically separate from other Greek-Turkish issues, most notably the Aegean dispute, it has overshadowed them as the most volatile arena in which their interests clashed.

Whilst the intercommunal negotiations were at an impasse, incidents over oil exploration in the Aegean erupted and brought Greece and Turkey to the brink of war. The crisis shocked both countries and their prime ministers, Papandreou and Turgut Özal, into recognizing the need for a conciliatory approach to their differences. Throughout April and May 1987, the two prime ministers, via their respective ambassadors, exchanged "messages not bullets."[55] During their first meeting at the 1988 World Economic Forum in Davos, the two leaders acknowledged that rapprochement would not be easy given the rigid mind-sets created in certain sections of their societies, and that past problems between the two countries were "at times exploited by certain" foreign powers.[56]

In a nine-point joint communiqué, the two prime ministers also agreed to a series of confidence-building measures, including the establishment of a bilateral political committee that would "define the problem areas, explore the possibilities of closing the gap and move towards lasting solutions"—its progress to be reviewed by the two prime ministers.[57]

Although officially the Cyprus problem did not constitute a bilateral Greek-Turkish issue, the presence of Turkish troops on the island provided Papandreou with the opening to propose to the Turkish leader the complete demilitarization of the island. As Papandreou explained to his parliamentary group, the proposal entailed "the withdrawal of the occupation forces, the simultaneous dissolution of the Cyprus National Guard, and the creation of a unified police force" that would be funded by the government of Cyprus. He also revealed that, although Özal did not accept the proposal, he did not reject it either. In regard to the missing persons, Özal assured Papandreou that none were in Turkey.[58] Kyprianou, who was kept fully informed, was optimistic that the Davos meeting meant that the Cyprus problem was entering a new, crucial phase.

The second meeting between Papandreou and Özal after a NATO summit resulted in a joint communiqué reiterating Greece's and Turkey's commitment to promoting rapprochement and refraining from any deed that might "undermine the spirit of Davos." For the first time the humanitarian issue of the missing persons in Cyprus was included by recommending that the Committee on Missing Persons be reactivated, which included the two prime ministers' direct input. Papandreou had again raised the issue of demilitarization, and Özal agreed to discuss the issue within the context of the international aspect of the Cyprus problem. Özal also accepted an official invitation to visit Greece on June 13–15, 1988.[59]

In the meantime, Denktash welcomed the change in the Greek Cypriot leadership and invited the newly elected Vassiliou to meet him. Although the meeting, which was hampered by protocol, did not eventuate, it was indicative of Davos's positive impact on Cyprus. In an attempt to emulate the Greek-Turkish confidence-building measures, Denktash released his "Good Will Measures" that, he argued, were aimed not at compromising either side's political positions but at "creating an atmosphere conducive to the re-establishment of trust and confidence." Denktash concluded that these measures would apply only if each side refrained from hampering each other's interests in the fields of trade, tourism, sport, transportation, communications, and other economic activities; and ceased the use of polemical language in all official and semiofficial publications.[60] Denktash's measures were rejected by Vassiliou since acceptance of the conditions would have deprived them of a major leverage—the lifting of the economic and sporting embargo on the TRNC.

As Özal's Greek visit approached, Vassiliou utilized the international platform of the General Assembly's Third Special Session on disarmament to promote the proposal for demilitarization—which he adopted with vigor. By taking advantage of the Davos climate, Vassiliou explained that a solution to the Cyprus problem would not only benefit the Cypriots but would "also promote good neighborly relations...between Greece and Turkey." He argued that, since "the withdrawal of Turkish troops and settlers [were] matters that necessitate action by the Turkish Government," it was only logical that he should meet Özal in order to discuss these matters. Vassiliou's demilitarization proposal entailed the dismantling of all forces in the island, which would be replaced by "an international peace force" under the auspices of the United Nations. Savings incurred from demilitarization would be rechanneled toward financing the peacekeeping force as well as toward developing the economically lacking regions of the island mostly inhabited by the Turkish Cypriots.[61]

The Turkish response to Vassiliou's overtures was interesting in that there appeared to be a new element of flexibility. Özal immediately ruled out the possibility of a meeting with Vassiliou, but he stated that if there were an agreement all Turkish troops would be withdrawn from Cyprus.[62] Two days later, Denktash announced that demilitarization could take place only after the formation of a transitional government. However, Turkey's foreign minister Mesut Yilmaz was more forthcoming, noting that some of the Turkish troops might be withdrawn if contacts between Denktash and Vassiliou were positive. Should they prove very positive, he continued, the possibility of a complete withdrawal could not be excluded.[63] However, it appeared that Turkey's Ministry of Foreign Affairs had a different view to that of their minister. In a public statement its director Inal Batu commented that no troops would be withdrawn if an agreement did not include effective guarantees for the Turkish Cypriots, adding that even after an agreement is reached a reduced number of Turkish troops would remain in Cyprus.[64] Eventually, Özal intervened to reaffirm the Turkish position that in the event of an agreement the force that was currently stationed in Cyprus would not be retained. He stressed that guarantees for Turkey and the Turkish Cypriots were a priority concern and that Turkey would not succumb to pressure from the EC. Furthermore, Özal indicated that although the Cyprus issue would not be officially discussed in his forthcoming visit to Athens, it would be discussed unofficially.[65]

During Özal's three-day state visit to Greece, Papandreou informed the Turkish leader that "progress [on] Greek-Turkish relations [was] influenced directly by a solution to the Cyprus Problem," which in turn was affected by the withdrawal of the Turkish troops from the island. In their private conversations Papandreou repeated the need for Cyprus's demilitarization—including the withdrawal of the settlers—believing that this would create a positive climate not only in Cyprus but also in respect to regional tension.[66]

Özal's response came during his speech at a luncheon given in his honor by the Foreign Correspondents Press Association, where he stated that the Cyprus issue was an international issue that depended very much on the intercommunal talks. He believed that Vassiliou was a successful businessman and a good leader for the Greek Cypriots and placed much importance on the forthcoming Denktash-Vassiliou meeting. Özal reiterated that the Turkish "troops will not stay there forever," and that Turkey "would like to see an agreement reached," at which point they would be withdrawn.[67] He clarified that the policy of "No War" adopted in Davos did not apply to Cyprus, noting that it was due to Turkey's intervention that democracy was restored in Greece. In concluding, Özal undertook to assist the International Committee of the Red Cross in its investigations of the missing Greeks and Greek Cypriots, pointing out that none of them were in Turkish jails.[68]

Although Cyprus once again was not mentioned in the Papandreou-Özal communiqué and Turkey's position on the withdrawal of its troops and the question of the missing persons had not changed since Davos, the climate generated by Özal's visit led Papandreou to declare optimistically that on the Cyprus issue "there [was] light at the end of the tunnel."[69]

However, after the Özal visit, the "Davos Spirit" began to dissipate. By 1989 it had completely evaporated. In June 1989, Papandreou lost the elections and political instability plagued Greece until ND was able to narrowly form a government in its own right. On the other side of the Aegean, Özal's accession to the presidency meant that his role as policy-maker and a stable influence over Turkish politics and the bureaucracy was marginalized.

When the new Greek and Turkish prime ministers, Konstantinos Mitsotakis and Yıldırım Akbulut, met in 1990 it became obvious that neither was equipped with the political will of their predecessors needed to sustain the Davos momentum. This was ironic since rapprochement with Turkey began as an ND policy by Karamanlis in 1976. However, throughout the Davos process, Mitsotakis had accused Papandreou of conducting "secret diplomacy" and dealing away Greece's strongest card (i.e., Greece's veto over Turkey's EC aspirations).

There was strong opposition to Davos in both Greece and Turkey, especially from the bureaucracies and the media who perceived every development through the conservative lens of "national interest." Three of Greece's senior ambassadors resigned in protest over the way the Cyprus issue had been taken off the agenda. When Özal visited Athens, Greek public opinion was swayed by demonstrations involving Turkish dissidents, Kurds, and Greek Cypriots, which forced Greek authorities to take extraordinary security precautions. There was also strong opposition from within Papandreou's own party, which viewed Davos as betraying PASOK's pledge on Cyprus. In Cyprus, despite Vassiliou's, AKEL's, and DISY's support, the militants of EDEK and DIKO attacked Davos.

In retrospect, the Davos experiment was made possible by the shock realization that an incident in the Aegean could escalate into war between the two countries. In reality, Davos was attributable largely to the strong personal diplomacy and leadership shown by Papandreou and Özal. In particular, the "Özal factor" was critical for Davos, as the Turkish leader gave priority to Greek-Turkish relations as part of his dual national policy of financial recovery and the resolution of Turkey's problems through dialogue.[70] Other factors also contributed to Davos, in particular the need for Turkey to eliminate Greece's obstruction to its European vocation and to U.S. aid, and Papandreou's need to disprove to the West and Turkey their allegations of Greek intransigence. Linked to the above motives was that both Turkey and Greece wanted to redirect their resources away from their rivalry. In Greece's case, whose economy was experiencing a downturn, defense expenditure in 1987 constituted 6.2 percent of Gross Domestic Product—the highest amongst NATO countries. Turkey, on the other hand, was just emerging from military rule and desperately needed to reestablish its credentials as a democratic nation, especially among the Europeans. Furthermore, Turkey needed to concentrate on the Kurdish insurrection, which was incurring a higher economic, social, and political cost than they openly admitted.

Regional and international impediments also contributed to a reassessment of Greek-Turkish relations. Improvement in U.S.-Soviet relations had diminished the strategic and political significance of both Greece and Turkey and forced them to shift their attention toward Europe.

Despite its brevity, the Davos experiment brought to the forefront once again the extent to which the Cyprus problem was linked to the broader Greek-Turkish relationship. The Davos rapprochement created the expectation that a more positive climate between the principal external powers, Greece and Turkey, would gradually evolve into a new "understanding" over the Cyprus issue. The argument was that the Aegean and Cypriot disputes could be politically linked, especially since development in one quarter was likely to impact on the other. But whereas a solution to the Cyprus problem would contribute to a positive resolution of the Aegean dispute, the reverse was not true.

The Davos experiment reinforced the need for the synchronization of a favorable climate in Greek-Turkish relations with sustained momentum in intercommunal negotiations. Immobility in the latter meant that any strategy to improve the Greek-Turkish relationship would eventually fail, as there was no reenforcement mechanism capable of persuading opponents and skeptics alike of the value of such an approach. Despite Papandreou's promise to lift Greece's objection to Turkey's European aspirations, it was unfortunate that the European factor had not been adequately integrated into the Davos process. Its introduction could have substantially improved Turkey's circumstances, thereby instilling the confidence it needed to adopt a more conciliatory position on Cyprus.

For Davos to have worked, it needed to be concurrently linked to progress in the intercommunal talks, which at the time were at an impasse. The limited time-span of the Davos process condemned the experiment to eventual failure. The departure of its two architects, Papandreou and Özal, from political center stage constituted a *prima facie* reason for Davos's termination, but its inability to integrate fully the Cyprus issue into its agenda meant that the process could not be sustained beyond the personality factor. The fact that there was no movement on the intercommunal negotiations compounded the difficulty of successfully linking Greek-Turkish rapprochement with the Cyprus issue. Davos nevertheless introduced a new political feature into the triangular relationship between Greece, Turkey, and Cyprus, namely, the potential role of the EC.

A Social Impact Statement

Collapse of the Davos process added to the litany of failed attempts to settle the Cyprus problem and intensified the social cost for both Cypriot communities. Protracted negotiations exhausted public faith in a settlement, and people began to disengage from the political process, seeking alterative ways to resolve their existential insecurity. This is best illustrated by reference to the precedence that tourism was accorded over traditional Cypriot norms, vistas, and settings.

Tourism's encroachment on the Greek Cypriot fishing village of Agia Napa reached such an extent that one day a *yiayia* (grandmother), after venturing to the nearby shops, could not find her way back home. Her village had changed so rapidly that she completely lost her way. Even more absurd, authorities built a "new" village and resettled the "traditional" villagers there, to keep them out of tourism's way.[71] The case of Agia Napa encapsulated the paradoxical changes Cypriot society was undergoing during the 1980s, where self-conscious anxiety over the peace process descended into incendiary forms of consumerism and self-indulgence.

Relocation, modernization, and urbanization, interfaced with the prolonging stalemate over the island's reunification, redefined Cypriot society throughout this period. Unknown to the participants, the 1980s would have a profound effect on the future discourse of the Cyprus problem. In conceptually mapping the interrelationship between the social and the political, we soon realize that the intercommunal talks had become firmly embedded in the psychological constitution of its people. Protracted negotiations, gridlocked in perpetual impasse, collapsing under their own weight, had accumulated a reservoir of expectations, disillusionment, and despair. By the 1980s, the intercommunal talks, in addition to becoming a perpetual fixture in the island's cultural vista, had acquired a fatalist quality that permeated all facets of Cypriot life. For different reasons, both communities deferred the handling of the Cyprus problem to the custody of their political elites, suspending anticipation and judgment.

The complex and fluid nature of Cypriot society and development problematique of its composite parts, in its post-1974 incarnation, requires a methodological approach that is responsive and reflexive of the changing contexts. In constructing our analytical framework we first need to be conscious of the bicommunal, biethnic composition of Cyprus's population and its transient physical context. The political, socioeconomic and psychological segregation of the two main ethnic groups, Greek and Turkish Cypriot, compounded by geographical and ethno-demographic dimension, inevitably renders the pertinent question whether we should be referring to Cypriot society in its singular, plural, or divided milieu?

Inevitably, protracted conflicts affect the economy and society of the afflicted communities and areas. The search for common intercommunal space, constrained by the physical divide, offered few opportunities for interaction during this period.[72] Notwithstanding their separateness, a peculiar trait began to emerge during this period: a growing sense of commonality in absentia. The circumstances created by 1974 offered a psychological buffer for intercommunal reflection. By the late 1980s there was a generation of Cypriots who never encountered members from the other community. And although isolation, from each other, lends itself to vilification of the unknown ("stranger"), it also concealed a curiosity for one another. Without overestimating its political significance, this ambiguous sense of Cypriotism—or what Doob terms "Cypriot patriotism"—rested on both communities' innate parochial need to differentiate themselves as Cypriots.[73]

Despite a policy of rapprochement, the 1980s were unable of shifting the ingrained divide separating the two communities. Rather, by the end of the decade, rapprochement began to display symptoms of its contradictory temperament. Idealized presumptions of the "Other" resulted in a flawed assessment of each other's interests, history, and positions, creating a false understanding and excessive expectations from each "Other." Compounded by the absence of outcome and reciprocity, rapprochement was adversely vilified by ethno-nationalist forces and discarded by the state.

The tension between partition and reconstruction was expressed more tangibly through the exasperation of the intercommunal talks, which were unable to confront the new challenges posed by the 1980s.

Attempts to build the new logic and language of rapprochement under the prevailing conditions of division were not only premature but deepened and extended the double (in)security complex within both communities. Rapprochement was especially vulnerable in the socio-economic climate of the 1980s, exacerbating intra-communal tensions and conflicts between Cypriotist and ethno-nationalist forces.

Whilst on one level the political constellation of the 1980s through the prism of the intercommunal negotiations had not been different, this was negated by partial and uneven socioeconomic realization of the principle of sovereignty. In this wider context, we begin to see how socioeconomic changes impinged on societal attitudes toward the politics, security, and resolution of the conflict. The convergence of contradictory trends in economic development, social-demographic mobility and national identity formation, formed the structural imperatives of an incontestable reality of the conflict. This was exemplified by the economic disparity between the two communities during the 1980s. Whilst Greek Cypriot living standards more than doubled, surpassing both that of Greece and Turkey, Turkish Cypriots per capita GNP staggered at $1,200 in 1985.[74]

Two other socio-demographic trends that impacted on Greek Cypriot political formation was resettlement and emigration. Although not a rigidly class orientated society, 1974 did insert a new cleavage amongst Greek Cypriots. The uprooting of nearly one-third of the population saw the relocation and resettlement of most Greek Cypriot refugees in urban dwellings. The divide between refugees and non-refugees was sharpened with the creation of refugee settlements scattered at the outskirts of Nicosia and other main cities in the south. Amongst other consequences, the resettlement of refugees accelerated urbanization, which by the end of the 1980s accounted for 64 percent of the population. A postwar demographic phenomenon, emigration had, by the 1970s, subsided considerably from its height in the mid-1950s (29,000 or 5 percent of the population) and 1960s (50,000 or 8 percent). As expected, 1974 saw a new wave of emigration that, as the economy recovered, had subsided by the early 1980s to net levels.[75]

Admittedly, there appeared to be coloration between economic prosperity and fluctuations in ethno-nationalism. As Paschalis Kitromilides and Caesar Mavratsas concur, the 1980s witnessed the reassertion of Greek Cypriot ethno-nationalism at the expense of Cypriotism. Whether we accost it to the "dialectic of intolerance," the lack of "political maturation,"[76] or as a by-product of the security-insecurity duplexity, the resurgence of Greek nationalism in Cyprus would impinge on the events of the ensuing decades.

Similarly, identity formation was emerging as a critical factor in Turkish Cypriot political discourse. The influx of settlers into northern Cyprus in conjunction with mass Turkish Cypriot emigration conditioned the emergence of an undercurrent of discontent that contested the brevity of Turkish nationalism in northern Cyprus. Increasingly, the sociopolitical landscape in northern Cyprus was being shaped by the divergent group consciousness of *Kıbrıslı* (Cypriot) and *Turkiyeliler* (people of Turkey). As with the Greek Cypriots, cultural differences ensuing from the everyday events saw the transformation of social reality in northern Cyprus, challenging the prevailing dictum that viewed the conflict in Cyprus as exclusively "ethnic."[77]

Whilst northern Cyprus offered itself as a frontline sanctuary for the ultranationalist *Bozkurtlar* (Grey Wolves),[78] by the 1980s Turkification began to lose its homogeneous allure amongst sections of the Turkish Cypriot community. Until 1974, Turkish Cypriot nationalism was in essence an extension of (mainland) Turkish nationalism that defined itself as countering Greek Cypriot *enosism*. However, as Niyazi Kizilyürek and Sylvaine Gautier-Kizilyürek acknowledged, 1974 began a process of differentiation and divergence, with Turkish Cypriots in search of their own connection to Cypriotism.[79] Artists, intellectuals, and the Left in general, in pursuit of alternative expressions, began to challenge the central tenets of Turkish nationalism as *anavatan* (motherland as saviour and liberator).[80]

Conclusion

An overall assessment of this period reveals that in addition to disparity with the content of the negotiations, the process itself begun to exhibit problems. As the social setting was changing, so was the texture of the problem. The fluid nature of Cypriot society and the stagnant disposition of the intercommunal talks erected two opposite realities of the conflict. In comparison with previous periods, the 1980s were characterized by a hardening of temperaments as both sides gravitated toward different directions. During this phase of the intercommunal talks, both sides, for the most part, pursued alternative avenues that lay outside the negotiating process.

However, a closer examination of the content of the negotiations reveals that, compared to previous phases, significant progress was achieved, narrowing the gap between the two sides considerably to the extent that a settlement seemed possible. The most important development to fill the emerging vacuum during this period was the brief interlude of improved Greek-Turkish relations. The potential of the Davos process can be appreciated only within the context of the Cypriot conflict. Throughout this book it has been stressed that the antagonistic relationship between the principal external powers, Greece and Turkey, frequently encroached on the relationship between the island's two communities. During the Davos interlude, which lasted less than six months, there was a dramatic improvement in the diplomatic atmosphere between Athens and Ankara, which aimed to transform the existing paradigm of hostility into the pursuit of common interests and mutual assistance. However, before the protagonists could reach this end point, they first had to resolve those contentious issues that had plagued them for over thirty years, chief among them being the Cyprus dispute.

In a way, when support did come, from the most unlikely quarters—improvement in Greco-Turkish relations,—the setting was not conducive to take advantage of this opportunity. In a different era, such development would have aided the process. However, in this instance, they cancelled rather than complemented each other. What this period shows is that there was a need for synchronization between the two sets of variables: internal progress at the negotiations and its external context (both political within the communities and its broader subregional context).

Chapter 4

The End of an Era?

> My father says
> Love your country
> My country is divided into two
> Which part should I love?
> —Neshe Yashin,
> "Love Your Country"[1]

Neshe Yashin's poem spoke for an entire generation of Cypriot peace activists whose voices, until the early 1990s, were silenced by the omnipresent ethno-nationalist discord. And then, for a fleeting moment in 1989, it appeared that fragments of the Berlin Wall might ricochet down Ledra Street, demolish the Green Line, and usher in a new epoch for Cyprus. The end of the Cold War, however, beyond some internal rumblings and existentialist angst caused to AKEL, barely impacted Cyprus. Third parties and foreign nongovernment organizations (NGOs) felt more euphoria than the afflicted communities who, throughout the crisis, remained stoic in the face of the new world order rhetoric.

For the Cyprus peace talks, the period from 1989 to 1994 was defined by three UN initiatives: Pérez de Cuéllar's Ideas of 1989, Boutros Boutros-Ghali's 1992 Set of Ideas, and the latter's subsequent 1993 Confidence Building Measures (CBMs). All three initiatives were interrelated and should be considered as phases of the same process. Without overstating UN influence on the Cyprus problem, during this period the international organization, through the office of the Secretary-General, played a more proactive role in overcoming the impasse impeding the intercommunal talks. All three initiatives transformed the UN Secretariat's mediating role from facilitation to instigation.

The UN initiatives took place in a changing international and regional climate, the most important development being the collapse of the Soviet Union and the emergence of the new post-Cold War security environment. This period saw a radical reevaluation of the United Nations, particularly of its peacekeeping and peacemaking role in conflict resolution. Parts of the world community, swept up in the euphoria of the end of the Cold War, believed that the "end of history" meant the United Nations could be a more effective mediator in international disputes. This view was fuelled by the United Nation's initial diplomatic successes in helping to end the Iran-Iraq war, facilitate the withdrawal of Soviet troops in Afghanistan, establish a broad-based coalition in Cambodia, and end the civil war in El Salvador. These successes, however, owed more to unique circumstances than to the ending of East-West rivalries.

In relation to the Cyprus negotiations, it was apparent that, despite strenuous and persistent UN efforts, the gap between Greek and Turkish Cypriots had never been wider, and even the patient United Nations was beginning to lose confidence. Overcommitted in other emerging trouble spots, the Security Council for the first time expressed its "concern about the chronic and ever-deepening financial crisis facing the United Nations Peacekeeping Force in Cyprus."[2]

Pérez de Cuéllar's Last Stand

When Pérez de Cuéllar launched his third attempt to resolve the Cyprus problem in August 1988, such was his conviction that he declared a settlement was within the parties' "grasp."[3] The Secretary-General optimistically believed that newly elected Greek Cypriot President Vassiliou president had a freshness that distinguished him from his predecessor. The recent rapprochement between Greece and Turkey had created a regional climate conducive to a new diplomatic offensive on Cyprus.

Pérez de Cuéllar's last initiative began with a set of modalities to recommence the intercommunal talks. Both sides then submitted proposals, and the initiative concluded with the Secretary-General's own ideas. Indicative of the new UN approach was the nature of the direct talks between Vassiliou and Denktash. Departing from official protocol, these took place at the Nicosia residence of the UN Secretary-General's Special Representative to Cyprus, Oscar Camilion. They were conducted on a one-to-one basis, with no minders, no agenda, and no formal minutes.

Denktash progressively unveiled the latest Turkish Cypriot proposals over the course of four different sessions: they constituted, in all, a package of nine subject-related papers.[4] Although they contained nothing particularly new, the Turkish Cypriot proposals further elaborated the rationale of their positions. On federalism, for example, they argued that there could be no progress until agreement was reached on three important tenets: "political equality of the partner(s)"; effective participation in the decision-making and implementation process; and "constitutional safeguards."[5] They stressed that discussions on the federal constitution would reveal whether the two peoples were willing to move toward power-sharing and an "equal Turkish-Greek partnership," reflecting the Turkish Cypriot belief that a "permanent duality" existed in Cyprus, such that the two peoples should peacefully coexist "in an environment of mutual respect for the other's reasonable and legitimate concerns, rights and interests." Applying this principle to the federal presidency, they argued that a ceremonial and rotating system would avoid entrenching power in one community, and that it would be an active symbol of equality and partnership between the two communities.[6] They insisted that "prominence to the concept of consensus" be enshrined in the federal constitution. This required separate majorities, weighted voting, and referenda as practical safeguards. The Turkish Cypriots envisaged that such "a functioning federation," while "open to evolution," would benefit from "the simplicity of its government machinery and the compatibility of its powers and functions with realities."[7]

The Greek Cypriots dismissed the Turkish Cypriot proposals as repetitive, accusing them of "attaching esoteric meanings to innocent-looking words." For them, it was "crystal clear that the Turkish Cypriot side [did] not want to talk about territory" and that "agreement on the constitution" was "a pre-condition to even talking about territory."[8] The Greek Cypriots interpreted the Turkish Cypriot constitutional proposals as a radical move toward confederation.

The subsequent Greek Cypriot proposals, tabled by Vassiliou on January 30, 1989, were unlike any others presented at the intercommunal talks. They did not pretend to tackle in detail either the complex constitutional legalities or the mechanical intricacies of the various issues; rather, they were a framework within which experts could flesh out the details. Vassiliou's document began by evaluating each community's main concerns. It assessed Turkish Cypriot apprehensions as being the preservation of their community's identity and the need for self-government in light of their minority predicament, and their fear of being dominated "by either the federal governmental power or by the Greek Cypriot province or community," including the "danger of erosion of their political power." Greek Cypriot concerns were gauged as being the fear that refugees would be prevented from returning to their homes; that due to the colonization of the north by Turkish settlers "the Greek Cypriots [would] be gradually squeezed out of Cyprus"; and that with its military superiority and increasing population, Turkey would one day "use northern Cyprus as a springboard for further expansionism." A related security concern was that Turkish Cypriot federal powers might "be used to frustrate the functioning of the State and that [a] result[ant] impasse [would] provide a pretext for a further invasion by Turkey at a tactically convenient time."[9]

In dealing with the three freedoms, Vassiliou attempted to shift the emphasis from communal to individual rights, while acknowledging that "practical difficulties" had to be taken into account during the initial implementation phase. Vassiliou was adamant that effective deadlock-resolving mechanisms should be in place to enable the government to function irrespective of any legislative or budgetary crisis. The Greek Cypriots were prepared to consider a system in which legislation affecting the Turkish Cypriot community would not be passed without Turkish Cypriot parliamentary support, including the activation of "reinforced majorities" when considering constitutional amendments.[10]

On the controversial question of the federal presidency, Vassiliou put forward two options. The first essentially restated the 1960 model, while the second proposed that the "president be elected by universal suffrage on a common roll and by an absolute majority of voters" where all citizens would have the right to nominate for the office. If a Greek Cypriot was elected president, all candidates for the vice-presidency would have to be Turkish Cypriots. Although Greek Cypriots would also vote in the vice-presidential elections, this would be communally weighted so that it formed the same percentage as the total Turkish Cypriot vote during the presidential elections.[11]

On the vexed subject of federalism, Vassiliou also proposed two options for the allocation of provincial powers and functions. In the first, there would be two lists, one federal and the other provincial, outlining in detail the powers and functions for each level. In cases of dispute, the federal supreme court would settle the matter by rule of interpretation. In the second, an additional third list would deal with issues that fell between the federal and provincial jurisdictions.[12]

Finally, Vassiliou tackled the economic aspect of the Cyprus problem, proposing a process of economic equalization and integration. Vassiliou believed that a political settlement would economically benefit all Cypriots, and particularly Turkish Cypriots. He contended that it would liberate resources consumed by the division of the island, and with increasing communal confidence, economic activity would intensify and lead to a boost in investment, especially in trade and tourism. This would require both federal and provincial government intervention to create the necessary conditions for reducing economic disparities and provide economic opportunities and adequate welfare provisions. Closer links with the EC would "help in promoting balanced regional development."[13]

The Turkish Cypriots criticized the Greek Cypriots for not responding to their proposals and castigated Vassiliou for embarking on "an exercise in public relations, rather than engaging in serious negotiations."[14] They believed that Vassiliou was out to impress the Europeans, the Americans, and the Secretary-General at a time when Cyprus was preparing to apply to join the EC. The Turkish Cypriots reiterated that "the security needs of the Turkish Cypriot people [were] a fundamental aspect of the Cyprus question," and they complained that other priority issues for the Turkish Cypriots, such as "bi-zonality and political equality, [were] not even mentioned." In addition, they were perplexed by Vassiliou's position on the question of guarantees, which were "an inseparable part of the question of security," and found his three freedoms "incompatible with the concept of bi-zonal federation." They totally rejected Vassiliou's criteria for territorial adjustments and considered his presidential "options" as an attempt, "through [a] complex and peculiar weighted voting system, to have a say in the election of a Turkish Cypriot vice-president."[15]

Equipped with the positions of both sides, Pérez de Cuéllar set out to piece together a discussion paper he felt would "prove helpful in arriving at an agreed outline" by identifying the issues and providing structure to the discussions.[16] Pérez de Cuéllar also aimed to establish a timetable for "a negotiated settlement of *all* aspects of the Cyprus problem by 1 June 1989" (my emphasis).[17]

Pérez de Cuéllar's Ideas proposed that an "overall agreement [was] to be negotiated as an integrated whole [and had to be] approved by both communities in separate referenda."[18] The objective of the agreement was to establish a constitutionally bicommunal and territorially bizonal federal republic based on the 1977 and 1979 high-level agreements. Its guiding principles would be to safeguard Cyprus's independence, territorial integrity, unity, bicommunality, security, and nonalignment. In doing so, the identity, integrity, and security of each community would be safeguarded and individual human rights—including political, economic, social, and cultural rights— would be protected.

The federal structure of the republic would comprise "two politically equal federated states" with identical powers and functions, and security and the administration of justice within each state would be the responsibility of each state. The federal republic would have a single international personality and citizenship. Advocating union or secession—in whole or in part—to any other country would be considered a federal criminal offence.[19]

Pérez de Cuéllar proposed that the bicommunal republic come into effect after approval by the two communities' separate referenda. Any amendments would have to be achieved through a similar process. Defining bizonality, Pérez de Cuéllar proposed that the states would be "administered by one community," where "the people of that community would have a clear majority of the population and of the land ownership." The federal government would not be able to encroach upon the powers and functions of the states.[20]

The legislature would consist of a lower house and an upper house. The lower house would have a 70:30 Greek Cypriot/Turkish Cypriot composition, and the upper house would have a 50:50 composition. The presidents of both houses could not come from the same community. All laws would have to be passed by a majority vote in both houses. Furthermore, in both houses, separate community majorities would be required for quorum. If a majority of either community in the lower house decided that a matter is "of vital interest to their community," separate majorities of both communities would be required. Measures were to be devised in the case of a deadlock so that both houses might initiate parallel proceedings while the federal government continued to function.[21]

The executive would comprise a president and vice-president who could not come from the same community. The president would be elected universally and the vice-president from separate rolls. Both would jointly appoint the ministry with a 7:3 Greek Cypriot/Turkish Cypriot ratio, and one of the three portfolios of foreign affairs, finance, or defense would be allocated to a Turkish Cypriot minister. These three ministries would rotate between the two communities, and in the first term the foreign minister could not come from the same community as the president. Decisions regarding foreign affairs, defense, security, budget, taxation, immigration, and citizenship would be taken by "weighted voting." The president and/or the vice-president would have the right to veto any law or decision regarding the above portfolio areas, or to return a decision to either parliament or the ministry for reconsideration.[22] A supreme court, comprising an equal number of Greek Cypriot and Turkish Cypriot judges, appointed jointly by the president and vice-president with the upper house's approval, would decide constitutional matters.

The three freedoms would be recognized in the federal constitution and their implementation would take into account the 1977 and 1979 guidelines, and it would be regulated by the states in a manner consistent with the federal constitution. More specifically: persons known to be involved in violent acts against the other community might be prevented entrance to the other state; freedom of movement would come into effect as soon as the federal republic was established; the rights of settlement and property would be implemented taking "into account the ceilings to be agreed upon." The Turkish Cypriots where always wary that in case of reunification the Greek Cypriots would overrun them in their communal state by taking advantage of the right to settlement and property. The imposition of "ceilings" was seen as a measure that would limit any potential trans-communal influx from altering the bizonal character of the federation. Displaced persons would be given priority listing, and once this arrangement was exhausted (and it was assumed that this would solve the question of displaced persons) others would follow. The president and vice-president would review jointly, at agreed intervals, the ceilings in question.[23]

On the issue of security, which was of special concern to the Turkish Cypriots, "demilitarization...remain[ed] an objective." Until demilitarization could be implemented, numerical balance between the Greek/Greek Cypriot and Turkish/Turkish Cypriot forces would be achieved by the time of the transitional stage. A UN-supervised timetable to reduce and withdraw all non-Cypriot forces not provided for under the Treaty of Alliance would be set in motion before the federal republic was established. As long as Greek and Turkish contingents were stationed in Cyprus, there would be a federal army, of equal community ratio, under the joint command of both the president and vice-president. On the question of guarantees, in general terms, the 1960 Treaties of Guarantees and Alliance would be updated during the preparation phase of the overall agreement.[24]

Pérez de Cuéllar did not elaborate on the territorial issue, other than to propose that any adjustments would be based on the 1977 agreement and take into account the 1984 Vienna "working points." He envisaged that the territorial adjustments "decided upon [would] enable a substantial number of Greek Cypriot displaced persons to return under Greek Cypriot administration." Furthermore, the return of the Greek Cypriots would require the satisfactory relocation and support of subsequent Turkish Cypriot refugees. Finally, as noted in the 1984 "working points," the United Nations would administer these areas during the transitional period.[25]

In principle, the "rights of Greek Cypriot and Turkish Cypriot displaced persons [were] recognized." In practice, priority would be given to those refugees who came under the territorial adjustment areas (that is, the area to be returned to the Greek Cypriots). The return of refugees to these areas would take precedence over any other arrangements. Those refugees whose pre-1974 homelands were under the other community's administration were to "be given the option to decide, within a specific time frame, whether they wish[ed] to return." Those who decided not to return were to be "compensated fairly." The return of refugees would take into consideration the three freedoms and practical difficulties arising from multi-residency. If the current residents were also refugees, their interests would have to be addressed. Persons who had been violent against the other community would be prevented, subject to due process, from returning to the state administered by the other community. Those who had property but did not reside in the state administered by the other community would be compensated. The option of long-term property leasing would be given serious consideration. A tripartite committee comprising the two communities and the Secretary-General would be set up during the transitional period to formulate criteria and procedures to deal with these matters, especially with the questions of compensation and long-term leasing. A federal bicommunal body would implement these arrangements, including establishing a special fund for the above purpose.[26]

As with Vassiliou's proposals, Pérez de Cuéllar concluded his plan on a positive note. Recognizing "the economic imbalance between the two communities," the first economic policy of the federal government would be to redress this disparity by aiding the Turkish Cypriot state. A special federal fund would be set up, administered by the Turkish Cypriots, for which foreign contributions would be solicited. Finally, transitional arrangements would be handled by a bicommunal committee of experts, supported by the UN Development Programme (UNDP), and would include taking the necessary steps for advancing Cyprus to full membership of the EC.[27]

While Vassiliou was willing to discuss the Ideas at a meeting scheduled for July 26, Denktash informed Camilion that he was unable to participate, owing to tensions created by incidents on July 19. Denktash was referring to the Greek Cypriot women's "walk home" demonstration, which saw some 1,000 women forcing their way through the UN buffer zone at two points in the Agios Kassianos area. Turkish

Cypriot police entered the UN zone, which led to clashes and the arrest of some 110 women.[28] The following days saw Greek Cypriot demonstrations over the detention of the women, and the blocking of all UN traffic through the Nicosia-Ledra Palace checkpoint. This followed an earlier women's demonstration, which had taken place in March, leading to the arrest of fifty-four demonstrators by the Turkish Cypriot police.[29]

The Turkish Cypriot position was finally clarified in late August when the TRNC legislative assembly rejected Pérez de Cuéllar's Ideas and resolved only to debate those proposals deriving from direct negotiations between the two parties.[30] When the UN Secretariat attempted to resurrect the talks in late 1989, Denktash wanted, as a precondition, both sides to sign a declaration in which both communities' "inherent right to self-determination" would be recognized.[31] When talks eventually resumed in early 1990 it became evident that the Turkish Cypriots had made a policy shift. Pérez de Cuéllar reported to the Security Council that talks broke down because of conceptual difficulties arising from the introduction of new terminology such as "self-determination" and "people."[32] The Turkish Cypriots argued that "recognition of the right of self-determination of each of the two peoples of Cyprus" was essential to give "meaning to the negotiations for the creation of a new partnership Republic"; and that if separate referenda were necessary to endorse any settlement, this first required the recognition of the right of self-determination for both peoples.[33]

Consistent with their previous stance, the Turkish Cypriot leadership now formally demanded that they be considered as a "people" rather than as a "separate minority" or even a "community." As illustrated previously, the Turkish Cypriots considered their efforts since 1964 as an evolution toward self-determination. The historical landmark in this evolution were the 1974 events, which provided them with a homogeneous territorial unit by which they were able in 1983 to declare their independence.[34] There is no doubt that examples of the emergence of newly formed nation-states in the wake of the collapse of the Soviet Union inspired them to pursue a similar path.

Pérez de Cuéllar recognized that such a "change in terminology could alter the conceptual framework" of the intercommunal talks. He felt that the negotiations had reached "an impasse of a substantial kind" and raised questions relating to the Secretary-General's mandate as provided by the Security Council.[35] Cyprus's application for full membership of the EC, on July 4, 1990, further infuriated the Turkish Cypriots. In a memorandum to the Council of Ministers of the European Communities, Denktash argued that the Greek Cypriots were not entitled "to make the application on behalf of Cyprus" or the Republic of Cyprus, since this was in contravention of the 1960 agreements, which recognized two separate legal communal entities.[36] He argued that the application was in violation of Article 1 of the Treaty of Guarantee and Article 185 of the constitution, which prohibited the Republic of Cyprus from "participat[ing], in whole or in part, in any political or economic union with any State whatsoever."[37] Denktash stressed that it was unacceptable for the Greek Cypriots to "impose their political will on the Turkish-Cypriots" in a matter that would affect future generations.[38] Although the Turkish Cypriots supported EC membership, under the current circumstances admission to the EC of a "uniquely Greek Cypriot state" could not "contribute to the resolution of the differences between the two communities."[39] Finally, Denktash argued that the admission of Cyprus to the EC would "mean a second vote for Greece," as the Greek Cypriot community would act as a "proxy for Greece."[40]

At this juncture of the negotiations it became apparent that the Greek Cypriot side was reassessing its strategic options. In a confidential memorandum to the National Council, Foreign Minister George Iacovou recommended reverting to the policy of internationalization. Iacovou believed that international reaction to the Turkish Cypriots' negative stance at the negotiations had not subsided, and that they, in cooperation with Athens, should adopt and advocate a common strategy to take advantage of this climate. In particular, he proposed broadening their strategy to encompass European institutions.[41]

At the behest of the Secretary-General, the Security Council adopted Resolution 649, expressing its "concern" at the collapse of the recent talks and reiterating that a solution should be sought from within the bicommunal/bizonal federal framework as per the 1977 and 1979 agreements and the agreed outline of June 1989. Failure of the 1989 talks also prompted the Security Council to further strengthen the mediating role of the Secretary-General. Specifically, it requested, for the first time, that the Secretary-General "assist the two communities by making suggestions to facilitate discussions" with a view to "developing an agreed outline of an overall agreement."[42]

Equally significant was the subsequent Resolution 716 in which the Security Council reaffirmed Pérez de Cuéllar's definition of political equality as advanced in his March 1990 report. For the Secretary-General, "political equality" did not necessarily mean "equal numerical participation in all federal" instruments, but that it should be reflected, inter alia:

> in the requirement that the federal constitution of the State of Cyprus be approved or amended with the concurrence of both communities; in the effective participation of both communities in all organs and decisions of the federal government; in safeguards to ensure that the federal government [would] not be empowered to adopt any measures against the interests of one community; and in the equality and identical powers and functions of the two federated states.[43]

Despite the resolution, Pérez de Cuéllar was so exasperated with the impasse that he concluded his July 1990 report with a stern warning that the "time has come for all concerned to give proof that they truly want to contribute to a solution of the Cyprus problem."[44] Without naming him, there is no doubt that Pérez de Cuéllar's statement was primarily directed toward Denktash, questioning his genuine commitment to a federal solution.[45]

Pérez de Cuéllar's doubts about Denktash's commitment became even more pronounced in 1991. Denktash's position, now entrenched, was "that each side possessed sovereignty which it would retain after the establishment of a federation, including the right of secession."[46] Denktash meant that the "Turkish Cypriots [could] only start from the present realities: two people, politically equal, living in their own separate zones, indeed two separate Republics, agreeing to a federal partnership."[47] This insistence on the introduction of sovereignty for the federated states would, according to Pérez de Cuéllar, "fundamentally alter the nature of the solution provided for in the 1977 and 1979 high-level agreements" and was against all UN resolutions on Cyprus.[48]

On June 28, 1991 members of the Security Council endorsed the Secretary-General's view that a high-level meeting, if properly prepared, "could give his efforts the necessary impetus [to] achieve an agreed outline of an overall settlement."[49] Despite strenuous UN efforts, by October 1991 no such progress had been achieved, and the Security Council, in Resolution 716 (1991), expressed its regret that it had not been possible to convene the high-level meeting. Nevertheless, it still considered "that convening a high-level international meeting, chaired by the Secretary-General, in which the two communities and Greece and Turkey would participate, represented an effective mechanism for concluding an overall framework agreement on Cyprus."[50]

During this period there was intense diplomatic and political involvement by the United States, which found the State Department's Special Coordinator for Cyprus, Nelson Ledsky, stating that he was "optimistic that in the next months we have a chance of at least reaching the first plateau of a Cyprus settlement, something that has eluded us since 1974."[51] However, the most succinct statement of U.S. commitment came from President George Bush during his address to the Greek Parliament on July 18, 1991, where he "pledge[d] that the United States will do whatever it can to help Greece, Turkey, and the Cypriots settle the Cyprus problem, and to do so this year."[52] He repeated the same message three days later in Ankara.[53]

Bush also made it clear that although the United States' role was "catalytic,"[54] and that he would "do whatever [he could] to facilitate…the UN Secretary General's good offices mission,"[55] "that the United States [could not] wave a wand, a magic wand, and solve [the] problem."[56] Bush told both Greece and Turkey that the "solution lies in your hands. Your friends can and will offer encouragement and support, but only Greeks, Turks and Cypriots can reach an effective lasting resolution."[57]

Proactive U.S. diplomacy on the Cyprus issue during 1991 was vigorous. According to Bush, its focus was to strengthen the latest efforts of the Secretary-General. In the post-Gulf War era, the United States utilized its new found status and renewed camaraderie with Greece and, in particular, Turkey to engineer a second tier of negotiations that culminated in Bush publicly proposing a "quadripartite meeting among Greece, Turkey and the Turkish and Greek communities in the island."[58] Promoting the quadripartite conference, the United States sponsored Security Council Resolution 716, in which the concept was described as "an effective mechanism for concluding an overall" agreement.[59]

In his last report to the Security Council on Cyprus, outgoing Secretary-General Pérez de Cuéllar concluded with the statement that "the mere maintenance of the status quo does not constitute a solution."[60] (A view reiterated by his successor Boutros Boutros-Ghali eight months later, who stated that it was time for the two communities to "take the important political decisions for an agreed, compromise solution."[61])

Fundamentally, the failure of Pérez de Cuéllar's last initiative can be attributed to his flawed assessment that prevailing conditions were conducive to finding an agreement. Pérez de Cuéllar had embarked on his plan confident that there was sufficient movement on three fronts ultimately to produce a positive setting for a settlement. Whilst he was correct in regarding Vassiliou as a more flexible Greek Cypriot leader than his predecessor, he miscalculated Özal's capacity to be a persuasive and moderating influence on Denktash.[62]

Pérez de Cuéllar had also overestimated the strength of the Greek-Turkish Davos rapprochement, which faded after the withdrawal of both Papandreou and Özal from the political helm. During this period, Greece experienced a phase of governmental stagnation, which also rendered the Davos experiment ineffectual. The failure of Davos, and Greece's political predicament, saw both principal external powers neutralized in respect of their role in the negotiations, with the decision-making process focusing again on the two primary agents: Vassiliou and Denktash. Within this political vacuum, Denktash was allowed to adopt a radically different posture from the one that Turkish Cypriots had hitherto maintained. This posture prevailed until 1999 and seriously jeopardized the delicate foundation on which the intercommunal talks had been conducted since 1975. Denktash's rejection of Pérez de Cuéllar's Ideas motivated the Greek Cypriots into reverting to their strategy of internationalization and pursuing EC membership with determination. Finally, the incidents of the summer of 1989, including clashes between Greek Cypriot protesters and Turkish Cypriot police for the first time since 1974, ensured the return to a confrontationist climate in Cyprus.

Boutros-Ghali's Set of Ideas: The Mediator Intervenes

The new UN Secretary-General Boutros-Ghali exhibited an even greater degree of tenacity than his predecessors when it came to the Cyprus conflict. Unrestrained by the conventional behavior of previous secretaries-general, boosted by Resolution 649, Boutros-Ghali signaled his intention "to undertake a new initiative and...to prepare a set of ideas [for] an overall framework agreement."[63] His pronouncement also came with a sharp warning that if this effort did not succeed, "consideration would have to be given to an alternative course of action in dealing with the Cyprus question."[64] Starting from the good work of his predecessor, Boutros-Ghali embarked on completing the initiative—a process that took nearly two years and which culminated in the 1992 "Set of Ideas on an Overall Framework Agreement on Cyprus"[65]—a document that should be seen as the sequel to Pérez de Cuéllar's Ideas.

In April 1992, the Security Council noted its "concern that there [had] been no progress in completing the set of ideas for an overall framework agreement" and, indeed, "in some areas there [had] even been regression." In Resolution 750, it endorsed the Set of Ideas as the basis of an agreement, subject to work being done on "the outstanding issues, in particular on territorial adjustments and displaced persons." It still believed that a high-level international meeting was the most effective mechanism for concluding an agreement. Finally, it requested that the Secretary-General report back to the Security Council by July 1992 to "make specific recommendations for overcoming any outstanding difficulty."[66]

In June 1992, in pursuit of Resolution 750, Boutros-Ghali invited both the Greek and Turkish Cypriot sides to New York for a series of proximity talks. During these talks the Secretary-General explored ideas around eight key topics aimed at bringing "the two sides within agreement range."[67] Over the course of his discussions with Greek and Turkish advisers, who were also in attendance, it became apparent that the Turkish Cypriot side prioritized bizonality, security, political equality, and its participation in the federal government. Greek Cypriot priorities were the territorial issue, displaced persons, the functioning of the federal government, and security.[68] At the second round of proximity talks, Boutros-Ghali submitted his Set of Ideas, which included an appendix of good will measures[69] and a map indicating the Secretary-General's territorial adjustments (see map 4.1 below).

Boutros-Ghali's Set of Ideas revamped Pérez de Cuéllar's earlier ideas and expanded in detail the sections on territorial adjustments, displaced persons, good will measures, and the transitional period.[70] The Secretary-General's intention was to "concentrate in the first instance on the two outstanding issues, territorial adjustments and displaced persons." Once he was satisfied that "reasonable progress had been made," and both sides were "within agreement range," discussions would proceed to the other issues. Both sides agreed with the proposed procedure.[71]

Boutros-Ghali's map was the sixth map relating to territorial adjustments tabled during the protracted negotiations, however, it was the first official map tabled by the United Nations. The map, together with the entire Set of Ideas, including suggested territorial adjustments, was endorsed on August 26 by the Security Council in Resolution 774 and subsequently reaffirmed in Resolution 789 (1992).

Boutros-Ghali clearly attached great importance to the question of the displaced persons and territorial adjustments, which "need[ed] to be addressed without delay." In a report submitted to the Security Council before the final Set of Ideas, Boutros-Ghali had signaled his

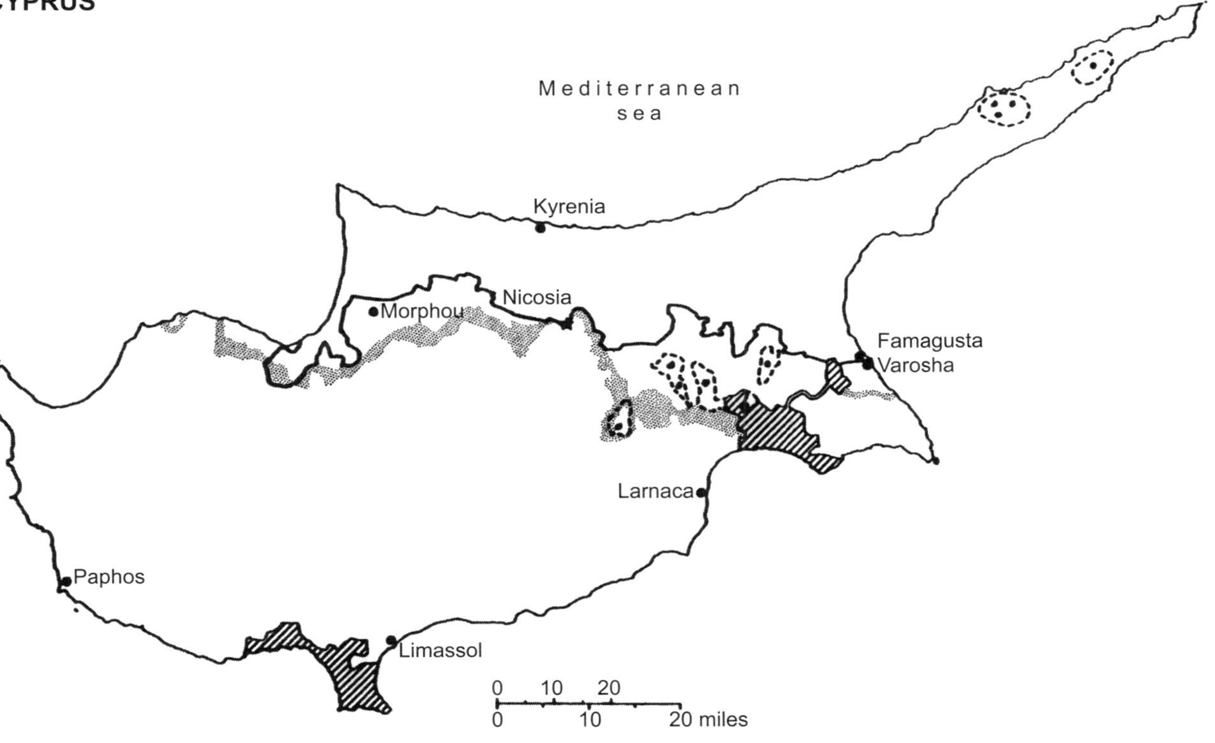

Map 4.1   Boutros-Ghali's Map of 1992
Source: UN S/24472, 1992.

intention to table a map within his overall framework to "delineate the two federated states so that a substantial number of Greek Cypriot displaced persons would be able to return to the area that [would] come under Greek Cypriot administration...[and to] address effectively the needs of Turkish Cypriots that would be affected by the territorial adjustments."[72]

The Secretary-General also considered the criteria Denktash had raised in previous discussions, namely, that territorial adjustments should ensure that Turkish Cypriots maintained control of the coastline currently in their possession; enable the Turkish Cypriot state to border the British sovereign base of Dhekelia in the east; respect the traditionally held Turkish Cypriot villages; take into account the distribution of water resources; and leave the Erçan (Tymbou) airport in the Turkish Cypriot state.[73]

On the related issue of displaced persons, Boutros-Ghali's principle position was that all "property claims...are recognized" and "dealt with fairly on the basis of a time-frame," "practical regulations" stipulated by the 1977 high-level agreement, and the "need to ensure social peace and harmony."[74]

The first group of displaced persons to be dealt with would be those from areas affected by the territorial adjustments, which would, according to Boutros-Ghali's map, come under Greek Cypriot administration. Turkish Cypriots who had resided in those areas before 1974 would have the option of remaining on their property or "receive comparable residence" in the Turkish Cypriot state. Turkish Cypriots who resided in those areas post-1974 would also have the same option, or could return to their former residence or have comparable residence in the same area. Immediately after the referenda approving the Overall Framework Agreement (OFA), a bicommunal committee would be set up to arrange housing for those affected by the territorial adjustments.[75]

Displaced persons who had arrived from other areas would be dealt with next. Both communities would set up an agency to deal with matters relating to displaced persons. The property of those displaced persons who sought compensation would be transferred "to the ownership of the community in which the property [was] located." All property titles would be "exchanged on a global communal basis between the two agencies at the 1974 value plus inflation." The owners would be compensated from their community's agency fund. These funds would be financed primarily from the sale of exchanged or transferred properties. The shortfall would be covered by the federal government through a special compensation fund that would be sourced through windfall taxes on the increased value of transferred properties, defense savings, and contributions from foreign governments and international organizations. Long-term leasing and other commercial arrangements might also be considered. Those entitled to compensation would be persons from both communities—or their heirs—who had resided or owned property in 1974 in the state administered by the other community, and Turkish Cypriots who were displaced after December 1963.[76]

Those refugees who were current residents in Cyprus, owned their permanent residence on the other side, and wished to resume their residency might "also select the option to return." Refugees who fell in the same category but had rented their permanent residence and wished to return would be given priority under the freedom of settlement arrangements. All claims would have to be filed within six months of the approval of OFA. The return of this category of refugees would be managed by the relevant federated state on a quota basis of an agreed number of refugees per year over an agreed number of years. The Maronite Cypriots, who in 1974 lived in the Turkish Cypriot administered state, could elect to return to their properties. These provisions would be reviewed by both states at the conclusion of the agreed period, taking into account the experience gained. The above process would commence after the resettlement and rehabilitation of those affected by the territorial adjustments.[77]

Refugees would only return to their former residences after those affected had been satisfactorily relocated. If the "current" occupant was also a refugee and wished to remain, or the premises had been substantially altered or converted into public use, then the former owner would be "compensated or provided with accommodation of similar value." Finally, those refugees who had been "actively or [were still] involved in acts of violence or incitement to violence and/or hatred against persons of the other community" might, subject to the due process of law, be prevented from returning.[78]

These arrangements were anticipated to yield, in the first instance, the relocation of at least 76,641 Greek Cypriot displaced persons to the areas defined under Boutros-Ghali's territorial adjustments. Given that the figure was much higher, based on the 1960 census, with an estimated 11 percent population increase from 1960 to 1973, the actual number was more likely to be around 85,000 Greek Cypriots. According to Boutros-Ghali's formula, approximately 3,982 Turkish Cypriots who had lived in these areas prior to 1974 would be entitled to remain in their villages.[79]

Boutros-Ghali's formula would have seen approximately half of the Greek Cypriot refugees return to their homeland. (Boutros-Ghali himself calculated that 160,000 Greek Cypriots had been displaced,[80] although the Cypriot government had always referred to a figure of 200,000, while Waldheim put the figure at 198,477 Greek Cypriots displaced.[81])

Denktash was displeased about the map, noting that it would create a second wave of Turkish Cypriot refugees from among those currently residing in the affected areas, have an economic impact on his community and in particular on the fertile citrus-producing lands of Morphou, and impact on Turkish Cypriot water supply. Denktash reiterated the Turkish Cypriot position that they would accept a reduction to no less than 29 percent of the territory of Cyprus, and he produced four alternative territorial arrangements. It was clear to the Secretary-General that the Turkish Cypriots were determined not to relinquish the Morphou area.[82]

Boutros-Ghali pointed out to Denktash that "the economic significance of the Morphou area had diminished with the decline in the value of citrus," and that Turkish Cypriots would retain 55 percent of the total Cypriot coastline, which was the island's most valuable natural resource. On the issue of water supply, he correctly pointed out to both leaders that supplies were "reaching a critical point" and "that the status quo would be a viable option for only a short time more." After the political problem, water shortage was indeed the second most important crisis facing Cyprus. As Boutros-Ghali explained, this was a general problem for all Cypriots, and it needed to be addressed at the federal level.[83] Indeed, Boutros-Ghali was adamant that "territorial adjustments [would] not affect the water supply available to each federated state" and that the water resources available throughout Cyprus would be allocated to the two states "at a proportion at least equal to their respective current demand."[84]

When they met under Boutros-Ghali's chairmanship at New York on August 12–14, 1992, both sides agreed to focus on displaced persons and then proceed to constitutional arrangements and territorial adjustments before tackling the remaining issues. Whilst Vassiliou appeared to endorse the Secretary-General's proposals, Denktash opposed its territorial adjustments and its proposed solution for displaced persons. He wanted negotiations to "recognize the validity of the 'title deeds' that the Turkish Cypriot authorities had issued to post-1974 occupants of properties of Greek Cypriots." Boutros-Ghali observed that the "Turkish Cypriot side need[ed] to show the necessary willingness to foresee an adjustment more or less in line" with his map.[85]

During the next joint meetings of October 28–November 11, Boutros-Ghali prepared a "non-paper" setting out the positions of both sides and where they coincided with the Set of Ideas and UN resolutions. Both sides agreed that the "non-paper" accurately reflected their respective positions. The Greek Cypriots fundamentally accepted the Set of Ideas and the map,[86] and the Turkish Cypriots affirmed they were in "basic agreement with 91 out of the 100 paragraphs."[87]

Commenting on the outcome, Boutros-Ghali stated that the joint meetings did not meet "expectations" and the "objectives set by the Security Council in Resolution 774." Essentially, an "overall framework agreement did not materialize." Although certain positions advanced by both sides were "variations of the provisions of the Set of Ideas, and should therefore [have been] amenable…the positions voiced by the Turkish Cypriot side were, in a fundamental way, outside the framework of the Set of Ideas."[88]

As argued earlier, Turkish Cypriots' concept of the federation was "based on the premise that there exist[ed]…two sovereign states with equal rights and that they [would] remain effectively sovereign in a future federation." Boutros-Ghali pointed out that this thread ran right through the negotiations, from the Turkish Cypriot attitude toward the overall objectives and guiding principles, to the Greek Cypriot properties in the north; transitional arrangements; having the two states trade as separate units; and constitutional preferences regarding immigration and citizenship, airports and ports, and the federal public service.[89]

Furthermore, Turkish Cypriots' refusal to discuss the map rested on their belief that it "would uproot 37,433 Turkish Cypriots." Denktash maintained that the Turkish Cypriot state should comprise of more than 29 percent of the territory and that "a map be drawn only following agreement on constitutional aspects of the federation and only when it [was] evident…that the Greek Cypriot side [had] agreed to power-sharing under a federal structure."[90]

On the question of displaced persons, Denktash requested a range of exceptions that would "in effect preclude the possibility that any Greek Cypriot…would be able to return."[91] Denktash argued that Greek Cypriot refugees could not "return to such properties…'owned' by Turkish Cypriots as they now hold 'legal title' on the properties concerned." As such, refugees could only be compensated for these properties.[92]

It became clear to the Secretary-General that Denktash's "position [was] to have two communities living separately, as practically homogeneous ethnic groups," a solution that was "incompatible with the

Set of Ideas...as well as with accepted international standards and practices."[93] On November 25, 1992, in Resolution 789, the Security Council not only reaffirmed its support for Boutros-Ghali's Set of Ideas and his map but noted that "certain positions adopted by the Turkish Cypriot side were fundamentally at variance with the Set of Ideas" and called on them "to adopt positions that [were] consistent" with the Secretary-General's proposals.[94]

As with Pérez de Cuéllar's Ideas, Denktash's conceptual shift regarding sovereignty meant he could not accept Boutros-Ghali's proposals. Furthermore, the tabling of a map by the Secretary-General, stipulating that the Varosha and Morphou areas be returned to the Greek Cypriots in order to accommodate approximately half their refugees, was a hard proposition for the Turkish Cypriots to accept. It was one thing for the Greek Cypriots, as their opponents, to demand territorial concessions, and another for the Secretary-General as the mediator to do so, and with Security Council endorsement.

Boutros-Ghali's Set of Ideas floundered on the same obstacle his predecessor had come up against: Denktash's rejection of the Secretary-General's entire framework. Nevertheless, Boutros-Ghali had adopted a different methodology and posture, and proved to be much tougher in his dealings with Denktash. By soliciting support from the Security Council and in particular the permanent five members, a fundamental shift transpired under Boutros-Ghali, transforming the Secretary-General's role from that of a neutral mediator to an advocate of a specific position. This shift was evident in the Security Council's willingness to blame the Turkish Cypriots for the failure of the talks. Still, Boutros-Ghali was conscious that outright condemnation might alienate the Turkish Cypriots and lead to the irreversible collapse of the intercommunal talks. Attempting to capitalize on Turkish Cypriot vulnerability, and encourage Turkey's intervention, Boutros-Ghali offered Denktash the opportunity to review his position, by proposing the CBMs.

The impending Greek Cypriot presidential elections also clearly influenced Denktash's approach to the negotiations. Failure of the talks would have strengthened Clerides's chances. During the presidential campaign, Clerides advocated a tougher line in the negotiations and opposed key clauses in the UN plan. Denktash harbored a personal grudge against Vassiliou and preferred dealing with Clerides who, as Camilion has argued, came from the same "school." Turkey also shared Denktash's conviction that more concessions could be extracted from Clerides than from Vassiliou. Both Turkey and Denktash soon discovered, however, that 17 years of opposition politics had transformed

President Clerides from the chief advocate of the pragmatists to the leader of the redeemed Greek Cypriot nationalists: he had adopted the ideological position of the hard-line militants.

Confidence-Building Measures

Concluding his 1992 report, Boutros-Ghali asserted that there was "a deep crisis of confidence between the two sides" and that there could be no "successful outcome to the talks for as long as this situation prevail[ed]."[95] Negotiations on the substantial issues of the Cyprus problem were not yielding any results, so Boutros-Ghali switched to tackling the peripheral issues, as his predecessors had done. Based on his goodwill measures of July 15, 1992, he forwarded to both sides a set of eight confidence-building measures.[96] Clerides and Denktash accepted this alternative approach, and preliminary discussions revealed a willingness from both sides to implement a series of CBMs above and beyond those proposed by the Secretary-General.[97]

As discussions progressed, the issues of Varosha and the Nicosia airport again occupied the epicenter of these CBMs. The United Nations proposed that the fenced area of Varosha (which was only a small part of the whole city and comprised some four kilometers north-south and about one-and-a-half kilometer east-west) be placed under its administration until an overall agreement was reached.[98] Denktash considered that there was "insufficient compensation for relinquishing" Varosha and tabled the idea of reopening the Nicosia airport for the benefit of both sides: the Turkish Cypriots were willing to consider a package deal of Varosha and the airport. The United Nations responded that it could be reopened for civilian and cargo traffic, under UN administration, in cooperation with the Council of the International Civil Aviation Organization (ICAO), until the Cyprus problem was settled. Traffic rights would be limited to foreign airlines, including those registered in Turkey. There would be free access from both sides and foreign visitors entering Nicosia airport would be able to travel between the two sides.

Not content with these arrangements, Denktash repeated his preconditions that the economic embargo be lifted, in particular, as it affected the Erçan airport and the northern seaports. Boutros-Ghali sought legal counsel from the President of the ICAO, who informed him that the Erçan airport could not operate "without recognizing a Turkish Cypriot state." To accommodate Denktash, it was accepted that the Cyprus Turkish Airlines, registered in Turkey, would operate from Nicosia airport. Clerides also assured Denktash that there would be an "unhindered flow of persons and goods," with the Greek Cypriots not impeding it with negative publicity or legal action. Finally, on Varosha, Denktash stated that his side wished to exclude a significant area north of Dimokratias Street from the UN administration, in order for it to serve as a buffer zone between the TRNC and the port of Famagusta. The package was once again adjusted, with Clerides's agreement.[99]

As Boutros-Ghali was ready to obtain a confirmation of the agreement on May 28, Denktash sought, and was granted by the Security Council, a delay until June 14 for consultation. Denktash also assured the international community that during his "consultations [he] would...promote acceptance of the proposals on Varosha and Nicosia International Airport."[100] However, it was becoming increasingly apparent to third-party intermediaries that Denktash was having difficulties in accepting the package.

This assessment was confirmed when Denktash made numerous statements, including one at Ankara airport on June 8 and another whilst addressing the Turkish Grand National Assembly on June 10, threatening to reject the Varosha/Nicosia airport package. On June 14 and 15, Denktash's representative in New York, Konan Atakol, conveyed the view that for the Varosha/Nicosia package to be accepted the northern part of Varosha would have to remain with the Turkish Cypriot side, and that all embargoes be lifted in north Cyprus.[101]

While negotiations over the CBMs were in progress, a series of internal and external developments impinged on UN and U.S. efforts to sustain the process. The most significant of these was the EC's decision to accept the Republic of Cyprus's application for membership. Despite strong protests from Turkish Cypriot authorities, the commission was convinced that Cyprus's inclusion would enhance security and assist in bringing the two communities closer. In particular, it foresaw that membership to the EC would guarantee "universally recognized political, social and cultural rights" throughout the island, while providing the Turkish Cypriot community with economic and social benefits. The EC admitted that its timing was coincidental, and that it wanted to send "a positive signal" to Cypriots in support of the Secretary-General's efforts.[102]

A year later, the European Court of Justice recognized the Republic of Cyprus as the only Cypriot state with which the European Community could trade. In effect, the ruling banned any exports from the TRNC to member-states of the EC, significantly affecting Turkish Cypriot attitudes toward the negotiations. By August 28, 1994, the National Assembly of the TRNC declared that "no good would come out of negotiations on the CBMs while the decision of the European Court of Justice on exports remained in force" and while the Greek Cypriots insisted on the unilateral pursuit of membership to the EU. The assembly reaffirmed the separate sovereignty of the TRNC and, more importantly, repealed previous resolutions that envisaged "federation as the sole form of settlement."[103]

Equally noteworthy were the insights that emerged from UN consultation into the dynamics of Turkish Cypriot domestic politics. Until then, the prevailing view had been that the Turkish Cypriot political landscape was solely shaped by the Left-Right divide. Yet Denktash revealed to the Secretary-General's Special Representative Joe Clark that there was a "deep political division" within the ruling nationalist establishment, which "prevented him from fulfilling effectively his function as negotiator."[104] Denktash was referring to a factional crisis that had exploded within his former party, the UBP, which saw nine deputies leave and form the centralist DP (*Demokrat Parti* [Democrat Party]). This split was entrenched at the elections of December 12, 1993, when UBP share dropped from 55 to 29.8 percent of the vote, to be matched by the DP's 29.2 percent. Among those who formed the DP was Denktash's own son, Serdar. It was also common knowledge that Denktash himself supported the DP. The crisis dated back to 1981 when Denktash's ex-political ally, the hard-line Derviş Eroğlu, took over as president of UBP and cemented his power base within the party. Denktash temporarily resigned as negotiator in 1993 after being attacked by Eroğlu (who with 34 members and two independents controlled parliament) for being too flexible. Even though Denktash's revelations could be construed as another delay tactic, there is some validity to the assertion that Eroğlu's strength within Turkish Cypriot politics had been largely underestimated.[105]

Clark's meeting with Turkish Cypriot political and business leaders also revealed three interesting points that lent weight to the idea that the United Nations should pursue a Turkish strategy that resonated throughout future deliberations. First, there was considerable confusion among Turkish Cypriots about the CBMs package. Second, Turkish Cypriots "looked to Turkey for guidance in deciding on the package." Third, "there was widespread interest in the package among Turkish Cypriots and a desire to consider it seriously."[106]

By this time, the UN Secretariat had realized Denktash was not interested in a federal settlement. A year later, he declared as such, pronouncing that a "federal solution in Cyprus [was] not possible any longer" and that the "Security Council [was] making a great error [in] bringing the two communities together by a superficial agreement."[107] To deal with Denktash's tenacity, the UN Secretariat sought to bypass his authority by appealing directly to Ankara and other Turkish Cypriot interest groups.

During the remainder of 1993 and throughout 1994 there were strenuous efforts by Boutros-Ghali and the Americans to revive the CBMs. Newly elected U.S. President William (Bill) J. Clinton also believed that Turkey should exercise its "special responsibility" to persuade Denktash to accept the package.[108] On September 20, 1993, the Security Council noted "that the Turkish Cypriot side [had] not yet shown the necessary goodwill and cooperation required to achieve an agreement" and "recognize[d] the important role that Turkey could play in this effort."[109] Boutros-Ghali underscored this idea in his September 1993 report, noting that despite a "campaign of disinformation" there was an encouraging and "widespread interest in the package and a desire to consider it seriously" among the Turkish Cypriot community, hoping that Ankara's support for the CBMs would be conveyed to the Turkish Cypriots.[110]

To increase momentum, Boutros-Ghali sent two teams of economic experts from the UNDP and the ICAO to Cyprus to study the "significant and proportional benefits" of the package,[111] which "would be relatively greater for the Turkish Cypriot side because of the relative size of its economy and their impact in alleviating the serious obstacles currently confronting the Turkish Cypriot economy."[112]

Boutros-Ghali soon discovered, however, that circumstances were not conducive for such a strategy. When Denktash objected to the modalities of March 21, 1994, Boutros-Ghali sought Ankara's intervention, but the Turkish government laconically responded that its position was one of "support" rather than "acceptance."[113]

Ankara was again unwilling, or unable, to offset Denktash on May 11–12 at a meeting in Vienna between Turkey, the United Nations, and the Turkish Cypriot community, initiated by the United States. Expecting the summit would cajole Denktash into cooperation, the UN Secretary-General's Deputy Special Representative Gustave Feissel instead found that the Turkish Cypriot side wanted to advance variants of a deal that went beyond the CBM package.[114]

When Clerides learned of the Vienna meeting, he too hardened his opposition to the March 21 proposal.[115] By this stage Clerides was reviewing his position as being too accommodative, as the previous December he expressed his willingness to demilitarize.[116]

Despite a last-ditch effort in October 1994 to retain the momentum around the CBMs, other issues had clearly intruded on the negotiating process, which was supposed to have been based on a minimalist document containing a set of specific measures.

Collapse of the CBMs had broad ramifications for peacemaking in Cyprus. The Secretary-General began to question the validity of the UN-led negotiations. In the most forthright report ever produced by a UN Secretary-General, Boutros-Ghali stated, with obvious frustration, that even after thirty years of endeavor there seemed to be no political will to resolve the conflict. He proposed five options for the Security Council to consider: one, given increasing demands, the United Nations could redirect its peacekeeping and peacemaking resources elsewhere; two, if the offices of the Secretary-General, which depended on the consent and cooperation of the parties involved, were not adequate to deal with the situation, then coercive measures should be investigated; three, put aside the CBMs and resume discussions on the essence of the Cyprus problem, based on the Set of Ideas; four, in consultation with members of the Security Council, the three guarantor powers, the two communities, and others, explore a wide range of options in a "fundamental and far-reaching reflection on how to approach the Cyprus problem"; and, five, based on the two communities' prior "in principle agreement" with the CBMs package, push ahead with a renewed effort to secure an agreement. Boutros-Ghali also stated that before the Security Council decided on a course of action, some form of international consultation—such as an international conference, a visit comprising some or all of the Security Council members, or a renewed effort by his special representative—might be appropriate. All except the first option required the continued presence of UNFICYP in Cyprus.[117]

As referred to earlier, UNFICYP had been confronted with a financial crisis, which was resolved when the Republic of Cyprus offered to contribute one-third of its annual costs on an ongoing basis. After the immediate financial problems of UNFICYP had been resolved, the Secretary-General felt the need to address the broader political question of "whether UNFICYP [was] not part of the problem in Cyprus rather than part of the solution," and questioning for how long the peacekeeping force could remain on the island. Advocating the continued presence of UNFICYP, Boutros-Ghali pointed that the Greek Cypriots, more than the Turkish Cypriots, had a "vital interest" in its maintenance. Furthermore, if the force was withdrawn, each side would seek to take over the UN-monitored buffer zone (3 percent of the island's territory). This would lead to incidents that "would escalate out of control," with grave consequences for both communities and the region. Moving past the status quo, through a negotiated settlement, was for Boutros-Ghali predicated on the "maintenance of tranquility" between the two sides.[118]

The situation was so grave after the collapse of the CBMs that Boutros-Ghali, in informal consultations, informed the Security Council that unless the two sides provided evidence, "through concrete actions, of their commitment to a negotiated settlement," he would "have to recommend that [his] mission of good offices be suspended."[119] True to his word, the United Nations under Boutros-Ghali undertook no new initiative on the Cyprus problem until a new Secretary-General took over in 1997.

Analysis of negotiations around the CBMs supports the view that mediation over the issues that had a lower profile produced greater progress than tackling the more complex, substantive problems that divided the two sides. As illustrated above, even though none where ever implemented, discussions on CBMs came very close to an agreed settlement. The experience gathered from these talks also confirmed the notion that timing was crucial to the final outcome of the mediation. A protracted process increased the possibility that either or both sides would renege on previous commitments and enhanced the likelihood that outside forces or events would endanger the fragile cohesion of the talks. Both sides entered the process with enthusiasm, even broadening the original Boutros-Ghali package. But as the process evolved, Varosha and the Nicosia airport again emerged as key obstacles, and the Turkish Cypriot leadership demonstrated their unwillingness to relinquish Varosha without an adequate exchange (the lifting of the embargo on the Erçan airport). Politicization of the CBMs, even at this level, brought into play the same dynamics that had plagued previous negotiations, allowing provocative statements to poison the climate, and ultimately producing an impasse. The eventual collapse of the CBMs saw, for the first time, a frustrated Secretary-General question the whole role of the United Nations in the Cyprus dispute.

The Neglected Track

Throughout this book, we have concentrated primarily on official (first-track) diplomacy. However, a less travelled pathway also exists. Second/third-track diplomacy is often overlooked by analysts, diplomats, and policy makers alike. There have been a succession of unofficial third-party mediation efforts, rapprochement encounters, and citizen-based bicommunal activities documented. Given the diversity and complexity of the "bicommunal movement," any summary runs the risk of oversimplification; and whilst it is not our intention to furnish a comprehensive survey of second-track diplomacy in Cyprus, it would be remiss if this alternative medium was not explicated in our analysis.

Characterized by their ad hoc demeanor, transitory temperament, and experimental disposition, bicommunalism in Cyprus is the progeny of two competing and parallel historical traditions. Grounded in proletariat internationalism, AKEL and the labor movement's policy of rapprochement offered itself as an antidote to sectarian ethno-nationalism and colonial imperialism.[120] Whilst rapprochement oscillated in postcolonial Cyprus, the emergence of conflict resolution as a research discourse designated Cyprus as one of its prime intrastate case studies. Beginning with John W. Burton's 1966 problem-solving workshop, unofficial third-party mediation in Cyprus included the following initiatives: the Cyprus Resettlement Project by a consortium of World Peace Brigade veterans, the International Peace Academy and others (1972–1974); Phillip Talbot's 1973 Rome Seminar; Doob's workshops in 1974 (aborted) and 1985; Herbert Kelman's University of Harvard interactive problem-solving workshops (1979 and 1984); the Canadian Institute for International Peace and Security seminars (1988–1989); meetings of political leaders facilitated by foreign embassies; Ronald J. Fisher's workshops in the early 1990s; the Cyprus Consortium Training Citizen Peacebuilders initiative (1991–1996); Benjamin Broome's Fulbright Training (1994–1996) program that expanded into the Cyprus Consortium intractability and brainstorming workshops (1997 and 1999–2000).[121]

The overall aim of the "bicommunal project," as with most conflict resolution processes, was to change the perception of the situation from "us" versus "them," negate the idea of "win-lose," and to strive for solutions that address the underlying needs of all parties. They were also about developing skills, forming relationships, and empowering participants to advance the cause of intercommunal dialogue. Specifically, their objectives were to bring to light any lingering areas of mistrust or misunderstanding, identify the values on which mutual respect should be based, and promote cooperation and joint activities locally, nationally, and within the diaspora.

The challenge confronting the burgeoning "bicommunal movement" during the 1990s was to translate such general principles into encounters, educational experiences, and practical activities that targeted the needs and operational environments of their communities within a specific conflictual setting. The hiatus resulting from the collapse of

Boutros-Ghali's initiative allowed for a plethora of bicommunal events, organizations, initiatives, and activities to flourish in the nebulous public space that linked the two communities. For the Turkish Cypriots, in particular, it would set the backdrop for the ensuing transformations that took place in northern Cyprus leading to the 2004 referendum.

Conclusion

The immediate post-Cold War period was heralded, prematurely, as "the last opportunity" to solve the Cyprus problem.[122] Despite being a period of extensive and vigorous mediation by the United Nations, it was not possible to achieve the final settlement so strenuously sought. The reasons for the failure of all UN initiatives can be identified both at a theoretical and an empirical level. Former U.S. State Department Cyprus counselor Nimetz outlined four dimensions that rendered the Cyprus problem "difficult to solve": first, the ambiguity of Cyprus's nationhood, born out of a compromise that most of its citizens "never really wanted," means that "a common set of shared experiences, national aspirations, or common heritage that might [form the] basis for trust and understanding" was lacking; second, antagonism between two ethnic groups was heightened in an "era of deepening animosities among nationalities"; third, both communities had "a nearby metropolitan power, Greece and Turkey"; and fourth, the success of UNFICYP in keeping the peace had also "made it less necessary...to find a lasting solution."[123]

Political scientist Cowher Rizvi agrees with Nimetz's first point that the Cyprus conflict was caused not so much because the constitution was "inherently defective" or even the "intransigence of a minority community," but because of the failure of "national integration and nation-building." Cypriot (civil) nationalism lacked the appeal to "web together both the Greek and Turkish communities."[124] On this basis, academics Maria Hadjipavlou-Trigeorgis and Lenos Trigeorgis have spoken of the need for Cyprus to go "first through a 'conciliation' stage (focusing on developing trust, cooperation and integration), followed by a (federal structure implementation) 'testing' phase, before expanding and ratifying full-scale implementation."[125]

Boutros-Ghali's reversion to CBMs was aimed at creating precisely such a climate. As indicated in previous chapters, both of Boutros-Ghali's predecessors, Waldheim and Pérez de Cuéllar, had attempted at various stages to switch their focus from tackling the substance of the Cyprus problem to creating favorable conditions that would lay the groundwork for an overall settlement. Inspired by the global doctrine established in his report *An Agenda for Peace*,[126] Boutros-Ghali set out to apply these principles in Cyprus through his CBMs. He believed that interaction and cooperation at various levels (for example, commercial joint ventures, cultural events, contact between the political parties, academics, scientists and journalists, common public projects, and people-to-people contact) by reducing restrictions of movement across the buffer zone (CBM 4) and soliciting bicommunal projects supported by the private and international sector (CBM 6) would dissolve the barriers of mistrust to such an extent that his Set of Ideas would be viable. In order for such interaction to be possible, it was necessary to establish bicommunal contact zones while simultaneously decreasing the military threat. This would be achieved by settling the low-level issues of Varosha and the Nicosia airport, both of which would initially come under the neutral administration of the United Nations.

The viability of this approach has merit if one considers the internal political situation in both the Greek and Turkish Cypriot communities. It has been the contention throughout this book that any successful unification of Cyprus would need a sociopolitical force composed of pro-intercommunal elements on both sides that could act in a dual political capacity: as a pressure group within their own community to confront the ethno-nationalist elements bent on dragging the community down a confrontationist path; and as a catalyst for the evolution, establishment, and functioning of pan-Cypriot institutions whose purpose would be to cater for their constituents above and beyond any interethnic considerations.

Throughout the book, it has also been argued that the Cyprus problem operates on three levels: the local, which entails the relationship between the two ethnic communities; the regional, which, as a product of geography, history, and demographics, is at the core of the bilateral dispute between Greece and Turkey; and the international, where the problem has preoccupied the United Nations since 1964 and involved NATO, the United States, and increasingly the EU and its instrumentalities. Political commentator Ronald Meinardus has argued, convincingly, that there have been two main reasons for third-party involvement in Cyprus: first, as an attempt to advance their own interests; and, because of the "pressure on these powers by the regional or local actors to get involved on their behalf." Meinardus has also argued that "both Athens and Ankara have in the past decades internationalized their bilateral disputes, hoping to mobilize in the international community support for their respective causes in the bilateral conflict."[127]

Empirically, for UN mediation to be successful, conditions on all three levels would have to be favorable. With the changing nature of the United Nations and indeed the world post-Cold War, and with the United States freed from past restrictions, the Cyprus dispute might have been resolved. However, international circumstances were dependent on the extent to which U.S. diplomatic intervention lent effective support to the United Nations during the negotiations, and in the end, the United States' "increased attention to the Cyprus problem" during this period proved to be "a short-lived spurt of optimism."[128]

Pérez de Cuéllar rightly assessed the climate in 1989 as positive enough to launch a diplomatic initiative. There had been a change of leadership in the Greek Cypriot community, with Vassiliou coming to power with the backing of the pro-rapprochement political forces headed by AKEL. The same could not be said of the Turkish Cypriot community, where Denktash maintained leadership. Still, with a moderate leader such as Özal in Turkey, and in the afterglow of Davos, both Pérez de Cuéllar and Boutros-Ghali rightly believed that the solution to Cyprus rested with Ankara. They gained confidence from the growing Turkish Cypriot opposition especially from left-wing moderates such as Özgür and Mustafa Akinci. As Clark realized, there were also encouraging signs to be found in the Turkish Cypriot business community, which was attracted to the potential financial benefits that would derive from the CBMs.

The fact that Denktash withheld from the Turkish Cypriot community the merits of the package compounded Boutros-Ghali's suspicion that there was a "Denktash problem." Although it would be an over-simplification to reduce failure of the talks to a single factor, evidence suggests that Denktash, in comparison with his counterparts in the Greek Cypriot community (with the possible exception of Makarios), wielded greater power in determining his community's stance than any other individual actor.[129] As seen previously, Denktash's motivations were derived from the events that both he and the Turkish Cypriot community experienced during their phase of isolation between 1964 and 1974. Denktash genuinely feared that reunification would once again reduce the Turkish Cypriot community to the minority status it suffered from 1964. Denktash's fear, which characterizes a whole generation of Turkish Cypriots, led him to the conclusion that he was destined to be a "father figure" (*babamiz*) for a Turkish Cypriot nation-state and that since 1975 his community has been involved in a national-liberation struggle. From this perspective, Denktash officially declared the Turkish Cypriot self-determination policy in 1989, to which he had eluded since 1975 and which nine years later became concrete with his confederation proposals.[130]

Finally, mention must be made of time as a key factor in the failure of all three UN initiatives. As demonstrated above, the fact that the last phase of the negotiations—the clinching of the deal—was so drawn out meant that the process was susceptible to adverse external influences. Denktash's delays eventually led the Greek Cypriots, especially under Clerides, to revert to a more hard-line position. In the years that followed, both communities pursued separate paths. Clerides embarked on a course for admission to the European Union, and the strengthening of the military apparatus of the Republic of Cyprus, while in response Denktash continued to forge still-closer ties with Turkey. The stage was set for a final encounter of the Cyprus conflict—one that implicated the European Union.

Chapter 5

Toward Annan's "European" Solution

In a statement immediately following the April 2004 referenda, the UN Secretary-General encapsulated his 1999–2004 effort—the Annan initiative—by explaining that his goal had been to facilitate "a reunited Cyprus to join the European Union."[1] Such was the momentum in the Cyprus peace talks that Kofi Annan had declared at his 2003 New Year press conference that "we are within striking distance of reuniting Cyprus."[2] All previous attempts to bring about a political settlement to the Cyprus problem had been unsuccessful in shifting the entrenched positions of the respective parties. In structural terms, failure to link advances in the negotiations with concurrent movements in their external context had meant a disjointed pattern of progress. Yet, what distinguished this period from previous ones was that the UN-negotiated process was both driven and matched by momentous external developments.

The introduction of the European factor into the Cyprus equation provided just the impetus necessary to shift the entrenched behavior paradigm. Integrating Cyprus and Turkey's EU accession pathways into the UN's mediating efforts, and the effects this unleashed within and between the parties, rendered this period as memontous as 1959 and 1974. The Annan initiative, however, was preceded by a period of intense and spasmodic third-party intervention, which seriously endangered Cyprus's fragile status quo.

Imminent Mutual Catastrophe:
Russian Missiles and U.S. Diplomacy

As with previous negotiating cycles, the collapse of Boutros-Ghali's efforts saw the Cyprus peace process descend into a passive lull, with high levels of tension, punctuated by feeble attempts to resuscitate the flagging negotiations. As the conflict reverted to a confrontational cycle, it emerged that Nicosia and Ankara were locked in a collision course, heading for the nebulous European centre.

Three significant developments defined this period as both sides edged toward mutual disaster and away from a delicate military equilibrium, both on the island and in the broader Greek-Turkish context. For the remainder of Boutros-Ghali's tenure as Secretary-General, there was no further UN initiative on the Cyprus problem. Collapse of the CBMs saw the Greeks embark with vigor on a policy of militarization. In November 1993, amidst repeated threats from Ankara that it would annex northern Cyprus in the event that the Republic of Cyprus joined the EU,[3] Nicosia and Athens formulated the Joint Defense Doctrine. Clerides' militarization aimed at establishing a "missile umbrella" covering all of Cyprus, included establishing the "Andreas Papandreou" airport at western Paphos, to enable the landing and refueling of Greek jet fighters. On March 5, 1995 the Joint Defense Doctrine was signed, committing Greece to aid the Republic of Cyprus in the event of war. The first sign of implementation was seen during the annual Greek Cypriot National Guard military exercise "Nikiforos '95," in which Greek air and naval force participated (the initial plan to airdrop Greek paratroopers on the island was abandoned following last minute U.S. intervention).

Militarization entered a new level when the Clinton Administration approved the $132 million sale of 120 MGM-140 ATACMS (Army Tactical Missile Systems) to Turkey in December 1995. The U.S. Department of Defense sought to reassure Greece and the Greek Cypriots that the sale would not "adversely affect either the military balance in the region or U.S. efforts to encourage a negotiated settlement of the Cyprus question."[4] With a range of 160 km, carrying a 450 kg payload of 950 M74 antipersonnel bomblets, a highly accurate inertial guidance system and update capability, the ATACMS, however, could easily strike targets in Cyprus from Turkey.[5]

Turkish military superiority and aggression had been a perennial fixation for Greek Cypriots: it defined their insecurity complex and determined their political behavior. Policies and strategies of dealing with Turkish military preeminence, especially since 1974, had been at the core of the militants-pragmatists debate. In military terms, the Greek side had—since the 1960s—grappled with the strategic dilemma of how to safeguard the air and naval corridor between Greece and Cyprus in the case of a Turkish military attack. In the past, Greece had attempted to address this "tyranny of distance" by sending a secret Greek contingent in 1964, though it was subsequently withdrawn in 1967.

One of the most significant consequences of the collapse of the peace process was tension and violence in Cyprus "unparalleled since 1974." Broader Greek-Turkish relations also deteriorated during this period. In 1995, Turkey threatened to consider it an act of war if Greece ratified the Law of the Sea Treaty, which would legally extend Greece's territorial waters, confirming that tension in Cyprus would always spill over into the Aegean. In February 1996, tension reached a crescendo, with a series of violent incidents along the cease-fire line resulting in the deaths of four Greek Cypriots and a Turkish soldier.[6] President Clinton had to intervene to head off a military confrontation over the disputed islets of Imia/Kardak. A visit to Cyprus by Greek Prime Minister Costas Simitis in August contained a double-edged message, calling for peace while warning that "any advance by Turkey [was] a cause of war."[7]

The most controversial development, however, was Clerides's decision to acquire the Russian S-300PMU-1 air-defense missile batteries in January 1997, to be installed within sixteen months.[8] The agreement entailed the safe delivery and installation of the S-300 by Russian engineers. Turkey threatened to destroy the missiles either en route or during installation. The escalating S-300 missile crisis threatened to embroil into conflict not only Greece and Turkey but also Russia and NATO. Relentless pressure on Clerides from the U.S. and European governments included threatening the Republic of Cyprus's EU application. Consequently, on December 29, 1998, in consultation with the Simitis government, Clerides announced that the missiles would not be deployed in Cyprus but would be redirected to Crete.[9]

Several aspects of the S-300 missile crisis deserve closer attention. The crisis brought into sharp focus the fragility of the Cyprus conflict and showed how rapidly it could deteriorate into an armed showdown involving Greece and Turkey. For our purposes, however, the most intriguing aspect of the S-300 crisis was the reasoning behind Clerides' risky policy. An interesting hypothesis advanced by *Phileleftheros* reporter Andreas Hatzikyriakou asserts that the S-300s were a "diplomatic weapon-warning" aimed at the United States and not Turkey. Clerides's logic rested on the belief that U.S. interest in Cyprus was as a point of tension in Greek-Turkish relations. As long as the Cyprus problem did not threaten their equilibrium, U.S. regional strategic interests were satisfied. This accounted for the lack of any serious or sustained U.S. engagement, as exemplified by Richard

Holbrooke's weak mediation attempt. In this context, Clerides intensified Cyprus's capacity to threaten Greek-Turkish relations.[10] The fact that subsequent events focused international attention on the missiles and not the problem of Cyprus should not diminish Clerides's reputation as the consummate pragmatist.

The psychology of the parties also shifted in this period, particularly for the Greek Cypriots, who had departed radically from their 1974 mood. Social, economic, and demographic divergence between the two sides continued throughout the 1990s, underpinned by an increasingly fluid conflictual context. Heightened insecurity created a defensive mindset that, in the absence of political dialogue, permeated throughout the social fabric of both communities. The double minority syndrome led to militarization that, coupled with hardening political rhetoric, contributed to the rise of ethno-nationalism. For the Greek Cypriots, a new, self-confidant, educated, and prosperous generation, who viewed the conflict through a different prism than those of their predecessors (they were uninhibited by the vulnerability and fatalism of the post-1974 period), led them to critique the prevailing orthodox precepts of passivism and even federalism, adding another layer to the militant-pragmatist dualism.

Within this context, the Russian missiles reaffirmed inter-Orthodox solidarity. Viewed by the Greeks as the traditional patron with muscle—both against the Ottomans and Western (Christian) powers—Russia occupied a unique space within Greek Cypriot nationalist discourse, even, ironically, during the "atheistic" Soviet era, which might account for AKEL's popular pro-Soviet posturing.

Another major feature of this period was Western diplomatic activity. The absence of UN efforts and deteriorating Greek-Turkish relations saw a renewed Anglo-American diplomatic effort. The seriousness of U.S. involvement was exemplified by the appointment of the architect of the (Bosnia) Dayton peace accords, Holbrooke, as Special Presidential Envoy for Cyprus. With the brief of "finding a solution," such was Holbrooke's confidence that he heralded 1996 as "Cyprus's year."[11] Two years later, Holbrooke conceded defeat, blaming Denktash's "unacceptable demands."[12]

Despite his failure, Holbrooke's foray into the Cyprus conflict made two noteworthy contributions. First, he confirmed the view that Denktash's role in the peace process was that of a "spoiler." Second, he reversed U.S. opposition on EU implication in the Cyprus conflict. In 2002, Holbrooke revealed that U.S. support for Cyprus's EU accession was only one component of a three-pronged strategy in the long-term stabilization of the region and Greek-Turkish relations. The other two elements were securing a "specific starting date" for Turkey-EU accession negotiations and convincing Ankara to pressure Denktash to move toward a settlement in Cyprus.[13]

The British also intensified their involvement. Using the impending EU-Cyprus talks as an opportunity to break the "log-jam," in December 1996 the British Foreign Secretary Malcolm Rifkind formulated a ten-point framework to reactivate the UN intercommunal talks. Rifkind wanted a comprehensive settlement to coincide with the commencement of Cyprus's EU accession talks, based on a bizonal-bicommunal federation that reflected the principle of political equality. The federation would have a single international personality attaining its mandate from separate referenda. There would be international guarantees and the territorial readjustment of two federated zones, contributing to a solution of the refugee problem. To accommodate these negotiations, both sides, in conjunction with UNFICYP, would undertake measures aimed at decreasing tension.

Rifkind's proposals were dismissed by Denktash, who castigated the European Union for only dealing with the Greek Cypriot Republic of Cyprus.[14] The Greek Foreign Minister Theodoros Pangalos also rejected Rifkind's position that the Cyprus problem had to be resolved before EU membership talks commenced. Pangalos threatened that there would be no EU enlargement without Cyprus.[15] Despite the collapse of Rifkind's framework, its focus on the UN-EU link resonated in future deliberations.

In the interim, after three years remission, two rounds of face-to-face UN-mediated discussions between Clerides and Denktash were held at Troutbeck, New York and Glion-sur-Montreux, Switzerland in July–August 1997. Despite a promising beginning, Denktash, citing the EU *Agenda 2000* report (which envisaged that accession talks would commence in 1998), withdrew from "any formal understanding or agreements."[16] Further hardening his position, Denktash insisted on interstate rather than intercommunal negotiations.[17]

British-American efforts culminated at the 1999 G8 summit, which provided diplomatic momentum for the ensuing Annan initiative. Recognizing that the Cyprus problem had gone "unresolved for too long," the G8 urged the UN Secretary-General to undertake a new mediating initiative. To aid the process, the G8 put forward four guiding principles: calling for "no pre-conditions," deliberation on all issues, commitment to an outcome-settlement, and consideration of all relevant UN resolutions.[18]

What emerged, as Greek-American academic Van Coufoudakis has suggested, was collusion between the UN Secretariat's role on Cyprus and U.S. and British interests.[19] Although UN dependence on U.S.-British support was well established prior to the Annan initiative, the new contextual environment integrated this relationship to such an extent that they became virtually indistinguishable. Unbeknown to the Cypriot communities, the scene was set for unprecedented intervention by the UN Secretary-General. The Annan Plan would alter the course of the Cyprus conflict.

However, before we examine the Annan initiative, we should first survey the Europeanization of the conflict as the prime reason for expediting the prospects of a political settlement more than any other attempt since the London-Zurich agreements of 1959.

Europeanization of the Conflict

When, on August 14, 1974, the Prime Minister of Turkey, Bülent Ecevit, ordered his troops to break the cease-fire and advance beyond the Kyrenia-Nicosia corridor, a frustrated British Foreign Secretary, James Callaghan, warned that "[t]oday, the Republic of Cyprus is the prisoner of the Turkish Army, but tomorrow the Turkish Army will find that it will be the prisoner of the people of Cyprus."[20] Three decades later, Callaghan's angry and prophetic words reverberated, as Ankara realized that Turkey's European aspirations depended not only on a successful outcome of the intercommunal talks, but, inexplicably, on the attitude the Greek Cypriot-controlled Republic of Cyprus adopted in the EU.[21] The asymmetric relationship that prevailed since 1974 had shifted over time, attributable in large part to the intervention of the EU.

Since the Republic of Cyprus applied for membership in 1990, the EU had progressively gained prominence as a player in the conflict, becoming increasingly entangled in the imbroglio of Greek-Turkish Cypriot relations. Analysts and policy-makers alike have come to see it as a "catalyst" for the resolution of the Cyprus conflict. By transforming the contextual framework of Greek-Turkish, EU-Cyprus, Turkey-EU, and (internal) Greek-Turkish Cypriot relations, the EU supplemented UN efforts. Greece's membership, Cyprus's accession, and Turkey's own candidature accelerated the EU's involvement in this region at a time when the West (both Europe and America) was refocusing its attention on the geopolitical significance of security in the East Mediterranean.

The Road to Brussels

To fully comprehend the role of the EU in the Cyprus conflict, one needs to trace its origins and evolution as a Greek strategy designed to alter the power configuration in Cyprus, given Turkey's predominance on the island following the events of 1974.

Thirty years earlier, the EC's role in the Cyprus conflict had been minimal, limited to exercising diplomatic pressure on Greece and Turkey—both of which had Association Agreements since the early 1960s—to accept a cease-fire and commence negotiations. The Europeans were unable to play a larger role in the armed conflict, largely because, following the fall of the Greek dictatorship, they were perceived by the Turks—and by U.S. Secretary of State Henry Kissinger—as being pro-Greek. Furthermore, the escalation of the conflict during the second phase of the invasion had demanded Turkey be restrained, and the Europeans possessed no military might independent of the United States.

After their initial attempt at crisis management, the EC's role in the Cyprus dispute amounted to no more than a second-tier intervention, providing support to the United States and for the UN Secretary-General's efforts at sustaining the intercommunal talks. Other factors also explain the EC's inability to play a more prominent role prior to the 1990s: notably, the divergent attitudes of its member-states toward the conflict, the lack of a common foreign policy approach, and Turkey's unwillingness to accept European mediation, which it considered biased in favor of the Greeks.

The idea that Cyprus should apply to join the EU as a strategy to enhance Greece's bargaining power vis-à-vis Turkey has its genesis in the early 1980s, after Greece joined the Economic European Community (EEC) and Andreas G. Papandreou was elected to government. In addition to pursuing a policy of internationalization throughout the 1980s, two of Papandreou's closest advisors, Periklis Nearchou and Andreas Christodoulou, also suggested that the Republic of Cyprus should join the EEC.[22] Once the internationalization strategy failed, the EU-Cyprus plan was resurrected and vigorously pursued by another Greek Cypriot PASOK advisor, Yiannos Kranidiotis, who is credited as the architect of the Cyprus-EU policy. The need for the Greek side to change policy direction was articulated by Simitis who, after his visit to Cyprus in 1996, became convinced that the Cyprus problem was at a standstill and that the island was at a critical juncture.[23] In 1987, the Republic of Cyprus concluded a Customs Union Agreement with the EC, which came into effect the following year.

It was not until July 1990 that Cyprus, under Vassiliou, formally applied for EU membership. The previous month, at its Dublin summit, the European Council reaffirmed its previous declarations in support of the unity, independence, sovereignty, and territorial integrity of Cyprus, as well as its support for UN efforts. More importantly, it reiterated that the Cyprus conflict was affecting EC-Turkey relations. Three years later, at its Luxembourg summit, the Council instructed the European Commission (hereafter also referred to as "Commission") to commence preliminary accession discussions with the Republic of Cyprus. The Council also confirmed the Community's support for the efforts made by the UN Secretary-General to produce a political settlement of the Cyprus question. If, despite these efforts, there was no prospect of a solution, the Council would reassess Cyprus's accession in January 1995, taking into account each party's behavior at the intercommunal talks. At the Corfu summit in June 1994, the European Council noted that Cyprus and Malta would be included in the next round of enlargement.[24] Turkish reaction to the Corfu decision was to warn that unilateral pursuit of EU membership would seriously jeopardize "federation as the sole form of settlement."[25]

By this time it was clear that Cyprus's accession to the EU had introduced a new dimension to the search for a political settlement. The evolution of the "European factor" emerged to such an extent that by January 1995 the newly appointed European observer on Cyprus, Serge Abou, confirmed that "Cyprus's membership of the EU [was] now fixed in the minds of all those concerned."[26]

The next important milestone in the Europeanization of the Cyprus problem occurred on March 6, 1995, when the General Affairs Council of EU Ministers, reconsidering Cyprus's application for membership, declared its "will to incorporate Cyprus at the next stage of its enlargement." The Council considered that "Cyprus's accession to the EU" would enhance "security and prosperity to both communities" and "allow the North to catch up economically" by improving "growth and employment" for the Turkish Cypriot community. The Council considered that the Turkish Cypriot community should recognize the advantages of EU accession and "its concerns at the prospect must be allayed." Finally, the Council reiterated the EU's intention to "support with all means at its disposal" UN efforts to "achieve a comprehensive settlement" of the Cyprus problem. In addition, the European Commission also regretted "the lack of progress in the intercommunal talks" and called on "all parties to step up their efforts to achieve a comprehensive settlement" in accordance with the UN Security Council resolutions and based on a "bi-communal and bi-zonal federation." The Council also instructed the Commission to make the necessary contacts with the Turkish Cypriot community, in consultation with the Government of Cyprus: it considered that accession "should benefit all communities and help bring about civil peace and reconciliation" to the island. It expected that negotiations would commence six months after the 1996 Intergovernmental Conference.[27]

Greek Cypriot desire for accession to the EU was guided by broader strategic considerations. Addressing the Cypriot Parliament on February 22, 1996, Republic of Cyprus Foreign Minister, Alecos Michaelides, placed the whole triangular predicament in context:

> for the first time since the invasion, [Turkey] has been faced with a dilemma to which it has to respond, within a specific time frame. The choice is clear. If Turkey insists on the policy of no solution to the Cyprus problem, then it will condemn the Turkish Cypriots to non-participation in the benefits deriving from accession. If it really wishes the Turkish Cypriots to share in the benefits, it will have to show goodwill and cooperate towards achieving a solution of the Cyprus problem…[T]he irrevocable [EU] accession course of Cyprus puts Turkey before this dilemma and that this course may act as a catalyst for the solution of the Cyprus problem.[28]

Turkey's immediate response was to warn the EU that the Council's decision could "lead to the permanent division of the island." If accession negotiations with Cyprus were to proceed, Turkey's Foreign Minister Murat Karayalçin cautioned, Turkey would be left with no other alternative than to take steps toward "integration with the Turkish Republic of Northern Cyprus."[29] When Turkey signed a Customs Union Treaty with the EU in December 1995, it was restated in more restrained terms. In a joint statement, Denktash and Turkish President Demirel reiterated that Cyprus's membership of the EU could be "taken up…after a final settlement" and should be discussed at the intercommunal talks. The Turks insisted that a federal Cyprus could "join the EU only simultaneously with Turkey's accession."[30]

Cyprus's efforts to join the EU had the potential both to exacerbate tensions between the Turkish Cypriots and Turkey and help resolve the conflict through some arrangement involving membership in return for a peace settlement. At this point, according to former Cypriot diplomat and academic Marios Evriviades, Washington reversed its opposition to Cyprus's accession to the EU. Holbrooke (then Assistant Secretary of State for European Affairs), in charge of the Cyprus triangle, saw the EU (unlike the UN) as capable of eliminating the outstanding Greek-Turkish issue, which had plagued NATO's eastern flank since the mid-1950s. Cyprus's accession could open the way to Turkey's own integration into Europe, thus providing stability and security to their troubled ally.[31] For the latter to occur, the processes of accession and settlement would have to be closely linked and take into account the multiple interrelationships at the heart of the Cyprus problem.

At its Dublin Summit on December 16, 1996, the European Council urged Turkey to use its influence to contribute to a solution of the Cyprus problem in accordance with UN resolutions.[32] But it was at the Luxembourg European Council Summit a year later that the enlargement process was formally launched, and the bilateral negotiations with Cyprus, Hungary, Poland, Estonia, the Czech Republic, and Slovenia were set to commence in the spring of 1998. The European Commission stipulated that Cyprus's accession should benefit all communities, aid civil peace and reconciliation, and make a positive contribution to solving the Cyprus problem. As in past declarations, political settlement should be achieved through the UN intercommunal talks based on a bicommunal bizonal federation. To achieve bicommunalism, the Commission requested that Turkish Cypriot representatives be included in Cyprus's negotiating delegation. With respect to Turkey, the Commission made it clear that its links with the EU would depend on its political and economic reforms, bringing human and minority rights into line with EU standards, its stable relations with Greece, and its support for UN negotiations based on the relevant UN Security Council resolutions.[33]

At the Helsinki European Council of 1999, the foreign ministers made two milestone decisions: first, they pronounced that settlement was not a precondition for Cyprus's accession, but that they would consider all relevant factors when making a final determination; second, by restating that compliance with the 1993 Copenhagen political criteria was a prerequisite, Cyprus's case was implicitly linked with Turkey's own candidature.[34]

At the crucial Copenhagen summit of December 2002, the European Commission declared that Cyprus would be admitted as a new member to the EU even in the absence of a settlement. It reiterated its strong preference for a united Cyprus joining the EU and endorsed the UN Secretary-General's proposals and timetable for reaching a settlement by February 28, 2003. In case of such a settlement, the EU would accommodate its terms in the Treaty of Accession. In respect of Turkey's candidature, the Council welcomed the legislative steps undertaken by the new AKP (*Adalet ve Kalkinma Partisi* [Justice and Development Party]) government and encouraged further reforms especially in relation to the political criteria—a reference to ensuring stable democratic institutions, the rule of law, human rights, and the protection of minority rights.[35]

As we will see, failure of Kofi Annan's first attempt to secure an agreement in 2003 saw the European Council adopt a firmer position on Turkey's EU candidature when it next convened in Brussels on December 12–13, 2003. Cloaked in diplomatic language, the Council, although noting Turkey's "political will," stipulated that Turkey's "membership aspirations" were linked to a settlement of the Cyprus problem. The European Council subsequently outlined a framework in which both the UN's peace process and Cyprus's EU accession were situated. Specifically, the Brussels framework reiterated the European Council's

> preference for a reunited Cyprus to join the Union on 1 May 2004...[urging] all parties concerned, and in particular Turkey and the Turkish Cypriot leadership, to support the UN Secretary General's efforts strongly...[call] for an immediate resumption of the talks on the basis of his proposals. The Union reiterates its willingness to accommodate the terms of a settlement...[and] welcomes the Commission's...assistance for a speedy solution within the framework of the acquis. Following a settlement, the Union is ready to provide financial assistance for the development of the northern part of Cyprus and the Commission would be called upon to prepare all necessary steps for lifting the suspension of the acquis.[36]

The significance of the Brussels declaration rests in its determination to incorporate the UN's process with its own enlargement designs as a way of dealing with the prevailing status quo over both Cyprus and Turkey.

EU's Dilemma over the Status Quo in Cyprus

British historian Perry Anderson best encapsulated European ambiguity over Cyprus's (divided) predicament when he noted that it constituted "an anomaly" in the new integrated Europe.[37] From the outset, the European Council's preference had always been for the accession of two parts to form a united Cyprus. As the accession process accelerated, however, the Europeans were confronted with an acute dilemma: how should they handle a candidate state whose 38 percent territory was under the control of another aspiring candidate. Inevitably, this predicament required the EU to survey future scenarios of the Cyprus conflict. The 1974 situation suggested three possible alternatives: (1) that the current status quo persists; (2) that the island be unified through a federal arrangement resulting from negotiations and based on either a strong or loose federation, or on some intermediate arrangement; (3) that Cyprus be formally or informally unified/annexed, in part or in whole, with Greece and/or Turkey. The last option implied high levels of instability and, given the volume of arms accumulated by both sides, the prospect of open hostility.

The fusion of scenarios 1 and 2 threatened to complicate Cyprus's accession to the EU. In particular, the Europeans were unsure how to deal with the Turkish Cypriot community, and how to treat northern Cyprus during the whole accession process. Initially there were three possible approaches to the problem: (1) delay Cyprus's admission until after a settlement had been achieved (the preferred Turkish position); (2) admit only the Republic of Cyprus with a view to including northern Cyprus if and when a solution was found (that is, following the German example); and (3) a variation on the second approach, which admitted the Republic of Cyprus while granting a special regime for northern Cyprus and the Turkish Cypriot community.

With the EU's decision to include Cyprus in its next round of enlargement, the first approach was rendered irrelevant. When the Laeken 2001 European Council decision established the timeframe for enlargement as between the end of 2002 and before the next European Parliamentary elections in 2004,[38] the question of handling northern Cyprus became critically important. Initial attempts by the European Council to include Turkish Cypriot representatives in the Cypriot negotiating delegation (including Clerides's 1998 invitation that Turkish Cypriot representatives be included in the Cypriot negotiating group[39]) were rebuffed by the Turkish Cypriot leadership, cutting short a mutually accepted approach by the Cypriots.[40]

For all practical purposes, the first approach had been replaced by a fourth strategy, which envisaged Cyprus's admission in conjunction with a political settlement. As we will see, a last minute UN effort to reach a settlement before the Republic of Cyprus officially joined the EU on May 1, 2004 was strongly pursued, with the EU offering economic incentives for northern Cyprus before and after settlement.[41]

The qualitative difference between the first and fourth approaches was that the course of European accession would drive the settlement process and not vice versa. Although the fourth approach was the preferred option for all concerned, it required enormous effort to synchronize four different processes (EU-Cyprus accession negotiations, European Commission-Turkey pre-accession strategy, UN-sponsored intercommunal talks, and Greek-Turkish bilateral discussions). As the deadline approached, the Europeans—having declared that a solution to the Cyprus problem was not a precondition to accession—were preparing to adopt some amended version of the third approach, a post-accession settlement and, in the interim, a transitional regime of economic and trade measures that would bypass the administrative authorities in the north.

The prospect of a post-accession settlement was incorporated within the Cyprus-EU Accession Treaty, signed in Athens on April 16, 2003. In a special protocol, the Accession Treaty suspended application of the *acquis communautaire* in the areas not controlled by the Republic of Cyprus (that is, northern Cyprus), which would be lifted in the event of a solution to the Cyprus problem. The Europeans would accommodate such a settlement, and the terms on which the Turkish Cypriot community would be integrated would be determined by the European Commission. In the meantime, measures promoting economic development in northern Cyprus were not excluded.[42]

As we will see, Greek Cypriot rejection of the Annan Plan and Cyprus's imminent accession rendered all other considerations superfluous. Post-accession settlement promptly mutated into a dilemma, as the EU searched for a formula that reconciled its legal predicament with political promises (extensively toward the Turkish Cypriots) while upholding the EU's visionary mantra of eradicating borders. The EU Council's immediate response was the "Green Line" regulation (April 29) that suspended the aquis "in the areas in which the Government of the Republic of Cyprus [did] not exercise effective control"—thereby establishing a new jargon with reference to northern (occupied) Cyprus.

As northern Cyprus did not constitute "an external border," the EU regulated "special rules" pertaining to the crossing of goods, services, and persons across the green line. As per scenario 3, denoting northern Cyprus as a "preferential regime," an ambiguous and convoluted system was constructed whereby all checks were carried out by the Republic of Cyprus authorities at two crossing points (Ledra Palace and Agios Dometios), while two other crossing points (Pergamos and Strovilia) came under the jurisdiction of the British Eastern Sovereign Base Area. Goods from the north acquired the "status of Community goods," requiring authorization from the Turkish Cypriot Chamber of Commerce, with the Republic of Cyprus's consent.[43] In many respects, the EU was reinforcing and incorporating the developments that emerged from the partial lifting of restrictions on movement along the cease-fire line, and from the Republic of Cyprus's Turkish Cypriot set measures of 2003.[44]

To deal with this "unique and complex situation," the EU began to articulate a Turkish Cypriot policy founded on the moral premise, as Commissioner Günter Verheugen explained, that "it would have been unfair" to leave them "out in the cold," given their overwhelming support for reunification. The European Commission proposed a comprehensive €259 million developmental aid package in July 2004 intended to end the isolation of the Turkish Cypriot community. The Europeans hoped that in addition to fostering economic development, trade from northern Cyprus would build new bridges between the two communities and sustain hope for the reunification of Cyprus.[45]

The potential shift in the conflict was overshadowed, however, by the broader subregional implications of Cyprus's accession. Much to its frustration, the EU quickly discovered what the United Nations had painfully learnt over decades: it had become an arena for Nicosia's and Ankara's enmity. As the fluidity of 2003–2004 dissipated, stalemate gave way to stagnation, the conflict reverted to familiar patterns of adversarial discourse. The EU, for its part, saw itself transformed from an agent of change to a dormant forum, with the Republic of Cyprus and Turkey vying for advantage and Europe's favor.

The next time the European Council focused on the Cyprus conflict was in June 2004. Clearly annoyed with the Greek Cypriots, the only reference to Cyprus was in the context of welcoming Ankara's "positive contribution" to Annan's efforts.[46] As Turkey's membership progressed, its refusal to recognize the Republic of Cyprus propelled the conflict into a new direction compounding Europe's dilemma over Turkey. But as the chair of the Turkish think tank (TESEV), Can Parker, noted, "suspension of efforts to solve the Cyprus issue...could pave the way for unwelcome developments in Turkey, the EU and in the region as a whole."[47]

From the Bosporus to Brussels (via the Green Line)

Greek Prime Minister Simitis aptly stated at a PASOK caucus in November 2002 that the "green line in Nicosia separates Ankara from Brussels," noting that the green line no longer served Turkey's interests.[48] Until 1974, international attention had focused primarily on Greece's role in the Cyprus conflict, but thereafter the pendulum swung toward Turkey's involvement in the island's affairs. During the Cold War, Turkey's reliance on the United States and its importance for the NATO alliance meant that Ankara was immune to UN and other external pressure to comply with international law. The end of the Cold War transformed regional and subregional security considerations, often challenging Turkey's centrality to Western interests. Although Turkey's geopolitical role was readdressed, post-September 11 and in the context of the U.S. "war on terror," the subsequent attitudinal and behavioral differentiation between the "European" and an Anglo-American West, with regard to the invasion of Iraq, placed Turkey and especially the AKP government in a precarious position. The transformation of European security and identity from "strategic culture" to "security identity" (with European identity at the centre of the EU's self-defining process) placed Turkey at its periphery as an unofficial European.[49]

Turkey's relationship with Europe had always been problematic, fraught with cultural complexities, misunderstandings, and security considerations, some dating back to the Ottoman period. In Europe, ambivalence regarding Turkey's candidature divided its members between those who did not consider Turkey a European country—as chair of the Convention on the Future of Europe, Valéry Giscard d'Estaing brusquely pointed out[50]—and those who viewed Turkey as a bridge to Central Asia and the Middle East, such as Jacques Chirac.[51]

Greek-Turkish "Earthquake" Rapprochement

Nowhere is Turkey's tumultuous relationship with Europe more clearly revealed than from the prism of Greek-Turkish relations. For over a century the prevailing dictum concerning Greek-Turkish relations was that it rested on primordial enmity. Such a predisposition would often provide European Occidentalism with a convenient cloak for their anti-Turkish sentiment. However, images of Greek and Turkish rescuers digging out a nine-year-old boy from the debris in Dermederek sent a powerful message that negated decades of ethno-nationalist polemics. Equally, Turkish rescuers were among the first foreign teams to arrive in Greece when the devastating earthquake shifted westward to Athens a month later.[52]

The Kocaeli earthquakes that struck western Turkey in 1999 proved to be a turning point in Greek-Turkish relations. In addition to empowering Turkish civil society, the generous, spontaneous, and sincere way in which Greece responded to Turkey's humanitarian need called into question the nationalist stereotyping of each other as the eternal enemy.[53] Another symbolic moment in this emotional Greek-Turkish reconciliation was the outcry from Turkey's civil society, media, and politicians over Health Minister Osman Durmus's claim that Turks did not need Greek blood. Durmus was forced to resign. The earthquake provided impetus for an emerging Greek-Turkish reconciliation process (dubbed "earthquake diplomacy"), heralding a new era in Greek-Turkish relations.[54]

Until 1999, the majority of EU states were content with, and indeed relied on, Greece's veto to block Turkey's accession to the EU. "Earthquake diplomacy," however, exposed European bias against Turkey's European orientation. Domestically, the Helsinki decision transformed Turkey's political landscape, providing space for a resurrected pro-EU lobby comprising business, liberal politicians, moderate elements of the Turkish Army, intellectuals, academics, journalists, and various NGOs.[55] This political force, although subservient, was enhanced by the success of Turkey's EU Accession Partnership Agreement, and it challenged the entrenched secular Kemalist nationalists, as well as offered a counter to the emerging populism of the Islamists. All three forces were competing for Turkey's political identity and destiny. At the center of this dispute was the vexed question of Turkey's EU membership and to what extent was it prepared to change. Nothing illustrated this dilemma more forcefully than the Cyprus issue.

Locating Cyprus in Turkey's European Vocation

Reassessing Turkey's foreign policy, prominent Turkish thinker Ahmet Davutoğlu in his seminal work *Strategic Depth* points out that Turkey has historically been plagued by the "Sèvres syndrome"—a reference to the post-First World War Treaty of Sèvres, which saw the disbanding of the Ottoman Empire. According to Davutoğlu, the "Sèvres syndrome" meant Turkish foreign policy was motivated by the twin fears of disintegration by external powers and imagined internal threats (that is, Kurds and Islamists), which led to a defensive strategic mindset.[56]

Turkey's strategic dilemma was exacerbated post-September 11: it could either embrace Europe and the West or assume a more independent stance, located somewhere between East and West.[57] Choosing to proceed with its EU ambitions, Turkey faced some fundamental decisions that would transform the Kemalist state and have far-reaching consequences for its external and internal constitution and behavior.[58]

In this context, Cyprus was central to Turkish nationalism and had been historically used to harness populist nationalism by civil governments at times of domestic crisis (for example, by Adnan Menderes in 1955, Ismet Inonü in 1964, and Ecevit in 1974). The Turkish military also saw Cyprus and its 1974 invasion as a source of prestige.[59]

Until the election of the AKP government, Turkey completely failed to assess accurately the extent of the damage inflicted by the Cyprus problem on its diplomacy, with regard to both its relationship with Greece and its policy for European integration.[60] This became evident when the European Commission rejected Turkey's 1987 application, citing "three sets of conditions": its poor human rights record, its lack of democracy, and the damaging effects of its dispute with another fellow member (Greece), in particular over Cyprus.[61] By the early 1990s, with the perception in Europe that Turkey's culture and religious identity were not European, the withdrawal of Turkish troops from Cyprus became the minimum price Turkey would have to pay to join the EU.[62]

As one of Turkey's strongest advocates in Europe, Britain intensified its message to Ankara that the Cyprus issue was linked to its European aspirations. In a parliamentary report on Turkey, the British Government agreed with the committee's conclusion that settlement of the Cyprus problem would enhance Turkey's European prospects.[63] The report confirmed that Turkish opinion and decision makers unanimously agreed that if a divided Cyprus joined the EU, it would constitute a serious setback not only for Turkey's EU prospects but also for domestic reform. Furthermore, a British parliamentary report concurred that once the Republic of Cyprus joined the EU, it would use its veto to block Turkey's candidature,[64] pushing Turkey's accession into the indefinite future and altering the Greek-Turkish détente climate into one of confrontation and bitterness.[65]

The European Commission in its 1999 Regular Report recognized Turkey's status as an applicant country and established the Cyprus issue as a political criterion for its accession. Specifically, the European Commission considered Turkey's stance on Cyprus as being at odds with UN resolutions and its own position, and that this was having an adverse effect on its ambitious Barcelona Process (Euro-Mediterranean Partnership) aimed at creating a new regional construct of peace, security, and prosperity.[66]

The following year, the Commission classified the Cyprus issue as one of the political criteria for Turkish entry, after EU-Turkish relations were enhanced by the December 1999 Helsinki European Council. The decision stipulated that bilateral EU-Turkish dialogue would be conducted on the basis of "progressing towards fulfilling the political criteria for accession with particular reference to the issue of human rights, as well as the issues referred to in paragraphs 4 and 9(a) (peaceful settlement of disputes and the Cyprus issue)." Although Turkey's position on Cyprus was still contrary to both the UN and EU policies, the Commission's assessment was that Turkey's candidate status had provided a "new impetus" to the Cyprus peace process.[67]

If there were any lingering doubts for Ankara about the link between a settlement in Cyprus and Turkey's EU prospects, then the Commission's 2003 progress report, and in particular the strategy paper, laid them to rest. Recalling that "efforts to resolve the Cyprus problem form part of the enhanced political dialogue between the European Union and Turkey," the Commission concluded that the "absence of a settlement could become a serious obstacle to Turkey's EU aspirations."[68]

Not surprisingly, the last sentence created a political storm in Turkey's political circles. Nevertheless, after initial protestations from Foreign Minister Abdullah Gül,[69] Turkey's policy-makers finally came to the same conclusion as former Foreign Minister İsmail Cem: a solution to the Cyprus problem was a prerequisite for Turkey's EU membership.[70] A month later, Turkey's Prime Minister Recep Tayyip Erdoğan publicly admitted that the two issues were connected,[71] and encouraged Annan to reactivate his initiative.

As predicted, the post-referendum climate reverted to a familiar con-flictual atmosphere. Exhausted by the Cyprus issue, the Commission reflected that the "Cyprus issue ha[d] dominated EU-Turkey rela-tions" and that "it was difficult to discern [Turkey's] clear position" on UN efforts toward a comprehensive settlement of the Cyprus problem, while acknowledging Turkey's "significant policy shift" in supporting the Annan Plan during the 2004 referendum.[72]

Following the 2004 referendum, it became clear that the EU was prepared to remove the Cyprus issue as a precondition for Turkey's accession. A precursor to this shift was the European Economic and Social Committee's stated opinion that "the EU cannot make the solution of the Cyprus problem a new condition" for Turkey's accession negotiations.[73] In exchange, the EU required from Turkey to make the small but symbolic gesture of lifting its restriction on Cypriot-flagged vessels from docking in its ports.[74]

At its Brussels summit on December 17, 2004, the European Commission agreed to commence membership negotiations with Turkey on October 3, 2005 within a framework of requirements. These included the expectation that Turkey would ratify the Adaptation Protocol, extending Turkey's association agreement with all EU members including the Republic of Cyprus.[75] Nevertheless, Turkey signed the protocol with a declaration that it did not recognize the Republic of Cyprus. The EU foreign ministers retaliated by issuing a counter-declaration requesting that Turkey recognize the Republic of Cyprus prior to accession and allow for the full and nondiscriminatory implementation of the additional protocol removing all obstacles to the free movement of goods and transportation.[76]

Turkey's subsequent refusal to open its ports to Greek Cypriot vessels, as per the additional protocol to the customs union, saw the EU impose punitive measures and partially freeze Turkey's membership negotiations in 2006.[77] The problem was further compounded in the foreign, security, and defense policy realms when Turkey resisted the inclusion of Cyprus (and Malta) in the EU-NATO strategic cooperation "Berlin Plus" agreement and blocked Cyprus's membership in the Wassenaar Arrangement on Export Controls for Conventional Arms and Dual-Use Goods Technologies.

In adopting the Republic of Cyprus, those forces opposing Turkey's admission into the EU reflected the wider cultural currents now swiping Europe. The view that Turkey instead be granted "privileged partnership" gained currency among key constituencies in Austria, Germany, and France. This created a nationalist backlash in Turkey (along with the Kurdish problem and the Iraq war), which transformed Cyprus into a contentious issue for the AKP government and the military-Kemalist establishment. Contradictory statements were issued by Erdoğan, as he attempted to link recognition of the Republic of Cyprus with the lifting of Turkish Cypriot isolation,[78] while insisting that the Cyprus problem be removed from Turkey's membership bid.[79] As Turkey entered a political crisis over Abdullah Gül's candidature for the presidency, many were concerned that deteriorating Turkish-EU relations would contribute to a "constant tension" between the AKP government and military-secular forces. The Turkish military, which had never favored EU membership, took comfort from the decline in public support for EU membership: from 55 percent (2005) to 44 percent (2006).[80]

By 2007, Turkey's accession to the EU depended on a wide range of factors—both external and internal, from short-term and middle-term—that would transform Turkey's polity, economy, and civil society. For this transition to take place, Turkey first needed to remove the "Cyprus problem" from the list of obstacles impeding its progress.

As veteran journalist Mehmet Ali Birand confirmed, Cyprus constituted one of three "basic issues" that impeded Turkey's progress and needed to be resolved in a conciliatory, and not an authoritarian nationalist, manner.[81] By then, the EU had demonstrated its capacity to transform Cyprus's domestic political space.

EU Impact on Inter- and Intra-Communal Political Space

On December 26, 2002, the largest ever Turkish Cypriot demonstration took place in Northern Cyprus. Waving EU flags, slogans, and olive branches, an estimated crowd of 30,000 called for the reunification of an EU-inducted Cyprus and demanded the resignation of Denktash.[82] Nineteen days later, an even larger crowd, estimated between 50,000 and 70,000 people, once again took to the streets of Nicosia and with taunting slogans such as "Denktash, if you don't have a pen, we have one" (referring to his refusal to sign-off on the Annan Plan), and continued to demand his resignation.[83] With Denktash typecast as a "spoiler" by the international community, the UN Secretary-General was not surprisingly "pleased that the people [were] out in the streets promoting peace, demanding peace, and demanding unification,"[84] nor that the U.S. State Department regarded that "people demonstrating in support of this opportunity to achieve to [*sic*] peace" were doing the right thing.[85] At the end of 2003, the pro-Denktash nationalist forces received an electoral shock. The opposition coalition, BDH (*Barış ve Demokrasi Hareketi* [Peace and Democracy Movement]),[86] gained a majority of the popular vote, but owing to the complicated electoral system secured only half (25 out of 50 seats) of the assembly seats. The EU and the Annan Plan were the core issues over which the election was fought between the pro-European opposition and the anti-unification nationalist governing forces.[87]

The challenge to Denktash's authority—both as a symbol and an institution of the dominant nationalist forces—was the result of local and external factors that provided an evolving and expanding social movement with political opportunities and resources to challenge the prevailing power structures. Although there had always been a left-wing Turkish Cypriot opposition to the nationalist or status quo parties, its political and electoral impact was always severely constrained by the spatial confinement and semi-authoritarian context it found itself in—what Navaro-Yashin expeditiously describes as "borders of imagination."[88] International isolation, embargo, and nonrecognition rendered their political space an illegal "non-state," interdependent and entangled with Turkey's Kemalist discourse.[89]

On this occasion, however, the opposition was able to appeal to a broader section of the North's population—even attracting support from some Anatolian settlers—and mobilize this mass movement into protests, civil disobedience, and eventually electoral support. Whether one applies breakdown or resource mobilization theory, two forces, operating at both supra- and substate level, converged to alter the territorial and other constraints that had silenced Turkish Cypriot dissent for decades. Utilizing the telecommunication and information tools provided by globalization, Turkish Cypriot civil society was able to communicate, network, mobilize, and consolidate support for their cause. The Turkish Cypriot mass movement drew on three different sources: the traditional Turkish Cypriot Left parties CTP and TKP, with their union affiliates; the peace and human rights movements and NGOs, which were Internet savvy; and finally, an economic or market sector including those Turkish Cypriots who had grievances against the ruling elite over issues of unemployment, corruption, and patronage.[90]

Prior to 2000, dissatisfaction with the regime in northern Cyprus had essentially come from two different sources: the traditional Turkish Cypriot Left opposition and dissatisfaction over deteriorating economic conditions. In 1996, these two streams merged and dissent acquired an overt political dimension, with the explosion of several small bombs at the CTP and DP offices. The event, however, that solidarized the trade union movement with the embryonic civil society groups was the protests over the killing of the left-wing journalist Kutlu Adali.[91]

The mass movement in northern Cyprus can be traced to July 19, 2000, when thousands protested against the arrest of three journalists and the editor of the oppositionist *Avrupa* newspaper ten days prior, charged with spying for the Republic of Cyprus government.[92] Five days later, on July 24, an angry crowd of 2,000 people raided the parliament, having lost their savings in the financial collapse of six banks.[93] Attempts by Denktash to blame the Greek Cypriots for both crises backfired, placing a considerable strain on the unity of the ruling nationalist forces—with a public fallout between Denktash and Eroğlu[94]—and strengthening the popular perception of a financial, political, and legal meltdown in northern Cyprus.

A year later, tear gas was used to disperse supporters of Group 41, who were protesting under the slogan "This Country is Ours." Group 41—later to expand to 86 organizations—was the solidification of Turkish Cypriot civil society, comprising the Left opposition parties, trade unions, professional associations, and other NGOs, and led by the KTTO (*Kıbrıs Türk Ticaret Odası* [Turkish Cypriot Chamber of Commerce]). To counter Group 41, nationalist forces attempted to establish their own civil society umbrella organization, the far-Right UHH (*Ulusal Halk Hareketi* [National People's Movement]), which was suspected of masterminding the bombing of *Avrupa* and other acts of intimidation. A few days later, there was a crackdown on all contacts with the Greek Cypriots. Meanwhile, Denktash accused the EU of pursuing a policy that gave "more importance to people who [were] against the establishment."[95]

The closer Cyprus got to EU accession, the more Turkish Cypriot dissent intensified. Frustration was directed at Denktash who as a symbol of the status quo appeared anti-European. The lifting of travel restrictions in 2003 promised to liberate northern Cyprus from both its external isolation and internal authoritarianism.[96]

Turkish Cypriot ethno-nationalism underestimated the allure of the EU, especially for young, professional, and middle-class Turkish Cypriots, many of whom had little or no memory of the pre-1974 situation to which Denktash made frequent reference. After nearly four decades of isolation, economic stagnation, and high unemployment, support for inclusion in the greater European family was reflected in public opinion polls. In a specially commissioned survey for the Cyprus Delegate of the European Commission, the KADEM Institute found in 2002 that 88 percent of Turkish Cypriots would vote in favor of EU membership at a referendum.[97] This confirmed previous reports that linked the potential economic benefits Turkish Cypriots would gain from EU membership with their strong desire to become part of Europe.[98] A report by the European Parliament found that productivity in the north was an estimated 38 percent of that of the Greek Cypriots in the south, and that their economy was heavily dependent on fiscal transfers from Turkey.[99]

European support for the opposition grew to the point that Denktash accused the EU of funding the Turkish Cypriot Chamber of Commerce's movement. Specifically, Denktash claimed that the EU gave the KTTO €270,000 and alleged that their protest activities started only then.[100]

As indicated earlier, throughout Cyprus's pre-accession period, the EU was unsure how it should manage northern Cyprus and the Turkish Cypriot community in different settlement/non-settlement scenarios. The EU's preferred option had always been for a unified Cyprus joining its ranks. At some point, there appeared to be a policy shift by EU officials to lend support to those civil society and market groups in northern Cyprus that shared their EU/settlement vision. The President of the European Commission, Romano Prodi, expounded this policy during his 2001 visit to Cyprus when he met with Turkish Cypriot trade union leaders who at the time were at the forefront of Group 41.[101]

The electoral gains by the main opposition party CTP, commencing with the 2002 municipal elections, followed by the 2003 and 2005 general elections and culminating with Mehmet Ali Talat's election as the new Turkish Cypriot leader, convinced the EU of its policy's electoral currency. The election of a new AKP government in Turkey was viewed as another positive contributing factor to the EU "catalyst" design. As soon as AKP was elected, Erdoğan, in an extraordinary TV interview in the northern city of Rize, commented that he was "not in favor of [a] continuation of [the] last 30–40 years' policy in Cyprus" and that Cyprus was "not the personal case of President Rauf Denktash." He pointed out that "if 30,000 people could hold a demonstration in Northern Cyprus, it means that Northern Cyprus has been heading to somewhere. It is not an ordinary event. We should well assess the situation. No one can ignore [the] views of the people."[102]

AKP government-Denktash relations became so tense that the president of Turkey, Ahmet Necdet Sezen, intervened in December 2002, assembling the stakeholders (the AKP government, Denktash, and the Turkish Armed Forces) in order to find a common Turkish position.[103] The dispute was not resolved and two weeks later Denktash threatened to resign if Turkey insisted that he sign the Annan Plan.[104] Denktash also declined to attend the four-way meeting in Switzerland.[105] Leading up to The Hague summit, the EU unsuccessfully pressured the Turkish government to pull Denktash into line.[106]

However, on a deeper level more substantial matters were at stake. As we have seen, until 2002 Turkey's national policy on Cyprus was affixed on the secure assumption that the problem was settled in 1974 and all subsequent deliberations were geared toward legitimizing the de facto status quo. Within this framework, Denktash's negotiating trademark of setting preconditions constituted an intricate component of the rejectionist doctrine. However, the new AKP government viewed Denktash's "disturbing idiosyncrasy" and skepticism as symptomatic of the 1964 generation's "siege mentality"—which essentially was a micro manifestation of the "Sèvres syndrome." Viewed from this perspective, as Halil Ibrahim Salih notes, the tension between

Erdoğan and Denktash was substantially a clash over prevalence of Turkish national policy—and the pertinent question of whether to persist with *taksim* or adopt a new way of thinking.[107]

Immediately following the UN's failure to achieve an agreement at The Hague, the European Commission made it clear where its sympathies lay in relation to the Turkish Cypriot internal political divide. After confirming that Cyprus's accession would proceed as scheduled and encouraging all parties, Turkey in particular, to reconsider the Annan Plan, the Commission candidly expressed its "solidarity with all Cypriots," acknowledged the "courage with which the Turkish Cypriots have expressed their European convictions," and recommitted itself to supporting projects that reduced economic disparities and built confidence between the two communities.[108]

The EU strategy of elevating the Turkish Cypriot opposition was further boosted when the Greek prime minister toured EU capitals. He first visited Cyprus and met with Turkish Cypriot political leaders, reassuring them that all Cypriots would share in the benefits of accession and settlement. Addressing the plenary session of the Cypriot parliament, Simitis sent a message to Turkey, calling on it to change its policy on Cyprus, and essentially marginalized the nationalists. Simitis repeated his impression that the Green Line separated Ankara from Brussels.[109]

On June 3, 2003, the European Commission proposed a package of special financial and other measures to "bring northern Cyprus closer to the EU." The financial component of the package amounted to €12 million, of which €9 million were earmarked for economic development (such as infrastructure projects in Nicosia, Famagusta, and Kyrenia; support for small- and medium-sized enterprises; and feasibility studies on economic integration of the North with the EU). The remaining €3 million would fund civil society and social partners, seminars, the translation of the *acquis communautaire*, and finance selected visits by Turkish Cypriot groups to EU institutions. The package also included trade promotion, by which the Turkish Cypriot Chamber of Commerce would be authorized to issue movement certificates of goods from the north to the Republic of Cyprus ports in the south. Finally, in case of a settlement, the Commission promised an additional €206 million for 2004–2006.[110] Denktash criticized the aid package, especially the provision of export certificates, claiming this was a "clear attempt to undermine the sovereignty of the TRNC."[111]

As EU intervention promised to shift the contextual parameters of the conflict, the stage was set for a major UN peacemaking offensive in the form of the Annan solution.

The UN Annan Plan

"This Saturday, each one of you has a difficult decision to make—one that will determine the destiny of your country...There is no other plan out there. This is it."[112] With this statement, four days before their historic referenda, the UN Secretary-General sought to impress upon the Cypriots a sense of destiny, determinism, and urgency. Annan was convinced that, for the first time, all external and internal elements were in constellation. One of the main problems with previous UN efforts had been the inability to harmonize external developments with the "ripe" moment for instigating the Cyprus talks.[113]

Annan Plan: A "Ripe" Moment?

Prior to 1999, there was little progress in either the intercommunal negotiations or the conflict's context. The warming of Greek-Turkish relations in the late 1990s suggested once again that progress on the Cyprus conflict relied heavily on the fluctuating Greek-Turkish barometer. Nonetheless, the catalyst for this newfound optimism was the increasing role played by the EU in the Cyprus conflict. The continued worth of the EU's contribution to the peace process relied on its capacity to adjust the asymmetric relationships between the four main parties: namely, Greece/Greek Cypriots, Turkey/Turkish Cypriots.

For the first time since 1974, it appeared that Greece/Greek Cypriots had some influence, indeed leverage, over Turkey's European aspirations. The change in this dynamic provided the preconditions for shifting the various entrenched positions, attitudes, and behavior, sufficient at any rate to convince the UN Secretary-General to launch a new initiative.[114]

Annan's strategy rested on a four-pronged "linkage" approach: first, to utilize Cyprus and Turkey's EU accession as a "catalyst" for settlement/membership; second, to enlist the active support of the key external parties: the United States and the United Kingdom; third, to lock in the support of the motherlands, Greece and Turkey; fourth, to use these pathways to alter the entrenched positions of the two communities.[115] Parallel to this "game plan," the intercommunal negotiations, through a combination of proximity and direct talks, would continue deliberating in order to narrow the parties' core differences (that is, those relating to constitutional, territorial, and security matters).

With little progress at the intercommunal talks and confronted with "conflicting calendars," Kofi Annan submitted his "Basis for

Agreement on a Comprehensive Settlement of the Cyprus Problem" in November 2002. A number of factors convinced the Secretary-General that this was an opportune time to intervene: which included a change of government following the Turkish elections (November 3); the Greek Cypriot presidential campaign to elect a successor to Clerides (February 2003); Denktash's recovery from open-heart surgery; and, most importantly, the forthcoming Copenhagen European Summit set to finalize Cyprus's accession and to consider Turkey's candidature (December 12–13).[116]

The Annan initiative consisted of two interventions. The first took place between the tabling of the plan (November 11, 2002) and The Hague summit (March 10, 2003), and the second covered the period from January 2004 to the April 24, 2004 referendum. Procedurally, the initiative was interlinked with the EU's enlargement process that aimed at inducting a reunified Cyprus into the European Union. The interfaced UN-EU timetable entailed interim agreement deadlines to culminate in simultaneous, but separate, referenda of both communities (in the first attempt, the referenda were set sixteen days before the signing of the EU Accession Treaty, and it eventually took place a week before the formal accession of Cyprus). The Annan strategy also incorporated Greece and Turkey into the negotiations, initially at a track-two level[117] and later at the second phase of the February 13 Agreement process in Bürgenstock.[118]

The Annan Plan was first submitted to both sides on November 11, 2002 (Annan I), followed by revisions on December 10, 2002 (Annan II), February 26, 2003 (Annan III), and March 29 (Annan IV). The fifth and final draft, "The Comprehensive Settlement of the Cyprus Problem," was submitted on March 31, 2004 in Bürgenstock, Switzerland. On April 18, corrigenda and clarifications were incorporated into the March 31 text

Timing emerged as a critical, albeit bewildering, ingredient in the Annan initiative, by pegging its deadlines against those of key EU decision-making dates. Three alternative EU-centric turning-points presented themselves. The first aimed at an agreement leading to the Copenhagen summit in December 2002. Despite failure to meet the December 2002 deadline, the Secretary-General's Special Adviser on Cyprus, Alvaro de Soto, declared that the parties had "never been closer" to agreement and that "the opportunity remained" for a "reunited Cyprus to accede to the European Union."[119] The second timeline anticipated a referenda/agreement prior to the signing of the Treaty of Accession on April 16, 2003 in Athens. The original intention was for separate and simultaneous referenda to take place among both communities on March 30, and toward that end the Secretary-General visited Cyprus on February 26–28 to lend weight to the final stage of the negotiations. Annan's "game plan," however, was complicated by a change of leadership in the Greek Cypriot community, as DIKO's Tassos Papadopoulos, backed by AKEL and EDEK, defeated Clerides at the presidential elections, therefore making Cyprus's formal accession, set for May 1, 2004, the third viable alternative deadline.

Despite high expectations of a major policy shift by the newly elected AKP government, Annan's first attempt collapsed. After the failure of Annan's first initiative at The Hague on March 10–11, 2003, the looming Iraq crisis shifted Turkey's regional and international attention away from Cyprus. The EU Commissioner for Enlargement, Verheugen, labeled Cyprus the "first casualty" of the Iraq war,[120] as it altered Greece's and especially Turkey's national priorities.

Beyond Track-One diplomacy, however, significant shifts were occurring within the Turkish/Turkish Cypriot dynamic. The challenge to the Kemalist establishment in Turkey began to alter the sociopolitical parameters in Northern Cyprus. Turkish Cypriot dissenters felt they could challenge Denktash's political hegemony. Pro-unification/anti-Denktash mobilizations sustained themselves throughout the year and fed into the domestic election campaign (December 14, 2003). The election result was a moral victory for the opposition parties but produced a "hung" parliament, comprising the pro- and anti–status quo parties. Eventually, Ankara compelled opposition leader Mehmet Ali Talat to form a coalition with Serdat Denktash's DP.

Despite declaring that it was the "end of the road" for his three-year Cyprus initiative,[121] by January 2004 Annan was ready to "resume negotiations"—cryptically alluding to his forthcoming meeting with Turkey's prime minister.[122] As seen above, changes in Turkish/Turkish Cypriot politics provided the impetus for the third deadline prior to Cyprus formally joining the EU. At their bilateral meeting on January 24, 2004, on the margins of the Davos World Economic Forum, Erdoğan made clear "his government's strong desire for the Turkish Cypriots to resume talks with the Greek Cypriots with a view of resolving outstanding issues by 1 May."[123]

Competing for attention with the looming Iraq crisis, Annan persevered with Cyprus during his meetings with European leaders, convinced of Turkey's willingness to "play a [proactive] role in the negotiation."[124] After consulting with the Greek government and the

Greek Cypriot leader, on February 4, 2004 Annan invited the Greek and Turkish Cypriot leaders to New York to "resume negotiations on the basis of his settlement plan," with the aim of putting "a completed text to referenda in April 2004, in time for a reunited Cyprus to accede to the European Union on 1 May." He also invited Greece, Turkey, and the United Kingdom to the table.[125]

The centrality of the New York summit cannot be underestimated, as it set "the ground rules of how to proceed and agree on a work programme" to conclude the process by May 1.[126] Heralding the significance of the impending summit, Annan declared that the "Cypriot people [would] have a historic opportunity to unify their country and enter the European Union together."[127] The Secretary-General declared at his press conference that although "[w]e have not yet solved the [Cyprus] problem…I really believe that, after 40 years, a political settlement is at last in reach." After three days of intense negotiations in New York, Denktash and Papadopoulos agreed, along with the three guarantor powers, to a three-stage process.

The February 13 agreement entailed that in the first stage the two leaders would negotiate in "good faith," on the basis of the Annan Plan, to agree on a finalized text by March 22, 2004, which would be put to a referendum before May 1. If they failed to reach an agreement, the process would be broadened, and Annan would convene a summit that included the participation of Greece and Turkey to reach agreement on the finalized text by March 29. If there was still no agreement, then "as a final resort" the parties authorized the UN Secretary-General to use his "discretion to finalize the text to be submitted to referenda."[128]

Both sides failed to agree to a finalized text by March 22, and the process moved to the next level. Reminiscent of the Lancaster House summit of 1959—which gave birth to the Republic of Cyprus[129]—negotiations moved to phase two, with Annan inviting the two parties and the guarantor powers to the Bürgenstock hotel outside Lucerne, Switzerland, on March 24. The summit was attended by Papadopoulos (flanked by the Greek Cypriot political leadership), Talat and Serdar Denktash, who had been authorized by Denktash to represent the Turkish Cypriot community, Greece and Turkey's foreign ministers Petros Molyviatis and Gül (later joined by prime ministers Kostas Karamanlis and Erdoğan), and EU Enlargement Commissioner Verheugen present in an observer-assistant capacity. The negotiations became convoluted, as direct talks were not possible and UN mediation "shuttled" between the two sides. Unable to secure an agreement, the process moved to phase three, and "close to midnight on 31 March 2004" Annan finalized the plan to be submitted for referendum.[130]

The Annan V Plan

The Annan Plan was a complex and comprehensive document comprising the foundation agreement with five appendices (constituent state constitutions, treaty matters, a draft act of EU accession, matters for UN Security Council decision, and measures for April 2004). The essence of the "Comprehensive Settlement of the Cyprus Problem" was located in the main articles of the foundation agreement and detailed in nine annexes (constitution, constitutional laws, federal laws, agreements between federal government and constituent states, list of international treaties, territorial arrangements, treatment of property affected by events since 1963, reconciliation commission, and coming into being of the new state of affairs).[131]

The Annan Plan committed both sides, as cofounders of the 1960 Republic of Cyprus, to a set of principles that renewed their bizonal partnership, renounced the violence of the past, and acknowledged that their "relationship [was] not one of majority and minority but of political equality." The foundation agreement purported to usher in a "new state of affairs" in which the 1960 treaties (establishment, guarantee, alliance) would *mutatis muntandis* apply to the new construct— excluding the British Sovereign Base Areas. Cyprus would sustain its special ties with Greece and Turkey, and as a member of the EU it would support Turkey's accession.

The United Cyprus Republic (UCR), as the new construct would be known, would comprise two equal constituent states, the Greek Cypriot State and the Turkish Cypriot State, with a single international personality. Federalism would be based on the Swiss model. There would be a single Cypriot citizenship, as well as an "internal constituent state citizenship," limiting Greek and Turkish nationals to 5 percent of their respective ethno-constituent state for 19 years—or until Turkey joined the EU. There would also be a five-year residency moratorium for persons hailing from the other state, and thereafter an incremental percentage limitation (6 percent of a village or municipality for 6–9 years, 12 percent for 10–14 years, and 18 percent until the 19th year or Turkeys' accession to the EU). As of the second year there would be no restriction to former inhabitants over 65 years and their partners or siblings.

The federal government would comprise two chambers, a Senate and a Chamber of Deputies, each with forty-eight members. There would be equal representation of Greek and Turkish Cypriots in the Senate, and proportional representation in the Chamber of Deputies with a minimal threshold of one-fourth heralding from each state. Decisions would require approval of both chambers by simple majority, requiring one-fourth senators from each state. A special majority of two-fifths from each state would be required in the Senate on specified matters.

Executive power would be exercised by a Presidential Council where the powers of Head of State was vested. The Council would comprise of six members elected from a "single list" by a senatorial special majority and a simple majority from the Deputy Chambers with at least one-third from each state. Decisions would be taken by simple majority, provided it was supported by at least one member from each state. Foreign affairs and EU affairs would not be allocated to members from the same state. The Council would elect two members from each state as president and vice-president to rotate every twelve months.

On security and military matters, the Treaty of Guarantee would be extended to cover the "territorial integrity, security, and constitutional order of the constituent states." Under the Treaty of Alliance, Greek and Turkish contingents would be stationed in Cyprus and would be phased out over time (6,000 until 2011; 3,000 until 2018 or Turkey's accession to the EU; and thereafter the Greek contingent would remain at 950 and the Turkish contingent at 650, subject to review in three years). A Monitoring Committee would be established to oversee security and military matters, comprising the guarantor powers, federal and state governments, and chaired by the UN. Besides an extended UN peacekeeping mission, all other military forces would be dissolved. Cypriot territory would not be used for international military purposes without the consent of the two states and, until Turkey joined the EU, of Greece and Turkey. Half the cost of the UN operation would be absorbed by the United Cyprus Republic during the first three years and two-thirds thereafter, which is to be reviewed in 2010.

As seen in Map 5.1 below, territorial adjustments pertaining to the boundaries between the two states would take place in a transitional six-phase period lasting forty-two months. According to the UN Secretary-General, these readjustments would allow the return of 86,000 (54 percent) Greek Cypriot refugees to their ancestral homelands and entail the return of Varosha and Morphou.[132]

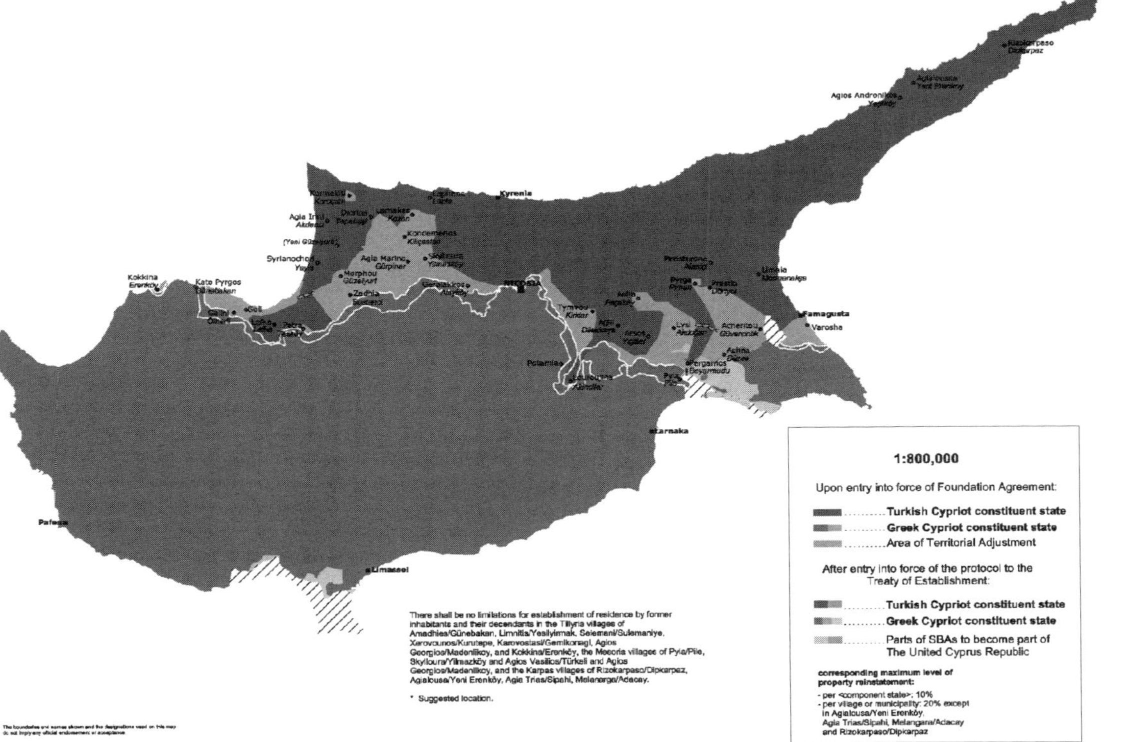

Map 5.1   Annan Map 2004

Source: United Nations, Map of Cyprus (Plan at a glance), 2004.

Concerning property claims, the agreement stipulated that they be "resolved in a comprehensive manner" on the basis of respecting the rights of the "dispossessed owners," the "current users," and the "principle of bizonality." All property claims would be dealt with by an independent Property Board. Property claims that lay outside the territorial adjustments would be resolved by reinstatement or compensation. Those who opted for compensation would be compensated immediately. All other dispossessed owners were entitled to one-third of the value and the area of their total property, and for compensation for the remaining two-thirds. For those who sought reinstatement, there was a series of options and arrangements, from outright reinstatement of their property to purchase by current users who had made "significant improvements" to the property. No current user would be required to vacate any property until alternative accommodation was made available to them. Finally, compensation claims and liabilities lodged prior to the agreement would "be dealt with by the constituent state from which the claimant hail[ed]."

To facilitate and promote intercommunal dialogue and understanding, a reconciliation commission would be established comprising an equal number of members from both states, with a non-Cypriot head appointed by the UN Secretary-General.

As mentioned before, the Annan Plan was unlike previous proposals in that it integrated the EU in settlement process and content. In addition to utilizing the EU accession as a "trigger," the EU served as a source of security, a mechanism for reducing Turkey's involvement in the island's affairs, and for guaranteeing Cyprus's (bicommunal-bizonal) exceptionalism.

"A United Cyprus in a United Europe"?

To comprehend the extent to which the EU had penetrated the Cyprus conflict and become an integral part of a political settlement, one need only examine the 192 pages of the Annan Plan (foundation agreement). From the outset, settlement was linked to Cyprus's EU accession, as illustrated by the text of the referendum that asked all Cypriots:

> Do you approve the Foundation Agreement with all its Annexes, as well as the Constitution of the Greek Cypriot/Turkish Cypriot constituent state and the provisions as to its laws to be in force, *to bring into being a new state of affairs in which Cyprus joins the European Union united?* Yes/No (my emphasis).[133]

Regulating the accession of Cyprus, the Annan package included a protocol, to be attached to the EU-Cyprus Accession Treaty, which—as with the document in its entirety—sought to reconcile two fundamentally conflicting political approaches: on one hand, to safeguard the human and civil rights of individual citizens, as enshrined in the European *acquis communautaire*;[134] and on the other hand, the basic tenets of a bizonal-bicommunal federal system that had underpinned the intercommunal negotiations since the mid-1970s. As a legal document and a product of political bargaining, the Annan Plan sought to bridge and minimize the divergence between the two parties. Leaving aside for a moment criticism of the UN's "win-lose" negotiating *modus operandi*, success or failure of the Annan Plan would be judged on its capacity to propel—or at least not thwart—the evolution of an ethnically integrated, nondiscriminatory polity in the future.

The 2004 Referendum and the "Ferment of Rejectionism"

Once Annan finalized his plan, the "time for negotiation [was] over, the time for decision and action [had] arrive[d]."[135] Echoing his chief, de Soto declared on April 24 that it was "now in the hands of the [Cypriot] people" to decide.[136]

While major shifts on the Turkish side saw Denktash sidelined by the AKP government and Talat campaigning vigorously for the "Evet" (yes) vote, attention focused on tribulations within the Greek Cypriot community. AKEL's General-Secretary Demetris Christofias termed the prevailing climate within the Greek Cypriot community leading to the referendum as a "ferment of rejectionism," which was being exploited by the nationalists who led the "No" campaign. As the campaign unfolded, ethno-nationalist forces in both Greek and Turkish Cypriot civil society found themselves in unison over their rejection of the Annan Plan.[137]

Rejectionists from both sides had been most vocal and effective in mobilizing against the UN plan. The rejectionists' advantage was primarily due to the fact that they played a politics of fear, uncertainty, and insecurity, appealing to groups such as the Greek Cypriot refugees who would not return to their homelands, and Turkish Cypriots and Anatolian settlers who would be relocated/resettled and possibly disadvantaged by the Annan Plan.[138] The mood of rejection was especially strong among the Greek Cypriot community who, with EU accession, considered they would be in a more advantageous negotiating position with the option of improving whatever settlement was being offered.[139]

Unlike the Greek Cypriots, Turkish Cypriot dissent was nurtured by the lack of alternatives and, as seen previously, by the dire future prospects for their community. The contrasting circumstances facing both communities leading up to the 2004 referendum helps explain why there had been no equivalent pro-settlement/pro-EU/pro-Annan Plan mobilization in the Greek Cypriot community.

The Greek Cypriot anti-Annan coalition comprised of diverse and unlikely allies. In addition to AKEL, it included the New Horizons and Cyprus Green minor parties, ultranationalist student and youth factions, local refugee and missing persons associations, the Cyprus Orthodox Church, public scholars such as Andreas Theophanous, Panayiotis Ifaistos, Van Coufoudakis, and Stephanos Konstantinidis, the "pan-Cyprian Citizens" Movement, renegade parliamentarians from DISY (who later formed EUROKO, *Evropaiko Komma* [European Party]), EDEK, Greek politicians and ex-ministers, the Greek Communist Party (*Kommounistiko Komma Ellados* [KKE]), the Archbishop of Greece, the *Simerini* newspaper, and most Greek and Greek Cypriot diasporic organizations.

There were also notable exceptions to this group, such as the Bishop of Morphou Neofitos, who castigated the church for its lack of vision and compassion during a time of uncertainty.[140] He joined the ranks of an equally diverse grouping of Greek Cypriots who supported the Annan Plan, such as DISY, EDI (*Enomemoi Dimokrates* [United Democrats]), former presidents Clerides and Vassiliou, the *Politis* newspaper, bicommunal and rapprochement NGOs, Simitis, George A. Papandreou, Takis Hadjidemetriou, AKEL ministers and high-ranking figures, public scholars, business figures, and intellectuals.

Besides UN, EU, U.S., and British officials, other foreign dignitaries tried to sway Cypriots in favor of the plan, including the former President of Finland, the UN envoy and EU negotiator Martti Ahtisaari, and the former foreign minister of Australia Gareth Evans, from the International Crisis Group. In a joint letter, they argued that in comparison to recent European precedents, the Annan Plan had three advantages: it addressed in a complete (if not satisfactory) way, the refugee and property issues; it "convincingly" dealt with demilitarization; and the structure of government was workable in terms of EU membership. It warned that rejection would "mean years of further stalemate" and contained a massage directed at the Greek Cypriots that international sympathy would be "nonexistent" for the side that rejected the plan.[141]

Three weeks before the referendum, the European Council underscored its strong preference for a united Cyprus to join the EU, reiterating its "strong support" for the Annan Plan, reassuring the parties that it would accommodate the terms of a settlement within its own aquis, and that it would hold an international donors conference.[142] Equally, the EU's High Representative for the Common Foreign and Security Policy Javier Solana joined the list of international celebrities to declare that "1 May marks Cyprus's date with Europe." He further stated, "On April 24, Cypriots have a date with themselves," reassuring them that Europe would be there to assist in reconstruction, construction, freedom and justice, security, and solidarity.[143] The British Helsinki Human Rights Group warned, however, that such "outside" intrusion "to influence the outcome of the referendum" was counterproductive.[144]

As with the Turkish Cypriot community, Greek Cypriot civil society was divided over the Annan Plan, and since its first appearance, there had been an intense anti-Annan Plan campaign against both the 2003 and 2004 referendum junctures. According to the various privately commissioned opinion polls, the anti-Annan campaign made a lot of headway: polls consistently indicated that a majority of Greek Cypriots, during both cycles of the Annan initiative, were against the plan as it stood. During the first Annan attempt, for example, the newspaper *Politis* polled 52 percent on November 17, 2002, with this figure rising only a week later to 68 percent. *Simerini*'s poll, published on December 11, 2002, counted 86 percent for rejection. In its online polling in late March 2003, the Web site European-Cyprus. net polled, 53 percent against and 47 percent for the Annan Plan as a basis for solution.[145]

During the second Annan attempt, opinion polls continued to reflect this trend. Polling by the Research and Development Centre, Intercollege, for the newspaper *Simerini*, which was conducted during the last week of February 2004, showed that 54 percent were against the Annan Plan, with just 11 percent in favor, and 34 percent undecided.[146] Likewise, the poll conducted by Ray Consultants for the newspaper *Phileleftheros* during the same period recorded a higher negative response toward the Annan Plan, with 62 percent against and only 24 percent in favor. The newspaper clarified that the "no" vote was likely to shift in the case that the president, the Greek government, and the party they supported took an open stand on the referendum.[147] Polling during the same period by the Communications Services Bureau (CSB) for the Greek newspaper *Paron* found 61 percent against the plan, 27 percent in favor, and 12 percent undecided.[148] AC Nielsen's two polls for *Politis* found during the third week of February that 40 percent were against, 31 percent were in favor, and

29 percent were undecided. This shifted in the first week of March when Nielsen's poll found that the "no" vote jumped by 13 percent to 53 percent.[149] Even if Papadopoulos supported the "Yes" case, 57 percent would still have voted against the Annan Plan, according to a pan-Cyprian poll a month prior to the vote.[150]

More revealing was Metron Analysis's polling conducted between April 2 and 6 in Nicosia (both sides), Istanbul, and Athens. It found that among the Greek Cypriots in Nicosia, 73 percent were against the plan, while in Athens 64 percent considered it unacceptable. In Istanbul, public opinion was divided, with 37 percent in favor and 37 percent against. Only in northern (Turkish) Nicosia were matters clearer, with 66 percent supporting the plan. Equally disconcerting was the Greek Cypriot response to the question of whether the Annan Plan was the last opportunity to reunify the island, and the alternative was partition and a two-state solution: only 44 percent opted for the former.[151]

Reasons Behind the Failure of the Annan Initiative

Just as a more active civil society was key in the transformation of political consciousness in Northern Cyprus—leading to Turkish Cypriot acceptance (64.9 percent) of the Annan Plan—it proved equally important, but to the opposite effect, in the Greek Cypriot rebuff of the Secretary-General's blueprint (75.8 percent). Complacently believing that Greek Cypriots supported Annan's plan, third parties were taken by surprise when most of their political leadership, spearheaded by President Tassos Papadopoulos in his declaration of April 7, 2004, called for a resounding "no" vote at the referendum for its failing to "satisfy the minimum targets" set by the Greek Cypriot side. Uncertainty facing the Greek Cypriots with the disbanding of the Republic of Cyprus, exasperation at Turkey's insufficient troop reduction and international guarantees, the workability of the state, the financial burden to the Greek Cypriots, and the safeguarding of the rights of the citizens underlined Papadopoulos's conviction that the negative consequences resulting from a "yes" vote far outweighed those from a "no" vote. Not convinced of the sustainability of a federal state, Papadopoulos was not prepared to disband the Republic of Cyprus. Visibly moved and with a sense of destiny, he stated that he "did not receive a State . . . to deliver a 'Community.' "[152]

There had been much criticism of the Greek Cypriot community over its rejection of the Annan Plan at the referendum. Despite repeated claims that the Greek Cypriots were rejecting a particular plan and not the reunification of the island or a federal settlement, the huge international political capital accrued by the Greek Cypriots since 1974 was severely depleted. On one level, as far as Western and international opinion was concerned, Greek Cypriot rejection of the Annan Plan absolved Turkey's 1974 invasion and nullified their sharp moral stance regarding the demographic partition of the island.

Closer scrutiny reveals that the international community had been naive, given that all opinion polls had most Greek Cypriots rejecting Annan's plan consistently since it appeared in November 2002. Despite strenuous efforts by third parties, this opposition did not waver prior to the referendum. Greek Cyprus's resounding rejection of the Annan Plan opened up an existential debate that transcended the conventional constitutional discourse associated with the Cyprus problem. The debate grappled with Greek Cypriots' relationship with their community, the way they saw themselves and the "Other," and the question of federalism. There is no intellectual shortcut to explain Greek Cypriot behavior. The reasons that the Annan initiative failed need to be addressed on two interconnected but distinct levels: the immediate causes and those attributed to middle- and longer-term factors.

Greek Cypriot rejectionism rested on a combination of historical and contemporary factors. Until Papadopoulos's rejection, the Greek Cypriot leadership, confronted with a long-standing dilemma, was divided over the Annan Plan. This split resonated with the overall anxiety that beset the Greek Cypriots, especially as they realized the inevitability of a deadline decision, while they were comforted by the certainty of EU accession.

This angst was epitomized by AKEL's contradictory position: they initially supported the "yes" case, then sought a postponement, only to support the "no" vote two days prior to the referendum. AKEL found itself caught between its historical legacy as the principle rapprochement institution in Cyprus and the "yes/no" imposition of an unconvincing settlement. Division and confusion began to spread among its leading cadres. This ambiguity was also exemplified in the opposing stands adopted by AKEL's two media outlets: the *Haravghi* newspaper opposed the plan while the radio station *Astra* advocated a "yes" vote. This division carried through to the party's chief decision-making organs, with AKEL's Politburo voting ten to four in support of the Annan Plan on April 6—Christofias abstained—while the Central Committee on April 10 recommended postponing the referendum. Finally, AKEL's pan-Cyprian congress, considering the sense of insecurity prevalent within the Greek Cypriot community and the plan's negative elements, called on the United Nations to "postpone the referenda for a few months," otherwise AKEL would have no choice but to oppose the Anna plan.[153]

Supporters of the plan were unable to counter the anti-Annan lobby effectively, and were initially hamstrung by Papadopoulos government's noncommittal stance, as indicated by its refusal to engage in a public information campaign. Rather, the Republic of Cyprus spokesperson considered public education the responsibility of the political parties.[154] Papadopoulos's intervention reinforced the adversarial (rather than dialogic) atmosphere prevailing among the Greek Cypriots. The majority of Greek Cypriots approached the referendum not as the beginning of a new era of collaboration, peace, and prosperity, but rather as a rearguard defense to safeguard their sovereignty and identity. Intervention by foreign dignitaries to influence the vote only exacerbated the situation and had the opposite effect.

The role of individuals cannot be underestimated in relation to Cyprus. Until 2003, Denktash was the most powerful person in the Cyprus conflict. Nevertheless, both Clerides and Denktash, who negotiated the bulk of the Annan Plan and took contrary positions to their respective communities, failed to realize the shift in public opinion and grasp the deeper socioeconomic dynamics at play, which ultimately determined the result of the referenda. The Greek Cypriot journalist Makarios Droushiotis held Clerides and Papadopoulos responsible for the Cyprus impasse, despite the fact that they came from two opposing schools (pragmatists and militants): Clerides, for "never prepar[ing] society for a solution" during his tenure, and Papadopoulos for not recognizing the "historic confluence of 2004" and negotiating assertively for a solution at a time when the external powers wanted to dispense with the Cyprus problem.[155]

Underpinning the quandary was the political and economic transformations that had transpired in both communities since the 1980s. Greek Cypriot prosperity rendered any economic incentive associated with the Annan Plan superfluous, and elevated security and functionality to their prime concerns. The risks associated with the proposal, in conjunction with reassurance from EU membership, entrenched the status quo. In contrast, Turkish Cypriot dissent was nurtured by the lack of alternatives and the dire future prospects for their community. The political and electoral ascendancy of the integrationist forces became possible only after a power shift among Turkish Cypriot (business) elites and the political and economic transformations away from the nationalist orientation of *taksim*.[156]

An assessment of the factors that undermined success suggests that, despite ample evidence to the contrary, the Secretary-General and others seriously miscalculated Greek Cypriot public opinion. In addition to being wedded to a timeline with predetermined goals, the negotiating process left little room for review. Its failure rested on three additional key errors of judgment.

First, the mediators failed to take into account the Greek Cypriots' historical dilemma over a federal solution. Skepticism over federalism had been prevalent among Greek Cypriots since its reluctant acceptance as a compromise toward reunification. New generations of Greek Cypriots, detached from the sentimentalities of 1974 and empowered by their newly acquired class status, questioned the intrinsic benefits of federalism. Greek Cypriot class reconfiguration also caused a challenge to the idea of bicommunal "equality," both in principle and practice, that permeated all constitutional federal arrangements. Greek Cypriots had always been uneasy with the concept of "equality," on the basis of their numerical superiority but also because of their sense of being the indigenous inhabitants of Cyprus. Their changing social-economic status caused them to question the benefit of federalism as a second-best solution. As one demonstrator wearing an "OXI" (No) t-shirt confidently exclaimed during the referendum: we "are no longer prisoners within the compromise zone."

Second, by interacting exclusively with the political elite, the mediators created a communicative comfort zone at the expense of identifying and engaging with their potential detractors. In this regard, they failed to gauge the patriotic attachment of many Greek Cypriots to the Republic of Cyprus. At a psychological level, the referendum was a test to affirm the Republic of Cyprus's legitimacy, which had eluded it since its inception.

On a broader level, the referendum saw a realignment of the two ideological forces that shaped Cypriot nationalism, Greek ethnonationalism and Cypriotism, along a rigid rejectionist fault line. Unlike previous altercations, the Annan referendum polarized Cypriot politics and society in a way reminiscent of the EOKA-B period during the 1970s. Ironically, the fiercest advocates of the Republic of Cyprus during the "No" campaign were those same militant *enosist* elements who prior to 1974 had striven to eliminate it—they had considered the Republic of Cyprus as an *ektroma* (abortion) of the Zurich-London regime and the tombstone of *enosis*.

Third, mediators overestimated the capacity of bicommunal groups to shift Greek Cypriot attitudes and behavior. The presumption that the same strategy that convinced the Turkish Cypriots would work with the Greek Cypriots revealed a fundamental misreading of Cypriot civil society and the conflict's internal dynamics. In this respect, the optimism of the opening of the Green Line in 2003 proved misplaced. The expectation that crossing-over would act as a catalyst to unleash a surge of people's power (akin to the collapse of the Berlin Wall) did not eventuate. Although construction of an intercommunal communicative space—a corridor of dialogue or a peace zone—is vital for the formulation of commonalities, the psychological imperative of overcoming the "incest barrier" has led to a transgression of attitudes.[157] After the initial enthusiasm to visit their lost homelands subsided, "checkpoint syndrome" contributed to rather than reduced (Greek) Cypriot rejectionism. As anthropologist Rebecca Bryant claims, crossing-over reconfirmed for Turkish Cypriot refugees from the south the finality of their predicament, while for Greek Cypriot refugees it reinforced their denial of the "new realities" emanating from 1974.[158]

Positive Outcomes of the Annan Strategy

Despite its weaknesses, the Annan initiative did have some positive effects. It served as a catalyst for radical change in the Turkish Cypriot leadership—sidelining Denktash. For the first time, both constituencies were forced to debate the future solution of the Cyprus problem. This, in turn, impacted on the two largest Greek Cypriot parties. The right-wing DISY split over the referendum, with the party endorsing the "yes" campaign, while the left-wing AKEL, as seen above, opted for a "soft no." The opposing positions of AKEL and the CTP elevated intercommunal dialogue to a more pragmatic level, where differences rather than commonalities were accentuated. The ensuing debate exposed the differences *within* each side, allowing the other side to observe, firsthand, internal divisions and disagreements. In its post-Annan incarnation, this fluidity promises to lend itself to cross-communal ideological trends by forging new political alliances and configurations beyond the traditional ethno-nationalist and Left-Right demarcation.[159]

The net effect in terms of conflict resolution was to dispel misconceptions regarding monolithic or one-dimensional attitudes on both sides. The pressure to repudiate intransigent (negotiating) behavior resulted in the lifting of travel restrictions over the Green Line, thus allowing for contact and interaction between Greek and Turkish Cypriots on a critical mass scale.[160] It remains to be seen whether the border opening constitutes an event capable of transforming the psychological configuration of the conflict. However, it has managed to break open the ubiquitous status quo in Cyprus, ushering—by default rather than design—changes incomprehensible to state-centric perception. The plan introduced another layer of communication to those dominated by the elites.

The Annan project gave the previously marginalized Turkish Cypriot civil society a new lease of life and created the conditions for joint collaboration. The referenda provided the Greek and Turkish Cypriot "yes" campaigns with the opportunity to collaborate and share resources and knowledge, and in doing so, create a collective memory and identity. The UN's mediating efforts showed that Greece and Turkey were amenable to formulating mutually supportive policies, and that a solution to the Cyprus problem was largely predicated on domestic developments in Turkey. Finally, the UN exercise introduced the EU as an indispensable component in the Cyprus equation.

What Prevented the Annan Strategy from Succeeding?

An in-depth analysis reveals that, in addition to the above reasons, the Annan initiative stumbled on the same cluster of factors that plagued previous mediating efforts.

Synchronizing external and internal processes proved once again elusive, and this ultimately frustrated an outcome. By interfacing the negotiating process with the EU-Cyprus accession calendar, Annan installed a definitive timeline as a mechanism to counter the cycle of indecision. In retrospect, the Annan "deadline" proved counterproductive, because it did not allow sufficient time for the new Turkish Cypriot leadership to adapt to the new conditions and (re)establish its working relationship with the AKEL. As mentioned above, the Annan strategy also rested on a flawed appraisal of the Greek Cypriot community and the assumption that the Greek government, as in the Turkish case, could influence its community's political behavior. Failure to differentiate the two sets of relationships and devise appropriate strategies was a grave miscalculation. Situational factors were also a crucial factor in the failure of the Annan initiative. The change of governments in Greece and, in particular, the Republic of Cyprus resulted in a diminished sense of ownership, in terms of both process and outcome, on the part of the new leaderships.

Closer scrutiny of Greek Cypriot politics reveals that Papadopoulos's rejectionism rested on three main factors: first, the revival of the hard-line militants and its diversification beyond traditional ideological constraints; second, the capacity of the "no" coalition to tap successfully into the population's uncertainty and insecurity; and third, securing EU accession boosted the sense among Greek Cypriots that they were in an advantageous negotiating position. Nevertheless, it does not follow that Papadopoulos was solely to blame for the "no" vote. Such an assessment is as naive as accosting Denktash exclusively for Turkish Cypriot detestation for unification prior to 2003 and fails to take into account the underlying causes of Greek Cypriot rejection. In essence, the Annan strategy failed to reassure the Greek Cypriots about their security concerns (troop reduction and guarantees) and satisfactorily address their emotional attachment to land (regarding property exchange and territorial adjustments). Reforms that aspire to usher in a new state of affairs require both popular legitimacy and a groundswell of support. Although the referendum became the apex for the Turkish Cypriot "quiet" revolution, this was not the case for their compatriots in the south. In campaigning terms, this reflected the inability of a third force in Cypriot politics to counter the excesses of ethno-nationalism.

The absence of the subjective factor in generating a spirit of commonality meant that there was no momentum in the final stages of the negotiating process to reach a settlement. Rather, confronted with a political dilemma, the majority of Greek Cypriots opted for the certainty of the status quo. Inevitably, failure of the referendum has been blamed on political and situational causes, but a deeper scrutiny reveals that polarization is a by-product of the negotiating culture. The way the negotiations were conducted and the proposals were framed reinforced communalism at the expense of individualism (for example, by stressing communal quotas, resettlement limitations, separate elections, and property rights). This is best illustrated by those provisions in the Annan Plan that restrict individuals' legal recourse, both domestically and through the European Court of Human Rights, in pursuing their property rights independent of the Cyprus Property Board.[161]

Finally, another factor contributing to the failure of the Annan initiative has to do with the EU's own inability to devise and pursue a consistent Cyprus policy. This is symptomatic of the EU's broader problem, namely, that the competing (and conflicting) interests of its member-states often render it incapable of constructing a common foreign and defense policy. The EU's internal difficulties meant that the EU itself became a larger arena within which the Cyprus conflict would be played out.

Compounded by its dilemma over whether settlement should be a precondition for Cyprus's accession, the EU failed in two important respects: first, by not dispelling Greek Cypriot hubris over unconditional accession, including its misplaced reliance on *acquis communautaire*; and second, being unable to offer itself as an alternative security source on both the macro and micro levels.[162]

Conclusion

Even though it was applied in what were especially favorable conditions, the Annan Plan offered a timely reminder that intercommunal negotiations, first-track diplomacy, and UN mediation—important as their contribution might be, both individually and collectively—were nevertheless inadequate. They were by themselves unable to overcome the constraints that steadfastly prevented the resolution of the Cyprus conflict. There appeared to be a missing link that prevented progress at the peace talks from resonating at either inter- or intra- communal relations.

A major problem contributing to the inadequacy of Annan's negotiating approach, not solely as a problem-solving mechanism, was the lack of effective communication. For reasons outlined above, the absence of a multifaceted communicative framework encompassing different agents and modes of interaction meant that the intercommunal talks (and their state participants) tended to monopolize the peace process. The systemic control of communication flows impacted on the conflict in two profound ways. The physical separation and isolation of the two communities from each other created, over time, a "fish-bowl" effect allowing the adversarial culture prevalent at previous intercommunal negotiations to permeate the societal spectrum of their relationship. Separatism and threat perception created a bipolar siege mentality that simultaneously deterred interactive processes between the two communities and reinforced the dominance of state-centric communalism over civil society.

Another related dilemma stemmed from the cultural development of group-identity socialization in colonial and postcolonial Cyprus. The inability of Cypriot public policy to distinguish between ethnic identity and political citizenship as well as between communalism and individualism hindered the emergence of an integrative civic nationalism.[163]

This said, regardless of the future evolution of the Cyprus problem, there can be little doubt that the Annan Plan has left an indelible mark on the island's political, social, and psychological landscape—including the Christofias-Talat direct negotiations launched in September 2008. (Demetris Christofias was elected President of the Republic of Cyprus and de facto leader of the Greek Cypriot community, defeating main rivals Tassos Papadopoulos and Ioannis Kassoulides in February 2008.) An analysis of the Annan initiative suggests that its most important legacy will be the EU's impact on the various primary actors. For decades, the obstacle to reaching a comprehensive settlement of the Cyprus problem has been the lack of movement on the part of the main parties, and especially from the Turkish side. Furthermore, the UN's peace enterprise also provided us with valuable lessons: changes in the external circumstances, whether planned or situational, can have a catalytic effect on a peace process, if these changes permeate through to domestic (inter- and intra-communal) relations. By introducing these new features into the conflict, in conjunction with broader internal and external changes, the Annan initiate inadvertently positioned Cyprus at the crossroads of transition. As a key new element, EU-ization/Europeanization of the Cyprus triangle offers a "unique historical process" to securitize the conflict across its various levels, groups, and sectors.[164]

A series of opinion surveys conducted by the Eurobarometer between 2004 and 2007 revealed that most Cypriots trusted the EU more than, or at least as much as, they trusted the United Nations. Such a positive image derived from the EU's perceived capacity to make Greek Cypriots feel safer (72 percent) whilst promising to deliver economic and political stability to the Turkish Cypriots (52 percent).[165] Although the propensity to view the EU as the panacea gave way to more realistic expectations, the opinion surveys are indicative of the EU's permanent rather than transitory role in the conflict. However, the EU's main contribution is likely to materialize in the middle to long term. Its success or failure would be judged in terms of its capacity to stabilize the (Greece-Turkey-Cyprus) subregion and to make the contextual relationship collaborative rather than adversarial. In addition, the EU's role in Cyprus's post-settlement phase would need to eradicate any residual resentment from disenfranchised groups and ensure that unresolved issues pertaining to civil liberties and past injustices are satisfactorily resolved, whilst providing all Cypriots with an enhanced sense of security.

Ultimately, Europeanization's success or failure depends on the extent to which this process is likely to have a *denationalizing* effect on both Greek Cypriot and Turkish nationalisms. If sustained in the longer term, Europeanization of the conflict would have a beneficial and transformative effect on the principal parties to the conflict so long as participation and interaction with EU instrumentalities, forums, and institutions were sensitively guided and sustained.

For any future peace initiative to have any chance of success, it is necessary to embrace a new negotiating paradigm and perhaps a new mediation model—one that is able to link domestic, regional, and international developments—and skillfully synchronize them with the core intercommunal negotiations. The implementation of such an approach also requires an appropriate third-party strategy—one that has political leverage, provides incentives to all parties, and commands legitimacy. The European Union might be able to perform such a mediating role so long as it complemented and reinforced, rather than replaced, the United Nations. One thing is certain: the intrusion of the EU into the Cyprus triangle is now a permanent fixture of the Cyprus conflict, offering all parties a common stage on which to deliberate their future relations. Whether a two-pronged mediation strategy of the kind envisaged here could produce the desired result, and whether the two communities themselves and Greece and, in particular, Turkey had the political will and leadership to support such a strategy, only time will tell.

Conclusion:
"And bring all Cyprus Comfort"[1]

When in 2001 Ibrahim Aziz filed a suit against the Republic of Cyprus and its three guarantor powers at the European Court of Human Rights (ECHR), one could have been forgiven for imagining that EU-ization was to empower the citizenry against the ubiquitous communal state.[2] Five years earlier, Titina Loizidou won a landmark lawsuit against Turkey for denying her access to her property in northern Cyprus.[3]

Although both cases lend themselves to polemical exploitation, in different ways and for different reasons, they aspired to higher expectations from any settlement of the Cyprus problem. At a more fundamental level, such narratives/images underscored the ethical dilemma compounding each attempt to resolve the conflict: how to construct a legal-constitutional order, dictated by a set of historical determinants, including the desire to rectify past injustices, which reconciles human rights and group security, with the expectation of upholding the fundamental precepts of liberal democracy, whilst fortifying the foundations for sequential integration/unification.

Conflicts and their settlements are neither inert nor eternal. Rather, particularism and historical contingency remain their abiding elements, thrusting them ever forward, even though they appear exceptional and insulated.

Throughout this study we have grappled with a key question: why, despite endless negotiations and countless proposals, has there been no resolution to the Cyprus conflict? Expressed a little more precisely, was failure of the Cyprus talks due to the belligerent nature of the negotiating parties? Or, are the underlying reasons to be found in the conflict's broader internal and external dynamics? Is it not possible, indeed likely, that we can find a close connection between these two questions? What is the precise distinction between them? Do the very structures and mind-sets underpinning the negotiations render them incapable of facilitating a political settlement?

As we have seen, the answers lie in the complex web of interacting factors—internal and external to Cyprus—that have shaped the overall negotiating process. Our approach has been to analyze those events, circumstances, and relationships that have impeded or facilitated a peaceful resolution of the Cyprus problem. It must be noted that the combination of factors was neither uniform nor consistent in its impact, and that complex interactions produced, at different times and phases, different processes and effects. In analyzing the relationships between the two sets of factors—internal and external— and their interconnected and often contradictory implications, it is possible to identify elements of continuity and change both within and between the phases that make up this period. In conceptualizing relevant trends and relationships, we have developed an overall assessment of the psychological and political dynamic that has thus far obstructed a resolution of the Cyprus problem.

Impending and Facilitating Factors

The intercommunal talks generally treated the Cyprus problem as an ethnic conflict and sought its resolution on this basis. As indicated earlier, the two communities had been politically, economically, socially, and psychologically separated over time, and the 1974 partition endowed this separation with a geographical, demographic, and military dimension. This deeply entrenched separation constituted the main impediment to any rapprochement. The net effect of the physical division of the island has been to hamper communication, interaction, and contact not only between the two communities but even between those forces that were prepared to pursue, or at least explore, common interests and objectives. In addition, postponement of a solution led at different times one or both parties to resort to unilateral actions outside the confines of the process, thereby exacerbating the conflict and further impeding negotiation and third-party mediation.

One of the key conclusions to emerge from this discussion is that both communities had, for different reasons and in different ways, become supporters of the status quo, which they viewed as, if not ideal, at least preferable to the uncertainties of any future regime that did not incorporate their maximum expectations. On one side, the Turkish Cypriots feared that reunification within a strong federation would see them revert to the pre-1974 situation as an isolated minority dominated by a larger and more powerful Greek Cypriot community. On the other side, the Greek Cypriots viewed any federal solution that did not encompass a strong central authority and the withdrawal of the Turkish troops as no better than their existing predicament. They would be sacrificing their legitimacy as the sole recognized Cypriot state and would be risking the total occupation of the island. Though the motivation and the rationale may have differed, the position of both parties was similar in one important respect: they both considered the incentives for change weaker than the security of the status quo. Fear of worst-case scenarios paralyzed the will and the capacity to pursue a riskier but ultimately more promising course.

Continuity and Change

To contextualize, during the thirty-to-forty-year-period under examination, the overall balance between negative and positive influences clearly favored the negative side of the ledger. The inescapable conclusion was that a set of closely interrelated obstacles consistently prejudiced the outcome of the negotiations. These may be briefly summarized as follows:

The "linkage" approach to negotiations has meant that there could be no settlement unless all aspects of the Cyprus problem (for example, constitution, territory, and security) were simultaneously agreed upon. As talks progressed, they inevitably became more complicated with the introduction of greater detail and new points of disputation. In addition, talks were often hampered by the introduction of different interpretations to concepts that had previously been agreed upon. Further hindering the process throughout this period were the contrasting motives, priorities, preferences, and objectives of the two sides, most starkly expressed in a series of dualisms: maintaining/changing the status quo, unification/separatism, federation/confederation, unitarism/decentralization.

The insecurity and distrust felt by each side in relation to the other created reluctance on both sides to risk any change to the existing arrangements. The close relationship and interdependence between the two communities on the one hand and the principal external powers (Greece and Turkey) on the other enhanced this phenomenon. The direct relationship between Greece and Turkey also impeded the negotiations and altered the political environment, forcing both sides, in line with a clearly recognizable action-reaction syndrome, to adopt confrontationist postures. This was especially so in the case of the Turkish Cypriot community, which had a different historical relationship with Turkey, was less self-sufficient, and lacked an opposition that could effectively challenge the prevailing orthodoxy. As the conflict became protracted, both communities chose to pursue their respective interests, with the aim of strengthening or promoting their legitimacy as independent international political actors.

When the two sides abandoned communication and the intercommunal talks were no longer considered a priority, the Cyprus conflict inevitably reverted to tension. In this context, unilateral actions designed to address military and/or political insecurities acquired potentially dangerous implications. The net effect was escalating military capabilities on both sides, intensification of international campaigns to bolster their respective causes, provocative statements, and the reemergence of nationalist sentiments. The Cyprus problem became the epicenter of the broader Greek-Turkish conflict, eventually embroiling both states.

Paradoxically, it was these confrontational phases, often followed by a more cooperative mood, that injected into the negotiating process renewed impetus for change and encouraged the two communities to break from their previously entrenched positions—a necessary condition for progress. For example, the 1985 High Level Meeting came about after the 1983 Turkish Cypriot UDI, the Pérez de Cuéllar and Boutros-Ghali initiatives of the early 1990s were heavily influenced by the Aegean crisis of 1988 and the Davos experiment; the CBMs were boosted by border clashes in 1993–1994, and the Annan initiative followed the S-300 missile crisis and the catalytic effect of Cyprus's and Turkey's EU accession pathways.

The overall conclusion arising from the preceding survey was that the intercommunal talks, in their current form and operating in isolation from other initiatives, cannot overcome the structural and psychological obstacles to a negotiated settlement. The relative failure of the intercommunal talks stemmed from their incapacity to address a number of political and organizational problems:

The negotiating process developed a logic and timing of its own, which did not necessarily correspond to the psychology of the political situation it was seeking to remedy. When, for example, dramatic developments occurred in the internal or external environment of the two parties, the intercommunal talks seemed incapable of capturing the conciliatory mood that ensued.

The history and geography of the region was such that to contemplate any exclusion of the two principal external powers, Greece and Turkey, from the resolution of the Cyprus problem was simply unrealistic. Yet, until 1999 no effective mechanism was found that would enable Greece and Turkey to be fully integrated in the resolution process, thereby encouraging a more positive congruence between internal and external influences.

The common interests shared by the two communities and the mutual benefits that could result from a negotiated settlement have not been sufficiently elaborated or emphasized during the intercommunal dialogue. Those elements in both communities who can discern mutual benefits and have an interest in establishing a constructive intercommunal relationship have not successfully done this, nor have the mediating parties adequately assisted them in this endeavor. The task of persuading their respective compatriots, and each other, of the value of rapprochement was compounded by the physical separation of the two communities. In these circumstances, in order for the advocates of rapprochement to be successful, their respective campaigns would need to be conducted with greater synchronization, and their advocacy needs must be supported by at least some practical tangible benefits even in the short term. Only such concrete evidence is likely to give force to the argument that reconciliation would work to the advantage of both communities. It was within this context that an interim settlement of such secondary issues as Varosha, the Nicosia International Airport, and implementation of CBMs might have helped to reverse the mistrust that has divided the country.

A final assessment of the intercommunal talks leaves us with the conclusion that since the acceptance of a bicommunal/bizonal federation, negotiations followed a repetitious cyclical pattern where disagreements on the substantial issues saw both sides retreat to their entrenched positions. As a result, the parties discussed all issues to the point of exhaustion, yet the two communities remained divided. In conceptual terms, disagreement over reunification fundamentally revolved around its structural form and, at least implicitly, the nature of power sharing. But underlying these differences was the intangible climate of mistrust between the two sides and their sense of insecurity, which meant the continuation of the status quo and contemplation of other unilateral options.

3+1 Settlement Scenarios: Unitary, Federal, or Two-state Solutions

With the collapse of the Annan initiative, we are able to visualize, more clearly, the contradictory trajectory of Cyprus's peace talks, characterized by the irresolvable tension between historical determinism and the unilateralist aspirations of pervasive ethno-nationalist sovereignty.

The tension between separatism and unification is expressed more tangibly in the new challenges posed by the doctrine of preemption during the post-referendum/post-accession phase. The difficulty of constructing a new peace paradigm in Cyprus is not only exacerbated by inter/intra-communal polarization, but is also vulnerable to internal and external tensions particularly as they relate to Turkey's European orientation.

In this wider context, a survey of the Cyprus conflict over the past thirty–forty-year- period suggests that the future of Cyprus is likely to unfold in the realm of any one of the following scenarios: (1) Cyprus is formally or informally unified/annexed, in part or in whole, by either Greece or Turkey—this option implies high levels of instability and, given the volume of arms accumulated by both sides, the prospect of open hostility; (2) the current status quo is retained in a context of perpetual ambivalence; (3) the island is united through some form of strong or lose federal—or intermediate—arrangement resulting from a negotiated outcome. By canvassing the three scenarios in this order, we are able to better assess the likelihood of their realization within different contexts and through the combination of various influences, domestic and international.

Since August 16, 1974, a cease-fire has technically been observed in Cyprus, and all parties have recoiled from a war scenario. This is because the risks involved clearly overrode any potential benefits. Both sides argue that acquisition of sophisticated weaponry constitutes part of their defense preparedness and, despite the risk of an accident that could trigger military confrontation, that the doctrine of mutual deterrence prevails. However, the main restraint against the outbreak of armed conflict in Cyprus has been the fact that it could quickly escalate into a broader Greek-Turkish war, which would immediately force NATO, the United States, and the Europeans to intervene.

Despite occasional ultranationalistic language, there has been no real evidence, thus far, that either Greece or Turkey wished to annex all of Cyprus, especially since this would burden them with a troublesome minority population that would, in turn, have far-reaching political repercussions for the aggressor. Annexation of northern Cyprus by Turkey is considered the most likely of the annexation scenarios, and such a radical development would lead to high levels of bilateral tension and regional instability. If this was to occur, then Turkey would, effectively, establish another hostile frontier with Greece—and the EU—with a perpetually hostile neighboring population at its vulnerable underbelly.

Between the second and third scenarios, a fourth category saw a solution based on a two-state, "loose federation," or some other confederate arrangement. Promoters of minimalist models range from partitionists, who argue for the formalization of the status quo, to gradualists who advocate an evolutionist approach to the Cyprus problem. For partitionists, for example, former UN Cyprus representative Hugo Gobbi, historical experience suggested that coexistence between the two communities within a "strong" federation was practically impossible.[4] In this view, it was expected that the Greek Cypriots would make concessions on sovereignty in exchange for territorial concessions from the Turkish side.[5]

More optimistically, the gradualists did not preclude the prospect for future reintegration once confidence was established. Rather, what was envisaged was a step-by-step transitional approach that addressed the minimum objectives of both sides. Initially this entailed a "second-best" settlement, such as confederation or "loose federation," accompanied by a series of CBMs. Conceptually, a "loose" federation rested on two interdependent propositions: that both sides voluntarily proceed to the next level of engagement; and the need for a conducive climate to sustain commonalities, which, within a EU framework, may lead to genuine unification.[6]

Building on such a sociopsychological premise, others argued that a long-term sustainable resolution to the conflict had to address the root causes of intercommunal friction and reconstruct a shared Cypriot identity.[7] This required Cyprus to undergo a "conciliation" stage ("healing of wounds," trust-building, negation of insecurities, cooperation, and integration), followed by a "testing" phase (for example, evolutionary federalism), before arriving at a durable political accord.[8] The success or failure of such a Cyprus conflict management initiative would ultimately be determined by the extent to which its proponents integrate the three aforementioned phases within a realistic timeline—one that monitored the consequences of actions and deliberations (including inaction) over the short, medium, and longer terms.

Over a thirty-five-year period the status quo was considered by every party as a transitional conflicting phase and all negotiating efforts concentrated on the federal option. In essence, negotiations over federalism were always impregnated with principles that surreptitiously competed with the parties' preferred positions (the Greek Cypriot penchant for a unitary state and the Turkish Cypriot preference for a two-state solution).

In the 2004 post-referenda context, uncertainty over federalism propelled a mood of despair and a readiness for both communities to surrender to the certainty of the status quo. Offsetting such contradictory developments are two opposing concepts: reinstituting the Republic of Cyprus as a metaphor for a unitarism, and a two-state solution. In what at first sight might appear as discontinuity, this approach in fact entails considerable continuity when projected in the conflict's entire historical continuum. It is worth noting here a number of qualifying differences between the old and new meanings of the unitary (Republic of Cyprus) and two-state solutions.

Dismissal of federalist solutions was always prevalent amongst both communities. A series of opinion polls since the 2004 referendum reveal an increasing trend, particularly among younger generations, rejecting federalism and supporting unitarism and/or two states.[9] Closer scrutiny, however, reveals a degree of volatility in attitudinal change and a distinct lack of clarity over what is understood by a unitary state or the difference between federal and two-state solutions.

In this context several aspects deserve closer attention. Greek Cypriot conceptualization of the unitary state is encapsulated in the Republic of Cyprus's pre-1974 milieu rather than its 1960 incarnation. Subsequently, rejection of the Annan Plan affirmed the Republic of Cyprus's legitimacy as "their" identity-based construct/polity. Such exclusivity has been challenged by the Turkish Cypriot integrationist, who, by utilizing the intercommunal space created by the Green Line corridor, seeks to resuscitate the republican project.[10]

The other anomaly that emerged was the resonance of the two-state solution amongst constituencies that traditionally abhorred the notion. Where previously the two-state solution was associated with partition and the separatists, it emerged as a proposition seriously contemplated by a sizeable number of Greek Cypriots. Greek Cypriot distaste for Annan's plan, coupled with a revamped attachment to the Republic of Cyprus, paradoxically converged with *taksim* to produce a situation where the two-state solution threatens to dislodge federalism as the second-best solution. Looking past its (political) implications, equally ominous are warnings that "creeping divergence" would mathematically lead, by osmosis, to partition.[11]

Whilst Turkish Cypriots are returning to the Republic of Cyprus, increasingly Greek Cypriots are trading federalism for the two-state solution as their preferred second-best solution. By embracing Gobbis's territory for sovereignty doctrine along the proposed Annan contour—with the addendum that northern Cyprus dovetails its European fortune with that of Turkey's—the two-state solution becomes a historical endgame for Greek and Turkish nationalism in Cyprus.[12]

Beyond the Discourse: Contemplating Certain Lessons

Whilst most conflicts are portrayed as unique, upon closer examination we soon realize that besides their contextual setting they are strikingly similar in their constitution, dynamics, and psychology. Our study of the Cyprus conflict suggests a number of lessons of considerable relevance to other conflicts. It is not our intention to exhaust the whole gamut of lessons learnt, but rather to focus on those ideas that conceptually lend themselves to other conflicts and related peace processes.

First, it brings into sharp focus the distinction between *interest-* and *value-based conflicts*. As we have noted, disagreement over a common constitution theoretically implies an interest-based conflict—since it involves power sharing and the distribution of positions and resources. However, the constitutional dispute reveals itself as much a value-based as an interest-based conflict. To the extent that a constitution constructs the legal-political framework to which both communities commit themselves, the ensuing agreement redefines their political status and identity. Turkish Cypriot insistence on decentralized constitutional arrangements stemmed from their emphasis on autonomy and self-determination. Similarly, Greek Cypriot insistence on a unified state reflected the high premium they placed on majority rights and trans-territoriality.

An equally important lesson has to do with the way we identify the parties to a conflict. By breaking down the Cyprus conflict into its micro-units, we derive a more encompassing overview of the respective roles of foreign parties in this internal conflict and the complexities of the ensuing relationships. Another consequence of such an approach is that it discloses the significant differences within the conflicting parties, thereby deconstructing and in this sense demystifying the "Other" in the eyes of each protagonist. In this respect, the Cyprus conflict presents itself as a prime example of linkage politics, operating as it does on three interrelated levels. The intercommunal talks, as the main negotiating process, have treated Cyprus as an internal ethnic dispute between the majority Greek Cypriot and the minority Turkish Cypriot communities. These negotiations evolved largely in the context of mediatory intervention by the UN as a third party, whose role has since been pivotal to their longevity. Yet by virtue of its history, geography, and demography, the Cyprus question has never been conterminous with its domestic parameters. It has always been the kernel of a broader and unresolved Greek-Turkish conflict. Greece's and Turkey's embroilment in Cyprus has been at odds with their common membership of NATO, their special relationships with the United States, their common European orientation, and their membership of the United Nations, thereby implicating these other actors at various stages of the conflict.

There is another lesson arising from the Cyprus experience that is worth noting. As with Sri Lanka, Northern Ireland, and Israel-Palestine, the Cyprus conflict, seen from a regional and social-psychological perspective, suffers from the *double minority complex*. In addition to blurring the inter/intrastate nature of the conflict, this notion provides us with an understanding of the *double (in)security* dilemma preoccupying both communities and their motherlands. Any useful analytical perspective must take note of this impediment and accurately map power relations between internal and external protagonists. Most analysts have treated the Cyprus dispute as either an intrastate conflict between two ethnic groups or as a manifestation of a broader Greek-Turkish rivalry. Invariably, conflict analysts explain the conflict using the symmetrical-asymmetrical vernacular, placing at its heart the double minority syndrome (that is, the Turkish Cypriot minority within the island, and the Greek Cypriot minority within its subregional context). Contrary to these two frames of reference, the Cyprus conflict has never centered purely on the island's two ethnic communities, or on the relationship between Greece and Turkey. A much more useful conceptualization suggests a conflict that pits one brand of *majoritarianism* against another: that is, the Greek Cypriot community against Turkey. Expressed differently, the main forces driving the Cyprus conflict have historically been Greek Cypriot nationalism and Turkey's national strategic interests. This dichotomy has recently been accentuated by the complex interactions between Turkey and the (Greek Cypriot controlled) Republic of Cyprus within the framework of EU institutions, forums, and deliberations.

Finally, our survey would not be complete if we did not dwell on the role of nationalism. Harold Saunders, after a lifetime in peacemaking, has argued that changing a conflictual relationship, rather than striving for a negotiated breakthrough, is a more significant productive approach.[13] Nowhere is the social-psychological imperative to transform a conflictual relationship more strikingly evident than in the elusive realm of (ethno) nationalism. As with most protracted conflicts, nationalism features prominently in the history of modern Cyprus, as competing ethno-nationalisms lay claim to territorial and historical legitimacy. A combination of insecurity, past injustices, and historical determinism lends nationalist discourse a psycho-political mystique.

Draped in iconoclastic symbols, surrounded by a legion of martyrs, and narrated with primordial enmity, nationalism is seen as the driving force that has shaped and transformed the conflict, propelling it in different directions. Until recently, most scholars have approached nationalism in Cyprus through an orientalist prism, underestimating its potency and allure as both a social movement and a force for historical change. As the furor before and since the 2004 referendum—in particular, but not exclusively, amongst the Greek Cypriot community—nationalistic behavior is the benign face of the legacy of the conflict inscribed at the moment of its creation. Nationalist behavior as a social code is shaped by the physical conditions and constraints within which the conflict is set. The study of Cypriot nationalism offers a pathway into the conflict's wider social-psychological realities and exposes the underlying factors that account for the prolongation of the conflict.

Furthermore, conflicts are rarely monocausal, one-dimensional, or static. Protracted conflicts develop their own language, culture, and processes. As with most protracted conflicts, the Cyprus conflict requires innovative and multidimensional approaches capable of introducing, at key junctures as circumstances change, new variables and parties, linking them at different levels into the central peace process.[14] The problem with concentrating exclusively on track-one diplomacy, striving for a political settlement while neglecting the need to shift the conflictive relationship on the ground, was borne out yet again by the Annan initiative.

Conflict resolution contains no certainties. They are thwarted by many unknown variables and susceptible to internal and external fluctuations. Besides security, the conflict's nagging presence becomes a constant reminder of the impossibility of sealing off one epoch from the next with any confidence in evolutionary progress. Asymmetry, inequality, disparity, and inclusion/exclusion, continue to define and redefine inter- and intra-communal relations, often underscoring class, gender, generational, and other social cleavages. The pervasive disposition of the status quo sits uncomfortably with Cyprus's historical order. In the interim, new trends have pegged Cyprus's particularism to regional and global transformations. Europeanization is but one manifestation of Cyprus's modernization as it teases out the boundaries of Western expansion and incongruous/contradictory convulsions of its own search/self-definition.

In this sense, for the EU the Cyprus challenge is fundamentally philosophical. Whether or not Cyprus could unify and transcend physical, ideological, and historical barriers goes to the heart of the

European project. Cyprus's accession to the European Union, and its conflict (and resolution), constitutes a pivotal test case for the European vision of "peace through unification." The Cyprus conflict throws up a series of challenges that threatens to compound rather than alleviate its "post-enlargement crisis." As an interstate conflict, Cyprus weighs into the whole question of Turkey's accession and the geopolitical and cultural issues this raises. It is not inconceivable that an unsuccessful outcome in the Cyprus-Turkey conundrum could render the "Green Line" a fault line, separating Europe from Turkey, further sharpening the West-Islam divide at Europe's southern border.

As an intrastate conflict, Cyprus also became a test case for the EU's peacemaking discourse and capacity to mitigate the causes and manifestations of conflict. Cyprus offered the EU the opportunity to trial its regional pattern/model in circumventing the internal/external divide when dealing with ethno-territorial contestations. On a cultural level, EU intervention also played on the need to forge a European identity to counter the excesses of ethno-nationalism.

If the Cyprus conflict is seen as driven by adversarial ethno-nationalism, both on the local and subregional levels, then imposing a political settlement from above without the necessary social renewal would simply add another divisive layer, heightening the intercommunal "trust" deficit and endangering any fragile peace settlement at its first major test. Drawing on the history of the conflict, relevant lessons should have been learned from the similar circumstances that had led to Cyprus's independence in the late 1950s. The London-Zurich agreements saw both communities caught within identity-based political visions and aspirations (*enosis* and *taksim*), and therefore totally unprepared for any compromise solution that emerged. The historic compromise of 1959 left a residue of bitterness, especially among the majority Greek Cypriot community, which had lived through four years of armed conflict. In the ethno-nationalist narrative, Republic of Cyprus independence became the *raison d'être* of the "unfulfilled" struggle, which festered over time, manifesting itself in inter- and intra-communal conflict. The fact that Cyprus's independence was externally manufactured, with little or no input by the Cypriots themselves, imposed by the colonial power with the consent of their neighboring motherlands, only added to the mythology of "betrayal" and "conspiracy."

Cypriot NGOs and civil society groups, which had pursued rapprochement and reconciliation between the two communities since the 1990s, consistently advocated track-two diplomacy as a precondition to transforming the conflict. By emphasizing the social factor in the conflict equation, the constructivists aspired to transform the conflictual relationship between the two communities by shifting the identity-based parties themselves. For this transformation to have taken place, however, the contextual frameworks in which they operated and the conflict structures that were in place needed to be changed.

Within such a context, the Europeanization of the Cyprus conflict promised to transform the conflict itself not only by providing the political, economic, and security incentives necessary for coexistence, but also by offering itself as an alternative source of identity (euro-nationalism) to that of primordial (Greek and Turkish) ethno-nationalism. Europeanization was much more than simply a normative process by which the EU's instrumentalities provided governance frameworks for readjusting national public policy. Inspired by Jean Monnet's postwar vision of a transnational Europe, the expectation was that EU-ization of the Cyprus conflict would potentially impact on the national identities.[15]

Ultimately, the EU's capacity to neutralize, or at least absorb, excessive ethno-nationalism, by presenting itself as a third identity source for conflicting groups, rests on its capacity to aid, and politically enhance, those civil society elements who advocate a multicultural perspective of Cypriot national identity.[16] This euro-nationalist perspective envisages an ideological intervention by which Europeanism interfaced with ethno-specific nationalism, enhancing those "shared" elements that, for historical reasons, had been prevented from steering the political culture toward civil nationalism. By integrating euro-nationalism with local nationalism, it was hoped that those ethnic, religious, and racial components negatively affecting trans-communal relations would be absorbed and eradicated.

The imposition, however, of a parallel—and rival—transnational identity raises a series of conceptual and normative difficulties. The premise that pan-Europeanism offered a strong, cohesive set of cultural ideas that would resonate with both communities and an alternative "shared" history was very much an untested premise. Such fluid identities could quite easily bring into the equation periphery versus metropolitan concentration of power, giving rise to separatism and subnationalism. Such an approach eventually brings into focus the broader question of deconstructing the nation-state by shifting and sharing its sovereignty. If Cyprus were to relinquish part of its sovereignty to Brussels, the EU might be able to impose measures, standards, norms, and values, and also act as an agent for the modernization and liberalization of the political, economic, and ethnic fabric that was Cyprus's divided society. Within such a framework, how the EU decides to deal with northern Cyprus in both its pre- and post-settlement context, either by inducting it into its Regional Economic and Social Cohesion policy or some other design, would ultimately determine both its overall Cyprus policy and its conflict intervention potential.[17]

Condensed to a singularity, the Cyprus conflict has been shaped by the clash of supra and sub state forces. However, it is important to recognize certain qualitative differences between the old internal/external and the new globalization/civil society dualisms. The rapid intensity of external intervention underscores the dramatic events experienced during the Annan initiative. In what, at first sight, appears as collusion by globalization and civil society to nullify the state's hegemonistic propensity is rather the combustion of accumulated social-economic containment. The relative fallacy of equating civil society with a progressive integrating dynamic is as inaccurate as it is misleading. In Cyprus's case, civil society (and capitalism) preceded the state, thus rendering their ideological interdependence inseparable. At the risk of oversimplification, the integrating (cosmopolitan) attributes of the financial sector/market, which presets profit as the overarching common interest, are more likely to create the necessary momentum for reunification in Cyprus.

In this milieu, locating second-track diplomacy and bicommunalism has proven problematic. Aside from the pertinent question of its impact on official mediation, high expectations of the effectiveness of bicommunalism during the Greek Cypriot referendum seriously jeopardized its value as a sociopolitical strategy. Whilst at first sight the number of bicommunal events appears to be encouraging—the years 2007 and 2008 saw 270 events involving 18,911 participants[18]—it has failed, thus far, to seriously and effectively engage with the harder and more resolute political dispositions in both communities.

Despite this dialectical incongruity, bicommunalism has carved out its own distinct, though highly susceptible, dialogical space in Cyprus. It is a dialogical discourse that aims to bring together people of different ethno-religious backgrounds and cultural traditions and promote mutual trust and more effective forms of communication, cooperation, and interaction. Bicommunalism offers, by virtue of its inclusiveness and wider agenda, a valuable antidote to prejudice and fear of the "Other," nurturing in its participants a strong sense of personal worth and belonging.

Finally, to ground the contestation more concretely, a fundamental imperative in conflict transformation is the prospect for dissent.

In addition to the dialectical attributes of fracturing ideological orthodoxies, dissent has a leveling effect, undermining the enemy-friend division, and reassuring the "Other" of its nonhomogenous demeanor. However, the threat to dissent comes from the most unsuspected quarters. The contradictory constellation of globalization has condensed rather than augmented dissent in Cyprus as it saturates communication with images, idioms, and narratives, which further entrench communalism and nationalism whilst alienating the individual from the decision-making and opinion-making processes.

To return to the contradictions of the peace talks, we have already consistently seen in the failed mediated efforts, and in a variety of circumstances, that impediments have prevailed over facilitating factors. To redress this balance and shift it in a more positive direction, a series of initiatives are needed to build confidence and trust amongst the Cypriot communities.

Whilst most short-term recommendations purport to create conditions that are conducive to the recommencement of settlement talks, as a "turning-point," EU-ization of the Cyprus conflict was premised on its capacity to alter the context and the scope of the conflict. EU activities have precipitated change in terms of processes, parties, issues, and history. In this respect, the challenge for the EU and the UN lies in their capacity to handle a process that strengthens peace-building measures through situational, procedural, institutional, structural, and cultural intervention. Attaining a sustainable peace within Cyprus requires reconciliation of competing values, interests, and needs: these can only be addressed in a consolidated democratic environment. The issues in dispute pertain essentially to the terms of coexistence, the meaning of equality, and ways of redressing the legacy of past injustices (restorative justice). From a transformative perspective, any political settlement of the Cyprus conflict needs to meet two fundamental prerequisites: it has to satisfy all stakeholders by limiting further victimization, and thus to safeguard against future discord; and a successful settlement must incorporate mechanisms, incentives, and processes for intercommunal integration rather than entrench communalism.

Much is to be gained from joint bicommunal partnerships, ventures, institutions, and projects that are diverse (for example, business, environment, local, epistemic) and conducive to more transparent and participatory processes (which are people-centered and democratic). The reestablishment of contacts between political parties could help to advance a process from which might emerge common policies across a wide range of issues not usually associated with the troublesome core of the Cyprus problem. Three interrelated areas lend themselves to common political deliberation: the distribution and depletion of resources, industrial relations, and environmental protection.

Another measure that would significantly aid the current climate is for third-party mediators to engage in political discourse with their detractors. By embarking on a consultation process with Greek and Turkish Cypriot civil society and commerce, the UN and the EU will encounter the whole spectrum of views not only on the details of a settlement plan, but more importantly on how they see the future of Cyprus. Such a "Cyprus Future Project" would allow the diversity of opinions from people and communities traditionally marginalized from the centre of power and decision-making forums to be taken into account.

As this book has been at pains to show, no settlement can be externally imposed on the internal parties without their consent and participation—a prerequisite for conferring on the peace process the necessary legitimacy. Without this legitimacy, the impeding factors that have been a constant in the negotiating landscape will once again hold sway. To succeed, such a strategy must be grounded in a proper analysis of the impeding and facilitating factors whose imbalance has militated against a successful settlement of the Cyprus problem. Such an effort needs to include an extensive process of consultation with the diverse societal, economic, and professional constituencies beyond the customary political elite. It would also require greater EU collaboration with the UN and the active involvement of other external powers besides the United States and United Kingdom.

The Cyprus conflict has many identities. The challenge confronting Cyprus ultimately lies in its capacity to transform itself into a postmodern society with a political arrangement that transcends its historical insecurities. Often a climate of uncertainty and ambivalence demands risk-taking. In this sense the EU offers itself as a surrogate for creative politics. As Cypriots need to overcome their past and create their own history, there is the danger that continual rejections will prolong stalemate, and stalemate will ensconce partition.[19]

Notes

Acknowledgments

1. Also known in Turkish as "Çatalköy (meaning forked village)."

Introduction: The Cyprus Conflict

1. George Mikes, *Eureka! Rummaging in Greece* (London: Andre Deutsch, 1965), 107.
2. Cyprus's ancient name during the Bronze Age.
3. Jay Rothman, "Conflict Research and Resolution: Cyprus," *The Annals of the American Academy of Political and Social Science* 518 (1991): 96.
4. Linda L. Putnam, "Challenging the Assumptions of Traditional Approaches to Negotiation," *Negotiation Journal* 10, 4 (1994): 337.
5. John W. Burton, *Global Conflict: the Domestic Sources of International Crisis* (University of Maryland, Center for International Development/ Wheatsheaf Books, 1984), 145.

1   Identifying the Sources of the Conflict

1. Benjamin Disraeli, *Tancred or the New Crusade* (London: Peter Davies, 1927), 244.
2. In analogizing Cyprus's East-West juxtaposition, the quintessential British Cypriotephile Harry Luke, *Cyprus—A Portrait and an Appreciation*, rev. ed. (London: George G. Harrap, 1964), 20–1, graphically described Cyprus's "conversion" from its "original (Asiatic) orientation" as "a spear of western Christianity poised against the strongholds of militant Islam."
3. The only serious exception appeared in December 1922 when, after Kemal Atatürk defeated the Greek army, a Turkish Cypriot delegation went to Ankara lobbying for Cyprus's return to Turkey. Atatürk did not support this claim. Halil Ibrahim Salih, *Cyprus, An Analysis of Cypriot Political Discord* (New York: Theo. Gaus Sons, 1968), 38.
4. See Michael Attalides, *Cyprus: Nationalism and International Politics* (Edinburgh: Q Press, 1979), 36–46; Charles Fraser Beckingham,

"Islam and Turkish Nationalism in Cyprus," *Die Welt des Islam* 5, 1–2 (1957): 65–83; and Niyazi Kizilyurek (2006) "The Turkish Cypriots from an Ottoman-Muslims Community to a National Community," in *Britain in Cyprus: Colonialism and Post-Colonialism, 1878–2006*, ed. H. Faustmann and N. Peristianis (Mannheim: Bibliopolis, 1994), 315–25.

5. In comparison to Greek Cypriot nationalism, Turkish Cypriot nationalism has attracted modest scholarly attention. In addition to the above, notable exceptions include, Huseyin M. Ateşin, *Kıbrıslı "Müslüma" larin "Türk" leşme ve "Laik" leşme Serüveni (1925–1975)* [Turkification and Securization Adventure of Cypriot Muslims] (Istanbul: Marifet Yayinlari, 1999); Altay Nevzat, "Nationalism Amongst the Turks of Cyprus: The First Wave" (PhD diss., University of Oulu, 2005); Nergis Canefe, "Communal Memory and Turkish Cypriot National History: Missing Links," in *National Identities and National Memories in the Balkans*, ed. Maria Todorova (London: Hurst and Company, 2003), 77–102; Niyazi Kiziliyürek, "The Turkish Cypriot Community and Rethinking of Cyprus," in *Cyprus in the Modern World*, ed. Michális S. Michael and Anastasios M. Tamis (Thessaloniki: Vanias, 2005), 228– 47; and Ahmet An, *Kıbrıs'ta Fırtınalı Yıllar* [The Stormy Years in Cyprus] *(1942–1962)* (Lefkoşa: Galeri Kültür Yayını, 1996); and *Kıbrıslı Türklerin Siyasal Tarihi (1930–1960): Basının Aynasında Kıbrıslı Türklerin Unutturulan Siyasal Geçmişi ve Liderlik Kavgaları* [The Political History of the Turkish Cypriots (1930–1960): The Forgotten Political History of the Turkish Cypriots and the Struggles for the Leadership in the Mirror of the Press] (Lefkoşa, 2006).

6. Peter Loizos, "The Progress of Greek Nationalism in Cyprus, 1878–1970," in *Choice and Change: Essays in Honour of Lucy Mair*, ed. J. Davis (London: Athlone, 1974), 114.

7. Lawrence Durrell, *Bitter Lemons* (London: Faber and Faber, 1957), 105. Throughout *Bitter Lemons* and in his correspondence with Henry Miller in 1953–1956, Durrell considered Cyprus "unGreek," a "piece of Asia Minor washed out to sea—not Greece" but rather part of the Middle East and the Levant more akin to Turkey, Egypt, and Syria. Following his disheartened departure from Cyprus, Miller consoled Durrell that he "should have no doubt that Cyprus will gain her independence or alliance with Greece," adding approvingly that "the down-trodden are coming into their own, it's inevitable. And there won't be any atom bomb wars either," George Wickens, ed., *Lawrence Durrell [and] Henry Miller: A Private Correspondence* (London: Faber and Faber, 1963), 294, 300, and 303.

8. Robert Holland and Diana Markides, *The British and the Hellenes: Struggles for Mastery in the Eastern Mediterranean 1850–1960* (Oxford: Oxford UP, 2006), 187–8.

9. John Thomson, *Through Cyprus with the Camera in the Autumn of 1878* (London: Sampson Low, 1879). As Mike Hajimichael, "Revisiting Thomson—The Colonial Eye and Cyprus," in Faustmann/Peristianis, *Britain in Cyprus*, 61–78, astutely notes, Thomson's work formed the template for how modern British society and polity "received and perceived" Cyprus, casting a "colonial eye" that was to dominate all subsequent British depiction of this newly acquired territory. It reenforced and articulated in a newly piercing medium of photos, with accompanied commentary, to a wider audience the confused combination of Philhellenism and colonialist/imperialist real politic.

10. Edward W. Said, *Orientalism* (New York: Routledge and Kegan Paul, 1978), xiii.

11. Four leading exemplars of Cypriot orientalism were Ronald Storrs, *Orientations* (London: Ivor Nicholson and Watson, 1937), George Hill, Harry Luke, and John Reddaway. Heavily influence by Storrs, Hill in the fourth volume of his nominal work, *A History of Cyprus: The Ottoman Province, the British Colony 1571–1948* (Cambridge: Cambridge UP, 1972 [1952]), sets the intellectual framework for Cypriot orientalism. Whilst not disputing the "Greekness of Cypriots," Hill contends that the (modern) "Greek idea of nationality" is different from that which is "understood by the Anglo-Saxons" or for that matter by the "ancient Greeks," in the sense that Greek irredentism dictates that all Greek territories come under the same sovereignty (489–90). Contextualizing Greek Cypriot nationalism in its Cold War demeanor, Luke views its "frenzied" manifestation caused by communist propaganda, blaming early British latitude for not countering the socialization of Greekness through the teaching of English. Finally, Reddaway, *Burdened with Cyprus: The British Connection* (London: Weidenfeld and Nicolson, 1986), 1–5—who, like Luke and Storrs, served in colonial Cyprus—presents a fatalistic detachment of Britain's role in subsequent events, and, like Luke, projects British complacency as a reluctant umpire between Greek and Turkish nationalist contestation.

12. In its review, "Cyprus in 1879," *The Times,* January 12, 1880, 4, suggested that it was far superior to any "elaborate" and "expensive" official report.

13. W. Hepworth Dixon, *British Cyprus* (London: Chapman and Hall, 1879).

14. Samuel White Baker, *Cyprus, As I Saw It in 1879* (London: Macmillan, 1879), 405.

15. Esmé Scott-Stevenson, *Our Home in Cyprus* (London: Chapman and Hall, 1880).

16. Kyriacos C. Markides, "Social Change and the Rise and Decline of a Social Movement: The Case of Cyprus," *American Ethnologist* 1, 2 (1974): 309–30.

17. Colonial Office, *Report on Cyprus for the Year 1952* (London: HMSO, 1953), 33, 52–3.

18. Colonial Office, *Colonial Reports: Cyprus 1953* (London: HMSO, 1954), 15.

19. This lends credence to Rebecca Bryant's, *Imagining the Modern— The Cultures of Nationalism in Cyprus* (London: I.B.Tauris, 2004), 24, and "Signatures and 'Simple Ones': Constituting a Public in Cyprus, circa 1900," in Faustmann/Peristianis, *Britain in Cyprus*, 79–81, claim that modernization, ushered during the first decades of British rule, served as a "precondition" for the transformation of parochial Cypriot public space by fusing Greek and Turkish nationalisms. Writing half a century prior, Irene B. Taeuber, "Cyprus: The Demography of a Strategy Island," *Population Index* 21, 1 (1955): 4–20, contested that Cyprus's modernization occurred after 1946 due to British economic and social reforms.

20. Kyriacos C. Markides, *The Rise and Fall of the Cyprus Republic* (New Haven: Yale UP, 1977), 18–9, profiling is correlated by the fact that according to the 1946 census, 55 percent of young men in towns were villagers. See D'Andrade (D. A.) Percival, "Some Features of a Peasant Population in the Middle East—Drawn from the Results of the Census of Cyprus," *Population Studies* 3, 2 (1949): 202–4.

21. Anita M. Walker, "Enosis in Cyprus: Dhali, a Case Study," *The Middle East Journal* 38, 3 (1984): 477–8.

22. John G. Peristiany, "Introduction to a Cyprus Highland Village," in *Contributions to Mediterranean Sociology: Mediterranean Rural Communities and Social Change*, ed. J. G. Peristiany (The Hague: Mouton, 1968), 79–80.

23. For a full description of the 1931 events, see Storrs, *Orientations*, 585–602, and G. S. Georghallides, *Cyprus and the Governorship of Sir Ronald Storrs: The Causes of the 1931 Crisis* (London: Cyprus Research Centre, 1986).

24. "Latest Intelligence: Cyprus," *The Times*, July 23, 1878, 5.

25. These early stances have been typified as "collaborationist," "adaptationist," and "absolute unionist," Costas P. Kyrris, *History of Cyprus* (Nicosia: Nicocles, 1985), 302. They later manifested into three broader trends: nationalist-autonomist-*enosist* (associated with the Left), nationalists-*enosist* (attached to the moderate Right), and pure nationalists (linked to the militant *enosists*), G. S. Georghallides, *Cyprus and…Storrs*.

26. Nancy Crawshaw, *The Cyprus Revolt: An Account of the Struggle for Union with Greece* (London: George Allen and Unwin, 1978), 22.

27. John Macdonald Kinneir, *Journey Through Asia Minor, Armenia and Koordistan in the Years of 1813 and 1814* (London, 1818), 185.

28. Harold Temperley, "Disraeli and Cyprus," *The English Historical Review* 15, 182 (1931): 274–9.

29. "Letter to Queen Victoria, 5 May 1878," in W. F. Monypenny and G. E. Buckle, *The Life of Benjamin Disraeli Earl of Beaconsfield*, vol. 2 (London: John Murray, 1929), 1163.

30. R. Hamilton Lang, *Cyprus: Its History, its Present Resources, and Future Prospects* (London: Macmillan, 1878), 197–8.

31. Great Britain, "Cabinet Meeting (Financial Situation; Proposed Cession to Greece of Cyprus without Cabinet Consent; Need for Smaller War Council)," CAB 37/136/26, October 21, 1915.

32. Percy Arnold, *Cyprus Challenge—a Colonial Island and its Aspirations: Reminiscences of a Former Editor of the "Cyprus Post"* (London: Hogarth Press, 1956), 118.

33. Cyrus Leo (C. L.) Sulzberger, "Greeks Preparing Territorial Claims," *New York Times*, August 8, 1944.

34. See C. L. Sulzberger, "U.S. Goals Outlined for East Europe," *New York Times*, January 1, 1945; and, James Reston, "Salonika Free Port, U.S. Aims in Policy to Freeze Borders," *New York Times*, March 22, 1946.

35. Mallony Browne, "Britain Plans Her Global Defense," *New York Times*, August 11, 1946.

36. Indicative of this conviction was an off-the-cuff statement by the Admiral of the British Fleet, Lord P. C. Chatfield, who on May 4, 1949 stated that "Cyprus was far too important to the British Empire, and therefore the world as a whole, for it to be lightly handed over to a country which found such difficulty in looking after itself. This was not the time to think of such a far-fetched idea as ENOSIS." The statement was made during an address by Reginald Thomas Herbert Fletcher, 1st Baron Winster, "Administrative Problems in Cyprus," *United Empire* 40 (ed. H. W. Elliot Bailey, 1949), 182, who served as Governor of Cyprus between 1946 and 1949, to the Royal Empire Society, which Chatfield chaired."

37. Department of State, "United States Policy in the Event of the Establishment of Communist Power in Greece," PPS/8 (Policy Planning Staff Paper under George F. Kennan), Top Secret, September 18, 1947.

38. Department of State, "Eastern Mediterranean and Middle East," PPS/14 (Policy Planning Staff Paper that emanated from conversations between the U.S. Department of State and the British Foreign Office with their military advisers), Top Secret, November 11, 1947.

39. Christopher Montague Woodhouse, "Cyprus: the British Point of View," in *Cyprus in Transition 1960–1985*, ed. J. T. A. Koumoulides (London: Trigraph, 1986), 86.

40. Winster, "Problems in Cyprus," 182.

41. George H. Kelling, "British Policy in Cyprus 1945–1955: The Pigeons Come Home to Roost," Faustmann/Peristianis, *Britain in*

Cyprus, 187. Also see *Countdown to Rebellion: British Policy in Cyprus, 1939–1955* (Westport, CT: Greenwood Press, 1990).

42. Reddaway, *Burdened with Cyprus*, 6.

43. "British Offer to Cyprus—Archbishop's Rejection," *The Times*, July 14, 1947, 3.

44. Thomas Ehrlich, *Cyprus 1958–1967: International Crises and the Role of Law* (Oxford UP, 1974), 7.

45. H. D. Purcell, *Cyprus* (London: Ernest Benn, 1969), 227.

46. Collin Cross, *The Fall of the British Empire 1918–1968* (London: Paladin, 1970), 125.

47. This was best exemplified by Henry Hopkinson's infamous statement (Undersecretary of State for the Colonies) that "there can be no question of any change of sovereignty in Cyprus," 531 *House of Commons Debates* (5th ser.) 507, 1954.

48. Great Britain, "Paper on Middle East Defence," FO 371/121370, V1197/22/G, December 26, 1956.

49. Anthony Eden, *Full Circle* (London: Cassell, 1960), 396.

50. E. H. Wyndham, "The European Scene," *Brassey's Annual: The Armed Forces Year-Book, 1956*, 67th ed. (London: William Clowes, 1957), 11.

51. Foreign Office, "Minutes" by J. H. A. Watson, FO 371/127757, V1075/39, July 3, 1957.

52. Robert Saundby, "Defence in the Nuclear Age," *Brassey's Annual: The Armed Forces Year-Book 1957*, 68th ed. (London: William Clowes, 1958), 29.

53. C. L. Sulzberger, "Cyprus: US Pressure on GB to Improve Air Bases," *New York Times*, June 6, 1952, 6.

54. In light of these strategic considerations, Britain redefined Cyprus's military purpose. A 1957 White Paper argued that: "Britain has undertaken in the Baghdad Pact to cooperate with the other signatory States for security and defence, and for the prevention of Communist encroachment and infiltration. In the event of an emergency, British forces in the Middle East area would be made available to support the Alliance. These would include bomber squadrons based in Cyprus capable of delivering nuclear weapons." Ministry of Defence, *Defence: Outline of Future Policy*, Cmnd. 124 (London: HMSO, 1957), para. 27.

55. "The text of the British proposals for Cyprus put to the Three Power Conference in London on 6th September 1955," Colonial Office, *Cyprus Report for the Year 1955* (London: HMSO, 1956): 89–91.

56. Eden, *Full Circle*, 402–3.

57. Nikos Kranidiotis, *Oi Diapragmatefseis Makariou-Harding* [the Makarios-Harding Negotiations] *(1955–1956)* (Athens: Olkos, 1987), 17.

58. Nikos Kranidiotis, *Diskola Hronia* [difficult years] (Athens: Estia, 1981), 174. "Dighenis" is a pseudonym Grivas adopted when he led EOKA

during 1955–1959. Dighenis Akritas is a legendary medieval Greek hero who defended the boundaries of the Byzantium empire against Arab incursions during the twelfth century.

59. Eden, *Full Circle*, 412.

60. AKEL was accused of developing "the whole paraphernalia of 'struggle' against established authority," joining the nationalists in demonstrations and riots, and serving international communism by stirring trouble over the bases (Cyprus Government, *Press Release*, December 14, 1955). The British managed to convince Eisenhower that communist infiltration in the Middle East had begun with the Gamal Abdel Nasser-Soviet "arms deal" and that Nasser was covertly aiding EOKA.

61. *Constitutional Proposals for Cyprus, Report Submitted to the Secretary of State for the Colonies by the Right Hon Lord Radcliffe*, Cmnd. 42 (London: HMSO, December 1956), A.I., 29.

62. *House of Commons Debates*, vol. 562, col. 1268–1272 (December 19, 1956).

63. Harold Macmillan, *Riding the Storm: 1956–1959* (London: Macmillan, 1971), 224.

64. Eden, *Full Circle*, 415.

65. Macmillan, *Riding the Storm*, 225.

66. Lord Harding of Petherton, "The Cyprus Problem in Relation to the Middle East," *International Affairs* 34, 3 (1958): 296.

67. *Cyprus: Statement of Policy*, Cmnd. 455 (London: HMSO, June 1958).

68. For example, the British authorized the preparation of electoral rolls for the election of the two separate communal assemblies, the establishment of separate Greek and Turkish Cypriot municipal councils, and invited the Greek and Turkish governments to appoint their representatives, to take "effect from 1st October," "Statement by the Prime Minister, 15th August, 1958," *Cyprus 1958*, 109–10.

69. "Hotel Diplomacy," *Time Magazine*, March 2, 1959, 17.

70. *Cyprus*, Cmnd. 1093 (London: HMSO, July 1960), 91–170.

71. Cmnd. 1093, 86–7.

72. John W. Burton considered the abandonment of *enosis* and *taksim* as the communities' compatibilization of interests. John Burton, *Deviance Terrorism and War: The Process of Solving Unsolved Social and Political Problems* (Oxford: Martin Robertson, 1979), 108.

73. Adamantia Pollis, "Intergroup Conflict and British Colonial Policy: The Case of Cyprus," *Comparative Politics* 5, 4 (1973): 599.

74. John W. Burton, *Conflict and Communication: The Use of Controlled Communication in International Relations* (New York: The Free Press, 1969), 34.

75. Vamık D. Volkan, "Trauma, Identity and Search for a Solution in Cyprus," *Insight Turkey* 10, 3 (2008): 95–110.

76. UNFICYP was under the direct mandate of the Security Council and was advised to "use its best efforts to prevent a recurrence of

fighting and, as necessary, to contribute to the maintenance and restoration of law and order and a return to normal conditions," SC Resolution 186, S/5575, March 4, 1964. In practical terms, UNFICYP was deployed in sensitive areas, placing itself between Greek and Turkish Cypriot military positions.

77. Edward Weintal and Charles Bartlett, *Facing the Brink: An Intimate Study in Crisis Diplomacy* (New York: Charles Scribner, 1967), in particular see chapter 2, "Aux Armes, Citoyens!," 16–36.

78. In a strongly worded letter to the Turkish Prime Minister Ismet Inonü, Johnson stated that he would not agree "to the use of any [US-] supplied military equipment for a Turkish intervention in Cyprus," and questioned NATO's "obligation to protect Turkey against the Soviet Union," "President Johnson and Prime Minister Inonü—Correspondence Between President Johnson and Prime Minister Inonü, June 1964, as released by the White House, January 15, 1966," *The Middle East Journal* 20 (1966): 386–8. On June 13, Inonü informed Johnson that, at his request, Turkey had "postponed [their] decision to exercise [their] right of unilateral action in Cyprus," ibid.: 288–93.

79. According to his biographer, before Acheson left for Geneva, "the State Department had concluded that the continuation of an independent state in Cyprus was a threat to American interests," Douglas Brinkley, *Dean Acheson: The Cold War Years 1953–1971* (New Haven: Yale UP, 1992), 215. For Acheson's account of the talks, see Dean Acheson, "Cyprus: Anatomy of the Problem," *Chicago Bar Record* 46, 8 (1965): 349–56.

80. George W. Ball, *The Past has Another Pattern: Memoirs* (New York: W. W. Norton, 1982), 357.

81. Tad Szulc, "Acheson Warns of Peril in Cyprus," *New York Times*, September 5, 1964, 4.

82. *Report of the United Nations Mediator on Cyprus to the Secretary-General* [September 28, 1964–March 26, 1965], S/6253, 19–28.

83. "Resolution 244: The Cyprus Question (December 22, 1967)," para. 4, http://daccess-ods.un.org/access.nsf/Get?Open&DS=S/RES/244%20(1967)&Lang=E&Area=RESOLUTION.

84. Fred Charles Iklé, *How Nations Negotiate* (London: Harper and Row, 1964), 2–3.

85. Glafcos Clerides, *Cyprus: My Deposition*, vol. 2 (Nicosia, Alithia, 1989), 265.

86. Polyvios G. Polyviou, *Cyprus in Search of a Constitution: Constitutional Negotiations and Proposals 1960–1975* (Nicosia: Chr. Nicolaou and Sons, 1976), 116.

87. Zaim M. Necatigil, *The Cyprus Question and the Turkish Position in International Law* (Oxford: Oxford UP, 1990), 67.

88. Rauf R. Denktash, "The Problem of Cyprus," *Review of International Affairs* 22, 544 (1972): 10.

89. Polyviou, *Cyprus in Search of a Constitution*, 138.

90. *Report by the Secretary-General on the United Nations Operation in Cyprus*, S/10401, November 30, 1971, para. 79.

91. EOKA-B preceded another *enosist* clandestine organization *Ethniko Metopo* [National Front], which in 1970 failed in its assassination attempt on Makarios. Greek officers loyal to Ioannidis and Makarios's former Minister for the Interior, Polycarpos Georgadjis, were implicated. In October 1973, EOKA-B also launched an assassination attempt on Makarios whereupon a series of coup plans were uncovered. See Spiros Papageorgiou, *Makarios dia Piros kai Sidirou* [Makarios through fire and steel] (Athens: Ladias, 1976), and Nikos Kranidiotis, *Anohiroti Politia* [unfortified state], vol. 2 (Athens: Estia, 1985).

92. Michael El. Dekleris, *Kipriako 1972–1974: I Teleftaia Efkairia* [Cyprus Problem 1972–1974: The Last Opportunity] (Athens: Estia, 1981), 141. For Turkish perceptions of Makarios's "*enosis* paradox," see Cyprus Turkish Information Office, "The Question of Cyprus: Can Makarios Abadon Enosis?" (Nicosia, 1971). Articulating a more sophisticated Turkish understanding, Kemal H. Karpat, "War on Cyprus: The Tragedy of Enosis," in *Turkey's Foreign Policy in Transition*, ed. K. H. Karpat (Leiden: E. J. Brill, 1975), 192–3, explains Makarios deviation from *enosis* in terms of class interest, AKEL's influence, and the allure of independence.

93. *Report by the Secretary-General on the United Nations operation in Cyprus for the period from 2 December 1973 to 22 May 1974*, S/11294, para. 60.

94. See also S/11008, October 3, 1973, Turkey's transmission of Denktash letter to the Secretary-General stating that the Turkish Cypriot community is seeking an agreed solution based on a permanent bicommunal independence; and S/10988 and S/11071, "Cyprus's letters," August 17 and November 2, 1973 stating the Greek Cypriots' objectives.

95. Until its official adoption by the Turkish leadership, federalism was muted as a potential legal-constitutional model. In a critique of Cyprus's central constitutional tenet as a failure in communalism, Catherine D. Papastathopoulos, "Constitutionalism and Communalism: The Case of Cyprus," *The University of Toronto Law Journal* 16, 1 (1965): 144, concludes by pondering whether federalism would have been a more appropriate model for the young Republic.

96. *Turkish News Bulletin* 2862, April 27, 1974.

97. Kemal H. Karpat, "Solution in Cyprus: Federation," in *The Cyprus Dilemma: Options for Peace* (New York: Institute for Mediterranean Affairs, 1967), 51.

98. Christopher Hitchens, *Cyprus* (London: Quartet Books, 1984), 164–5.

99. "Interview on MEGA TV with Michael Ignatiou, Secretary Colin L. Powell Washington, DC, April 16, 2004," 2004/416, April 17, 2004, www.state.gov/secretary/former/powell/remarks/31532.htm.

100. Vamık D. Volkan, *Cyprus—War and Adaptation: A Psychoanalytic History of Two Ethnic Groups in Conflict* (Charlottesville: UP of Virginia, 1979), 111–9.

101. An examination of the military forces on the island at the time of the Turkish invasion shows: the (Greek) Cypriot National Guard consisted of 11,500 men who were mainly infantry, with some light armaments, and 950 mainland Greek officers; while the Turkish Cypriot fighting force consisted of 11,000 well-trained militia under the control and command of 650 mainland Turkish officers. In addition, there were approximately 2,200 UNFICYP and some 8,000 British troops at the bases.

102. "Declaration by the Foreign Ministers of Greece, Turkey and the United Kingdom of Great Britain and Northern Ireland," S/11398, July 30, 1974.

103. Alan Watkins, "A Modest Success for Jim," *New Statesman* 2262 (July 26, 1974), 102.

104. A. M. Rendel, "Cyprus Agreement Finally Settled without Call for Turkish Withdrawal," *The Times*, July 31, 1974, 1.

105. "Mr Ecevit Cautious over Nato Links with Greece," *The Times*, August 1, 1974, 4.

106. During this diplomatic hiatus, Greek Cypriot refugees fleeing the Kyrenia enclave numbered 20,000. The United Nations confirmed that the Turkish army was forcibly expelling the remaining Greek Cypriots from the areas under Turkish control, "An Island Coming Apart at the Seams: The Blood Debt," *The Economist*, August 10, 1974, 33–4.

107. "Ecevit: The Poet Premier," *Time*, August 12, 1974, 29.

108. Mario Modiano, "Athens and Ankara May Start Talks Next Week," *The Times*, August 1, 1974, 4.

109. "The Six-Day Struggle to End the Ten-Day War: The Greeks Are Not Themselves," *The Economist*, August 3, 1974, 25.

110. Polyviou, *Cyprus in Search*, 423–4.

111. Clerides proposed a revision of the 1960 Constitution that provided for autonomous communal administrations, with increased powers over grouped Greek and Turkish areas, and legislation exercised by a bicommunal parliament. Once Callaghan's efforts for a joint UN-U.S.-British "determined stand" failed, he advised Clerides to reach the "best possible accommodation" under the circumstances. Callaghan's proposals called for "two autonomous administrations, within boundaries, united under a central government," within the context of a sovereign, independent, and integral Republic of Cyprus, Polyviou, *Cyprus in Search*, 420–5.

112. Clerides confirms that after sounding out Callaghan about the possibility of U.S.-British intervention in case of a further Turkish offensive, he propositioned the Soviets, through their Ambassador Sergei Astavin, that he was willing to give them a military base in exchange for Soviet intervention. Astavin replied to Clerides just before he left for Geneva that the Soviet Union was prepared to intervene only in conjunction with the United States. Glafkos Clerides, *I Katathesi Mou* [my deposition], vol. 4, (Nicosia: Alithia, 1991), 42 and 76.

113. This statement was issued at the August 13, 1974 Department of State press briefing, see Henry Kissinger, *Years of Renewal* (London: Weidenfeld and Nicolson, 1999), 229–31.

114. Kissinger stated at a news conference that the "situation in Cyprus tilted toward Turkey not as a result of American policy but as a result of the actions of the previous Greek Government which destroyed the balance of forces as it had existed on the island." "Secretary Kissinger's News Conference of August 19," *Department of State Bulletin* 71/1836, September 9, 1974, 354.

115. "Ankara Says US Backs Federal Solution," *The Times*, August 16, 1974, 8. Commenting on the United States' role, Ecevit also stated that the "United States, as a friend of all the three states…followed the developments closely [and was] able to evaluate the situation, the problem, objectively. They have refrained from taking sides. They have refrained from putting pressures, but I think they have tried to be understanding and to be constructive," "The Cyprus Situation: Ecevit Speaks," *The Middle East* 3, September/October 1974, 10.

116. "Britain Proposes Plan for Cyprus," *Washington Post*, August 13, 1974, 1.

117. John Saar, "The Turks Push Ahead in Cyprus Drive," *Washington Post*, August 15, 1974, 1.

118. "The Turks Carve their Slice," *Newsweek*, August 26, 1974, 16.

2   A Prisoner's Dilemma

1. Doob's ten-day workshop was to be held at the Hotel Fermeda in Tyrol, with the participants scheduled to depart from Nicosia International Airport on Saturday morning, July 20, 1974. Leonard W. Doob, "A Cyprus Workshop: An Exercise in Intervention Methodology," *Journal of Social Psychology* 94 (1974): 161–78.

2. In 1971, Malvern Lumsden, "The Cyprus Conflict as a Prisoner's Dilemma Game," *The Journal of Conflict Resolution* 17, 1 (1973): 7–32, a social psychologist from the University of Bergen conducted a clinical survey of 185 Greek and Turkish Cypriot student teachers, to assess how they perceived Cyprus five years into the future, under four contingencies (peace, war, *enosis*, and *taksim*).

3. In an interview with Oriana Fallaci, *Interview With History* (Boston: Houghton Mifflin, 1976), 313–4, Makarios stated: "What do you mean by a bad agreement? ... Turkey is going to insist on a geographical federation, and I will never accept a federation on a geographical basis. It would lead to a partition of the island and to double Enosis: half of Cyprus consigned to Greece and half to Turkey. It would mean the end of Cyprus as an independent state." Nevertheless, Makarios did not rule out federation, as evidenced in the rest of his answer: "I'm more than ready to discuss a federation, yes, but on an administrative basis not a geographical one. It's one thing to have areas governed by Turks and areas governed by Greeks; it's quite another to divide ourselves into two parts."

4. Clerides, *I Katathesi Mou*, 153–6.

5. See George Karouzis, *Proposals for a Solution to the Cyprus Problem* (Nicosia, 1976), 96–9, 146–56. At the time, Karouzis was head of the Cyprus Land Consolidation Authority and president of the Cyprus Geographical Association.

6. Critics of Cypriotism facetiously referred to the New Cyprus Association as *neokiprioi* (neo-Cypriots), implying they did not have continuous Hellenic lineage.

7. *Ta Nea*, November 8, 1974.

8. Ezekias Papaioannou, "Analisi tis Kipriakis Tragodias" [analysis of the Cyprus tragedy], *Neos Dimokratis* 43 (April 1975), 3–6.

9. *Ta Nea*, November 10, 1974.

10. Vassos Lyssarides, "Agonistikos Realismos me Vasi to Triptiho tis Ethnikis Sotirias" [fighting realism based on the triptych of national salvation], *ANTI* 46 (May 29, 1976), 19.

11. *Ta Nea*, May 11, 1975.

12. Mümtaz Soysal, "Political Parties in the Turkish Republic of Northern Cyprus and their Vision of 'the Solution,'" in *Cyprus, A Regional Conflict and its Resolution*, ed. N. Salem (New York: St. Martin, 1992), 40.

13. Rauf R. Denktash, *The Cyprus Triangle* (London: Allen and Unwin, 1982), 80.

14. As Nergis Canefe, "Refugees or Enemies? The Legacy of Population Displacements in Contemporary Turkish Cypriot Society," *South European Society and Politics* 7, 3 (2002): 1–28, argues, denying the existence of Greek Cypriot refugees by Turkish Cypriot nationalists was a key factor in their rejectionist posturing at the intercommunal negotiations; such denial stemmed from their pre-1974 victimization/ marginalization that created a "zero-sum" mentality toward the negotiations by justifying the population shifts emanating from 1974 as a "casualty of war."

15. Metin Tamkoç, *The Turkish Cypriot State: The Embodiment of the Right of Self-determination* (London: Rustem, 1988), 111.

16. David Tonge, "Oi Apopseis ton Tourkokiprion" [the views of the Turkish Cypriots], *ANTI* 51–2, August 7, 1976, 14.

17. *Haravghi*, October 2, 1989.

18. Tonge, "Apopseis ton Tourkokiprion."

19. *Halkin Sesi*, May 24, 1978.

20. The Republican Turkish Party, founded in 1970, was based on socialist principles and on an anti-imperialist platform. Berberoglu contested the 1976 vice-presidential elections polling 22 percent of the vote. He was succeeded as leader by Özgür (1976–1996).

21. *Halkin Sesi*, August 16, 1979.

22. The first post-1974 Greek Cypriot proposals comprised nine general principles: (1) "Cyprus shall be an independent and sovereign Republic"; (2) its "Constitution shall be that of a bi-communal multi-regional federal state"; (3) this included "a substantial area in the north extending on both sides of the Nicosia-Kyrenia axis to the sea"; (4) the other regions "shall be formed where Turkish Cypriot villages are mainly concentrated"; (5) the areas that should come under Turkish Cypriot administration shall "correspond approximately to the present ratio of the Greek and Turkish population" (that is, 18–20 percent); (6) the Republic shall "fund the cost of resettlement for those Turkish Cypriots who wish to settle in the Turkish Cypriot administered regions and who originally lived in the Greek Cypriot region"; (7) the "Central Government of the Federal State [shall have] substantial powers"; (8) the legal status of the Greek Cypriots and the Turkish Cypriots under each other's administration shall "be defined and entrenched"; (9) finally, human rights shall be ingrained in the constitution, including the three freedoms of movement, settlement, and ownership of property for all Cypriots. The document concluded by stating that these principles should not affect the provisions of the UN General Assembly Resolution 3212, especially those that pertained to the withdrawal of foreign troops and the return of all refugees. See "Constitutional proposals submitted by Mr. Clerides on 10 February 1975," *Special Report of the Secretary-General on Developments in Cyprus*, S/11624/Annex I, February 18, 1975.

23. Denktash tabled eleven constitutional principles proposing that Cyprus be an independent and secular republic (point 1); with a constitution that defined it as a bicommunal and bizonal state (point 2); federal laws would not discriminate against the Greek and Turkish federal states and be legislated in a way that neither community would dominate economically or/and politically (point 3); given the fact that the two communities cannot coexist, "only those powers necessary for the establishment of the Federation shall be left to the Federal State so as to enable the smooth functioning of the state. All other powers shall be vested in the federated state" (point 4); joint institutions be established,

on an equal basis, so as to prevent *de jure* and *de facto* sovereignty of one community against the other (point 5); foreign affairs would not be conducted at the expense of either of the federal states (point 6); there be a federal court independent of those of the states (point 7); citizens of the federal republic be allowed to travel between the two states (point 8); basic human rights and freedoms be respected (point 9); a transitional government, agreed by both communities, be established (point 10); and finally, the 1960 international agreements remain (point 11). See "Constitutional proposals submitted by Mr. Denktas on 13 February 1975," S/11624/Annex III.

24. Denktash, *Cyprus Triangle*, 80.
25. S/11449/Rev. 1, August 15, 1974.
26. *Report of the Secretary-General on the United Nations Operation in Cyprus for the Period from 23 May to 5 December 1974*, S/11568, paras. 63 and 81.
27. S/11557, November 14, 1974.
28. S/11657, March 12, 1975.
29. *Interim Report of the Secretary-General Pursuant to Security Council Resolution 367*, S/11684, May 4, 1975.
30. See "Turkish Cypriot Proposals of 18 July 1975 for a Joint Transitional Government," S/11770/Annex, July 22, 1975.
31. The agreement stipulated that: "1. The Turkish Cypriots at present in the South of the island [would] be allowed, if they wanted to do so, to proceed North with their belongings under an organized program with the assistance of UNFICYP. 2. Mr Denktash reaffirmed, and it was agreed, that the Greek Cypriots at present in the North of the island [were] free to stay and that they [would] be given every help to lead a normal life, including facilities for education and for the practice of their religion, as well as medical care by their own doctors and freedom of movement in the North. 3. The Greek Cypriots at present in the North who, at their own request, and without having been subjected to any kind of pressure, wish[ed] to move to the South, [would] be permitted to do so. 4. UNFICYP [would] have free and normal access to Greek Cypriot villages and habitations in the North. 5. In connection with the implementation of the above agreement, priority [would] be given to the reunification of families, which [might] also involve the transfer of a number of Greek Cypriots, at present in the South, to the North." "Text of the Press Communiqué on the Cyprus Talks Issued in Vienna on 2 August 1975," S/11789/Annex, August 2, 1975.
32. Turkish Republic of Northern Cyprus, *Questions of Cyprus: A Documented Story of 28 Years (1960–1988)* (Nicosia, 1988), 30–1.
33. Denktash, *Cyprus Triangle*, 81.
34. Glafkos Clerides, interview by author, Nicosia, January 11, 1984.
35. Robert McDonald, *The Problem of Cyprus* (Adelphi Paper 234, 1988/9), 20.

36. Kurt Waldheim, *The Challenge of Peace* (London: Weidenfeld and Nicolson, 1980), 70–1.

37. The text of the Brussels Accord (December 12, 1975) was jointly released by the Greek and Turkish Foreign Ministers, Dimitrios Bitsios and Ihsan Sabri Caglayangil, on May 22, 1976. See Necati Münir Ertekün, *In Search of a Negotiated Cyprus Settlement* (Nicosia, 1981), 283.

38. Clerides, *Katathesi Mou*, 415.

39. Ibid., 463–70.

40. "Proposals of the Greek Cypriot Side on the Various Aspects of the Cyprus Problem," S/12093/Annex I, June 5, 1976, 3–9.

41. These criteria included bizonal federalism; accommodating Turkish Cypriots wishing to live in the north; security requirements; restitution of Turkish Cypriots displaced prior to and following 1963; economic self-reliance; and communications latitude. "Proposals of the Turkish Cypriot Side on Various Aspects of the Cyprus Problem, Nicosia, 17 April 1976," S/12093/Annex II.

42. Kurt Waldheim, *In the Eye of the Storm: The Memoirs of Kurt Waldheim* (London: Weidenfeld and Nicolson, 1985), 78–92.

43. Waldheim, *Challenge of Peace*, 60–1.

44. The Makarios-Denktash High-Level agreement stated that: "(1) The participants [were] seeking an independent, non-aligned, bi-communal federal Republic; (2) The territory under the administration of each community should be discussed in light of economic viability and productivity and land ownership; (3) Questions of principles like freedom of movement, freedom of settlement, and the right of property and other specific matters [would be] open for discussion, taking into consideration the fundamental basis for a bi-communal federal system and certain practical difficulties which may arise for the Turkish Cypriot community; [and,] (4) The powers and functions of the Central Federal Government [would] be such as to safeguard the unity of the country, having regard to the bi-communal character of the state." See *Report of the Secretary-General in Pursuance of Paragraph 6 of Security Council Resolution 401 (1976)*, S/12323, April 30, 1977, para. 5.

45. *UN Press Release*, UN SG/T/752, Vienna, February 17, 1977.

46. Turhan Feyzioglu and Necati M. Ertekün, *The Crux of the Cyprus Question* (Nicosia, 1987), 40.

47. Rauf R. Denktash, "Memorandum Setting Out the Factual Position Regarding the Questions of 'Bizonality' and 'Security' (28 June 1979)," in Necati M. Ertekün, *The Cyprus Dispute and the Birth of the Turkish Republic of Northern Cyprus* (London: Rustem, 1984), 280–3.

48. Criton G. Tornaritis, *Cyprus and Its Constitutional and Other Legal Problems*, 2nd edn. (Nicosia, 1980), 116.

49. Even Pierre Oberling, *The Road to Bellapais: The Turkish Cypriot Exodus from Northern Cyprus* (New York: Columbia UP, 1982), 205—often a critic of Greek Cypriot obstinacy—conceded that the agreement was a

"major concession" by Makarios in that it recognized that the territory under each community's administration should be economically viable.

50. *Phileleftheros*, August 6, 1977.

51. Polyvios G. Polyviou, *Cyprus: Conflict and Negotiations 1960–1980* (London: Duckworth, 1980), 207.

52. Ibid., 10.

53. "Basic Principles which should Govern the Constitutional Structure of the Federal Republic of Cyprus Presented by the Greek Cypriot Side on 6.4.1977," S/12323/Annex III.

54. According to the Turkish Cypriot proposals, the areas that would come under the federal government's jurisdiction were: foreign affairs, defense, banking and foreign exchange, federal budget, customs, federal communications, citizenship and passport, federal medical services, weights and measures, and the setting up of federal advisory organizations, S/12323, 295–6.

55. "Constitutional Proposals of the Turkish Cypriot Side (submitted on April 1, 1977)," S/12323/Annex IV.

56. Public Information Office (PIO), "Statement by the Greek Cypriot Interlocutor on the Territorial Proposals of the Greek Cypriot Side on 31/3/77," *Cyprus Intercommunal Talks: New Series, First Round, Vienna, 31 March–7 April 1977* (Nicosia, 1977), 9.

57. "Comment made by the Greek Cypriot Interlocutor at the Meeting on 2.4.1977 on the Proposals Presented by the Turkish Cypriot Side on 1st April 1977 on the Constitutional Aspect," ibid., 18.

58. Zaim M. Nejatigil, *Our Republic in Perspective* (Nicosia: Tezel, 1985), 26–7.

59. Nancy Crawshaw, "Cyprus after Makarios: Prospects for a Settlement," *The World Today* 34, 1 (1978): 32.

60. Paragraph 5 proved controversial, going to a separate vote, as it recommended that the Security Council, monitoring the Cyprus issue, should *"adopt all practical means to promote the effective implementation of its relevant resolutions in all their aspects"* (my emphasis). But when the Security Council adopted Resolution 422 on December 15, 1977, it ignored the General Assembly's recommendation and instead placed its confidence in the Secretary-General "to continue the mission of good offices entrusted to him," UN Security Council Resolutions 1977, www.un.org/documents/sc/res/1977/res422e.pdf.

61. *Report of the Secretary-General on the United Nations Operation in Cyprus for the Period 1 December 1977 to 31 May 1978*, S/1273, paras. 47–9.

62. Proposals submitted by the Turkish Cypriot interlocutors on April 13, 1978 (which was referred to as the Soysal proposals) comprised two sets of documents: the actual proposals themselves, "Main Aspects of the Turkish Cypriot Proposals," and an "Explanatory Note of the Turkish Cypriot Proposals for the Solution of the Cyprus Problem" (incorporated as S/12723/Annex).

63. "Explanatory Note," ibid., 16.

64. "Main Aspects," ibid., 8–9.

65. Ibid., 12–5.

66. "Proposals on the Territories of the Federated States and a Joint Water Project," ibid., 20.

67. "Proposals on Maras (Varosha)," ibid., 21.

68. "Statement by the President of the Republic, Mr. Spyros Kyprianou," *Press Release* 8, Nicosia, April 19, 1978.

69. "Turkey's Ambiguous Offer" (editorial), *The Times*, April 15, 1978, 15.

70. The ten-point agreement stipulated that: "(1) It was agreed to resume the intercommunal talks on 15 June 1979; (2) The basis of the talks [would] be the Makarios/Denktash guidelines of 12 February 1977 and the UN Resolutions relevant to the Cyprus question; (3) There should be respect for human rights and fundamental freedom of all citizens of the Republic; (4) The talks [would] deal with all territorial and constitutional aspects; (5) Priority [would] be given to reaching agreement on the resettlement of Varosha under UN auspices simultaneously with the beginning of the consideration by the interlocutors of the constitutional and territorial aspects of a comprehensive settlement. After agreement on Varosha [had] been reached it [would] be implemented without awaiting the outcome of the discussions on other aspects of the Cyprus problem; (6) It was agreed to abstain from any action which might jeopardize the outcome of the talks, and special importance [would] be given to initial practical measures by both sides to promote good will, mutual confidence and the return to normal conditions; (7) The demilitarization of the island [was] envisaged and matters relating thereto [would] be discussed; (8) The independence, sovereignty, territorial integrity and non-alignment of the Republic should be adequately guaranteed against union in whole or in part with any other country and against any form of partition and secession; (9) The intercommunal talks [would] be carried out in a continuing and sustained manner, avoiding any delay; (10) The intercommunal talks [would] take place in Nicosia," S/13369, paras. 47–51.

71. Ibid., para. 44.

72. Rauf R. Denktash, "Letter to Dr Kurt Waldheim, Secretary-General of the United Nations, Nicosia, 28 June 1979," in Ertekün, *Cyprus Dispute*, 279–80.

73. S/13672, para. 46.

74. Ibid., para. 47.

75. *Aydinlik*, October 19, 1979.

76. *Olay*, July 16, 1979.

77. *Aydinlik*, August 10, 1980.

78. *Haravghi*, May 29, 1980.

79. *Report by the Secretary-General on Efforts to Bring about a Resumption of the Intercommunal Negotiations in Cyprus*, S/14100, August 11, 1980.

80. Ibid., annex.
81. "Greek Cypriot Proposals of October 8, 1980," 1–2 and 18–20.
82. "Turkish Cypriot Proposals, Draft Constitution of the Federal Republic of Cyprus," 1981, 1–2.
83. Ibid., 3.
84. Ibid., 17.
85. Ibid., 13–6.
86. Ibid., 30–1.
87. *Report of the Secretary-General on the United Nations Operation in Cyprus for the Period 28 May to 30 November 1981*, S/14778, para. 55.
88. Waldheim's guidelines were first published in *Cyprus Weekly*, November 6–12, 1981.
89. A decade later, Kyprianou's former foreign minister Nikos Rolandis revealed the existence of a UN map presented to him by Gobbi in New York on October 2, 1981 (*Agon*, March 31, 1991). According to Rolandis, the "Gobbi Map" would have allowed approximately 86,000 Greek Cypriot refugees to return to their homes, and defined the territorial size of the two provinces as being 72.5:27.5 percent (*Phileleftheros*, May 3, 1991). Furthermore, Rolandis stated that the map was proposed as a final solution to the territorial issue and that both Famagusta and Morphou would have been returned to the Greek Cypriots—although, according to Rolandis, Gobbi foresaw problems with Turkish Cypriots returning Morphou. Finally, Rolandis claimed that Kyprianou did not take the Gobbi map seriously (*Agon*, April 2, 1991). Kyprianou's response was that the map constituted Gobbi's personal opinion and this was verified by the fact that it was not included in Waldheim's proposals fifteen days later, nor was it ever mentioned in any future discussions (Democratic Party, *Press Release*, May 3, 1991). Rolandis retaliated by claiming that Gobbi would not have undertaken such an initiative if it was not authorized by the Secretary-General. The matter did not proceed further because Gobbi's map did not receive any encouragement from the Greek Cypriot side (*Phileleftheros*, May 4, 1991.)
90. Metin Munir, "Kissinger Proposes Cyprus Solution," *The Middle East* 4, November/December 1974, 12.
91. S/12723, para. 73.
92. "Statement by Mr. Denktash issued on 22 May 1978," A/33/107-S/12715/Annex, May 23, 1978.
93. This resulted in Resolution 33/15, which called on the Security Council to set a "time-frame" for the implementation of all resolutions on Cyprus and, if not adhered to, then to adopt "all appropriate and practical measures" accorded by the UN Charter for ensuring their implementation. The controversial paragraph 8 went to a separate vote and was passed by eighty in favor, seven against, and forty-eight abstentions (including the United States).

94. "A Promising Initiative on Cyprus" (editorial), *The Times*, November 23, 1978, 19.

95. U.S. Foreign Assistance Act 1961, Section 16 (A), Sec. 620B and C.

96. "Framework for a Cyprus Settlement Prepared by the US, British and Canadian Governments," PIO, *Cyprus Intercommunal Talks: Following the Turkish Invasion of July-August 1974* (Nicosia: April 1982), 88–91.

97. "AKEL Central Committee, Press Release, 4 December 1978," *Neos Dimokratis* 55, December 1978, 3–7.

98. Main elements of the paper, "Observations on the Document Entitled 'Framework for Regulating the Cyprus Problem,'" are found in PIO, *Cyprus Intercommunal Talks*, 42–6.

99. Yiannos Kranidiotis, "Oi Diapragmateseis gia tin Epilisi tou Kipriakou [negotiations for the resolution of the Cyprus problem] (1974–1981)," in *Kipros: Istoria, Provlimata kai Agones tou Laou tis* [Cyprus: History, Problems and Struggles of Its People], ed. Giorgos Tenekidis and Yiannos Kranidiotis (Athens: Estia, 1981), 616–7.

100. For the most articulate critique of the U.S. plan by the militants, see Chrysostomos Perikleous, *To Kipriako Provlima* [Cyprus problem] (Nicosia: Onisillos, 1986), 152–3.

101. DISY, *Analisi Enos Lathous: I Aporipsi tou Ditikou Schediou gia tin Kipro* [Analysis of a Mistake: The Rejection of the Western Plan for Cyprus], Nicosia: May 1980, 14–21.

102. "Tenth Report on Cyprus: Message to the Congress, November 30 (1978)," *Department of State Bulletin* 79/2023, February 1979, 44.

103. Famagusta Refugee Movement, "The Case for Famagusta," Nicosia, 1981, 28.

104. Denktash's first offer (May 22, 1978) was reiterated—ominously—on July 20, 1978, which had Varosha come under UN supervision that included municipal and police functions. However, the offer was contingent on the Greek Cypriots restarting the intercommunal talks ("Open Message dated 20 July 1978 to the Greek Cypriot Leadership from the Turkish Cypriot Leader, Mr. Rauf R. Denktash," S/12782). Kyprianou rejected the proposal on the grounds that it was territorially insufficient, and five days later issued his own proposals, which entailed the withdrawal of Turkish troops from the city and the safe return of its Greek Cypriot inhabitants. Furthermore, before it reverted to Greek Cypriot jurisdiction, the city would, for a period of time, be under UN control (S/12789, July 25, 1978).

105. Specifically, the Nimetz Plan stipulated that the resettlement of Varosha would be conducted in cooperation with the UN Secretary-General, according to the following guidelines: that the area in question be defined broadly to encompass land from "the east of the village Agios Nikolaos…to the south of the old Nicosia-Famagusta Road" and to take into consideration Turkish Cypriot

security concerns regarding old Famagusta and its harbor; that the territory be administered by the United Nation with Greek and Turkish Cypriot liaison officers; that there be no fixed numerical limit for resettlement of former residents; and that the Varosha refugees not be subject to further involuntary displacement. "Framework for a Cyprus Settlement," 88–91.

106. S/12723, para. 78.
107. *Cyprus Mail*, January 9, 1981.
108. Denktash Press Conference, Nicosia, January 8, 1981.
109. *Bozkurt*, January 8, 1981.
110. For example, the newspaper *Kurtulus*, November 7, 1980, declared that "the arguments put forward by the government attributing the misery…to the Greek embargo [were] not true."

3 Faltering UN Involvement

1. Waldheim, *Challenge of Peace*, 77–8.
2. Kurt Waldheim, *Building the Future Order: The Search for Peace in an Interdependent World* (New York: Free Press, 1980), 42.
3. For example, on December 10, 1981, Papandreou stated that "as far as the great national issue of Cyprus, I placed it on an entirely new basis. The essence of the Cyprus problem has never been, nor is the conflict, between the two communities, the Greek-Cypriot and the Turkish-Cypriot…The dialogue between the two communities is not a dialogue between two communities! It is a dialogue between Nicosia and Ankara, which has a tremendous military presence in occupied Cyprus." *Logoi Prothipourgou Andrea G. Papandreou* [prime minister Andreas G. Papandreou's speeches] *1981–1982*, (Athens: Press and Information General Secretariat, 1983), 52.
4. S/15002, December 1, 1982, para. 59.
5. Besides strengthening, even further, the mediating role of the Secretary-General, Resolution 37/253 entailed two additional paragraphs pertaining to the withdrawal of all occupational troops and a timeframe for its implementation.
6. Aide Memoire, August 8, 1983.
7. A/38/452-S/16148/Annex.
8. *For the Liberty, Equality, Dignity and Security of our People: The Declaration and Resolution Adopted by the Turkish Cypriot Parliament on 15 November 1983*, Article 24, 11–2.
9. UN Security Council Resolution 541 (1981), November 18, 1983, http://daccessdds.un.org/doc/RESOLUTION/GEN/NR0/453/99/IMG/NR045399.pdf?OpenElement.
10. Kyprianou proposed that in the first instance all Turkish troops and settlers be withdrawn, followed by the Greek and Turkish contingents, and the disbanding of the Cyprus National Guard and the Turkish Cypriot Security Forces. An expanded UN peacekeeping force, drawn

from countries that had no direct involvement with the conflict, would be in charge of internal security.

11. "Framework for a Comprehensive Settlement of the Cyprus Problem," S/16549/Annex, January 11, 1984.

12. DISY, ["Clerides Plan"], Nicosia, January 27, 1984.

13. "Press Release dated 17 November 1983," S/16159/Annex.

14. S/16246/Annex, January 3, 1984.

15. Specifically, President Ronald Reagan sought budget approval from the Congressional Appropriations Committee for funds to modernize Turkey's F-16 fighter aircrafts. The committee resolved to withhold the $39 million package whilst the Senate Foreign Relations Committee also decided to suspend $215 million in military aid to Turkey until Varosha was placed under UN administration. This prompted Reagan to make a statement, three days before the Security Council vote on Resolution 550, in which, while recognizing the frustration felt by Congress over the need for progress on Cyprus, he nevertheless proposed that, rather "than punishing Turkey," Congress needed to work with his Administration in creating the conditions conducive for successful diplomacy. In this connection Reagan argued that he was prepared to establish a "Special Cyprus Peace and Reconstruction Fund" of $250 million. "Statement by President Reagan, May 8, 1984," *American Foreign Policy Current Documents, 1984* (Washington: Department of State, 1986), doc. 138, 386–7.

16. Denktash's response to the five-point package were as follows: he argued that if the Turkish Cypriots refrained from implementing the UDI, then the Greek Cypriots should also cease from asserting that they were the "Government of Cyprus"; he also argued that for a high-level meeting to proceed, there had to be a total ban on the internationalization of the Cyprus issue; on the resettlement of Varosha, Denktash set a series of conditions. Varosha would be divided into two zones, east and west of Dherinia. The section east of Dherinia would be placed under interim UN administration and, provided that the Greek Cypriots did not contravene the ban on internationalization for one year, they would be allowed to resettle. Furthermore, its resettlement would be subject to a final settlement being reached within five years, otherwise in both cases it would revert back to Turkish Cypriot jurisdiction. In addition, tourists would be allowed to visit the above section through Turkish and/or Greek Cypriot air and sea ports. The resettlement of Varosha west of Dherinia would not come under Greek Cypriot jurisdiction until a final settlement was reached, S/16519/Annex IV.

17. S/16519/Annex III.

18. UN Secretary-General's "Working Points," August 1984.

19. Necatigil, *Cyprus Question*, 242.

20. These points were: the actual deadlock-resolving mechanisms for the legislature; the structure of the presidency and executive government;

the territorial adjustments; the conclusion of the UN interim administration of Varosha, the six areas delineated in the 1981 Turkish Cypriot map, and the Nicosia Airport; and the setting of the date for the inauguration of the transitional federal government. Pérez de Cuéllar, "Agenda for the Third Round of the Secretary-General's Proximity Talks on Cyprus, Preliminary Draft for a Joint High-Level Agreement," November 1984.

21. "Non-Paper No. 1" and "Non-Paper No. 2," New York, December 1984.

22. Spyros Kyprianou, "Letter to Secretary-General of the United Nations," New York, December 13, 1984.

23. Mario Mindiano, "Reagan's Letter Generates Cyprus Breakthrough," *Sunday Times*, December 16, 1984.

24. Information about an airport at the outskirts of the village Lefkoniko being constructed and financed by the United States was first revealed by the news article "Cyprus Tension Rises over US 'Base Plan,'" *Sunday Times*, May 27, 1984. This was followed by Christopher Hitchens's, "Minority Report: Cyprus," *Nation*, August 18–25, 1984, 104. In their editorial on the proximity talks, *The Times* mentioned the airport by linking it to the U.S. Central Command ("More Discreet Proximity on Cyprus," November 27, 1984, 15). These reports prompted a denial by Richard N. Haass, "US Views on Cyprus," *The Times*, December 20, 1984, 11. Glen D. Camp, "Cyprus Between the Powers: 1980–1989," *The Cyprus Review* 1, 2 (1989): 74, believed that reports of the Lefkoniko airport were part of a disinformation campaign that originated with a forged letter published on the front page of the Greek Cypriot newspaper *Simerini* on November 26, 1985.

25. "Politics Today," *International Review* 1 (London: Conservative Research Department, January 25, 1985), 12.

26. S/16858/Add.2, Annex II, February 2, 1985.

27. The four issues comprised: a timetable for the withdrawal of non-Cypriot troops; the question of guarantees; the three freedoms; and the exact areas the Turkish Cypriots would return to the Greek Cypriots.

28. Richard N. Haass, *Conflicts Unending: The United States and Regional Disputes* (New Haven: Yale UP, 1990), 71–2.

29. Interview by Pérez de Cuéllar, *BBC Four Radio* (January 24, 1985).

30. *Guardian*, January 27, 1985.

31. AKEL Central Committee, "1985 Parliamentary Results," *Neos Dimokratis* 89, 1986, 7–10.

32. *Halkin Sesi*, May 17, 1979.

33. Christos Ioannides, *In Turkey's Image: The Transformation of Occupied Cyprus into a Turkish Province* (New Rochelle, NY: A. D. Caratzas, 1991), 163–5.

34. *Richard Haass, Special Cyprus Coordinator, Testimony Before the Subcommittee on Europe and the Middle East* (Washington, DC, November 2, 1983), 27.

35. *Halkin Sesi*, May 24 and 25, 1978.

36. See *Milliyet*, March 13, 1984; and, *Günaydin*, March 3, 1984.

37. *Günaydin*, January 7–14, 1986.

38. S/11859/Annex, October 24, 1975.

39. Turkey Ministry of Foreign Affairs, *Foreign Policy of Turkey at the United Nations*, vol. 3 (Ankara, 1983), 502.

40. See Colonial Office Cyprus reports for the years 1955–1959.

41. See Republic of Cyprus, *Statistical Abstracts, 1965 and 1973* (Nicosia).

42. *Yenidüzen*, February 15, 1989.

43. *Ortam*, May 18, 1989, and *Yenidüzen*, February 2, 1990.

44. *TRNC Statistical Yearbook, 1987* (Nicosia, 1988), 12.

45. See *Rozanne Ridgway, Assistant Secretary of State for European and Canadian Affairs, Testimony before Subcommittee on Europe and Middle East* (Washington, DC, June 19, 1986), 51–2; UK House of Commons, Foreign Affairs Committee, *Report on Cyprus* (London: HMSO, May 1987), xvii. Demographist Aaron Segal, *An Atlas of International Migration* (London, 1993), 162, estimated that there had been 80,000 Turkish settlers by the 1990s, while Özgür stated that 50,000 settlers were officially imported into northern Cyprus between 1974 and 1986, *Humanité*, April 7, 1984. The most accurate figure, however, was provided by *Yenidüzen*, February 15, 1989, which revealed that 46,216 Turkish nationals settled in the TRNC in 1974–1986. It is worth noting that even Denktash admitted that 45,000–50,000 Turkish nationals had migrated to the TRNC, *El Pais*, July 20, 1988.

46. Using the 1996 census data and updates, Mete Hatay in a PRIO report, *Beyond Numbers: An Inquiry into the Political Integration of the Turkish "Settlers" in Northern Cyprus* (PRIO Report 4/2005), estimated Turkish "settlers"—defined as Turkish-mainland migrants granted TRNC citizenship—to be around 32,000–35,000, accounting for 16.4 percent–18.4 percent of a total TRNC citizenship of 190,000. He also pointed out that there was an estimated additional 102,000 temporary residents from Turkey in northern Cyprus (viii–ix). Hatay places the figure of "settlers" at around 20 percent–30 percent of the TRNC population/electorate (57).

47. *Aydinlik*, April 18, 1980.

48. Necatigil, *Cyprus Question*, 290–1.

49. "Letter dated 21 April 1986 from His Excellency Mr. Denktash addressed to the Secretary-General," S/18102/Add.1/Annex V.

50. "Letter dated 20 April 1986 from President Kyprianou Addressed to the Secretary-General," S/18102/Add.1/Annex IV.

51. A/41/96-S/17752/Annex, January 21, 1986.

52. Spyros Kyprianou, "Letter to His Excellency Mr. Javier Pérez de Cuéllar, Secretary-General of the United Nations," Nicosia, March 10, 1987.

53. In a confidential report, the Republic of Cyprus's (RoC) Ministry of Foreign Affairs (1987), "Cypriot Recourse to the 42nd Session of the UN General Assembly [Greek]," Confidential, File number A.24/17,

GAPOLPAR/VM/MZM, was optimistic that with the support of the nonaligned countries such a resolution could be adopted.

54. Richard N. Haass, "Cyprus: Moving Beyond Solution?" *The Washington Quarterly* 10, 2 (1987): 188–9.

55. "Messages, not Bullets," *Athena Magazine* 16, May–June 1987, 152–3.

56. Greek PIO, *Greece: Background, News, Information* 27, London, February 25, 1988. It appeared that foreign exploitation of Greek-Turkish differences was a widely held view amongst many left-wing political leaders in both Greece and Turkey. For example, Ecevit asserted that after "World War II, when other countries were too occupied with their own problems and left Turkey and Greece alone, excellent relations and co-operation between the two countries were established in the 1950s, and were only disrupted as a result of the events in Cyprus. So the elimination of outside influences is essential for a solution of the problems between Turkey and Greece and for a solution of the Cyprus problem." Bulent Ecevit, "Turkey's Security Policies," in *Greece and Turkey: Adversity in Alliance*, ed. J. Alford, (Adelphi Library 12, 1984), 141.

57. Other measures included an economic committee and a joint business council, and the encouragement of military, media, and business contacts. A hotline would link the two leaders, who would meet reciprocally at least once a year, and their diplomats would cooperate in international organizations. "Davos Joint Press Communiqué," January 31, 1988.

58. *Greece: Background…27.*

59. Özal also agreed to repeal the 1964 decree that froze Greek properties in Turkey, and in exchange the Greek side would give its consent to reactivate the Turkey-EC Association Agreement. "Brussels Communiqué," March 4, 1988.

60. Raoul Denktash, "Good Will Measures Proposed by the Turkish Cypriot Side on 3 March 1988," A/42/928-S/19578.

61. "Address by the President of the Republic of Cyprus, Mr. George Vassiliou, to the 3rd Special Session of the UN General Assembly Devoted to Disarmament," *Press Release* 7, June 2, 1988, 6–7.

62. Özal Press Conference, UN Headquarters, New York, June 2, 1988.

63. *Tercüman*, June 4, 1988.

64. (Turkish) *Daily News*, June 4, 1988.

65. *Milliyet*, June 6, 1988.

66. Greek Press and Information Secretariat, "Events of the Week: 10–17 June 1988," 6–7.

67. Greek PIO, *Greece: Background, News, Information* 31, June 30, 1988.

68. "Events of the Week," 9, 12–13.

69. Papandreou's Press Conference after Departure of Ozal, June 15, 1988.

70. Mehmet Ali Birand, "Turkey and the 'Davos Process': Experience and Prospects," in *The Greek-Turkish Conflict in the 1990s: Domestic and External Influences*, ed. D. Constas (London: Macmillan, 1991), 27–9.

71. Theodore Stanger, "A Town Moves out of Town; Too much Tourism for the People of St. Napa," *Newsweek* 113/1, March 13, 1989, 39.

72. Such common space was to be found at the periphery of Cypriot society, such as in the mixed village of Pyla—caught in the nebulous UN buffer zone separating the Turkish Armed Forces and the (Greek) Cyprus National Guard, on the edge of the Dhekelia British Sovereign Area. The Greek and Turkish Cypriot diaspora, especially in the UK and to a lesser extent in Australia and North America, also offered themselves as common space for bicommunal rapprochement.

73. Leonard W. Doob, "Cypriot Patriotism and Nationalism," *Journal of Conflict Resolution* 30, 2 (1986): 383–96.

74. According to the World Bank, in 1978 Cyprus's GNP per capita was $2,120, whilst Turkey's was $1,200 and Greece's $3,250, all ranked as middle-income countries, *World Development Report 1980* (Washington, DC, August), 111 and 159. In 1989, Cyprus's GNP per capita raised to $7,040, which, according to the World Bank, ranked as a high-income economy, surpassing Greece at $5,350 and Turkey at $1,370, World Bank, *World Development Report 1991: The Challenge of Development* (New York: Oxford UP), 205 and 271. Independent Turkish Cypriot figures for this period are hard to find, as they were not registered by international financial monitors. This account is attributed to David Barchard, *Financial Times*, December 3, 1985, in Demetrios Christodoulou, *Inside the Cyprus Miracle: The Labours of an Embattled Mini-Economy* (Minnesota Mediterranean and East European Monographs 2, 1992), xiv–xivi.

75. In 1974–1979, approximately 51,500 Greek Cypriots emigrated from the island. Between 1980 and 1986 this figure dropped to approximately 2,000, whilst for the same period 2,850 repatriated back to Cyprus.

76. See Paschalis M. Kitromilides, "The Dialectic of Intolerance: Ideological Dimensions of Ethnic Conflict," *Journal of the Hellenic Diaspora* 6, 4 (1979): 5–30; and Caesar V. Mavratsas, "The Ideological Contest between Greek-Cypriot Nationalism and Cypriotism 1974–1995: Politics, Social Memory, and Identity," *Ethnic and Racial Studies* 20, 4 (1997): 717–37.

77. Yael Navaro-Yashin, "De-ethicizing the Ethnography of Cyprus: Political and Social Conflict between Turkish Cypriots and Settlers from Turkey," in *Divided Cyprus: Modernity, History and an Island in Conflict*, ed. Y. Papadakis, N. Peristianis, and G. Welz (Bloomington: Indiana UP, 2006), 84–99.

78. The fact that its founder, Alparslan Türkeş, was a Turkish Cypriot compounds the association between Cyprus and Turkish (ultra) nationalism, whilst drawing interesting parallels with the instance of George Grivas.
79. Niyazi Kizilyürek and Sylvaine Gautier-Kizilyürek, "The Politics of Identity in the Turkish Cypriot Community and the Language Question," *International Journal of the Sociology of Language* 168 (2004): 37–54.
80. Christoph Ramm, "Assessing Transnational Re-negotiation in the Post-1974 Turkish Cypriot Community; 'Cyprus Donkeys,' 'Black Beards' and the 'EU Carrot,'" *Southeast European and Black Sea Studies* 6, 4 (2006): 523–42.

4   The End of an Era?

1. The poem was written in 1976 and appeared in Neshe Yashin's collection, *Hyacinth and Narcissus* (Istanbul: Cem, 1979), 36.
2. UN SCR 682, December 21, 1990.
3. "Report of the Secretary-General on the work of the Organization," *Yearbook of the United Nations, 1989,* vol. 43 (New York, 1997), 6.
4. "The Turkish Cypriot Proposals" of 1988/89 do not carry any distinguishable title and are referred to as simply "The Turkish Cypriot Proposals." The set of documents submitted on January 9, 1989 comprised an introductory document, "The Turkish Cypriot Position"; and the following: (1) "The Turkish Cypriot approach to the question of the so-called 'three freedoms' as part of an integrated whole"; (2) "The Turkish Cypriot approach to the question of Cypriot and non-Cypriot Forces as part of an integrated whole"; (2/A) "The Turkish Cypriot approach to the question of Cypriot and non-Cypriot Forces as part of an integrated whole (expanded version)"; (3) "The Turkish Cypriot approach to adequate and effective guarantees as part of an integrated whole"; (4) "Federal structure, as part of an integrated whole, is the key to a comprehensive settlement"; (5) "The Turkish Cypriot approach regarding the future course of the talks"; (6) "The Turkish Cypriot approach to the question of 'deconfrontation'"; (6/A) "The Turkish Cypriot approach to the question of 'deconfrontation' (expanded version)"; (7) "The Turkish Cypriot approach to the federal constitution as part of an integrated whole"; (8) "The Turkish Cypriot approach to the federal executive as part of an integrated whole."
5. Paper No. 4.
6. Paper No. 8, 1–3.
7. Paper No. 7, 2–3.
8. The Greek Cypriot response was presented in a detailed working document prepared by the RoC foreign ministry, "Analysis of Mr. Denktash's Papers Formally Tabled on 9.1.1989," Nicosia, January 26,

1989, comparing them to their previous positions, 2, 7–10, and 42–5.

9. George Vassiliou, "Outline Proposals for the Establishment of a Federal Republic and for the Solution of the Cyprus Problem," Nicosia, January 30, 1989, 2–3.

10. Vassiliou, 19.

11. In an earlier version, Vassiliou originally excluded the Greek Cypriots from voting for the vice-president in situations where the vice-president had to be a Turkish Cypriot, "The Future Federal Republic of Cyprus: Turkish Cypriot Participation and Other Related Matters," Nicosia, January 14, 1989, 3. It appeared that, on reflection, Vassiliou believed cross-voting should apply to both communities, otherwise the proposals would lose their purpose of integrating communal politics.

12. Vassiliou, 21.

13. Vassiliou, 25.

14. "Memorandum by the Turkish Cypriot Side Presented on 13 February 1989 at the Intercommunal Talks in Lefkosa," *New Cyprus*, February 1989, 18.

15. "An Appraisal of the Greek Cypriot 'Outline Proposals' of January 30, 1989," ibid., 19–23.

16. *Report of the Secretary-General on his Mission of Good Offices in Cyprus*, S/21393, July 12, 1990, para. 3.

17. "Statement by the President of the Security Council," S/20330, December 15, 1988.

18. "Pérez de Cuéllar's Ideas," July 25, 1989, 1.

19. Ibid., 2.

20. In particular, the federal government would have jurisdiction over foreign affairs (with the states being able to enter into foreign agreements provided they were consistent with the federal constitution and with federal government policy), monetary affairs, international trade and customs (including ports and airports), immigration and citizenship, national defense, budget and federal taxation, postal and telecommunications, trademarks and patents, appointment of federal civil servants, the establishment of a Cypriot university, federal judiciary and federal police, the coordinating of tourism and industrial policy, and the setting of standards for health, environment, natural resources, transportation, weights and measures. All other matters would have state jurisdiction with the option of jointly conferring additional powers and functions to the federal sphere. Each state would decide its own government arrangements, ibid., 2–3.

21. Ibid., 4.

22. Ibid., 5.

23. Ibid., 6–7.

24. Ibid., 7–8.

25. Ibid., 9.

26. Ibid., 9–10.

27. Ibid., 10–1.

28. "Statement by Secretary-General on Events of 19 July in United Nations Buffer Zone in Nicosia," *Press Release,* UN SG/SM/4310, New York, July 21, 1989.

29. *Report of the Secretary-General on his Mission of Good Offices in Cyprus,* S/21010, December 13, 1989.

30. S/20821, August 28, 1989.

31. "Draft Joint Declaration, (together with) Explanatory Note and Draft Outline of a Comprehensive Settlement in Cyprus" were submitted to the UN Secretary-General, October 11, 1989, 2.

32. *Report of the Secretary-General on his Mission of Good Offices in Cyprus,* S/21183, March 8, 1990, para. 13.

33. TRNC, *The Right to Self-Determination of the Turkish-Cypriot People* (Nicosia, 1990), 3–4.

34. Ibid., 11–19.

35. S/21393, para. 8.

36. "Turkish Cypriot Memorandum Addressed to the Council of Ministers of the European Communities in Respect to an 'Application' for Membership by 'the Republic of Cyprus,'" (July 12, 1990), para. 2, http://www.cypnet.com/.ncyprus/cyproblem/articles/bolum1.html. This point was further elaborated by reference to the Zurich/London Agreements' minutes of February 19, 1959, "A Supplementary Note to the Turkish Memorandum of 12 July 1990 on the Greek Cypriot 'Application' for Membership of the European Communities," http://www.cypnet.com/.ncyprus/cyproblem/articles/bolum10.html. Denktash pursued this further by seeking a legal opinion on his community's right to sovereignty and self-determination, the legal status of the two communities, and the Greek Cypriots acting as the Republic of Cyprus and applying for EC membership. See Elihu Lauterpacht, "Turkish Republic of Northern Cyprus—the Status of the Two Communities in Cyprus," Monroe Leigh, "The Legal Status in International Law of the Turkish Cypriot and Greek Communities in Cyprus," Lauterpacht and Leigh, "On Sovereignty in Cyprus and its Relationship to Proposals for a Solution on the Cyprus Problem Along Federal Lines," in *The Status of the Two People in Cyprus,* ed. N. M. Ertekün (Nicosia: TRNC Foreign Affairs and Defense, 1997).

37. Turkish Cypriot Memorandum, para. 16.

38. Ibid., para. 15.

39. Ibid., para. 2 and 3, 18, 22.

40. Ibid., para. 19 and 20.

41. Eisigiseis tou Ipourgou Exoterikou pros to Ethniko Simvoulio gia tin Peraitero Diethnopoiisi tou Kipriakou [proposals by the minister of foreign affairs toward the national council in the further internationalization of the Cyprus problem], Confidential Document, Nicosia, June 1, 1990, 1.

42. UN SC Resolution 649/90, March 13, 1990, para. 4 and 7.

43. S/21183/Annex I, para. 11, 7.

44. S/21393, para. 25.

45. "Pérez de Cuéllar's Statement," March 2, 1990.

46. *Report of the Secretary-General on his Mission of Good Offices in Cyprus*, S/23121, October 8, 1991, para. 17.

47. R. Rauf Denktash, "Federalism-Economic and Political Issues," *Turkish Review* 3, 16 (1989): 11.

48. S/23121, para. 19.

49. "Statement by the President of the Security Council, 28 June 1991," S/22744, 29.

50. Resolution 716, 29–30.

51. Senate Committee on Foreign Relations, *Cyprus: International Law and the Prospects for Settlement: Hearing before the Subcommittee on European Affairs*, 102nd Congress, 1st sess., April 17, 1991, 5.

52. "Address by President Bush before the Greek Parliament, Athens, July 18, 1991," U.S. Department of State, *American Foreign Policy Current Documents 1991* (Washington, DC: Government Printing Office, 1994), doc. 146, 288.

53. Specifically, Bush stated that: "We've seen too much change in the world to settle for the status quo between your two great countries...We have seen too much change in this region and throughout the world to stand for the status quo in Cyprus." "Statement by President Bush, Istanbul, July 21, 1991," ibid., doc. 208, 381.

54. "Press Conference by President Bush and Prime Minister Mitsotakis, Athens, July 18, 1991," ibid., doc. 130, 260.

55. "Letter from President Bush to the Speaker of the House of Representatives, May 3, 1991," ibid. doc. 129, 260.

56. Ibid., 261.

57. Ibid., doc. 208.

58. "Press Conference by President Bush and President Özal, Ankara, July 20, 1991," ibid., doc. 131, 262. Despite Bush's claim to ownership of the "quadripartite" proposal, it appears to have come from Özal himself. The fact that Turkey offered to directly involve itself, for the first time since 1974, in the Cyprus talks, appeared to signal to the Americans Turkey's (or at least Özal's) willingness to apply pressure on Denktash to be more cooperative. William E. Broomfield, "The Eastern Mediterranean in the Post-Gulf Crisis: Unresolved Issues," *Mediterranean Quarterly* 2, 3 (1991): 21–2.

59. Resolution 716, October 11, 1991.

60. *Report of the Secretary-General on His Mission of Good Offices in Cyprus*, S/23300, December 19, 1991.

61. *Report of the Secretary-General on His Mission of Good Offices in Cyprus*, S/24472, August 21, 1992, para. 14.

62. Quite the contrary, as Pérez de Cuéllar's assistant, Camilion, revealed, Özal disliked Denktash and "couldn't give a damn about him." High Commission of Australia, "Records of Meetings by

Dr. A. Theophanous, MP, with Mr Oscar Camilion and Foreign Minister George Iacovou, October 6, 1992," Nicosia, 1. The experience revealed another aspect of the Turkish Cypriot leader's relationship with Turkey's governing elite, namely, that Denktash was capable of deflecting any potential pressure from the civilian politicians if their views did not meet his purpose.

63. *Report of the Secretary-General on his Mission of Good Offices in Cyprus*, S/23780, April 3, 1992, para. 1.

64. Ibid., para. 43.

65. "Set of Ideas on an Overall Framework Agreement on Cyprus," S/24472/Annex and Appendix, July 15, 1992.

66. Resolution 750 (April 10, 1992), *Resolutions and Decisions of the Security Council 1992* (New York: United Nations, 1993), 92.

67. These eight topics were: (1) overall objectives; (2) guiding principles of federation; (3) constitutional aspects: (i) powers and functions of the federal government; (ii) structure, composition, and functioning of the federal government; (iii) fundamental rights, including the three freedoms, and political, economic, social, and cultural rights; (4) security and the question of external guarantees; (5) territorial adjustments; (6) displaced persons; (7) economic development and safeguards; and, (8) transitional arrangements, S/23780, para. 4.

68. Ibid., para. 6.

69. This program would be introduced once both communities, through separate referenda, reached an overall agreement. It consisted of fourteen goodwill measures: (1) the embargo on the flow of persons and goods, services, capital, communication, and international assistance to and from Cyprus be lifted; (2) all restrictions on travel of the Turkish Cypriots be lifted; (3) the restrictions on the movement of tourists be lifted; (4) that objections to the participation in international sport and cultural events be lifted; (5) that the freedom of movement, subject to agreement and with minimal procedure, be facilitated; (6) that Varosha be placed under UN administration and a program for its restoration be prepared and implemented; (7) that all military modernization and strengthening of positions cease, and that the two sides would cooperate with UNFICYP in extending the unmanning of positions along the buffer zone to all areas where their troops are in close proximity to each other and ensure that UNFICYP has free access to the whole of the island; (8) that a bicommunal committee be established to review school textbooks which may have offensive aspects to each community; (9) that both communities would promote goodwill between themselves and toward Greece and Turkey; (10) that both communities terminate all recourse to international bodies against each other and Greece and Turkey; (11) the establishment of a bicommunal committee to review the water supply situation and make appropriate recommendations; (12) the establishment of a bicommunal committee to prepare a

program for the restoration of historical and religious sites through-out Cyprus; (13) that a bicommunal committee be established to undertake a population census; and, (14) that the two communities would support the efforts of the Committee for Missing Persons in an extensive investigation of each individual case. "Programme of Action to Promote Goodwill and Close Relations between the Two Communities (CBMs)," S/24472/Appendix.

70. Transitional arrangements would have to be completed within eighteen months, including two separate referenda to approve the Overall Framework Agreement, the federal constitution, and elect their federal officials. In the interim, each side would continue to handle its internal affairs on a day-to-day basis, while external affairs would be conducted in line with the principles of the Overall Framework Agreement and with the consensus of the two leaders. Each community would prepare its own state constitution, and elections would be streamlined with those of the federal republic. They would all be required to come into effect at the time of the establishment of the federal republic (paras. 93–9). Other additions included: the maintenance of special friendship ties with Greece and Turkey; that separate majorities in the lower house would be required on matters of foreign affairs, defense, budget, taxation, immigration, and citizenship; that a deadlock on decisions or bills would be referred to a "consensus mechanism" comprised of two Greek Cypriot and two Turkish Cypriot parliamentarians; a time-table for military reduction would be in "phases parallel to imple-mentation of [a] good will programme"; personnel of the Greek and Turkish contingents would be of equal numerical strength and would not exceed a certain number; they would be stationed and administered in their corresponding community's state and not be permitted to enter the other state; the same provisions would apply to the Greek Cypriot and Turkish Cypriot component of the federal army; there would be no reserve army, and no military or paramili-tary training of civilian groups; ownership of weapons, other than licensed hunting guns, would be disallowed. Importation or transit of military equipment other than those authorized by the federal government would be prohibited. Security and guarantee provi-sions would be the responsibility of, and overseen by, an interim monitoring committee comprising the three guarantor powers, the two communities, and the UNFICYP; a supervision and verifica-tion committee comprising the three guarantor powers, the presi-dent, and vice-president would be established with UN support to investigate any threat to either community or the federal republic; this would be done by on-site inspections or any other methods deemed necessary; the verification committee would make recom-mendations if there were contraventions of the Treaties of Guarantee and Alliance and the parties would be obliged to implement the

recommendations promptly. Furthermore, any person could be employed anywhere in the republic on equal pay; special safeguards and measures were to be in place to protect the Turkish Cypriot economy from adverse effects; each state could establish and administer its own tax regime; membership of the EU required approval from both communities in separate referenda. "Set of Ideas," para. 7, 14, 33–38, 50, 57–66, 87–92.

71. S/24472, para. 15.
72. S/23780, para. 25.
73. S/24472, para. 18.
74. "Set of Ideas," para. 72.
75. Ibid., para. 73–5.
76. Ibid., para 76–8.
77. Ibid., para. 79–83.
78. Ibid., para. 84–5.
79. See Table 5.1 Pre-1974 Population Distribution of Areas Affected by Boutros-Ghali's Territorial Adjustments, in Michalis S. Michael, "Proposals for Resolving the Cyprus Problem (1974–1994)" (PhD diss., La Trobe University, 1998), 271.
80. S/24472, 13.
81. *Report of the Secretary-General on the United Nations Operation in Cyprus for the Period 7 December 1976 to 7 June 1977*, S/12342, para. 36.
82. S/24472, para. 19–21.
83. Ibid., para. 25.
84. "Set of Ideas," 15.
85. S/24472, para. 12, 13, 28, 31, 35.
86. *Report of the Secretary-General on his Mission of Good Offices in Cyprus*, S/24830, November 19, 1992, para. 9.
87. The nine paragraphs—and eight issues—with which the Turkish Cypriots disagreed and considered to be of significant value were: (1) the insistence that the president and vice-president should rotate between the two communities; that each community should elect their federal officials separately; (2) that there should be an equal number of Turkish and Greek Cypriot ministers; and that "the council of ministers should function on the basis of consensus." Others of less significance referred to were: (3) transitional arrangements; (4) the elimination of economic disparities; (5) participation in international bodies in which Greece and Turkey are not both members. The last three: (6) modalities regarding the principle of "one sovereignty"; (7) displaced persons; and (8) territorial adjustments, were all at the heart of the problem.
88. These positions related to the three last categories: (a) federation, (b) displaced persons, and (c) territorial adjustments, S/24830, para. 44–7.
89. Ibid., para. 48.

90. Ibid., para. 8 and 34.
91. Ibid., para. 50.
92. Ibid., para. 52.
93. Ibid., para. 55.
94. S/RES/789, November 25, 1992.
95. S/24830, para. 63.
96. The CBMs were subsequently endorsed by the SC Resolution 789 and entailed: the reduction of the Turkish armed forces to a level of a decade before, reciprocated by a suspension of weapons' acquisition by the Greek Cypriot side; the extension of the 1989 "unmanning" agreement to all UN-controlled buffer zones where the two sides were in close proximity; Varosha to come under control of UNFICYP; the promotion of people-to-people contact between the two communities by reducing restrictions of movement across the Buffer Zone; a similar reduction of restrictions to apply to foreign visitors; to stimulate intercommunal cooperation, each side would propose bicommunal projects—especially those pertaining to the private sector—which donor nations and international institutions would be encouraged to support; for both sides to commit to a Cyprus-wide census under UN auspices; and, a UN feasibility study on resettlement and rehabilitation of Turkish Cypriots affected by territorial adjustments. Ibid., para. 63.
97. In particular, they included expert cooperation on Cyprus's water problem and electricity supply, on educational matters by way of promoting intercommunal harmony and friendship, and on health and the environment; joint cultural and sporting events; meetings of political party leaders; journalists crossing to the other side without UN authorization; meetings of chambers of commerce to develop joint commercial ventures; intercommunal cooperation in Pyla; extension of the 1989 unmanning agreement; cooperation between the two sides to identify and develop joint projects; international assistance to benefit both sides; both sides to meet periodically to review progress and propose additional CBMs. *Report of the Secretary-General on his Mission of Good Offices in Cyprus*, S/26026/Annex I, July 1, 1993.
98. In particular, Varosha would function as "a special area for bicommunal contact and commerce, a kind of free-trade zone in which both sides could trade goods and services," whose territory would be opened in two phases: the first area to be opened would be that to the south of Dimokratias Street, and the second, north of Dimokratias Street, would be opened at an agreed date. Owners of property in these areas would be able to reclaim their properties. There would be freedom of movement to and from the area from both sides by Greek Cypriots, Turkish Cypriots, and foreign visitors without much formality. Ibid., para. 38.

99. Ibid., para. 21–6.

100. "Statement Made to the Press on 1 June 1993 on the Joint Meetings with the Leaders of the Two Communities in Cyprus," S/26026/ Annex II.

101. S/26026, para. 32–5.

102. *Commission Opinion on the Application by the Republic of Cyprus for Membership*, Com(93) 313 final, Brussels, June 30, 1993, para. 8, 10, 46, 48. Although the Commission was of the opinion that "Cyprus'[s] integration implie[d] a...[political] settlement" (para. 47), it felt that should the negotiations fail to achieve such a settlement, then the Commission would reassess the situation and reconsider Cyprus's accession in January 1995 by taking into account "the positions adopted by each party" in the negotiations (para. 51).

103. *Kibris*, August 29, 1994.

104. *Report of the Secretary-General on his Mission of Good Offices in Cyprus*, S/26438, September 14, 1993, para. 9.

105. Clement H. Dodd, *The Cyprus Issue: A Current Perspective*, 2nd ed. (Huntington: Eothen Press, 1994), 37n, makes the pertinent point that the Greek Cypriots wrongly blamed everything on Denktash and contributed to "Denktashphobia" abroad.

106. S/26438, para. 10.

107. Anatolia News Agency, June 27, 1994.

108. "Letter from U.S. President," August 19, 1993, 3.

109. S/26475, September 20, 1993.

110. S/26438, para. 18–9.

111. *Report of the Secretary-General in Connection with the Security Council's Comprehensive Reassessment of the United Nations Operation in Cyprus*, S/26777, November 22, 1993, para. 46–8.

112. *Report of the Secretary-General on his Mission of Good Offices in Cyprus*, S/1994/262 Annex I, March 4, 1994.

113. S/1994/384.

114. *Report of the Secretary-General on his Mission of Good Offices in Cyprus*, S/1994/629, May 30, 1994.

115. "Letter to the UN Secretary-General (Boutros-Ghali)," A/48/962-S/1994/794, July 5, 1994.

116. Clerides proposed to "repeal the National Guard Law, disband the Guard and hand all its arms and military equipment to the custody" of UNFICYP; "undertake the total cost of a substantially numerical increase" in UNFICYP; and deposit in the United Nations account all money saved from the disbanding of the National Guard, "to be used after the solution of the problem for the benefit of both Communities." This offer was made with the proviso that the Turkish side agreed that, parallel with the above, the Turkish Forces would be withdrawn from Cyprus, the Turkish Cypriot armed forces disbanded and their weapons and equipment handed to the UN. "Letter to the UN Secretary-General (Boutros-Ghali)," Nicosia, December 17, 1993.

117. S/1994/629, para. 57–62.

118. Boutros-Ghali argued that although the Turkish Cypriots had no objection to UNFICYP, they did not "particularly desire its continued presence, as security and stability [were] assured by the large-scale presence of Turkish forces," S/26777, para. 101.

119. Report (decision 49/406).

120. See Pantelis Varnava, *The Common Labour Struggles of Greek and Turkish-Cypriots (Events through History)* (Nicosia, 1997).

121. For an overview, see Ronald J. Fisher, "Cyprus: The Failure of Mediation and the Escalation of an Identity-Based Conflict to an Adversarial Impasse," *Journal of Peace Research* 38, 3 (2001): 307–26; Benjamin J. Broome, "Bridging the Divide in Cyprus: The Role of Bicommunal Activities," in Michael and Tamis, *Cyprus in the Modern World*, 266–304.

122. Nancy Crawshaw, "Cyprus: A Crisis of Confidence," *The World Today* 50, 4 (1994): 73.

123. Mathew Nimetz, "The Cyprus Problem Revisited," *Mediterranean Quarterly* 2, 1 (1991): 59–62.

124. Cowher Rizvi, "Ethnic Conflict and Political Accommodation in Plural Societies: Cyprus and Other Cases," *The Journal of Commonwealth and Comparative Politics* 31, 1 (1993): 57.

125. Maria Hadjipavlou-Trigeorgis and Lenos Trigeorgis, "Cyprus: An Evolutionary Approach to Conflict Resolution," *Journal of Conflict Resolution* 37, 2 (1993): 342.

126. *An Agenda for Peace, Preventive Diplomacy, Peacemaking and Peacekeeping*, A/47/277-S/2411, June 17, 1992.

127. Ronald Meinardus, "Third-Party Involvement in Greek-Turkish Disputes," in Constas, *Greek-Turkish Conflict*, 157.

128. Helen Laipson, "US Policy Towards Greece and Turkey Since 1974," ibid., 174.

129. Tazun Bahcheli, "Cyprus in the Post-War Environment: Moving toward a Settlement?" in *Cyprus and its People: Nation, Identity, and Experience in an Unimaginable Community, 1955–1997*, ed. V. Calotychos (Boulder: Westview Press, 1998), 114–6.

130. "President Denktash Proposes Confederation to Greek Cypriots (September 1, 1998)," http://www.trncwashdc.org./News/98_09_01.html.

5   Toward Annan's "European" Solution

1. "Statement Attributable to the Spokesman of the Secretary-General on Outcome of Referenda in Cyprus," April 24, 2004, http://www.un.org/apps/sg/sgstats.asp?nid=888.

2. "Transcript of Press Conference by Secretary-General Kofi Annan at United Nations Headquarters," *Press Release* SG/SM/8581, January 14, 2003.

3. Philip H. Gordon, "Turkey Overreacts, but the EU Is Not Blameless," *International Herald Times*, December 20, 1997. Such threats were repeated several times, see Joseph Fitchett, "Turkey's Warning on Cyprus Vexes Western Allies," *International Herald Times*, November 9, 2001.

4. Department of Defense, "Memorandum for Correspondents (267-M 4, Dec. 1995)," www.defenselink.mil/news/Dec1995/m120495_m267-95.html.

5. See congressional debate in Senate, especially Senator Larry Piessler, "Missile Sales to Turkey," *Congressional Records*, December 18, 1996, S18996-7.

6. *Report of the Secretary-General on the United Nations Operation in Cyprus, for the Period from 30 June to 10 December 1996*, S/1996/1016, para. 2–13.

7. "Greek Prime Minister Warns Turkish Troops on Cyprus," *CNN World News*, August 17, 1996, http://www.cnn.com/WORLD/9608/17/cyprus.pm/index.html.

8. Glafkos Clerides, *Ntokoumenta mias Epohis* [documents of a period] *1993–2003* (Nicosia: Politeia, 2007), 131–2.

9. See Michael Barletta, "The Missile Crisis over Cyprus: Countdown to a Crisis?" Centre for Nonproliferation Studies, 1998, http://cns.miis.edu/research/cyprus/countdown.htm; and Erik Jorgensen, "Conflict Averted: The Decision Not to Deploy on Cyprus," Centre for Nonproliferation Studies, 1999.

10. "To Megalo Dilemma tou k. Kliridi" [Mr. Clerides big dilemma], *To Vema*, August 23, 1998.

11. "New Hopes for Cyprus," *Cumhuriyet*, January 26, 1996.

12. "U.S. Envoy Drops Talks on Reunifying Cyprus," *New York Times, May 5, 1998*.

13. Richard C. Holbrooke, "Europe's Chance for Trifecta," *The Washington Post*, November 29, 2002.

14. "Denktas Turned Down Rifkind Call for New Guarantee Plan for Cyprus" (December 17, 1996), http://www.byegm.gov.tr/YAYINLARIMIZ/CHR/ING/12/96X12X17.TXT.

15. "Britain Plays 'Worst Role' in Cyprus, says Greek FM," *Cyprus News Agency*, December 8, 1996.

16. *Report of the Secretary-General on his Mission of Good Offices in Cyprus*, S/1997/973, December 12, 1997, para. 6.

17. "Inter-State Talks Only Viable Course," *Kibris*, February 6, 1998.

18. G8 Information Centre, University of Toronto, G8 Summit Wirtschaftsgipfel Cologne, Köln 1999, "G8 Statement on Regional Issues" (June 20, 1999), www.g8.utoronto.ca/summit/1999koln/regional.htm.

19. Van Coufoudakis, *Cyprus: A Contemporary Problem in Historical Perspective* (Minnesota Mediterranean and East European Monographs 15, 2006) 26–35.

20. A. M. Rendel, "Mr Callaghan Blames Talks Failure on Turks," *The Times*, August 15, 1974. Callaghan's statement was made in response to Turkey's foreign minister withdrawing from the second Geneva conference. The conference between the three guarantor powers took place between August 8 and 14, 1974, and in addition to the three foreign ministers, it was attended by the two Cypriot leaders, Clerides and Denktash, U.S. Assistant Secretary of State Arthur Hartman, Soviet representative Victor Menin, and UN Secretary-General Waldheim.

21. This historical paradox was not lost on Turkey's former foreign minister, İsmail Cem, who at a lecture in Istanbul criticized the current government's foreign policies on Cyprus and the EU stating that "Turkey's EU membership is at the mercy of the Greek Cypriot Administration," *Afrika*, October 30, 2003.

22. Conversation between the author and Periklis Nearchou, Bangkok, August 10, 2002.

23. Kostas Simitis, *Politiki gia mia Dimiourgiki Ellada* [politics for a creative Greece] *1996–2004* (Athens: Polis, 2005), 107.

24. "European Council at Corfu 24–25 June 1994: Presidency Conclusions," *Press Release* 00150/94, Brussels, June 24, 1994.

25. *Kibris*, August 29, 1994.

26. *European Observer's Report on Cyprus*, Brussels, January 23, 1995, para. 11.2(ii).

27. European Council, "General Affairs Council of Ministers Decision," SN 1661/95, Brussels, March 6, 1995.

28. "The Course of Cyprus Towards the European Union: Speech by the Minister of Foreign Affairs Mr Alecos Michaelides before the House of Representatives, 22 February 1996," Nicosia: PIO, 1996, 11.

29. "Statement by Murat Karayalçin, Foreign Minister of Turkey, on Greek Cypriot application for EU Membership on 6 March, 1995, during the EU-Turkey Association Council in Brussels," http://www.cypnet.com/.ncyprus/cyproblem/articles/bolum31.

30. "Joint Declaration by the President of Turkey and the President of the Turkish Republic of Northern Cyprus, Ankara, 28 December 1995," http://www.cypnet.com/.ncyprus/cyproblem/articles/bolum32.

31. Marios L. Evriviades, "Europe in Cyprus: The Broader Security Implications," *The Brown Journal of World Affairs* 10, 1 (2003): 241–3.

32. "Dublin European Council, 13 and 14 December 1996: Presidency Conclusions," CFSP Presidency Statement SN401/1/96, Brussels, December 16, 1996.

33. "Luxembourg European Council: Presidency Conclusions," *Press Release* SN400/97, Luxembourg, December 12, 1997.

34. "Helsinki European Council: Presidency Conclusions," *Press Release* NR 00300/1/99, Brussels, December 11, 1999.

35. "Copenhagen European Council 12 and 13 December 2002—Presidency Conclusion," 15917/02, Brussels, January 29, 2003.

36. "Brussels European Council 12 and 13 December 2003—Presidency Conclusions," 5381/04, Brussels, February 5, 2004, para. 42.

37. Perry Anderson, "The Divisions of Cyprus," *London Review of Books* 30, 8 (2008), 7.

38. "Presidency Conclusions—Laeken, 14 and 15 December 2001," SN300/1/01 REV1, para. 8.

39. "Statement by President Clerides relating to Turkish Cypriot Participation, 12th March 1998," http://www.cyprus-eu.org.cy/eng/07_documents/document005.htm.

40. The British EU Presidency at the time strongly reiterated their preference "to see a mixed delegation negotiating," especially since the Turkish Cypriot community "would actually benefit more, because their standard of living [was] lower they would gain much more from membership," Carole Andrews, "EU Enlargement: The Political Process," House of Commons Library Research Paper 98/55, 1985, 18–19.

41. *Continuing Enlargement Strategy Paper and Report of the European Commission on the Progress Towards Accession by Bulgaria, Romania and Turkey*, http://europa.eu.int/comm/enlargement/report_2003/pdf/strategy_paper2003_full_en.pd.

42. "Protocol No 10 on Cyprus," *Treaty of Accession to the European Union 2003*, AA2003/ACT/P10/en. 4803.

43. "Green Line Regulation" (Council Regulation No 866/2004 of 29 April 2004) http://eur-lex.europa.eu/smartapi/cgi/sga_doc?smartapi!celexplus!prod!CELEXnumdoc&lg=en&numdoc=304R0866R(01).

44. The lifting of travel restrictions offered a new space for social-economic interaction, forcing the Greek Cypriot leadership, as de facto custodians of the RoC, to develop a policy and implement a set of measures that integrated their citizens into a whole range of activities. See RoC, "Memorandum: Government Policy Vis a Vis the Turkish Cypriots (Set of Measures)," Nicosia, April 30, 2003.

45. "Commission Proposes Comprehensive Measures to End Isolation of Turkish Cypriot Community," *Press Release* IP/04/857, Brussels, July 7, 2004. After a two-year delay, €229,650,000 was approved in two instalments for developing infrastructure, promoting economic and social development, fostering reconciliation, confidence building measures, supporting civil society, bringing the Turkish Cypriot community closer to the European Union, and preparing the Turkish Cypriot community to introduce and implement the *acquis communautaire*.

46. Council of the EU, "Presidency Conclusions–Brussels European Council 17 and 18 June 2004," 10679/2/04 REV2, Brussels, July 19, para. 32, 6.

47. Mensur Akgün, Ayla Gürel, Mete Hatay, and Sylvia Tiryaki, "Quo Vadis Cyprus?" TESEV Working Paper, 2005, 5.

48. "Cyprus' Hour has Arrived, PM Simitis Says," *Athens News Agency*, November 29, 2002.

49. Gülnur Aybet and Meltem Müftüler-Bac, "Transformations in Security and Identity after the Cold War: Turkey's Problematic Relationship with Europe," *International Journal* 55, 4 (2000): 567–82.

50. "Pour ou contre l'adhésion de la Turquie à l'Union européenne" [for or counter the accession of Turkey to the European Union], *Le Monde*, November 9, 2002.

51. "Interview with Jacques Chirac, President of the Republic, by Patrick Poivre D'Arvor," *TF1 - 8:00 Journal*, December 15, 2004, http://www.elysee.fr/elysee/elysee.fr/anglais_archives/speeches_and_documents/2004/interview_with_mr_jacques_chirac_french_president_by_mr_patrick_poivre_d_arvor_tf1–800_journal-elysee_palace.27965.html.

52. This narrative is in stark contrast to another boy's intercultural encounter a few years prior while visiting Turkey. After a few days, the young boy Nikos complained to his parents that he had not seen any Turks. His parents explained that most of the people he saw were Turkish, but he exclaimed, "You don't understand! I don't want to see people, I want to see Turks!" Lily Hamourtziadou, "Greek Myths or the Boy Who Wanted to See Turks," *Internationale Schulbuchforschung* 21 (1999): 369.

53. Faruk Sen, "Earthquakes and Foreign Policy," *Turkish Daily News*, September 18, 1999.

54. Ilnur Cevik, "Ankara and Athens Must Listen to their People," *Turkish Daily News*, September 2, 1999.

55. Ahmet Sözen, "The Role of the European Union as a Third Party in Resolution of External Conflicts: The Case of the Cyprus Problem" (paper presented at the 15th annual meeting for the International Association for Conflict Management, City Park, Utah, June 8–12, 2002), 5, ft. 1.

56. Ahmet Davutoğlu, *Stratejik Derinlik: Turkiye'nin Uluslararasi Konumu* [strategic depth: the international position of turkey] (Istanbul: Küre Yayınları, 2001). Davutoğlu's views are important if one bears in mind that he was Prime Minister Erdoğan's chief foreign policy advisor and subsequent foreign minister (2009–). Reassessing Turkey's foreign policy, his book aims to provide a theoretical formulation of a new multidimensional foreign policy and proposed a new Turkish geostrategy, which utilizes its vast historical geostrategic position (which he calls "strategic depth"). On AKP's new foreign policy, see also Sözen, "A Paradigmatic Shift: New Principles of Turkish Foreign Policy Making" (a paper presented at the annual conference for International Studies Association, San Francisco, March 26–29, 2008).

57. Gregory R. Copley, "The Turkish Schism Deepens," *Defence and Foreign Affairs Strategic Policy* 29, 11–12 (2001): 12.

58. The Institute for the Study of Diplomacy at Georgetown University identified eight key challenges confronting Ankara: economic frailty, an ossified political elite, division over the military's domestic role, perception of its importance to the Western alliance, lack of foreign policy vision, lack of reform, regional tensions, and the U.S.-led war on terror; Aleksandar D. Jovovic, "A Turning Point for Turkey," *Schlesinger Working Group on Strategic Surprises* (2001): 1.

59. Philip Robins, "Confusion at Home, Confusion Abroad: Turkey between Copenhagen and Iraq," *International Affairs* 79, 3 (2003): 557. By surveying online discussion of Turkish tertiary students, Lemi Baruh and Mihaela Popescu, in "Guiding Metaphors of Nationalism: The Cyprus Issue and the Constriction of Turkish National Identity in Online Discussions," *Discourse & Communication* 2, 1 (2008): 79–96, locate Cyprus's metaphoric function as a source for replenishing Turkish nationalism.

60. Heinz A. Richter, "Ankara's Policy Towards Cyprus and the European Union," *Cyprus Review* 13, 2 (2001): 29–45.

61. "Commission Opinion on Turkey's Request for Accession to the Community," SEC (89) 2290, final/2, 1989, para. 9.

62. John Redmond, *The Next Mediterranean Enlargement of the European Community: Turkey, Cyprus and Malta?* (Aldershot: Dartmouth, 1993), 54. For Turkey's reaction to the EU's Cyprus "conditionality," see Birol A. Yesilada, "Turkey's Candidacy for EU Membership," *Middle East Journal* 56, 1 (2002): 94–111.

63. UK House of Commons, Sixth Report from the Foreign Affairs Committee, *Turkey, Response of the Secretary of State for Foreign and Commonwealth Affairs* (London: HMSO, cm 5529, 2002), 9.

64. At a breakfast policy briefing organized by the European Policy Centre, Tassos Papadopoulos stressed that it would be unwise for Cyprus to veto Turkey's EU accession course, "Unwise to Veto Turkey's EU Accession" (October 16, 2003), http://www.cypria. com/news24/cyprus/article.html?article_id+20157.

65. UK House of Commons, *Sixth Report from the Foreign Affairs Committee on Turkey* (London: HMSO, April 23, 2002), para. 86.

66. *1999 Regular Report from the Commission on Turkey's Progress Towards Accession*, November 13, 14–15, and 41.

67. *2000 Regular Report from the Commission on Turkey's Progress towards Accession*, November 8, 66–7.

68. *Continuing Enlargement Strategy Paper* (2003), 16.

69. "Turkey Rattled by EU Reference to Cyprus," *Turkish Daily News*, November 6, 2003. While in opposition as the AKP's Deputy Chair, Gül pointed out that the Cyprus problem was the most crucial obstacle on Turkey's European path, *Turkish Daily News*, July 29, 2002.

70. Cem's press release was issued as the leader of the oppositional Young Turkey Party (YTP), and in it he claimed, for the first time, that the

EU set a Cyprus solution as a prerequisite to Turkey's membership, "Cem: EU Bid Depends on Cyprus Solution," *Turkish Daily News*, November 6, 2003. Columns and editorials of the leading Turkish dailies ran the line—more or less—exemplified by Sami Kohen, that the EU was sending Turkey a message that the Cyprus issue would be, in practice, an obstacle and that Turkey should adhere to the warning and initiate a solution, "EU Message," *Milliyet*, November 6, 2003.

71. Specifically, Erdoğan stated: "I am not saying that the Cyprus issue can be totally isolated from our membership. But it was not useful for the EU Commission to establish a link in written form between our membership bid and the Cyprus issue," "Turkey Criticizes EU's Terror Response," *Turkish Daily News*, December 6, 2003.

72. *2004 Regular Report on Turkey's Progress Towards Accession*, Com(2004) 656, Brussels, SEC(2004) 1201, October 6, 51–2.

73. "Opinion of the European Economic and Social Committee on EU-Turkey Relations with a View to the European Council of December 2004," REX/172-CESE 965/2004, Brussels July 1, para. 3.8.

74. "Issues Arising from Turkey's Membership Perspective," Commission Staff Working Document Com(2004) 656, Brussels, SEC(2004) 1202, October 10, 2004, 7 and 25.

75. "Brussels European Council, December 16/17, 2004—Presidency Conclusions," Brussels, February 1, 2005, 16238/1/04 REV 1, para.17–23.

76. *Turkey 2006 Progress Report*, COM(2006), 649 final, Commission Staff Working Document SEC(2006), 1390, Brussels, November 8, 24–5.

77. "Brakes on the European Train," *Radikal*, December 12, 2006.

78. Kirsty Hughes, "Turkish Crash Looms for Europe," *BBC News*, September 6, 2006, http://news.bbc.co.uk/go/pr/fr/-/2/hi/europe/5314194.stm.

79. "Erdoğan Slams Embargoes, EU-Cyprus Link," *Turkish Daily News*, July 21, 2006.

80. "Public Opinion in the European Union, Turkey National Report—Executive Summary," *Eurobarometer 67* (Spring 2007), 2.

81. Mehmet Ali Birand, "Why Are we so Afraid to Change?" *Turkish Daily News*, August 14, 2007, linked Cyprus and Armenia as one issue relating to Turkey's foreign policy. The other two (the Kurdish issue and secularism versus Islam) related to Turkey's domestic developments. According to Professor Rıdvan Karluk, former PM Mesut Yılmaz believed that the Kurdish issue was the main obstacle to Turkey's EU accession, when in reality it was Cyprus that regulated Turkey-EU relations. EU-Turkey Information Network ABHaber, "Prof. Dr. Karluk: 'The Cyprus Issue had Became a Precondition for

Turkey to get a Full Membership to the EU,'" September 11, 2007, http://www.abhaber.com/news_page.asp?id=3589.

82. "Turkish Cypriots Call for Reunification," *BBC News*, December 26, 2002, http://bbc.cco.uk/2/hi/Europe/2607099.stm.

83. *BBC News World* edition, http://news.bbc.co.uk/2/hi/europe/2656211.stm.

84. UN SG/SM/8581, January 14, 2003.

85. State Department, *Daily Press Briefing*, Richard Boucher, Spokesman, Washington, DC, January 14, 2003, http://www.state.gov/r/pa/prs/dpb/2003/16641.htm.

86. The BDH, comprising three political parties and sixteen NGOs, was announced on June 29, 2003 with the distinct aim of gaining enough votes at the forthcoming elections to replace Denktash as chief negotiator at the UN intercommunal talks. The leading personalities of the movement were Mehmet Ali Talat, Mustafa Akinci, and Ali Erel; H. Smith, "United Front Take on Denktash," *Guardian*, June 30, 2003. After internal consultations the three parties agreed on a protocol that would "terminate the duties of President Denktash as negotiator," strongly oppose the "pro status-quo parties in collaboration with the anti-EU forces in Turkey," and "achieve an agreement on the basis of the Annan Plan by May 2004 and put it to a referendum." The Protocol was agreed to by the Peace and Democracy Movement (PDM), the Republican Turkish Party-United Forces, and the Solution and EU Party (SEUP), Nicosia, September 4, 2003.

87. "Draw in Turkish Cypriot Elections," *BBC News*, December 15, 2003, http://news.bbc.co.uk/1/hi/world/europe/3317125.stm.

88. Yael Navaro-Yashin, "Confinement and Imagination: Sovereignty and Subjectivity in a Quasi-State," in *Sovereign Bodies: Citizens, Migrants, and States in the Postcolonial World*, ed. T. B. Hansen and F. Stepputat (Princeton: Princeton UP, 2005), 103–19.

89. For critical articles, reports, and updates on Turkish Cypriot opposition, see the Web site of the Cyprus Action Network (CAN), a grassroots anti–status quo human rights NGO, at www.cyprusaction.org; for example, "Overall View of Political Oppression in North Cyprus," http:www.cyprusaction.org/humanrights/terrorism/longintro.html.

90. For a more extensive survey of the social-political transformations in northern Cyprus, see Hannes Lacher and Erol Kaymak, "Transforming Identities: Beyond the Politics of Non-Settlement in North Cyprus," *Mediterranean Politics* 10, 2 (2005): 147–66.

91. See Centre for International Development and Conflict Management, University of Maryland, Minorities at Risk, "Assessment for Turkish Cypriots in Cyprus," http://www.cidcm.umd.edu/mar/assessment.asp?groupId=35201.

92. "Big Demo in Turkish Cyprus," *BBC News*, July 19, 2000, http:// news.bbc.co.uk/1/hi/world/europe/840800.stm.

93. "Bank Victims Storm KKTC Parliament, 10 Detained," *Turkish Daily News*, July 25, 2000.

94. "Denktas Calls on Eroglu Government to Resign," *Turkish Daily News*, July 27, 2000.

95. Helena Smith, "Northern Cypriots Turn Against Turkey," *Guardian*, September 25, 2001.

96. Yael Navaro-Yashin, "'Life Is Dead Here'—Sensing the Political 'No Man's Land,'" *Anthropological Theory* 3, 1 (2003): 107–25.

97. "Public Opinion 2002—First Results—Northern Cyprus," Brussels, November 2002. The survey was conducted by KADEM Institute from Northern Cyprus, which was commissioned by the Cyprus Delegation of the European Commission. Using the same question-naire method as Eurobarometer, KADEM surveyed the opinions of 500 Turkish Cypriots for the period September 1–30, 2002.

98. Furthermore, according to the European Parliament and Commission, the approval rate among Turkish Cypriots in 2001 was as high as 90 percent; *Report on Cyprus' Membership Application to the European Union and the State of Negotiations*, Final A5–0261/2001/Par 1, para. 38; and *Regular Report on Cyprus' Progress Towards Accession*, SEC(2001) 1745, Brussels, 2001, 23.

99. *Report on Cyprus's Membership Application to the European Union and the State of Negotiations*, RR\446036EN.doc, July 17, 2001, para. 21–2, 15/88. The Commission estimated that Turkey provided €100–200 million per annum to the North's economy, but in the highly inflationary Turkish lira, and warned that the economy faced severe shortages of capital, skills, and business as there was the ten-dency for highly educated young people to seek employment over-seas. *2002 Regular Report on Cyprus's Progress Towards Accession*, COM (2002) 1401, Brussels, October 9, 28–9.

100. *Kibris*, December 30, 2002. A claim rejected by KTTO Chair Ali Erel, who called on Denktash to apologize, *Otam*, December 30, 2002.

101. "Romano Prodi, President of the European Commission, Speech to the House of Representatives, Cyprus, 25 October 2001," Speech/01/495 *Press Release*, October 26, 2001.

102. "Politics is an Art of Creating Solutions Instead of Problems," *Anadolu News Agency*, January 2, 2003.

103. According to Birand, the Cankaya Summit on Cyprus, of December 18, 2003, resolved to support Denktash, have the Annan proposals amended, and reverse the impression that the Turkish side did not favor negotiations, "Denktash Leaves the Door Open," *Turkish Daily News*, December 20, 2002.

104. "Denktash Says Would Resign if Turkey Presses Him," *Turkish Daily News*, December 31, 2002.

105. "Denktash Declines to Attend Swiss Meetings; Other TRNC Officials to Attend Instead," TurkishPress.com: Press Review 3/18/04, enews@anatolia.com, Thu 18/03/2004 11:24 PM.

106. Ian Black and Helena Smith, "EU Tells Turkey to Push Cypriot Leader into Line," *Guardian*, March 12, 2003.

107. Halil Ibrahim Salih, *Cyprus, Ethnic Political Counterpoints* (Dallas: University Press of America, 2004), 290–3.

108. "Commission Regrets Failure of UN Efforts to Solve the Cyprus Problem and Confirm Accession Process will go Ahead as Scheduled," *Press Release* IP/03/359, Brussels, March 11, 2003.

109. "Greek Presidency, Tour of EU Capitals: Nicosia 18/19 April," *Press Release*, April 19, 2003.

110. "The Commission Proposes a Goodwill Package to Bring Northern Part of Cyprus Closer to the EU," *Press Release* IP/03/786, Brussels, June 3, 2003.

111. TRNC President's Office, "Doubts over EU Aid," *Press Release*, June 5, 2003, http://www.trncpresidency.org/press/news/doubts.htm.

112. "Secretary-General, in Message to Cypriot People, says Reunification Plan will Determine Destiny of Divided Island," *Press Release* SG/SM/9264, April 21, 2004.

113. Furthermore, Edward Newman, "The Most Impossible Job in the World: The Secretary-General and Cyprus," in *The Work of the UN in Cyprus: Promoting Peace and Development*, ed. O. P. Richmond and J. Ker-Lindsay (New York: Palgrave, 2001), 127–8, adds the post-Cold War pressure for more activists Secretary-General and how the SG's efforts were not synchronized with external actors political will.

114. *Report of the Secretary-General on his Mission of Good Offices in Cyprus*, S/2003/398, April 1, 2003, para. 6.

115. David Hannay, *Cyprus: Search for a Solution* (London: I.B. Tauris, 2005), 96–115.

116. S/2003/398, para. 42.

117. Ibid., para 50.

118. *Report of the Secretary-General on his Mission of Good Offices in Cyprus*, S/2004/437, May 28, 2004, para. 30–41.

119. "Following Consultations on Cyprus under aegis of Special Representative of Secretary-General, 'An Opportunity Remains; for Solution to Problem,'" *Press Release Note* 5772, December 13, 2002.

120. Sophia Kannas, "Verheugen: Cyprus Was the First Casualty of Looming War in Iraq," *Cyprus Mail*, March 15, 2004.

121. "Secretary-General says 'End of Road' Reached Concerning Current Cyprus Talks but 'Plan Remains on the Table,'" *Press Release* SG/SM/8630, March 11, 2003.

122. "Secretary-General Activities in Baden Baden, 21 January; Receives German Media Prize," *Press Release* SG/T/2393, January 22, 2004.

123. "Activities of Secretary-General in Davos, 22–25 January," *Press Release* SG/T/2394, January 26, 2004.

124. "Iraq, Cyprus Continue to be Focus of Annan's Talks with European Leaders in Belgium," *UN News Centre*, January 29, 2004.

125. "Annan Invites Greek Cypriot and Turkish Cypriot Leaders to New York for Talks," *UN News Service*, February 4, 2004.

126. "Secretary-General's Press Encounter on Arrival at UN Headquarters, New York, 9 February 2004," www.un.org/apps/sg/printoffthecuff.asp?nid=538.

127. "Cypriots Have 'Historic' Chance to Join European Union as One, Annan Says Ahead of Talks," *UN News Service*, February 9, 2004.

128. "Transcript of Press Conference by Secretary-General Kofi Annan at United Nations Headquarters, 13 February," *Press Release* SG/SM/9159, February 13, 2004.

129. Both Papadopoulos and Clerides were at Lancaster House, where Papadopoulos (together with AKEL) voted against the London-Zurich agreements.

130. S/2004/437, para. 30–41.

131. *The Comprehensive Settlement of the Cyprus Problem*, http://www.cyprus-un-plan.org/Annan_Paln_April2004.pdf.

132. By factoring a 40 percent growth in the Greek Cypriot population since 1974, Annan estimated that the figure would be closer to 120,000, S/2003/398, para. 118.

133. "Commitment to Submit the Foundation Agreement to Approval at Separate Simultaneous Referenda in Order to Achieve a Comprehensive Settlement of the Cyprus Problem," ibid.

134. "Community acquis," meaning the entire accumulated body of legislation, rights and obligations, binding all member-states within the European Union.

135. "Secretary-General Presents Final Settlement Plan for Cyprus, Says 'Offer Best and Fairest' Chance for Peace," *Press Release* SG/SM/9239, March 31, 2004.

136. "Opening Statement and Unofficial Transcript of Remarks to the President by Secretary-General's Special Adviser on Cyprus, Alvaro de Soto, Füringen Hotel, near Bürgenstock, Switzerland," March 31, 2004, http://194.154.157.106/Press_conference_in_Burgenstock_de_Soto_Mar31.pdf. Initially the date for the referendum was set for April 20, 2004, "Date for Referenda on Cyprus set for 20 April—UN," *UN News Service*, March 9, 2004.

137. "Omilia tou GG tis K.E. tou AKEL, D. Christofias stin Ektakti Pagkypria Sindiaskepsi tou AKEL gia to Dimopsifisma tis 24is Apriliou" [address by G.S. of the C.C. of AKEL, D. Christofias at the special pan-Cyprian congress of AKEL for April 24, 2004 referendum] http://www.akel.org.cy/archive-omilies-2004.html.

138. Ann-Sofi Jakobsson Hatay, "The Orphan Peace Plan: Kofi Annan's Proposal for a Reunited Cyprus," Transnational Foundation for Peace

and Future Research, *Meeting Points Forum* (Lund, Sweden, 2004), http//:www.transnational.org/forum/meet/2002/JakobssonHatay_Cyprus.html. For Greek Cypriot attitude variance toward Turkish Cypriots and Turkish settlers/immigrants, see Liana Danielidou and Peter Hortvath, "Greek Cypriot Attitudes toward Turkish Cypriots and Turkish Immigrants," *The Journal of Social Psychology* 146, 4 (2006): 405–21.

139. Interview by Van Coufoudakis, "Ishiri Oso Pote I Diapragmateftiki mas Thesi" [as strong as ever our negotiating position], *Simerini*, February 15, 2004.

140. "Mitropolitis Morphou: Apanto 'Nai' sto Schedio Anan" [Bishop of Morphou: I answer "Yes" to the Annan Plan], *Politis*, April 22, 2004.

141. Martti Ahtisaari and Gareth Evans, "Three Advantages of the Annan Peace Plan," *International Herald Tribune*, April 19, 2004.

142. "Brussels European Council 25 & 26 March 2004, Presidency Conclusions, (Brussels 19 May 2004)," 9048/04 POLGEN 20 CONCL 1, para. 49 and 50.

143. Javier Solana's article, "A European Solution for Cyprus," was translated into several languages and published in several newspapers between April 18 and 21, 2004, such as *Zaman, Kathimerini, Le Soir, Kibris Gazetesi, Phileleftheros, Süddeutsche Zeitung,* and *International Herald Tribune*.

144. British Helsinki Human Rights Group, "Cyprus 2004: Curtains for the Annan Plan," http://www.bhhrg.org/CountryReport.asp?CountryID=29.

145. Web site European-Cyprus.net available at http://www.european-cyprus.net/cgi-bin/poll.cgi?poll=000003&viewresults=1.

146. "Vrontero 'Ohi' 54.3% sto Schedio Annan" [thundering "no" 54.3 percent to the Annan Plan], *Simerini*, March 7, 2004.

147. *Phileleftheros*, March 7, 2004.

148. "Vrontero 'Ohi' tou Laou sto Schedio Annan" [public's thundering "no" to the Annan Plan] *Simerini*, February 20, 2004.

149. *Politis*, March 7, 2004.

150. The figure increased to 94 percent in the event that the UN rejected the Greek Cypriot proposals, *Simerini*, March 28, 2004.

151. *Elefherotypia*, April 8, 2004.

152. "Diaggelma tou Proedrou tis Dimokratias Tassou Papadopoulou gia to Dimopsifisma tis 24is Apriliou 2004" [address by the President of the Republic Tassos Papadopoulos regarding the referendum of April 24, 2004], http://www.cyprusnet.gr/CyprusnetPages/Kypriako/Enimerosis/Papadopoulos_Diagelma.htm.

153. "Proposal of the C.C. AKEL to the Pancyprian Conference that will Decide on Annan's Plan," Nicosia, April 10, 2004, http://www.akel.org.cy/English/akel.html.

154. "Daily Briefing by the Government Spokesperson" [in Greek], February 17, 2004, http://www.pio.gov.cy/greek/news/spokesman/spokesman454.htm.

155. Makarios Droushiotis, "The Bankrupt Policy of 'All or Nothing,'" *Cyprus Mail*, August 7, 2005.

156. Sertaç Sonan, "From Bankruptcy to Unification and EU Membership?: The Political Economy of Post-Nationalist Transformation in Northern Cyprus," RAMSES Working Paper 9/07, University of Oxford European Studies Centre, 2007.

157. Avner Falk, "Border Symbolism," *Psychoanalytic Quarterly* 43 (1974): 650–60.

158. Rebecca Bryant, "A Dangerous Trend in Cyprus," *Middle East Report* 235 (2005), http://www.merip.org/mer/mer235/bryant.html.

159. Yücel Vural and Nicos Peristianis, "Beyond Ethno-nationalism: Emerging Trends in Cypriot Politics after the Annan Plan," *Nations and Nationalism* 14, 1 (2008): 39–60.

160. From April 23, 2003 to 2008 there had been over 16 million crossings from the north to south and vice versa at the Ledra, Ayios Dometios/Metehan, Pergamos, and Strovilia crossing points. A further impetus was provided with the opening of Ledra Street in Nicosia on April 3, 2008. Furthermore, between August 2004 and November 2008 there was a flow of goods worth $13 million from north to south and worth $3.6 million from south to north. *See Report[s] of the Secretary-General on the United Nations Operation in Cyprus,* S/2007/328, June 4, 2007, para. 23; S/2207/699, December 3, 2007, para. 20; S/2008/353, June 3, 2008, para. 24; S/2008/744m November 28, 2008, para. 26. (Countering this phenomenon have been the 1544 violations and incidents along the Green Line between 2007 and 2008, S/2007/328, para. 13, S/2207/699, para. 10, S/2008/353, para. 11, S/2008/744 para. 18).

161. Specifically, Article 5: "Suspension of dealings, proceedings or alterations with respect to affected property," suspends any "transaction, dealing, or any proceeding in any court or legal or administrative body in Cyprus…with respect to any *affected property* shall be suspended or prohibited upon entry into force of the Foundation Agreement, until the Property Board" deals with it. More significantly was the second clause of article 5, which stipulated that the United Cyprus Republic, in "invoking the fact that the Foundation Agreement is providing a domestic remedy for the solution of all questions related to *affected property*" would "inform the European Court of Human Rights…that the United Cyprus Republic shall therefore be the sole responsible State Party and request the Court to strike out any proceedings currently before it concerning *affected property*, in order to allow the domestic mechanism agreed to solve these cases to proceed," Annex VII, "Treatment of Property

Affected by Events since 1963," "Part II: Regulation of Exercise of Property Rights," Article 5 and attachment 5, "Letter to the President of the European Court of Human Rights."

162. Nathalie Tocci, *EU Accession Dynamics and Conflict Resolution: Catalysing Peace or Consolidating Partition in Cyprus?* (Burlington, VT: Ashgate, 2004), 159–67.

163. For an in-depth analytical account, see Harry Anastasiou, *The Broken Olive Branch: Nationalism, Ethnic Conflict, and the Quest for Peace in Cyprus* (New York: Syracuse UP, 2008).

164. Olli Rehn, "Cyprus: One Year After Accession," Speech/05/278, Nicosia, May 13, 2005.

165. Between 2004 and 2007, Greek Cypriots' trust for the EU fluctuated between 54 percent and 61 percent whilst trust for the UN ranged at 25–33 percent; amongst the Turkish Cypriots the two institutions maintained a parity of trust levels (UN: 41–48 percent v. EU: 36–51 percent). See *Standard Eurobarometer National Reports Cyprus* 62 (Autumn 2004), 63.4 (Spring 2005), 64 (Autumn 2005), 65 (Spring 2006), 66 (Autumn 2006), 67 (Spring 2007), http://ec.europa.eu/public_opinion/standard_en.htm. Cyprus's surveys are subdivided for "Areas under the Control of the Cyprus Government" (Greek Cypriot community) and "Turkish Cypriot Community."

Conclusion: "And bring all Cyprus Comfort"

1. Cassio, Act II/Scene I, William Shakespeare (1603–1604) *Othello, the Moore of Venice.*

2. Aziz complained that "he was prevented from exercising his voting rights (at the 2001 elections) on the grounds of national origin and/or association with a national minority." Declared partially inadmissible, the Court found that there had been a violation of Article 3 of Protocol No. 1 (right to free elections) as well as a violation of Article 14 (prohibition of discrimination) of the Convention for the Protection of Human Rights and Fundamental Freedoms, awarding Aziz €3,500 for costs and expenses, ECHR, *Case of Aziz v. Cyprus Judgement*, application on. 69949/01, Strasbourg, June 22, 2004.

3. The Court found Turkey guilty of denying Loizidou "access to and interference with property rights in northern Cyprus," ECHR, *Case of Loizidou v. Turkey (Merits) Judgement* 40/1993/435/514, Strasbourg, December 18, 1996. Furthermore the Court found the applicant entitled to compensation and "still the legal owner of the property [and] no issue of expropriation arise[d]," *Case of Loizidou v. Turkey* (Article 50) Judgement, Strasbourg, July 1998. Faced with noncompliance sanctions in November 2003, Turkey agreed to pay Loizidou £CYP 450,000 in compensation.

4. Hugo Gobbi, "Partition May be the Only Solution," *Cyprus Mail*, February 26, 1996, viewed "separation" as the best solution for

Cyprus. He argued that unification of the island would come at a very high cost for the Greek Cypriots, who would lose their "free determination," abandon their Hellenic destiny, and accept Turkish Cypriot vetoes in a reproduction of the 1960 political structure, whilst separation would damage the Turkish Cypriot community in economic terms.

5. Hugo J. Gobbi, *Rethinking Cyprus* (Tel Aviv: Aurora, 1993), 49–55; and Tozun Bahcheli, "Searching for a Cyprus Settlement: Considering Options for Creating a Federation, a Confederation, or Two Independent States," *Publius* 30, 1 (2000), 214–7.

6. Andreas Theophanous, *The Political Economy of a Federal Cyprus* (Nicosia: Intercollege Press, 1996), 175–7. Although Theophanous, *The Political Economy of a Cyprus Settlement: The Examination of Four Scenaria* (Oslo: PRIO Report 1/2008), purports "functional federalism with loose bizonality" as an alternative model, in essence it belongs to Cyprus's quest for federalism.

7. Nathalie Tocci, *The "Cyprus Question": Reshaping Community Identities and Elite Interests within a Wider European Framework* (Brussels: Centre for European Policy Studies, 2000), 23–6.

8. Trigeorgis, "Cyprus," 342; and Vamık D. Volkan, "Turks and Greeks of Cyprus: Psychopolitical Considerations," in Calotychos, 278.

9. CYMAR in June 2004 found that 28.2 percent of Greek Cypriots (G/Cs) preferred division either as continuation of present status quo or two-state solution (35.4 percent amongst 25–34-year-olds and 41 percent amongst 18–24-year-olds), 14.6 percent preferred a federal solution (7.5 percent amongst younger age groups), Craig Webster and Christophoros Christophorou, *Greek Cypriots, Turkish Cypriots, and the Future: The Day after the Referendum*, Executive Report, Nicosia, CYMAR Market Research, June 17, 2004, 2–7. Lordos's study found that 22.7 percent rejected federation, whilst 71.1 percent found unitary state solution acceptable, 29 percent did not oppose a two-state solution, and concurred with CYMAR that there was a "gradual shift" in G/C attitudes toward acceptance of two-state solution (strongly prevalent amongst the 25–34 age group), Alexandros Lordos, *Can the Cyprus Problem be Solved? Understanding the Greek Cypriot Response to the UN Peace Plan for Cyprus* (an evidence-based study in cooperation with Cymar, October 2004), 11–16. In April 2006 a Cyprus Broadcasting Corporation poll found that 48 percent of G/Cs preferred permanent separation from the Turkish Cypriots (T/Cs) (in contrast to 67 percent in 2003), amongst the 18–25-year-olds this figure was as high as 63 percent, "Do G/Cs Want Coexistence-Solution?" *Politis*, April 9, 2006. Similarly, according to a 2007 KADEM poll, 65 percent of T/Cs preferred a two-state solution whilst support for a federal solution dropped to 20 percent, "65% Say Taksim," *Afrika*, January 29, 2007. These are in contrast to Lordos's April 2006 poll that found amongst G/Cs 36 percent to favour two-state solution,

federal solution favoured by 28 percent, and unitary-state solution favoured by 63 percent; whilst amongst T/Cs 75 percent rejected two-state solution, 52 percent accepted federal solution and 57 percent rejected a unitary-state solution. *Building Trust: An Intercommunal Analysis of Public Opinion in Cyprus* (Nicosia: CYMAR and KADEM, April 2006), 15–16. Equally perplexing was the UN poll that found that 65 percent of G/Cs and 70 percent T/Cs considered a federal solution as tolerable/or satisfactory, "The UN in Cyprus: An Inter-communal Survey of Public Opinion by UNFICYP," *Press Release,* Nicosia, April 24, 2007, 5.

10. This includes Mustafa Akinci's proposals that the Republic of Cyprus incubate an "intermediate solution," *Kibris,* October 7, 2005; as well as the Turkish Cypriot Cyprus EU Association's (Ali Erel and Mustafa Damdelen) recourse to the ECHR attempting to reactive the Turkish Cypriot clauses of the 1960 constitution ("Turkish Cypriots Seek Parliamentary Rights through European Rights Court," *Cyprus Mail,* September 7, 2007).

11. South East European Studies at Oxford, *Cyprus After Accession: Getting Past "No"?* Workshop Report and Responses, May 2007, 6–9.

12. See Dan Lindley, "Historical, Tactical, and Strategic Lessons from the Partition of Cyprus," *International Studies Perspectives* 8 (2007): 224–41.

13. Harold H. Saunders, *A Public Peace Process: Sustained Dialogue to Transform Racial and Ethnic Conflicts* (New York: Palgrave, 2001), xvii–xix.

14. Such an example is the two-day visit to Cyprus by three members of The Elders, Lakhdar Brahimi, Jimmy Carter, and Desmond Tutu, in early October 2008. By meeting with young people, civil society groups, political parties, and those involved with official mediation, their mission was to lend support and encouragement to the community leaders, Christofias and Talat, in their peace talks. For more information and regular updates, see "Summary Report of The Elders' Visit to Cyprus, 8–9 October 2008," at www.TheElders.org.

15. A view that held currency not only amongst scholars but also decision makers, including Greece's foreign minister George Papandreou, who considered the Europeanization of national policy interests the next challenge to a European model of cultural integration. George A. Papandreou, "The Future of Europe after Iraq: A Lecture Delivered at St. Anthony's College, University of Oxford, 6/5/03," http://www.eu2003.gr/en/articles/2003/5/8/2707.

16. Thomas Diez, ed., *The European Union and the Cyprus Conflict: Modern Conflict, Postmodern Nation* (Manchester UP, 2002), 10–2.

17. A policy aimed to assist those regions suffering economic disadvantage due to structural deficiencies, inadequate physical and human capital, lack of innovative capacity, business support and low environmental

capital. See *Third Report on Economic and Social Cohesion: A New Partnership for Cohesion: Convergence-Competitiveness–Cooperation*, Luxembourg: Office for Official Publications of the European Communities, 2004. By adopting a provincial or localized approach, the EU hoped to address, at least for a period, the socioeconomic disparities between the Greek Cypriot south and Turkish Cypriot north. An additional benefit in linking northern Cyprus into the EU's regional cohesion policy was that it would alleviate the minority-security problem affixed to the territorially determined states. As Olga Demetriou, "Catalysis, Catacresis: The EU's Impact on the Cyprus Conflict," in *The European Union and Border Conflicts: The Power of Integration and Association*, ed. T. Diez, M. Albert, and S. Stetter (Cambridge: Cambridge UP, 2008), 64–92, argues, Cyprus's accession, although a legitimate structural prevention mechanism, was a peacemaking policy failure as it was ineffective in transforming the conflict's interethnic power dynamics.

18. S/2007/328, para. 25, S/2207/699, para. 24, S/2008/353, para. 25, S/2008/744 para. 27.

19. Özger Özgür, "I Arnisi Prokalei mi Lisi Kai i mi Lisi Dihotomisi" [Rejection provokes no solution and no solution partition], *Philelefteros*, January 16, 2005.

Bibliography

Primary Sources

Unpublished

Australia, High Commission. "Records of Meetings by Dr A. Theophanous, MP, with Mr Oscar Camilion and Foreign Minister George Iacovou, 6 October 1992." Prepared by P. M. Edwards, First Secretary, file 828/1, October 20, in confidence.

Clerides, Glafcos. "Letter to the UN, Secretary-General (Boutros-Ghali)." Nicosia, December 17, 1993.

Cyprus, Republic of, Ministry of Foreign Affairs. "Cypriot Recourse to the 42nd Session of the UN General Assembly." Confidential, File number A.24/17, GAPOLPAR/VM/MZM, 1987.

———. "Analysis of Mr. Denktash's Papers Formally Tabled on 9.1.1989." Nicosia, January 26, 1989.

———. "Eisigiseis tou Ipourgou Exoterikou pros to Ethniko Simvoulio gia tin Peraitero Diethnopoiisi tou Kipriakou." [Proposals by the minister of foreign affairs toward the national council in the further internationalization of the Cyprus problem]. Confidential Document, Nicosia, June 1, 1990.

Denktash, Rauf R. "Draft Joint Declaration, Explanatory Note and Draft Outline of a Comprehensive Settlement in Cyprus." October 11, 1989.

Great Britain. "Paper on Middle East Defence." FO 371/121370, V1197/22/G, December 26, 1956.

———. "Cabinet Meeting (Financial situation; Proposed cession to Greece of Cyprus without Cabinet Consent; Need for smaller War Council)." CAB 37/136/26, October 21, 1915.

"Greek-Cypriot Proposals of 8 October 1980" (Nicosia).

Greek Cypriot Side. "The Future Federal Republic of Cyprus: Turkish Cypriot Participation and Other Related Matters." Nicosia, January 14, 1989.

———. "Outline Proposals for the Establishment of a Federal Republic and for the Solution of the Cyprus Problem." Nicosia, January 30, 1989.

Kyprianou, Spyros. "Letter to His Excellency Mr Javier Pérez de Cuéllar, Secretary-General of the United Nations." Nicosia, March 10, 1987.

"Turkish-Cypriot Proposals, Draft Constitution of the Federal Republic of Cyprus." January 1981.

"The Turkish Cypriot Position." Nicosia, November 1, 1988.

"The Turkish Cypriot Approach to the Federal Legislature as Part of an Integrated Whole." Paper No. 9, Nicosia, January 30, 1989.

UN Secretary-General (Javier Pérez de Cuéllar). "Aide Memoire." August 8, 1983.

———. "Working Points." August 1984.

———. "Agenda for the Third Round of the Secretary-General's Proximity Talks on Cyprus, Preliminary Draft for a Joint High-Level Agreement." November 1984.

———. "Non-Paper No.1" and "Non-Paper No. 2." New York, December 1984.

———. "Pérez de Cuéllar's Ideas." July 25, 1989.

———. "Pérez de Cuéllar's Statement." March 2, 1990.

U.S. Department of State. "Eastern Mediterranean and Middle East." PPS/14, Policy Planning Staff Paper that emanated from conversations between the U.S. Department of State and the British Foreign Office with their military advisers, Top Secret, November 11, 1947.

———. "United States Policy in the Event of the Establishment of Communist Power in Greece." PPS/8 Policy Planning Staff Paper under George F. Kennan, Top Secret, September 18, 1947.

Published

Cyprus, Republic of. *Cyprus Intercommunal Talks: New Series, First Round, Vienna, 31 March–7 April 1977.* Nicosia: PIO, 1977.

———. *Cyprus Intercommunal Talks: Following the Turkish Invasion of July–August 1974.* Nicosia: PIO, April 1982.

———. "Address by the President of the Republic of Cyprus, Mr. George Vassiliou, to the 3rd Special Session of the UN General Assembly Devoted to Disarmament." *Press Release* 7, PIO, June 2, 1988.

———. "The Course of Cyprus Towards the European Union: Speech by the Minister of Foreign Affairs Mr Alecos Michaelides before the House of Representatives, 22 February 1996." Nicosia: PIO, 1996.

———. "Memorandum: Government Policy Vis a Vis the Turkish Cypriots (Set of Measures)." Nicosia, April 30, 2003.

DISY. *Analisi Enos Lathous: I Aporipsi tou Ditikou Schediou gia tin Kipro.* [Analysis of a Mistake: The Rejection of the Western Plan for Cyprus]. Nicosia, May 1980.

———. ["Clerides Plan"]. Nicosia, January 27, 1984.

European Commission. *Commission Opinion on Turkey's Request for Accession to the Community.* SEC (89) 2290, final/2, 1989.

———. *Commission Opinion on the Application by the Republic of Cyprus for Membership.* COM (93) 313 final, Brussels, June 30, 1993.

———. *1999 Regular Report from the Commission on Turkey's Progress Towards Accession.* November 13, 1999.

———. *2000 Regular Report from the Commission on Turkey's Progress Towards Accession.* November 8, 2000.

———. *2001 Regular Report on Cyprus' Progress Towards Accession.* SEC (2001) 1745, Brussels.

———. *Public Opinion 2002—First Results—Northern Cyprus.* Brussels: Directorate General Press and Communication, November 2002.

——— *Continuing Enlargement Strategy Paper and Report of the European Commission on the Progress Towards Accession by Bulgaria, Romania and Turkey.* November 5, 2003.

———. *2004 Regular Report on Turkey's Progress Towards Accession.* COM (2004) 656, Brussels, SEC (2004) 1201, October 6, 2004.

———. "Issues Arising from Turkey's Membership Perspective." Commission Staff Working Document COM (2004) 656, Brussels, SEC (2004) 1202, October 6, 2004.

———. *Turkey 2006 Progress Report.* COM (2006) 649, final Commission Staff Working Document SEC (2006) 1390, Brussels, November 8, 2006.

———. *Eurobarometer 67.* Public Opinion in the European Union, "Turkey National Report—Executive Summary," Spring 2007.

European Council. "European Council at Corfu 24–25 June 1994: Presidency Conclusions." *Press Release* 00150/94, Brussels, June 24, 1994.

———. "General Affairs Council of Ministers Decision." SN 1661/95. Brussels, March 6, 1995.

———. "Dublin European Council, 13 and 14 December 1996: Presidency Conclusions." CFSP Presidency Statement SN401/1/96. Brussels, December 16, 1996.

———. "Luxembourg European Council: Presidency Conclusions." *Press Release* SN400/97. Luxembourg, December 12, 1997.

———. "Helsinki European Council: Presidency Conclusions." *Press Release* NR 00300/1/99. Brussels, December 11, 1999.

———. "Presidency Conclusions—Laeken, 14 and 15 December 2001." SN300/1/01 REV1.

———. "Copenhagen European Council 12 and 13 December 2002—Presidency Conclusion." 15917/02. Brussels, January 29, 2003.

———. "Brussels European Council 12 and 13 December 2003—Presidency Conclusions." 5381/04. Brussels, February 5, 2004.

———. "Brussels European Council 25 and 26 March 2004, Presidency Conclusions." 9048/04 POLGEN 20 CONCL. Brussels, May 19, 2004.

———. "Presidency Conclusions—Brussels European Council 17 and 18 June 2004." 10679/2/04 REV2. Brussels, July 19, 2004.

European Council. "Brussels European Council, 16/17 December 2004—Presidency Conclusions." 16238/1/04 REV 1. Brussels, February 1, 2005.

European Court of Human Rights. *Case of Loizidou v. Turkey (Merits) Judgement* (40/1993/435/514). Strasbourg, December 18, 1996.

———. *Case of Loizidou v. Turkey* (Article 50) Judgement. Strasbourg, July 1998.

———. *Case of Aziz v. Cyprus Judgement* (application no. 69949/01). Strasbourg, June 22, 2004.

European Economic and Social Council. "Opinion of the European Economic and Social Committee on EU-Turkey Relations with a View to the European Council of December 2004." REX/172-CESE 965/2004, Brussels, July 1, 2004.

European Parliament. *Report on Cyprus's Membership Application to the European Union and the State of Negotiations.* RR\446036EN.doc. July 17, 2001.

———. *Report on Cyprus' Membership Application to the European Union and the State of Negotiations* (Final A5-0261/2001/Par 1), 2001.

European Union. "Protocol No. 10 on Cyprus." *Treaty of Accession to the European Union 2003.* AA2003/ACT/P10/en. 4803.

European Union Council of Ministers. *European Observer's Report on Cyprus.* Brussels, January 23, 1995.

Famagusta Refugee Movement. "The Case for Famagusta." Nicosia, 1981.

Turkish Cypriot Administration. *For the Liberty, Equality, Dignity and Security of our People: The Declaration and Resolution Adopted by the Turkish Cypriot Parliament on 15 November 1983.*

Turkish Cypriot Side. "An Appraisal of the Greek Cypriot 'Outline Proposals' of 30 January 1989." *New Cyprus*, February 13, 1989, 19–23.

———. "A Supplementary Note to the Turkish Memorandum of 12 July 1990 on the Greek Cypriot 'Application' for Membership of the European Communities." http://www.cypnet.com/.ncyprus/cyproblem/articles/bolum10.html.

Turkish Republic of Northern Cyprus. *Questions of Cyprus: A Documented Story of 28 Years (1960–1988).* Nicosia:Turkish Cypriot U.N. Association, 1988.

———. *TRNC Statistical Yearbook, 1987.* Nicosia: State Planning Organization, Statistics and Research Department, 1988.

———. *The Right to Self-Determination of the Turkish-Cypriot People.* Nicosia: Public Information Office of TRNC, 1990.

"Turkish Cypriot Memorandum Addressed to the Council of Ministers of the European Communities in Respect to an 'Application' for Membership by 'the Republic of Cyprus.'" (July 12, 1990), http://www.cypnet.com/.ncyprus/cyproblem/articles/bolum1.html.

United Kingdom. *Constitutional Proposals for Cyprus, Report Submitted to the Secretary of State for the Colonies by the Right Hon Lord Radcliffe G.B.E.* Cmnd. 42. London: HMSO, December 1956.

———. *Cyprus: Statement of Policy.* Cmnd. 455. London: HMSO, June 1958.

———. *Cyprus.* Cmnd. 1093. London: HMSO, July 1960.

United Kingdom, Colonial Office. *Report on Cyprus for the Year 1952.* London: HMSO, 1953.

———. *Colonial Reports: Cyprus 1953.* London: HMSO, 1954.

———. *Cyprus Report for the Year 1955.* London: HMSO, 1956.

———. *Cyprus Report 1956.* Nicosia: HMSO, 1957.

———. *Cyprus Report 1957.* Nicosia: HMSO, 1958.

———. *Cyprus Report for the Year 1958.* London: HMSO, 1959.

———. *Cyprus Report 1959.* Nicosia: HMSO, 1961.

United Kingdom. House of Commons. Foreign Affairs Committee. *Report on Cyprus.* London: HMSO, May 1987.

———. *Sixth Report from the Foreign Affairs Committee on Turkey.* London: HMSO, April 23, 2002.

———. *Sixth Report from the Foreign Affairs Committee: Turkey, Response of the Secretary of State for Foreign and Commonwealth Affairs.* Cm 5529, London: HMSO, July 2002.

United Kingdom. Ministry of Defence. *Defence: Outline of Future Policy.* Cmnd. 124. London, HMSO, 1957.

United Nations. *Report of the United Nations Mediator on Cyprus to the Secretary-General.* S/6253, March 26, 1965.

———. *Report by the Secretary-General on the United Nations Operation in Cyprus.* S/10401, November 30, 1971.

———. *Report by the Secretary-General on the United Nations Operation in Cyprus for the Period from 2 December 1973 to 22 May 1974.* S/11294.

———. Declaration by the Foreign Ministers of Greece, Turkey and the United Kingdom of Great Britain and Northern Ireland. S/11398, July 30, 1974.

———. *Report of the Secretary-General on the United Nations Operation in Cyprus for the Period from 23 May to 5 December 1974.* S/11568, 1974.

———. *Special Report of the Secretary-General on Developments in Cyprus.* S/11624, February 18, 1975.

———. *Interim Report of the Secretary-General Pursuant to Security Council Resolution 367.* S/11684, May 4, 1975.

———. "Turkish Cypriot Proposals of 18 July 1975 for a Joint Transitional Government." S/11770/Annex, July 22, 1975.

———. *Report of the Secretary-General in Pursuance of Paragraph 6 of Security Council Resolution 401.* S/12323, April 30, 1977.

———. *Report of the Secretary-General on the United Nations Operation in Cyprus for the Period 7 December 1976 to 7 June 1977.* S/12342.

———. *Report of the Secretary-General on the United Nations Operation in Cyprus for the Period 1 December 1977 to 31 May 1978.* S/12723.

———. *Report by the Secretary-General on Efforts to Bring About a Resumption of the Intercommunal Negotiations in Cyprus.* S/14100, 1980.

United Nations. *Report of the Secretary-General on the United Nations Operation in Cyprus for the Period 28 May to 30 November 1981. S/14778.*
———. *Report of the Secretary-General on His Mission of Good Offices in Cyprus.* S/21010, December 13, 1989.
———. *Report of the Secretary-General on his Mission of Good Offices in Cyprus.* S/21183, March 8, 1990.
———. *Report of the Secretary-General on his Mission of Good Offices in Cyprus.* S/21393, July 12, 1990.
———. *Report of the Secretary-General on his Mission of Good Offices in Cyprus.* S/23121, October 8, 1991.
———. *Report of the Secretary-General on his Mission of Good Offices in Cyprus.* S/23300, December 19, 1991.
———. *Report of the Secretary-General on his Mission of Good Offices in Cyprus.* S/23780, April 3, 1992.
———. *Report of the Secretary-General on his Mission of Good Offices in Cyprus.* S/24472, August 21, 1992.
———. *Report of the Secretary-General on his Mission of Good Offices in Cyprus.* S/24830, November 19, 1992.
———. *Report of the Secretary-General on his Mission of Good Offices in Cyprus.* S/26026, July 1, 1993.
———. *Report of the Secretary-General on his Mission of Good Offices in Cyprus.* S/26438, September 14, 1993.
———. *Report of the Secretary-General in Connection with the Security Council's Comprehensive Reassessment of the United Nations Operation in Cyprus.* S/26777, November 22, 1993.
———. *Report of the Secretary-General on His Mission of Good Offices in Cyprus.* S/1994/262, March 4, 1994.
———. *Report of the Secretary-General on His Mission of Good Offices in Cyprus.* S/1994/629, May 30, 1994.
———. *Report of the Secretary-General on the United Nations Operation in Cyprus, for the Period from 30 June to 10 December 1996. S/1996/1016.*
———. *Report of the Secretary-General on His Mission of Good Offices in Cyprus.* S/1997/973, December 12, 1997.
———. *Report of the Secretary-General on His Mission of Good Offices in Cyprus.* S/2003/398, April 1, 2003.
———. *Report of the Secretary-General on His Mission of Good Offices in Cyprus.* S/2004/437, May 28, 2004.
———. *Report of the Secretary-General on the United Nations Operation in Cyprus.* S/2007/328, June 4, 2007.
———. *Report of the Secretary-General on the United Nations Operation in Cyprus.* S/2207/699, December 3, 2007.
———. *Report of the Secretary-General on the United Nations Operation in Cyprus.* S/2008/353, June 3, 2008.
———. *Report of the Secretary-General on the United Nations Operation in Cyprus.* S/2008/744, November 28, 2008.

————. *Resolutions and Decisions of the Security Council 1992.* S/INF/48, New York, 1993.

————. *Yearbook of the United Nations, 1989.* Vol. 43, New York, 1997.

————. Secretary-General. Framework for a Comprehensive Settlement of the Cyprus Problem (January 11, 1984). A/38/812-S/16549/Annex, May 10, 1984.

————. *An Agenda for Peace, Preventive Diplomacy, Peacemaking and Peace-keeping.* A/47/277-S/2411, June 17, 1992.

————. *Set of Ideas on an Overall Framework Agreement on Cyprus.* S/24472/ Annex and Appendix, July 15, 1992.

————. *Programme of Action to Promote Goodwill and Close Relations between the Two Communities (CBMs).* S/24472/Appendix, August 21, 1992.

————. *The Comprehensive Settlement of the Cyprus Problem.* http://www. cyprus-un-plan.org/Annan_Paln_April2004.pdf.

Turkey, Ministry of Foreign Affairs. *Foreign Policy of Turkey at the United Nations.* Edited by Yuksel Soylemez, Ankara: Department of International Organizations, 1983.

U.S. Congress. Senate. Committee on Foreign Relations. *Cyprus: International Law and the Prospects for Settlement: Hearing Before the Subcommittee on European Affairs.* 102nd Cong., 1st sess., April 17, 1991.

U.S. Department of State. *American Foreign Policy Current Documents, 1984.* Washington DC: Government Printing Office, 1986.

————. *American Foreign Policy Current Documents 1991.* Washington DC: Government Printing Office, 1994.

World Bank. *World Development Report 1980.* Washington, DC, August 1980.

————. *World Development Report 1991: The Challenge of Development.* New York: Oxford University Press, 1991.

Secondary Sources

Acheson, Dean. "Cyprus: Anatomy of the Problem." *Chicago Bar Record* 46, 8 (1965): 349–56.

Akgün, Mensur, Ayla Gürel, Mete Hatay, and Sylvia Tiryaki. "Quo Vadis Cyprus?" TESEV Working Paper, April 2005.

An, Ahmet. *Kıbrıs'ta Fırtınalı Yıllar (1942–1962)* [The Stormy Years in Cyprus (1942–1962)]. Lefkoşa: Galeri Kültür Yayını, 1996.

————. *Kıbrıslı Türklerin Siyasal Tarihi (1930–1960): Basının Aynasında Kıbrıslı Türklerin Unutturulan Siyasal Geçmişi ve Liderlik Kavgaları* [The Political History of the Turkish Cypriots (1930–1960): The Forgotten Political History of the Turkish Cypriots and the Struggles for the Leadership in the Mirror of the Press]. Lefkoşa, 2006.

Anastasiou, Harry. *The Broken Olive Branch: Nationalism, Ethnic Conflict, and the Quest for Peace in Cyprus.* Syracuse, NY: Syracuse University Press, 2008.

Anderson, Perry. "The Divisions of Cyprus." *London Review of Books* 30, 8 (April 24, 2008): 7–16.

Andrews, Carole. "EU Enlargement: The Political Process." *House of Commons Library Research Paper* 98/55 (1998).

Arnold, Percy. *Cyprus Challenge—A Colonial Island and Its Aspirations: Reminiscences of a Former Editor of the "Cyprus Post."* London: Hogarth Press, 1956.

Ateşin, Huseyin M. *Kıbrıslı "Müslüma" larin "Türk" leşme ve "Laik" leşme Serüveni (1925–1975)* [Turkification and Securization Adventure of Cypriot Muslims]. Istanbul: Marifet Yayinlari, 1999.

Attalides, Michael. *Cyprus: Nationalism and International Politics.* Edinburgh: Q Press, 1979.

Aybet, Gülnur, and Meltem Müftüler-Bac. "Transformations in Security and Identity after the Cold War: Turkey's Problematic Relationship with Europe." *International Journal* 55, 4 (2000): 567–82.

Bahcheli, Tozun. "Searching for a Cyprus Settlement: Considering Options for Creating a Federation, a Confederation, or Two Independent States." *Publius* 30, 1 (2000): 203–16.

———. "Cyprus in the Post-War Environment: Moving Toward a Settlement?" In Calotychos, *Cyprus and Its People*, 105–19.

Baker, Samuel White. *Cyprus, As I Saw It in 1879.* London: Macmillan, 1879.

Ball, George W. *The Past has Another Pattern: Memoirs.* New York: W. W. Norton, 1982.

Baruh, Lemi, and Mihaela Popescu. "Guiding Metaphors of Nationalism: The Cyprus Issue and the Constriction of Turkish National Identity in Online Discussions." *Discourse & Communication* 2, 1 (2008): 79–96.

Beckingham, Charles Fraser. "Islam and Turkish Nationalism in Cyprus." *Die Welt des Islam* 5, 1–2 (1957): 65–83.

Birand, Mehmet Ali. "Turkey and the 'Davos Process': Experience and Prospects." In *The Greek-Turkish Conflict in the 1990s: Domestic and External Influences*, edited by D. Constas, 27–39. London: Macmillan, 1991.

Brinkley, Douglas. *Dean Acheson: The Cold War Years 1953–1971.* New Haven: Yale University Press, 1992.

Broome, Benjamin J. "Bridging the Divide in Cyprus: The Role of Bicommunal Activities." In Michael and Tamis, *Cyprus in the Modern World*, 266–304.

Broomfield, William E. "The Eastern Mediterranean in the Post-Gulf Crisis: Unresolved Issues." *Mediterranean Quarterly* 2, 3 (1991): 15–26.

Bryant, Rebecca. *Imagining the Modern—The Cultures of Nationalism in Cyprus.* London: I. B. Tauris, 2004.

Burton, John W. *Conflict and Communication: The Use of Controlled Communication in International Relations.* New York: The Free Press, 1969.

———. *Deviance Terrorism and War: The Process of Solving Unsolved Social and Political Problems.* Oxford: Martin Robertson, 1979.

———. *Global Conflict: the Domestic Sources of International Crisis.* Brighton, Sussex: University of Maryland, Center for International Development/Wheatsheaf Books, 1984.

Calotychos, Vangelis, ed. *Cyprus and Its People: Nation, Identity, and Experience in an Unimaginable Community, 1955–1997.* Boulder, CO: Westview Press, 1998.

Camp, Glen D. "Cyprus Between the Powers: 1980–1989." *The Cyprus Review* 1, 2 (1989): 65–90.

Canefe, Nergis. "Communal Memory and Turkish Cypriot National History: Missing Links." In *National Identities and National Memories in the Balkans,* edited by Maria Todorova, 77–102. London: Hurst and Company, 2003. "Refugees or Enemies? The Legacy of Population Displacements in Contemporary Turkish Cypriot Society." *South European Society and Politics* 7, 3 (2002): 1–28.

———. "Communal Memory and Turkish Cypriot National History: Missing Links." In *National Identities and National Memories in the Balkans,* edited by Maria Todorova, 77–102. London: Hurst and Company, 2003.

Christodoulou, Demetrios. *Inside the Cyprus Miracle: The Labours of an Embattled Mini-Economy.* Vol 2, Minnesota Mediterranean and East European Monographs. Minneapolis, MN: University of Minnesota, 1992.

Clerides, Glafcos. *Cyprus: My Deposition.* Vol. 2, Nicosia: Alithia, 1989.

———. *I Katathesi Mou* [my deposition]. Vol. 4, Nicosia,: Alithia, 1991.

———. *Ntokoumenta mias Epohis 1993–2003* [documents of a period 1993–2003]. Nicosia: Politeia, 2007.

Copley, Gregory R. "The Turkish Schism Deepens." *Defence and Foreign Affairs Strategic Policy* 29, 11/12 (2001): 12–14.

Coufoudakis, Van. *Cyprus: A Contemporary Problem in Historical Perspective.* Minnesota Mediterranean and East European Monographs 15; University of Minnesota, 2006.

Crawshaw, Nancy. "Cyprus after Makarios: Prospects for a Settlement." *The World Today* 34, 1 (1978): 31–8.

———. *The Cyprus Revolt: An Account of the Struggle for Union with Greece.* London: George Allen and Unwin, 1978.

———. "Cyprus: A Crisis of Confidence." *The World Today* 50, 4 (1994): 70–3.

Cross, Collin. *The Fall of the British Empire 1918–1968.* London: Paladin, 1970.

Danielidou, Liana, and Peter Hortvath. "Greek Cypriot Attitudes Toward Turkish Cypriots and Turkish Immigrants." *The Journal of Social Psychology* 146, 4 (2006): 405–21.

Davutoğlu, Ahmet. *Stratejik Derinlik: Turkiye'nin Uluslararasi Konumu* [Strategic Depth: The International Position of Turkey]. Istanbul: Küre Yaınları, 2001.

Dekleris, Michael El. *Kipriako 1972–1974: I Teleftaia Efkairia* [Cyprus Problem 1972–1974: The Last Opportunity]. Athens: Estia, 1981.

Demetriou, Olga. "Catalysis, Catacresis: The EU's Impact on the Cyprus Conflict. In *The European Union and Border Conflicts: The Power of Integration and Association*, edited by T. Diez, M. Albert, and S. Stetter, 64–92. Cambridge: Cambridge University Press, 2008.

Denktash, Rauf R. "The Problem of Cyprus." *Review of International Affairs* (Belgrade) 22, 544 (1972): 9–11.

———. *The Cyprus Triangle*. London: Rustem/Allen and Unwin, 1982.

———. "Federalism-Economic and Political Issues." *Turkish Review* 3, 16 (1989): 5–12.

Diez, Thomas, ed. *The European Union and the Cyprus Conflict: Modern Conflict, Postmodern Nation*. Manchester: Manchester University Press, 2002.

Disraeli, Benjamin. *Tancred or the New Crusade*. London: Peter Davies, 1927.

Dixon, W. Hepworth. *British Cyprus*. London: Chapman and Hall, 1879.

Dodd, Clement H. *The Cyprus Issue: A Current Perspective*. 2nd ed. Huntington: Eothen Press, 1994.

Doob, Leonard W. "A Cyprus Workshop: An Exercise in Intervention Methodology." *Journal of Social Psychology* 94 (1974): 161–78.

———. "Cypriot Patriotism and Nationalism." *Journal of Conflict Resolution* 30, 2 (1986): 383–96.

Durrell, Lawrence. *Bitter Lemons*. London: Faber and Faber, 1957.

Ecevit, Bulent. "Turkey's Security Policies." In *Greece and Turkey: Adversity in Alliance*, edited by Jonathan Alford, 136–4. Adelphi Library 12, Aldershot: Grower International Institute of Strategic Studies, 1984.

Eden, Anthony. *Full Circle*. London: Cassell, 1960.

Ehrlich, Thomas. *Cyprus 1958–1967: International Crises and the Role of Law*. London: Oxford University Press, 1974.

Ertekün, Necati Münir. *In Search of a Negotiated Cyprus Settlement*. Nicosia: ULUS, 1981.

———. *The Cyprus Dispute and the Birth of the Turkish Republic of Northern Cyprus*. London: Rustem, 1984.

———, ed. *The Status of the Two People in Cyprus*. Nicosia: TRNC Ministry of Foreign Affairs and Defence, 1979.

Evriviades, Marios L. "Europe in Cyprus: the Broader Security Implications." *The Brown Journal of World Affairs* 10, 1 (2003): 241–57.

Falk, Avner. "Border Symbolism." *Psychoanalytic Quarterly* 43 (1974): 650–60.

Fallaci, Oriana. *Interview With History*. Boston: Houghton Mifflin, 1976.

Faustmann, Hubert., and Nicos Peristianis, eds. *Britain in Cyprus: Colonialism and Post-Colonialism, 1878–2006*. Mannheim: Bibliopolis, 2006.

Feyzioglu, Turhan, and Necati M. Ertekün. *The Crux of the Cyprus Question*. Nicosia, 1987.

Fisher, Ronald J. "Cyprus: The Failure of Mediation and the Escalation of an Identity-Based Conflict to an Adversarial Impasse." *Journal of Peace Research* 38, 3 (2001): 307–26.

Georghallides, G. S. *Cyprus and the Governorship of Sir Ronald Storrs: The Causes of the 1931 Crisis.* London: Cyprus Research Centre, 1986.

Gobbi, Hugo J. *Rethinking Cyprus.* Tel Aviv: Aurora, 1993.

Haass, Richard N. "Cyprus: Moving Beyond Solution?" *The Washington Quarterly* (1987): 183–90.

———. *Conflicts Unending: The United States and Regional Disputes.* New Haven: Yale University Press, 1990.

Hadjipavlou-Trigeorgis, Maria, and Lenos Trigeorgis. "Cyprus: An Evolutionary Approach to Conflict Resolution." *Journal of Conflict Resolution* 37, 2 (1993): 340–60.

Hamourtziadou, Lily "Greek Myths or the Boy Who Wanted to see Turks." *Internationale Schulbuchforschung* 21 (1999): 369–85.

Hannay, David. *Cyprus: Search for a Solution.* London: I. B. Tauris, 2005.

Harding of Petherton. "The Cyprus Problem in Relation to the Middle East." *International Affairs* 34, 3 (1958): 291–6.

Hatay, Ann-Sofi Jakobsson. "The Orphan Peace Plan: Kofi Annan's Proposal for a Reunited Cyprus." Transnational Foundation for Peace and Future Research, *Meeting Points Forum*, 2002.

Hatay, Mete. *Beyond Numbers: An Inquiry into the Political Integration of the Turkish "Settlers" n Northern Cyprus.* Nicosia: PRIO Report 4, 2005.

Hill, George. *A History of Cyprus: The Ottoman Province, the British Colony 1571–1948.* Vol. 4. Cambridge: Cambridge University Press, 1972 [1952].

Hitchens, Christopher. *Cyprus.* London: Quartet Books, 1984.

Holland, Robert, and Diana Markides. *The British and the Hellenes: Struggles for Mastery in the Eastern Mediterranean 1850–1960.* Oxford: Oxford University Press, 2006.

Iklé, Fred Charles. *How Nations Negotiate.* London: Harper and Row, 1964.

Ioannides, Christos. *In Turkey's Image: The Transformation of Occupied Cyprus into a Turkish Province.* New Rochelle, NY: Aristide D. Caratzas, 1991.

Jovovic, Aleksandar D. "A Turning Point for Turkey." *Schlesinger Working Group on Strategic Surprises.* Washington, DC: Institute for the Study of Diplomacy, Georgetown University, 2001.

Karouzis, George. *Proposals for a Solution to the Cyprus Problem.* Nicosia: Kosmos Press, 1976.

Karpat, Kemal H. "Solution in Cyprus: Federation." In *The Cyprus Dilemma: Options for Peace*, 35–54. New York: Institute for Mediterranean Affairs, 1967.

———. "War on Cyprus: The Tragedy of Enosis." In *Turkey's Foreign Policy in Transition*, edited by K. H. Karpat, 186–205. Leiden: E. J. Brill, 1975.

Kelling, George H. *Countdown to Rebellion: British Policy in Cyprus, 1939–1955.* Westport, CT: Greenwood Press, 1990.

Kinneir, John Macdonald. *Journey Through Asia Minor, Armenia and Koordistan in the Years of 1813 and 1814.* London, 1818.

Kissinger, Henry. *Years of Renewal.* London: Weidenfeld and Nicolson, 1999.

Kitromilides, Paschalis M. "The Dialectic of Intolerance: Ideological Dimensions of Ethnic Conflict." *Journal of the Hellenic Diaspora* 6, 4 (1979): 5–30.

Kiziliyürek, Niyazi. "The Turkish Cypriot Community and Rethinking of Cyprus." In *Cyprus in the Modern World*, edited by Michális S. Michael and Anastasios M. Tamis, 228–47. Thessaloniki: Vanias, 2005.

Kizilyürek, Niyazi, and Sylvaine Gautier-Kizilyürek. "The Politics of Identity in the Turkish Cypriot Community and the Language Question." *International Journal of the Sociology of Language* 168 (2004): 37–54.

Kranidiotis, Nikos. *Diskola Hronia* [Difficult Years]. Athens: Estia, 1981.

———. *Anohiroti Politia* [Unfortified State]. Vol. 2, Athens: Estia, 1985.

———. *Oi Diapragmatefseis Makariou-Harding (1955–1956)* [The Makarios-Harding Negotiations (1955–1956)]. Athens: Olkos, 1987.

Kranidiotis, Yiannos. "Oi Diapragmatefseis gia tin Epilisi tou Kipriakou (1974–1981) ["Negotiations for the Resolution of the Cyprus problem (1974–1981)"]. In *Kipros: Istoria, Provlimata kai Agones tou Laou tis* [Cyprus: History, Problems and Struggles of Its People], edited by Giorgos Tenekidis and Yiannos Kranidiotis, 585–662. Athens: Estia, 1981.

Kyrris, Costas P. *History of Cyprus.* Nicosia: Nicocles, 1985.

Lacher, Hannes, and Erol Kaymak. "Transforming Identities: Beyond the Politics of Non-Settlement in North Cyprus." *Mediterranean Politics* 10, 2 (2005): 147–66.

Laipson, Helen. "U.S. Policy Towards Greece and Turkey Since 1974." In Constas, 164–82 (1991).

Lang, R. Hamilton. *Cyprus: Its History, Its Present Resources, and Future Prospects.* London: Macmillan, 1878.

Lindley, Dan. "Historical, Tactical, and Strategic Lessons from the Partition of Cyprus." *International Studies Perspectives* 8 (2007): 224–41.

Loizos, Peter. "The Progress of Greek Nationalism in Cyprus, 1878–1970." In *Choice and Change: Essays in Honour of Lucy Mair*, edited by J. Davis, 114–33. London: Athlone, 1974.

Lordos, Alexandros. "Can the Cyprus Problem be Solved? Understanding the Greek Cypriot Response to the UN Peace Plan for Cyprus." An evidence-based study in cooperation with CYMAR, October 2004.

———. "Building Trust: An Inter-communal Analysis of Public Opinion in Cyprus." Nicosia: CYMAR and KADEM, April 2006.

Luke, Harry. *Cyprus—A Portrait and an Appreciation.* London: George G. Harrap, 1964.

Lumsden, Malvern. "The Cyprus Conflict as a Prisoner's Dilemma Game." *The Journal of Conflict Resolution* 17, 1 (1973): 7–32.

Macmillan, Harold. *Riding the Storm: 1956–1959.* London: Macmillan, 1971.

Markides, Kyriacos C. "Social Change and the Rise and Decline of a Social Movement: The Case of Cyprus." *American Ethnologist* 1, 2 (1974): 309–30.

———. *The Rise and Fall of the Cyprus Republic.* New Haven: Yale University Press, 1977.

Mavratsas, Caesar V. "The Ideological Contest between Greek-Cypriot Nationalism and Cypriotism 1974–1995; Politics, Social Memory, and Identity." *Ethnic and Racial Studies* 20, 4 (1997): 717–37.

McDonald, Robert. *The Problem of Cyprus.* Adelphi Paper 234, International Institute of Strategic Studies, 1988/9.

Meinardus, Ronald. "Third-Party Involvement in Greek-Turkish Disputes." In Constas, 157–63 (1991).

Michael, Michalis S. "Proposals for Resolving the Cyprus Problem (1974–1994)." PhD diss., La Trobe University, 1998.

Michael, Michális S., and A. M. Tamis, eds. *Cyprus in the Modern World.* Thessaloniki: Vanias Press, 2005.

Mikes, George. *Eureka! Rummaging in Greece.* London: Andre Deutsch, 1965.

Monypenny, William Flavelle., and George Earle. Buckle. *The Life of Benjamin Disraeli Earl of Beaconsfield.* Vol. 2, London: John Murray, 1929.

Navaro-Yashin, Yael. " 'Life is Dead Here'—Sensing the Political 'No Man's Land.' " *Anthropological Theory* 3, 1 (2003): 107–25.

———. "Confinement and Imagination: Sovereignty and Subjectivity in a Quasi-State." In *Sovereign Bodies: Citizens, Migrants, and States in the Postcolonial World*, edited by Thomas Blom Hansen and Finn Stepputat, 103–19. Princeton: Princeton University Press, 2005.

———. "De-ethicizing the Ethnography of Cyprus: Political and Social Conflict between Turkish Cypriots and Settlers from Turkey." In *Divided Cyprus: Modernity, History and an Island in Conflict*, edited by Y. Papadakis, N. Peristianis, and G. Welz, 84–99. Bloomington: Indiana University Press, 2006.

Necatigil, Zaim M. *Our Republic in Perspective.* Nicosia: Tezel, 1985.

———. *The Cyprus Question and the Turkish Position in International Law.* Oxford: Oxford University Press, 1990.

Nevzat, Altay. "Nationalism Amongst the Turks of Cyprus: The First Wave." PhD diss., University of Oulu, 2005.

Newman, Edward. "The Most Impossible Job in the World: The Secretary-General and Cyprus." In *The Work of the UN in Cyprus: Promoting Peace and Development*, edited by O. P. Richmond and J. Ker-Lindsay, 127–53. Basingstoke: Palgrave, 2001.

Nimetz, Mathew. "The Cyprus Problem Revisited." *Mediterranean Quarterly* 2, 1 (1991): 59–62.

Oberling, Pierre. *The Road to Bellapais: The Turkish Cypriot Exodus from Northern Cyprus.* New York: Columbia University Press, 1982.

Papageorgiou, Spiros. *Makarios dia Piros kai Sidirou* [Makarios Through Fire and Steel]. Athens: Ladias, 1976.

Papandreou, Andreas G. *Logoi Prothipourgou Andrea G. Papandreou 1981–1982* [Prime Minister's Andreas G. Papandreou Speeches 1981–1982]. Athens: Press and Information General Secretariat, 1983.

Papastathopoulos, Catherine D. "Constitutionalism and Communalism: The Case of Cyprus." *The University of Toronto Law Journal* 16, 1 (1965): 118–44.

Percival, D'Andrade (D.A) "Some Features of a Peasant Population in the Middle East—Drawn from the Results of the Census of Cyprus." *Population Studies* 3, 2 (1949): 192–204.

Perikleous, Chrysostomos. *To Kipriako Provlima* [The Cyprus Problem]. Nicosia: Onisillos, 1986.

Peristiany, John G., ed. *Contributions to Mediterranean Sociology: Mediterranean Rural Communities and Social Change.* The Hague: Mouton, 1968.

Pollis, Adamantia. "Intergroup Conflict and British Colonial Policy: The Case of Cyprus." *Comparative Politics* 5, 4 (1973): 575–99.

Polyviou, Polyvios G. *Cyprus in Search of a Constitution: Constitutional Negotiations and Proposals 1960–1975.* Nicosia: Chr. Nicolaou and Sons, 1976.

————. *Cyprus: Conflict and Negotiations 1960–1980.* London: Duckworth, 1980.

Purcell, H. D. *Cyprus.* London: Ernest Benn, 1969.

Putnam, Linda L. "Challenging the Assumptions of Traditional Approaches to Negotiation." *Negotiation Journal* 10, 4 (1994): 337–46.

Ramm, Christoph. "Assessing Transnational Re-negotiation in the Post-1974 Turkish Cypriot Community; 'Cyprus Donkeys,' 'Black Beards,' and the 'EU Carrot.'" *Southeast European and Black Sea Studies* 6, 4 (2006): 523–42.

Reddaway, John. *Burdened with Cyprus: The British Connection.* London: Weidenfeld and Nicolson, 1986.

Redmond, John. *The Next Mediterranean Enlargement of the European Community: Turkey, Cyprus and Malta?* Aldershot: Dartmouth, 1993.

Richter, Heiz A. "Ankara's Policy Towards Cyprus and the European Union." *Cyprus Review* 13, 2 (2001): 29–45.

Rizvi, Cowher. "Ethnic Conflict and Political Accommodation in Plural Societies: Cyprus and Other Cases." *The Journal of Commonwealth and Comparative Politics* 31, 1 (1993): 57–83.

Robins, Philip. "Confusion at Home, Confusion Abroad: Turkey between Copenhagen and Iraq." *International Affairs* 79, 3 (2003): 547–66.

Rothman, Jay. "Conflict Research and Resolution: Cyprus." *The Annals of the American Academy of Political and Social Science* 518 (1991): 95–108.

Said, Edward W. *Orientalism.* New York: Routledge and Kegan Paul, 1978.

Salih, Halil Ibrahim. *Cyprus, An Analysis of Cypriot Political Discord*. New York: Theo. Gaus Sons, 1968.

———. *Cyprus, Ethnic Political Counterpoints*. Dallas: University Press of America, 2004.

Saunders, Harold H. *A Public Peace Process: Sustained Dialogue to Transform Racial and Ethnic Conflicts*. New York: Palgrave, 2001.

Scott-Stevenson, Esmé. *Our Home in Cyprus*. London: Chapman and Hall, 1880.

Segal, Aaron. *An Atlas of International Migration*. London: Hans Zell, 1993.

Simitis, Kostas. *Politiki gia mia Dimiourgiki Ellada 1996–2004* [Politics for a Creative Greece 1996–2004]. Athens: Polis, 2005.

Sonan, Sertaç. "From Bankruptcy to Unification and EU Membership? The Political Economy of Post-Nationalist Transformation in Northern Cyprus." RAMSES Working Paper 9/07, European Studies Centre, University of Oxford, 2007.

South East European Studies at Oxford. "Cyprus after Accession: Getting Past 'No'?" Workshop Report and Responses, May 2007.

Soysal, Mümtaz. "Political Parties in the Turkish Republic of Northern Cyprus and Their Vision of 'the Solution.'" In *Cyprus, A Regional Conflict and Its Resolution*, edited by N. Salem, 39–43. New York: St. Martin's Press, 1992.

Sözen, Ahmet. "The Role of the European Union as a Third Party in Resolution of External Conflicts: The Case of the Cyprus Problem." Paper presented at the 15th annual meeting for the International Association for Conflict Management, City Park, Utah, June 8–12, 2002.

———. "A Paradigmatic Shift: New Principles of Turkish Foreign Policy Making." A paper presented at the annual conference for the International Studies Association, San Francisco, March 26–29, 2008.

Storrs, Ronald. *Orientations*. London: Ivor Nicholson and Watson, 1937.

Taeuber, Irene B. "Cyprus: The Demography of a Strategy Island." *Population Index* 21, 1 (1955): 4–20.

Tamkoç, Metin. *The Turkish Cypriot State: The Embodiment of the Right of Self-determination*. London: Rustem and Brother, 1988.

Temperley, Harold. "Disraeli and Cyprus." *The English Historical Review* 15, 182 (1931): 274–9.

Theophanous, Andreas. *The Political Economy of a Federal Cyprus*. Nicosia: Intercollege Press, 1996.

———. *The Political Economy of a Cyprus Settlement: The Examination of Four Scenaria*. Oslo: PRIO Report 1, 2008.

Thomson, John. *Through Cyprus with the Camera in the Autumn of 1878*. London: Sampson Low, 1879.

Tocci, Nathalie. "The 'Cyprus Question': Reshaping Community Identities and Elite Interests within a Wider European Framework." Brussels: Centre for European Policy Studies, 2000.

Tocci, Nathalie. *EU Accession Dynamics and Conflict Resolution: Catalysing Peace or Consolidating Partition in Cyprus?* Burlington, VT: Ashgate, 2004.

Tornaritis, Criton G. *Cyprus and Its Constitutional and Other Legal Problems.* 2nd ed., Nicosia, 1980.

Varnava, Pantelis. *The Common Labour Struggles of Greek and Turkish-Cypriots (Events through History).* Nicosia, 1997.

Volkan, Vamık D. *Cyprus—War and Adaptation: A Psychoanalytic History of Two Ethnic Groups in Conflict.* Charlottesville: University Press of Virginia, 1979.

———. "Trauma, Identity and Search for a Solution in Cyprus." *Insight Turkey* 10, 3 (2008), 95–110.

———. "Turks and Greeks of Cyprus: Psychopolitical Considerations." In Calotychos, *Cyprus and its People,* 277–84.

Vural, Yücel, and Nicos Peristianis. "Beyond Ethno-nationalism: Emerging Trends in Cypriot Politics after the Annan Plan." *Nations and Nationalism* 14, 1 (2008): 39–60.

Waldheim, Kurt. *The Challenge of Peace.* London: Weidenfeld and Nicolson, 1980.

———. *Building the Future Order: The Search for Peace in an Interdependent World.* New York: Free Press, 1980.

———. *In the Eye of the Storm: The Memoirs of Kurt Waldheim.* London: Weidenfeld and Nicolson, 1985.

Walker, Anita M. "Enosis in Cyprus: Dhali, a Case Study." *The Middle East Journal* 38, 3 (1984): 474–94.

Webster, Craig, and Christophoros Christophorou. "Greek Cypriots, Turkish Cypriots, and the Future: The Day after the Referendum." Executive Report, Nicosia, CYMAR Market Research, June 17, 2004.

Weintal, Edward, and Charles Bartlett. *Facing the Brink: An Intimate Study in Crisis Diplomacy.* New York: Charles Scribner, 1967.

Wickens, George, ed. *Lawrence Durrell [and] Henry Miller: A Private Correspondence.* London: Faber and Faber, 1963.

Winster, Lord (Reginald Thomas Herbert Fletcher, 1st Baron). "Administrative Problems in Cyprus." In *United Empire* 40, edited by H. W. Elliot Bailey, 178–82, 1949.

Woodhouse, Christopher Montague. "Cyprus: The British Point of View." In *Cyprus in Transition 1960–1985,* edited J. T. A. Koumoulides, 82–94. London: Trigraph, 1986.

Yashin, Neshe. *Hyacinth and Narcissus.* Istanbul: Cem Publications, 1979.

Yesilada, Birol A. "Turkey's Candidacy for EU Membership." *Middle East Journal* 56, 1 (2002): 94–111.

Index